W9-DCZ-802

CARLYLE AT HIS ZENITH

MR. WILSON'S LIFE OF CARLYLE

Vols. V and VI to follow.

CARLYLE

AT HIS ZENITH

(1848—53)

BY

DAVID ALEC WILSON

LONDON
KEGAN PAUL, TRENCH, TRUBNER & CO., LTD.
NEW YORK: E. P. DUTTON & CO.
1927

Printed in Great Britain at
The Mayflower Press, Plymouth. William Brendon & Son, Ltd.

PREFACE

THIS is the fourth volume of a *Carlyle* to be completed in six. The first volume, *Carlyle till Marriage* (1795–1826), appeared in 1923; the second, *Carlyle to "The French Revolution"* (1826–37), in 1924; and the third, *Carlyle on Cromwell and Others* (1837–48), in 1925. The fifth is to be *Carlyle to Threescore and Ten*, and the sixth and last, *Carlyle in Old Age*. These remaining two volumes shall appear in due course, if I am spared, as soon as the work of condensation can be completed. That is all I can promise; but a prophecy may be ventured, that the work may be finished before the end of 1929.

The Preface in the first volume applies to all the rest. So nothing in it needs to be repeated. To the acknowledgments in it and later Prefaces, I have now to add my thanks to Mr. C. O. Gridley, a trustee of the Carlyle House, who in 1925 lent me a fine collection of Carlyleäna, arranged and annotated by his friend, Mr. R. H. Shepherd, the author of *Memoirs of Thomas Carlyle* (2 vols., 1881). I have also to thank the librarians of Trinity College, Cambridge, and of the Advocates' Library, Edinburgh, for help in respect of unpublished letters of Carlyle; and also Glasgow University for an unusual favour. During my absence in Burma on business, from 1907 to 1911, the librarian of Glasgow University, Mr. Galbraith, took faithful charge of all my Carlyle MSS. and notes, and kept them safe in the University Library. Further, I have the pleasure of thanking the daughters of Sir Charles Gavan Duffy, who are his executrices, for assigning to me by a formal deed in 1925 his rights in his book, *Conversations with Carlyle*, the better to enable me to do as he wished,—use it as freely as if it were my own. The best of Book XVII of this volume is taken from it; and in many other parts of this work I have benefited by his writings and advice. For help in correcting proofs, I have to thank my friends James Tennant, Samuel Scott and Robert Carson.

D. A. WILSON.

AYR, 1st *January*, 1927.

CONTENTS

XVI

AMID DISTURBANCES (1848–49)

XVII

TOURING IN IRELAND (1849)

XVIII

CONTEMPORARIES (1849)

LIST OF ILLUSTRATIONS

BOOK XVI

AMID DISTURBANCES

1848–49

I

CARLYLE'S IDEA OF HEAVEN &c.

WHEN 1848 began Carlyle was still enjoying himself, reading at large. Americans wondered to hear him say 'sometimes in a laughing mood'—"My idea of Heaven would be to be turned into an inexhaustible library of new and good books, where I could browse to all eternity." [1] The infinite curiosity which made him a reader in boyhood was never abated, and seemed to grow stronger as he grew older. Among books he was like a fire among dry wood.

Perhaps the most like him, of all the records of his talk about books, is what an Edinburgh lawyer, John Hunter, who came to London occasionally on business, had been writing some time before this in his private diary. [2] What brought him into Carlyle's company was his admiration of Leigh Hunt. To meet Leigh Hunt John Hunter was frequenting the house of George Craik, and once when he was there Carlyle came in, and here is what was written.—

'Carlyle and Hunt were in great force, and came out in the course of the evening in their full strength, decided contrasts to each other. I never saw Carlyle in such vigour. The conversation lasted from five till near twelve o'clock, and embraced the most multifarious subjects, the Scottish Kirk, the Church of England, Wordsworth, Petrarch, Burns, Knox and Hume, Dante, Heaven and Hell, and strange work was made of them. . . .

'Hunt told us someone had been talking against eternal punishment and the like, when Lamb turned round on

[1] *Thomas Carlyle*, by Prof. R. E. Thompson, *The Penn Monthly*, March, 1881, p. 214.

[2] *Reminiscences of Carlyle and Leigh Hunt*, by Walter C. Smith, D.D., in *Good Words*, Feby., 1882, pp. 99–103.

him with—" No, that won't do for me, I can't give up my Hell!" . . .'—Or as another reporter[3] put it, on some similar occasion—" Oh, G-G-Godwin, don't try to d-d-deprive me of my H-H-Hell!"

'Wordsworth Carlyle represented as inferior to Cowper, adding—" From the débris of Robert Burns a thousand Wordsworths might have been made." '

Hunter had previously called on Carlyle in the company of Craik and they had debated about Petrarch. 'He told me,' Hunter wrote, 'that if the works of Petrarch were crushed together, you could extract nothing but the words, " I love Laura, I love Laura." I asked him if he could see nothing that answered to an inward feeling in his heart in such words as '—four quotations in Italian. 'But he only laughed at me and said they were toys and prettinesses. This is provoking, to find people boast of wanting a perception which you know to be one of the finest of your spiritual possessions.'

Dean Swift being mentioned—" What a burst of laughter," said Carlyle, " lay within that man over the present scene of things! What a legion of fancies! But what an awful tragedy he had, at last, to enact! If he had foreseen the part he had to play "—outliving his sanity—" would he have stayed to play it (out)?" The awful pause that followed this was pleasantly broken by Leigh Hunt retelling the joke of Swift at the expense of Partridge the almanac maker, making believe that Partridge was dead, and discrediting all Partridge's remonstrances.

At Craik's house, when the battle about Petrarch was joined again, Craik himself and Leigh Hunt supported Hunter in praising the Italian poet, and it is written by Hunter—' At last Carlyle said—" All I have to say is that there is one son of Adam who has no sympathy with his weak, washy twaddle about another man's wife. I cast it from me as so much trash, unredeemed by any quality that speaks to my heart and soul. And now you may say whatever you like of him or me."

'I answered hastily—" Then I would say of you that you are to be pitied for wanting a perception which I have, and which I think, and the world in general will think, I am the

[3] Charles Cowden Clark, reported in an undated newspaper cutting, a letter signed " A. J.," apparently in the *Times*, and perhaps about 1884.

richer for possessing; and I would just speak of what you have now uttered in these words :—

> 'Say, canst thou paint a sunbeam to the blind,
> Or make him feel a shadow with his mind?'"

A slight shade passed over his face at this, and he said—"Well, I admit you are right to think so, whatever I may think of the politeness of your saying it as you have now done." Hunt interposed to the rescue with, "Well, that's very good. Carlyle knocks down all our idols with two or three sweeps of his arm, and having so far cleared his way to us, he winds up by knocking down ourselves; and when we cry out against this rough work, he begins to talk of—politeness!" This was followed by a peal of laughter, in which Carlyle joined'—so heartily that "his lungs crowed like chanticleer," wrote Hunter elsewhere—'and then addressed me cordially and kindly—"I believe, after all, you are quite right. I ought to envy you. I have no doubt you have pleasures and feelings manifold from which I am shut out, and have shut out myself, in consequence of the habit I have so long indulged of groping through the sepulchral caverns of our being. I honour and love you for the lesson you have taught me." This was felt to be very noble. "There is Carlyle all over," said Hunt; "that's what makes us all love him. His darkest speculations always come out to the light by reason of the human heart which he carries along with him. He will at last end in glory and gladness."' But it has to be added that Carlyle never changed his opinion about Petrarch, "that wearisome creature."[4]

'Towards the conclusion of the evening we had a regular discussion between Carlyle and Hunt, involving the whole merit of their several systems, if I may so call Hunt's fantastic framework of *agreeabilities*, which Carlyle certainly shattered to pieces with great ease (though without disconcerting Hunt in the slightest degree) in order to substitute his eternal principles of right and wrong, responsibility, awe of the Unseen—the spiritual worship of the soul, yearning out of the clay tenement after the infinitely holy and the infinitely beautiful. Hunt's system, I told him, would suit nobody but himself.' To which it is needful to add only that John Hunter's solution of what he called "the hidden mystery" of life was orthodox belief in Jesus.

[4] Letter of T. C. to John Forster, quoted in Forster's *W. S. Landor, a Biography*, p. 438.

II

HENRY JAMES REPORTS WELL

ANOTHER reporter equally free from any bias in favour of Carlyle was the American theologian Henry James—Sandemanian-Swedenborgian, and above all Henry-Jamesian—who came much about his house in the forties and afterwards. He was careless about dates, but appears to have been prompt and accurate in using his note-books; and here is what may fall about the beginning of the revolutionary disturbances, or a little before then.[1]—

'I happened to be in Carlyle's Library the other day, when a parcel was handed in which contained two books from some American admirer. One proved to be *Lectures on the Natural History of Man*, by Alexander Kinmont of Cincinnati; the other a book of Poems. Carlyle read Mr. Kinmont's title-page, and exclaimed: "The Natural History of Man, forsooth! And from Cincinnati too, of all places on this earth! We had a right, perhaps, to expect some light from that quarter in regard to the Natural History of the hog; and I can't but think that if the well-disposed Mr. Kinmont would set himself to study that unperverted mystery he would employ his powers far more profitably to the world. I am sure he would employ them far less wearisomely to me. There!" he continued, handing me the book, "I freely make over to you all my right of insight into the natural history of man, as that history dwells in the portentous brain of Mr. Alexander Kinmont of Cincinnati, being more than content to wait myself till he condescend to the more intelligible animal." And then opening to the blank leaf the volume of Poems, and without more ado, he said—"Permit me to write my friend Mrs. James's [2] name

[1] *Some Personal Recollections of Carlyle*, by Henry James, *Atlantic Monthly*, May, 1881, and reprinted by his son, William James, in the *Literary Remains* of Henry James, pp. 421–68.

[2] The name is a guess, that in the text being "So-and-so."

here, who perhaps may get some refreshment from the poems of her countryman; for, decidedly, I shall not." '

Then Henry James felt his sympathy go out in a flood to the unread philosopher of Cincinnati and to the poet, and he at once, according to his own report, 'suggested' to Carlyle 'that he himself did nothing all his days but philosophize in his own way, and that his prose habitually decked itself out in the most sensuous garniture of poetry,' whereupon 'he affected the air of M. Jourdain in Molière'—the Bourgeois gentilhomme, who did not know till he was told it that he had been talking prose all his life—'and (he) protested, half fun, half earnest, that he was incapable of a philosophic purpose or poetic emotion.'

To Henry James the contemporary Lord John Manners, heir to a Dukedom, appeared 'a sincere sentimentalist, who believes that by reviving old English sports' and so on he could make the aristocracy popular, and Mr. James was sympathetically indignant at Carlyle's treatment of such a 'distinguished swell.' He tells us with a shudder how Carlyle 'laughed as if he would rend the roof' after telling how 'Lord John Manners and some other of the dilettanti aristocratic reformers had called upon him to take counsel. "They asked me," he said, "with countenances of much interrogation, what it was, just, that I would have them to do. I told them that I had no manner of counsel to bestow upon them; that I didn't know how they lived at all up there in their grand houses, nor what manner of tools they had to work with. All I knew was, I told them, that they must be doing something ere long, or they would find themselves on the broad road to the Devil." ' This may have been a sequel to either *Past and Present* or *Latter-Day Pamphlets*.

On another occasion when the publisher Mr. Moxon was present as well as several others including Alfred Tennyson, Henry James seems to have heard Carlyle delivering his opinion on William the Conqueror, already told.[3] ' "Nothing," Carlyle said, "nothing will ever pry England out of the slough she is in, but to stop looking at Manchester as Heaven's Gate, and Free Trade as the (only)[4] everlasting God's Law man is bound to keep holy. The human stomach, I admit, is a memorable

[3] *Carlyle on Cromwell and Others*, p. 313, B. XIV, Ch. VI.
[4] Conjectural correction, by D. A. W.

necessity, which will not allow itself, moreover, to be long neglected; and Political Economy no doubt has its own right to be heard among all our multifarious jargons. But I tell you the stomach is not the *supreme* necessity our potato-evangelists make it, nor is Political Economy any tolerable substitute for the *eternal veracities*. To think of our head men *believing* the stomach to be the man, and legislating for the stomach, and compelling this old England into the downright vassalage of the stomach! Such men as *these*, forsooth, to rule England—the England once ruled by Oliver Cromwell! No wonder the impudent knave O'Connell takes them by the beard, shakes his big fist in their faces, does his own dirty will, in fact, with England, altogether! *Oh, for a day of Duke William again!*"' (meaning, of course—to deal with Dan O'Connell).

Then follows what reads like a rough note of Carlyle's words, but as good as a shorthand report of Tennyson's, for the reporter himself added that it was what Tennyson said that fixed the thing in his memory and 'set its colours, so to speak.' As for the historical question in issue, anyone can see to-day in Green's and other histories how far the others were wrong and Carlyle right. He was almost as much a pioneer in esteeming the character of the Conqueror as in vindicating Mahomet or Cromwell.

Tennyson 'protested that England was no longer the England of Duke William' (the Conqueror), 'nor even of Oliver Cromwell, but a totally new England, with self-consciousness all new and unlike theirs.' Carlyle only repeated, "Oh, for a day of Duke William again!" At last the 'suffering' Tennyson cried, "I suppose you *would* like your Duke William back, to cut off some twelve hundred Cambridgeshire gentlemen's legs, and leave their owners squat upon the ground, that they mightn't be able any longer to bear arms against him!" "Ah!" replied Carlyle, "That *was* no doubt a very sad thing for the Duke to do; but somehow he conceived he had a right to do it—and upon the whole, he had!" "Let me tell your returning hero one thing then," cried Tennyson, "and that is that he had better steer clear of my precincts, or he will feel my knife in his guts very soon."

Which only made Carlyle laugh again. David Masson used to tell [5] how he was once ushered in to where Carlyle and Tennyson were sitting together, and was just in time

[5] To D. A. W. and others.

to see Tennyson resume his pipe after a long harangue, while between two puffs Carlyle remarked—" Eh, you're a wild man, Alfred ! " The words remained in his memory because they puzzled him till by and by explained—by Mrs. Carlyle, it seems likely—as a bit of coterie talk. He was told that that had been the usual rejoinder of an old country-wife to the strong language of her husband.

III

MORE ABOUT TENNYSON

DURING the forties Tennyson 'was in the habit of walking with Carlyle at night,' according to his son and biographer,[1] and Carlyle would rail against the "governments of Jackasserie which cared more for commerce than for the greatness of our empire"; or against the stuccoed houses in London as "acrid putrescence," inasmuch as they were deliberately ill-built and often of bad materials, 'cheap and nasty.' It is curious that in this connection Carlyle does not anywhere appear to have cursed the badness of the English land-laws, which allowed landlords to lease ground for building for ninety-nine years or less, and made the buildings the property of the landlord when the lease expired. Such a ridiculous kind of building lease made it stupid to build substantially. Every extra pound spent on building was like a voluntary addition to the rent paid for the land. The bad laws shaped for the convenience of the landowners make most English buildings "shoddy."

It may have been the badness of the buildings [2] which led Carlyle when walking with Tennyson in the suburbs to rail against the "jumble of black cottages where there used to be pleasant fields"; and they would both agree that it was growing into "a strange chaos of odds and ends, this London." According to what Tennyson told his son, 'they were not in the least afraid of one another, although many were afraid of them, and they had long and free discussions on every conceivable subject, and once only almost quarrelled, when Carlyle asserted that my Father talked of poetry as "high art," which he flatly contradicted, saying—"I never in my life spoke of 'high art.'"' The poet was

[1] *Alfred, Lord Tennyson*, by his son, I, p. 267.
[2] *Ibid.*, and see *Personal Rems. of Carlyle*, by A. J. Symington, pp. 102–4.

quibbling. If Carlyle had said that he *treated* poetry as if it were 'high art,' there would have been no room for contradiction. Perhaps that was what he did say, and the contradiction came all the same—one cannot expect a poet to be "reasonable," and Tennyson was very touchy.

'For Tennyson the man,' says Espinasse,[3] 'Carlyle had a considerable affection. He told me he found "Alfred"—thus he always spoke of him—"an intelligent listener." Of course, he recognised Tennyson's poetic genius, but he thought it largely wasted on that which profiteth not. Of the lovely "Princess" Carlyle said curtly that it "had everything but common sense"'—a stern judgment, but much the same as Edward Fitzgerald wrote to Tennyson's brother.[4]

According to Emerson,[5] Carlyle called Tennyson "the best man in England to smoke a pipe with." He resorted so much to Cheyne Row that there was a hole in the garden wall "for Tennyson's pipe."

It should not be supposed that Tennyson thought of his poetry as his son and biographer did. He had to write something for a living, and it is easy to imagine how he might excuse the *Princess* to Carlyle. Nothing in all the books about him is so good as what he said himself at the dinner-table about this very time.[6]—"I don't think that since Shakespeare there has been such a master of the English language as I," said he, and when the others were looking astonished, he calmly added—"To be sure, I've got nothing to say."

At that time Tennyson was not shy and reserved, as he afterwards became. He was in the first flush of his glory and enjoying it, and particularly enjoying the abundant lionising during his occasional visits to London.

One forenoon Carlyle was found by Espinasse 'deep in the *Acta Sanctorum*' (Acts of the Saints), a compilation of holy old legends, and 'full of the story of the dealings of an early Christian missionary with some Scandinavian and heathen potentate.' "Alfred," he declared, "would be much better employed in making such an episode interesting and beautiful than in cobbling his odes"—which was what

[3] *Literary Recollections*, by F. Espinasse, pp. 213–4.
[4] *Letters of Ed. Fitzgerald*, 1894, Vol. I, pp. 237–8.
[5] *R. W. Emerson*, by J. E. Cabot, II, pp. 157–9.
[6] The *Author*, 1.12.1897, reported by "Senex," saying,—"I had this from one who was present."

he had found him doing, when visiting him some time before. He there and then "reproached him with the futility" of what he was doing. "Did Tennyson not stand up for his literary procedure?" asked Espinasse eagerly. "No! He lay down for it," was the answer.

IV

ON BOOKS AND AUTHORS

CARLYLE told Espinasse [1] once how Miss Barrett (Mrs. Browning) had sent him some of her poems, and he had advised her to stick to prose, and received " so touching a rejoinder " from the delicate lady that in short—" I had to draw in my horns."

He was little more tolerant of the novel than of poetry, and used to say that to write a novel was " on the whole, to screw one's-self up on one's big toe " ; but he owned that ' there were some very clever men among the novelists, and that if he " were to be hanged," he could not imitate their successes.' He ' called the day on which he first read *Roderick Random* one of the sunniest of his life, and a good biography of Smollett, he thought, was among the few things of the kind which then remained to be done.' He praised Mrs. Gaskell for her novel of *Mary Barton*, as it revealed ' romance in the prosaic life of cotton-spinning Manchester ' ; but Anthony Trollope's novels he called " alum ", and Jane Austen's, " dish-washings."

He never recanted the mockery of *Pelham* in *Sartor*, though pleased by Bulwer-Lytton's friendliness in spite of it. Mrs. Carlyle, in the heat of her sympathy for Bulwer-Lytton's wife, called him " a lantern-jawed quack " ; but it was probably John Forster's outspoken adoration of the great man that once provoked Carlyle to call him " a poor fribble." Mrs. Carlyle told Espinasse that her husband had refused " I know not how many invitations to dine with him "—which shows, at least, Bulwer-Lytton's good-will, and she should have added that her husband did not refuse them all.

' Current literature ' in general, according to Espinasse,[1] Carlyle rather despised, maintaining that ' a man was much better employed smoking his pipe, even with " a moderate

[1] *Literary Recollections*, by F. Espinasse, pp. 214–28.

glass of beer," than in reading "such books as come out now."' Nevertheless, he read many of the books of the day recommended to him, and he dipped into most of the books and pamphlets presented to him by their authors in considerable numbers. . . . Speaking of the London publishers, he said—"Considering what is behind, it is well to have in them such a deadwall of dullness."

'Mrs. Carlyle occasionally read a novel aloud to him. I found her once thus occupied with a weird story of Emily Brontë's, not much to her husband's taste. It was in old books that Carlyle chiefly delighted. He lived very much in the past.

'Mr. Bohn's issue of the Standard Library he greeted with rare cordiality, especially the Antiquarian and Classical sections.' I had heard him 'protest against Lord Brougham's pretentious Society for the Diffusion of Useful Knowledge, which had books of various kinds written to order for publication under its auspices. "They treated literature," said Carlyle, "as if it were a *tabula rasa*" (or blank sheet), whereas good books already existed in abundance, but needed to be brought within the reach of readers of moderate means." That was what Bohn was doing, and he deserved "a Parliamentary Grant in aid of his useful enterprise."' One of the earliest volumes of Bohn's Classical Library was Cary's translation of Herodotus. Carlyle read it with delight, pronouncing the Father of History "a beautiful old fellow." In a general way Carlyle cared little about the classics, and never read them in the original.

'As might be expected, he protested strenuously against the time devoted to Latin and Greek in our modern education, and did not estimate very highly the importance of classical scholarship. "It was not," he would say, "by studying Egyptian that the Greeks came to produce their literature. There was Goethe, who was not a profound classical scholar, but he knew better than all your pedants what a Roman or Greek man thought and felt."'

When Forster's fine *Life of Oliver Goldsmith* came out he, of course, sent a copy to Carlyle, and received a letter commending the book, but telling him that Carlyle objected to 'Goldsmith being made the central figure of a group composed of some of the most distinguished men of his time.' In conversation Carlyle told this to Espinasse, and said that "Goldsmith was an Irish blackguard," 'but had the grace to add—" he wrote some of the most elegant things in the English language." ' Then they discussed who had kept England from revolution in 1789. Espinasse thought Burke's *Reflections* had had most effect. Carlyle admitted there were " gleams of insight " in Burke, but thought that ' instead of denouncing the French Revolution, Burke had better have promoted reform at home.' He 'always insisted' on what he had said first in his essay on Boswell long ago, that it was not Burke but Dr. Johnson mainly who had kept England ' loyal to the old,' and safe from revolution.

There was nothing but what might have pleased Biographer Lucas in all he said of Charles Lamb—" He did very well with that little mousetrap of his," meaning his mouth. And De Quincey himself would have bowed his acknowledgments if he had heard as Espinasse did Carlyle declaring—" De Quincey sees into the fibres of a thing." But as for Byron, all he said was—" he will be forgotten in fifty years "—a prophecy clearly needing correction as to date, or, as Lord Kelvin was told in his laboratory by a student, when he stated in plain figures the duration of the earth—" Your figures are *far too exact to be accurate*."

History was his favourite reading, but he did not always enjoy, even in its simplest shape, biography. The *Life of Keats* by his friend Monckton Milnes he called " fricassee of dead dog," which he declined to swallow. He told Espinasse—" The account in the book of Keats's last days and death in Rome is as painful as anything I have ever read." He plainly told Milnes [2] himself—" Keats is a miserable creature, hungering after sweets which he can't get ; going about saying, ' I am so hungry, I should so like something pleasant.' " Milnes wrote the words in his commonplace book ; and on further reflection Carlyle wrote in his journal, 1848 :—' Milnes on Keats. . . . A truly unwise little book. The kind of man that Keats was gets ever more horrible to me. Force of hunger for pleasure of every kind, and want of all other force—such a soul, it would once have been very evident, was a chosen " vessel of Hell " ; and truly, for ever there is justice in that feeling. At present we try to love and pity, and even worship such a soul. . . . There is, perhaps, no clearer evidence of our universal *immorality* and cowardly untruth than such sympathies.'

Carlyle met Hallam often at dinner-tables, but confided to Espinasse that as a writer Hallam was " Dryasdust."

[2] *R. M. Milnes, Lord Houghton*, by T. Wemyss Reid, I, p. 435.

Macaulay, too, as an historian, seemed " limited " and unsatisfactory ; and Ranke's elaborate *Prussian History* he declared a " complete failure " and " broken-backed." He explained to Espinasse that he had seen and talked with Ranke, when he was in London working among the MSS. of the Record Office and the Museum, and that " something was so much the matter " with his backbone that it was " linked together with an iron hook." Espinasse was fairly puzzled to hear the *writings* of Ranke called " broken-backed " ; but the adjective fitted—Michelet, too, has remarked in Ranke a lack of moral backbone.

When reminded by Espinasse of what he had done to make German literature known in England, Carlyle replied abruptly, " It only increased the confusion." There are many erudite persons who fancy Fichte gives a key to *Sartor*, which may explain why Espinasse was astonished to hear him remark, " Fichte is a thick-skinned fellow." But " Kant," he said, " taught me that I had a soul as well as a body." The great Humboldt's *Kosmos* he called " dreich " or tedious, but said Humboldt had done fairly well in " his own sentimental-atheistic way."

" In Political Economy," he once wrote to an enquiring young man,[3] " I consider (Adam) Smith's *Wealth of Nations* to be still the best as well as the pleasantest to read of all the books."

" Poor John Mill," Carlyle said one night to the theologian James,[4] " is writing away there in the *Edinburgh Review* about what he calls the Philosophy of History ! As if any man could ever know the road he is going, when once he gets astride of such a distracted steed as that ! " When in 1848 Mill sent him his *Political Economy*, Espinasse tells us that ' Carlyle called Mill's a " very clever book," ' comparing its complex treatment of its subject to the operation of " extracting the cube root in Roman numerals. It could be done, but was not worth doing," said he, and went on to talk of Mill as usual with kindness, as if regretting he saw him no more. Mill used to insist on " having everything demonstrated," he said, describing how ' Mill used at one time to come to him every Sunday for a walk,' and adding :— " On one point we were agreed. If the Bible could be buried for a generation and then dug up again, it would in that case be rightly enjoyed."

[3] Jos. Lawton : letter in Mr. Gridley's cuttings, from a newspaper of about 1886. [4] See Note 1, Chapter II of this book.

V

MRS. JAMESON STANDS UP FOR HAPPINESS, &c.

MRS. JAMESON had helped Mrs. Carlyle to make a good bargain with Fraser about *Heroes*. She was a woman of letters and a year older than Carlyle himself, and always welcome at Cheyne Row. Reporting without a date, she tells us :—'I have had arguments, if it be not presumption to call them so, with Carlyle on this point,'—the happiness of virtue and the misery of vice.[1] 'It appeared to me that he confounded happiness with pleasure, with self-indulgence. He set aside with a towering scorn the idea of living for the sake of happiness so-called (which), he styled,—" the philosophy of the frying-pan." '

'Speaking of education, Carlyle said to me :—" I want to see some institution to teach a man the truth, the worth, the beauty, the heroism of which his present existence is capable. Where's the use of sending him to study what the Greeks and Romans did and said and wrote ? Do you think the Greeks and Romans would have been what they were, if they had just studied only what the Phenicians did before them ? " ' Mrs. Jameson afterwards wrote, 'I should have answered, had I dared,—Yet perhaps the Greeks and Romans would not have been what they were if the Egyptians and Phenicians had not been before them.' Which would have been irrelevant. The Greeks and Romans did not make their best young men waste their early years on Phenician or Egyptian grammatical gibberish.

Mrs. Jameson describes without naming 'a celebrated orator,' whom Carlyle apostrophised :—" You blasphemous scoundrel ! God gave you that gifted tongue of yours and set it between your teeth, to make known your true meaning to us, not to be rattled like a muffin-man's bell ! " Which was like what the Rev. George Gilfillan seems to have heard him say of Brougham : [2]—" an eternal grinder of commonplace and pretentious noise, like a man playing on a hurdy-gurdy."

[1] *A Commonplace Book of Thoughts, &c.*, by Mrs. Jameson, pp. 9, 34, 111–12, 1854. [2] *History of a Man*, by Rev. G. Gilfillan, p. 152.

VI

CARLYLE AS OTHERS SAW HIM

(1848)

ANOTHER interview without a date, which can hardly be later than 1848 and may be some years earlier, is reported by a young man who had come to London to push his fortune, and had a letter of introduction to Carlyle, perhaps from the Rev. David Aitken.[1] —

'I waited upon Mr. Carlyle one morning about ten o'clock, delivering my letter to a domestic who answered the bell, and in a few minutes was ushered into the presence of the great man. He received me with a cordial and rather vice-like grip of the hand. He had just had breakfast and was about to *resume* work, he said. He desired me to sit down beside him on the sofa, enquired as to the health of his friend who gave me the letter to him, and as to my own views in coming to London, and said :—" I have no connection with what is called the Press, and, I fear, if you expect any service from me in that way, I can do nothing or almost nothing."

'I at once said that I had no intention of asking an obligation, and had accepted the letter of introduction for the opportunity of seeing an eminent countryman. " Scot all over," he said to himself, looking towards the window, and after a pause, " Well," he said, " You seem self-reliant, and it is a quality generally characteristic of Scotsmen, but I have found myself in a situation not only to need, but to ask a favour ; and in doing so it was like treading upon burning marl. Well, then, if you are intent upon a literary career, I must warn you that it is a hazardous and most ungracious one, in which there are many blanks and few prizes, aye, and much disappointment and absolute humiliation ; but, after all, a facility of literary composition may be turned to a useful account in life, and success would be more general if young writers would only stick to the

[1] *An Hour with Thomas Carlyle*, by John Wilson, *West Middlesex Advertiser*, 23.8.84.

veracities, and tell us all about what they themselves have seen and known, whether in the way of prose or poetry, for I see my friend says you have written verses."

'I acknowledged the fact, and told him they had received commendation from Robert Chambers of Edinburgh. "Then you ought to feel a little flattered, for there could be no more competent judge, but my advice would be not to continue to write poetry except as an occasional amusement." "But," I said, "I do not mean to follow a literary career. I have come to London to assist a Mr. Wilson in a newspaper, *tho not as a writer*." "Oh, do you mean James Wilson?"' After making sure he meant James Wilson the economist, Carlyle went on.—' "He was an indigo merchant and was in other lines of business. I know Wilson; he is a remarkable man, and as sure as Fate will reach some position of eminence, unassuming as he is, and shy of manner."'

It is easy to agree with the reporter that this foresight showed 'sagacity,' for Wilson was a wonderfully good exponent of right principles in trade and finance. Tho he did not enter Parliament till 1847, he had started the *Economist* in 1843; and it might with some truth be said that while Cobden persuaded the voters that the Corn Laws should be abolished, James Wilson persuaded Peel and his like; and everybody agreed that the £10,000 presented to Wilson in 1846 by the Anti-Corn-Law League was well deserved. He was afterwards a successful Minister of State, and in India in a single year put right the finances after all the confusion of the Mutiny, and made many changes which experience has justified. If Carlyle was speaking before 1847, the insight he showed was wonderful; but the reporter leaves us guessing as to that,—telling only that Carlyle gave him in conclusion 'much sound practical advice, tendered in a courteous, almost affectionate manner,' and leave to call again.

Another witness, whose evidence cannot be later than 1848 and may be a little earlier, is David Lester Richardson, once of the Bengal Army, but in 1848 a man of forty-seven, with much experience as a newspaper editor. Here is his report.[2]—

'Carlyle rather startled me. I expected to see a pale, scholar-like, or half-parson-like sort of man, something

[2] *Literary Chit-Chat, &c.*, 1848, by Col. David Lester Richardson, pp. 194–5.

rather of the recluse than the man of the world. He is a tall athletic Scotchman, with some ungainliness, but no timidity or *mauvaise honte*. His features are a little coarse, but very expressive, and by no means unpleasing. His look is shrewd, yet kindly. His voice is loud, his accent broad Scotch, his movements angular. You see at once that he is no ordinary person. (When) he begins to converse freely, you discover that he has both strength and refinement of intellect and great fervour of feeling.

'In conversation he is not so neat, brilliant and epigrammatic as Macaulay, but he is more cordial and exhibits greater ardour and generosity. Carlyle opens the hearer's heart—Macaulay closes it. There is an undercurrent of sarcasm and contempt in Macaulay. Carlyle exhibits none of this offensive condescension. His associates feel *safe* in his presence, and do not anticipate that he will laugh at his guest as soon as the door is closed.'

VII

HOPE REVIVED

(1848)

SOLILOQUIZING in February, 1848, on what to write about, Carlyle remarked that this was a '*Scavenger Age*, really up to nothing better than the sweeping out the gutter. Might it but do that well! It is the indispensable beginning of all.' This was his habitual feeling, one of complete detachment from passing squabbles; but even as the 1830 Revolution in Paris made him look anew at current events, and was one of the reasons why he wrote *The French Revolution*, so the 1848 disturbances, when he had rested enough after Cromwell to be looking for fresh work, led him into contemporary politics. First of all he articulated what was really needed,—efficient administration of public business; and when it seemed too much to hope for any heed about that from the 'public men' in power, he turned him to the task of showing in *Frederick the Great* what the efficient administration of public business was like. Incidentally in holding up the mirror to reality, he revealed eighteenth century Europe as it really was,—giving us a movie-picture of men's souls, like the best of Tacitus.

It was before the end of February that the pleasant news came from Paris of another revolution; and immediately, instead of merely buying as usual a newspaper for his wife to read, and remaining himself content with whatever she distilled to him, or others told him in private, he now began to take in the *Times* and study it closely, as well as a French daily paper. Soon he was complaining to Espinasse [1] that he had expected from the *Times* "cleverer writing than he found in it," with its "Johnsonian" articles and "sentences all properly balanced." He spoke of the clever journalists,—enquiring, "What are these fellows doing? They serve only to cancel one another." To which Espinasse as a journalist at once replied, "They are like barristers who

[1] *Literary Recollections*, by F. Espinasse, pp. 224–5.

put neatly and concisely the cases of their clients, the political party which the newspaper supports, and which supports the newspaper." To which there was no rejoinder, perhaps because Carlyle was, at this very time,[2] recommending Espinasse to John Forster for employment, and was therefore content to see him rate highly his occupation of "guiding the people forward from day to day."

As early as 27.2.48 Carlyle himself was offering Forster an article for the *Examiner* on French affairs, and an article of his appeared there on 4.3.48.[3] It welcomed the downfall of 'Sophist Guizot' and 'Sham-King Louis Philippe,' and their 'cunningly devised system of iniquity in all its basest shapes.' Matthew Arnold and other young men admired the article much ; [4] but the cautious editor had had to cut it, and he suppressed altogether another meant to follow it, lest Carlyle's excessive candour might damage the circulation of the *Examiner*. What frightened him then may be interesting now.

Carlyle in talk would call Louis Philippe 'a royal Ikey Solomon' [5] ; but in writing he was altogether serious. He said bluntly that the worst feature of a Republic such as that at Paris was that it had to be a Government of Talkers, a self-cancelling Government. 'Nevertheless, essentially there are Republics, even with this sad feature, that keep going for some time. We ourselves are to most practical intents a Republic surmounted by civil lists, and various theatrical fringings and inert heraldic supporters, animate and inanimate, inert all of them :—whether now a Republic, surmounted by a bit of tricolour bunting, can subsist, without any fringing or inert heraldic supporters at all ? That is verily the question. Alas ! If the horoscope of England itself, to the thinking man that looks even a few years ahead, is very doubtful, what may that of this new French Republic at the Hôtel de Ville be ? For we English, moreover, are used to our Government of Talkers ; are of quiet, even sluggish nature, capable of holding on by phantasms, generations after the substance has vanished.'

If the Czar sought to crush the French Republic, 'nearly the one *casus belli* we could imagine in England would be a

[2] Letters in the John Forster Collection, South Kensington Museum.
[3] Reprinted in *Rescued Essays of Thomas Carlyle*, by P. Newberry, Leadenhall Press.
[4] *Letters of Matthew Arnold*, by G. W. E. Russell, I, pp. 3 & 4.
[5] *Rems. of my Irish Journey*, by T. Carlyle, p. 175.

war, not against France, but by the side of France ; a truly sacred war, in defence of France, and of her cause and ours.'

It was not for lack of sympathy that Forster shuddered at such sentiments. It may have been to him that Leigh Hunt was writing (3.3.48) :[6] —' The state of things in France is DIVINE. I am republican, in spite of pension, Queen and all, when I read every day what these glorious men are doing. . . . Why did not Shelley live to see it ? . . . Perhaps he does . . . ! ! ! ' Of course, the Queen had had nothing to do with his pension, which was given by the Liberal Government, mainly as compensation for what he had suffered from George IV and the Tories.[7]

The day after his first article appeared, Carlyle, who objected to being muzzled, was writing what can now be called a draft of his plan for the *Latter-Day Pamphlets*.—

' March 5.—Scheme of volume : *Democracy*. What one might have to say on it ? (1) Inevitable now in all countries ; regarded vulgarly as *the* solution. Reason why it cannot be so ; something farther and ultimate. (2) Terrible disadvantage of the Talking Necessity ; much to be said here. What this comes from. Properly an insincere character of mind. (3) Follows deducible out of that ! Howardism. Regard every Abolition Principle man as your enemy, ye reformers. Let them insist not that punishment be abolished, but that it fall on the right heads. (4) *Fictions*, under which head come Cants, Phantasms, alas ! Law, Gospel, Royalty itself. (5) Labour question. Necessity of government. Notion of voting to all is delirium. Only the vote of the wise is called for, of advantage even to the voter himself. Rapid and inevitable progress of anarchy. Want of bearing *rule* in all private departments of life. Melancholy remedy : " Change as often as you like." (6) Tho men insincere, not all equally so. A great choice. How to know a sincere man. Be sincere yourself. *Career open to talent. This actually is the conclusion of the whole matter.*[8]

' Six things. It would make a volume. Shall I begin it ? I am sick, lazy, and dispirited.'

He can be seen through the eyes of Emerson on

[6] *Correspondence of Leigh Hunt*, II, p. 90.

[7] See *Athenæum* newspaper article, 18.6.1881, quoting the letter of the Prime Minister and giving the full text of Carlyle's " memoranda concerning Mr. Leigh Hunt."

[8] Italics added.

9.3.1848.[9]—'Carlyle is in the best humour at the events in France. For the first time in his life he takes in a daily paper—the *Times*—and yet I think he has not much confidence in the ability of the French to carry such great points as they have to carry. He interests himself a good deal in the Chartists, and in politics generally, tho with abundant contempt for what is called *political* . . . speaking the best opinions one is likely to hear in this nation. . . The guiding genius of the man, and what constitutes his superiority over other men of letters, is his commanding sense of justice and incessant demand for sincerity.'

In conversation with Matthew Arnold, Emerson added :—"Carlyle is much agitated by the course of things ; he had known, he said, a European Revolution was inevitable, but had expected the old state of things to last out his time."[10]

[9] *Life of R. W. Emerson*, by A. Ireland, p. 202.
[10] *Letters of Matthew Arnold*, by G. W. E. Russell, p. 7.

VIII

PEEL AND OTHERS

(1848)

MUCH was to happen before the *Latter-Day Pamphlets* appeared; but some talk reported in the opening pages of the first of them gives a good idea of what Carlyle was now saying at dinner-tables.—

'Not long ago, the world saw a real miracle, a Reforming Pope. A good country-priest, unexpectedly' made Pope, 'takes the New Testament [for] his rule of governing,—no more finesse, chicanery, hypocrisy, or false or foul dealing: God's truth shall be spoken on the throne called of St. Peter: an honest Pope shall preside there. The European populations everywhere hailed the omen; with shouting and rejoicing: thinking people listened with astonishment. To such it was very clear how this poor devoted Pope would prosper. . . .

'"Reforming Pope?" said one of our acquaintance often in those weeks, "Was there ever such a miracle? About to break-up that huge imposthume too, by curing it? Turgot and Necker were nothing to this. God is great; and when a scandal is to end brings some devoted man to take charge of it in hope, not in despair!"

'"But cannot he reform?" asked many. . . .

'"Reform a Popedom,—hardly. A wretched old kettle, ruined from top to bottom, and consisting mainly now of foul *grime* and *rust*: stop the holes of it, as your antecessors have been doing, with temporary putty, it may hang together yet a while; begin to hammer at it, solder at it, to what you call mend and rectify it,—it will fall to sherds, as sure as rust is rust; go all into nameless dissolution,—and the fat in the fire will be a thing worth looking at, poor Pope!"

'The Sicilians were the first notable body that set about applying this new strange rule . . . the law of veracity.' So 'by favour of Heaven and the Pope' the fighting began, 'insurrection fiercely maintained in the Sicilian Cities' against Neapolitan Officials,—the news of which 'aggravated the feeling of every Frenchman, as he looked on a Louis-Philippism which had become the scorn of all the world, repression, corruption, dishonesty,' and so on. 'We know what France became in February; and can trace a share in that event to the good simple Pope with the New Testament in his hand. Close following which all Europe exploded. Everywhere Democracy rose monstrous, bellowing [to] Kings and reigning persons, "Begone, ye imbecile hypocrites, histrios not heroes! Off with you, off!" What was notable, the Kings all made haste to go, as if exclaiming, "We *are* poor histrios," play-actors, "we, sure enough;—did you want heroes? Don't kill us; we couldn't help it!" They fled precipitately, some of them with what we may call an exquisite ignominy,—in terror of the treadmill or worse! . . .'

In an article in the *Examiner*, 4.3.48,[1] Carlyle described the reign of the runaway 'Sham-King Louis Philippe' with candour.—'Here is a man accepting the supreme post among his fellow-men, and deliberately, with steadfast persistence, for seventeen years . . . appealing to what was bad and false and sordid, and to that only. His management has been a cunningly devised system of iniquity in all its basest shapes. Bribery has flourished; scandalous corruption, till the air was thick with it, and the hearts of men sick. Every serviceablest form of human greed and lowmindedness has this "source of honour" patronized,'—as if 'sovereign ruler' meant 'supreme swindler.'

It is difficult to imagine now how very perplexing talk to this effect would sound in London Society, where even such as Macaulay were haranguing as if the current shibboleths of English Political Economy were laws of Nature.[2] Conventional people in England who could see no need for revolution naturally felt there was no excuse for the continental disturbances. But when Carlyle was present, Macaulay was never allowed to spout without contradiction his do-nothing gospel of 'laissez-faire' or let alone, so that the most philanthropic of the aristocrats, Lord Shaftesbury, was writing in his diary:—[3]

[1] Reprinted in *Rescued Essays of T. Carlyle*, by P. Newberry, pp. 3–13.

[2] See, e.g. *G. O. Trevelyan's Lord Macaulay*, Ch. XI, Lord Carlisle's journal, entry of 4.3.48.

[3] *The Life, &c., of the Earl of Shaftesbury*, by E. Hoddin, II, p. 239.

'March 10th.—Breakfasted with Mahon, to meet Macaulay and Carlyle; pleasant, but strange.' This would be Lord alias Viscount Mahon, afterwards Earl Stanhope, the historian and the champion of copyright, who by and by did much in Parliament for the National Portrait Gallery.

Two days later, on 12.3.48, Mrs. Austin was writing to Dr. Whewell, "the harmonious blacksmith." Her husband was the Utilitarian jurisprudent known to law-students as the flunky-philosopher, and she quoted him with wifely docility as abusing Carlyle for being "worse than foolish," showing "gross insensibility to the sufferings of others" by "exulting in this awful ruin."[4] The Austins had been living in Paris from 1844, but the fear of revolution-rows had now sent them home. Their irritation was natural. But even where 'some were his warm friends,' Emerson remarked this month[5] that the talk of Carlyle found 'little reception. The aristocrats say, "Put that man in the House of Commons, and you will hear no more of him."' Which may have been why he was now thinking of going into the Commons, as he afterwards confessed. It could have been easily arranged.

On 14.3.48 Carlyle was dining at the American Ambassador Bancroft's, in the company of Bunsen and Macaulay, Milman and Emerson; and on the Saturday following, 18.3.48, the night of the bloody Berlin insurrection, he was at the dinner-table of the Barings, sitting next to Sir Robert Peel, but rather listening than talking. Peel was delighting him by his humour, speaking of "Milnes Ouvrier," [working-man], 'with an innocent archness, in allusion to our coming revolution.' Milnes had changed sides in politics at the end of 1847, quitting the Carlton Club and going over to the Whigs,[6] while rejoicing like Leigh Hunt at the victory of Liberty and the Republic, so that jealous wits were saying he wanted to be available if needed for the Presidency of an English Republic.

As long ago as 1840 Guizot had noticed what best explains how Peel and Carlyle drew together :—"What struck me most of all in the private talk of Sir Robert Peel was his perpetual and earnest anxiety about the condition of the

[4] *Three Generations of Englishwomen*, by Mrs. Ross, I, p. 216.
[5] *R. W. Emerson*, by J. E. Cabot, II, pp. 148–9.
[6] *R. M. Milnes, Lord Houghton*, by T. Wemyss Reid, I, pp. 401–6 and 414.

working classes in England. His anxiety was as much moral as political; and one could see through his calm and measured words the feelings of the man as well as the foresight of the statesman."[7]

By 1848 Peel was sixty, and appeared to Carlyle to be 'a finely made man of strong (and) elegant stature; stands straight, head slightly thrown back, and eyelids modestly drooping; every way mild and gentle, yet with less of that fixed smile than the portraits give him.' He looked his age, 'especially in his complexion, when you are *near* him: clear, strong blue eyes which kindle on occasion, voice extremely good, low-toned, something of *cooing* in it, rustic, affectionate, honest, mildly persuasive.'

He said he had *seen* General Dumouriez, and in discussing French Revolutions generally he appeared to be 'well read in all that,' noted Carlyle, who added that he was 'reserved seemingly by nature, obtrudes nothing of diplomatic reserve.' His best story was about a body of rioters who in the Reform Bill time had been set to howl down the Lords in their coat-of-arms coaches. "Why don't you shout?" cried one to another. "No, I reserves myself for the tulip," said the other, meaning the Mitre on a bishop's coach.

Even the old Pope was now seeking change of air, and on Monday, 20.3.48, Mazzini was calling to take leave. He was in high spirits, according to Mrs. Carlyle, with nothing to complain about but the prospect of being allowed to go home to Genoa in peace. That seemed "*extremely distressing* to him!!!"[8] Even in sleepy London special constables were being enrolled as a protection to property against a Chartist rising, announced for the approaching tenth of April,—it should have been the first!

Carlyle was intently surveying what he called the "General Bankruptcy of Humbug"[9] in all directions. A letter of 24.3.48 to his friend "St. Thomas" (Erskine of Linlathen) reveals his mind.—

'Hardly since the invasion of the wild Teutons and wreck of the old Roman Empire has there been so strange a Europe, all turned topsy-turvy, as we now see. What was at the top has come, or is rapidly coming, to the *bottom*.

[7] *Memoirs of Sir Robert Peel*, by M. Guizot, p. 83, and *Peel*, by J. R. Thursfield, p. 187.
[8] *Jane Welsh Carlyle, Letters, &c.*, by Leonard Huxley, p. 308.
[9] Letter to Thomas Aird, p. xxxvii of the Memoir prefixed to the *Poetical Works of Thomas Aird*, by Rev. J. Wallace.

'All over London people are loud upon the French. Right to hurl out Louis Philippe, most of us said or thought, but there I think our approval ended. The what next upon which the French had been thinking, none of our people will seriously ask themselves. I, in vain, strive to explain that this of the "organization of labour" is precisely the question of questions for all governments whatsoever; that it vitally behoved the poor French Provisional to attempt a solution; that by their present implements and methods it seems impossible they should succeed; but that they, and what is better, all governments, must actually make some advance towards success and solve said question more and more, or disappear swiftly from the face of the earth without successors nominated. There seems to me only that alternative; and, however it may fare with the French, I calculate that we here at home shall profit inexpressibly by such an example, if we be wise to try the inevitable problem while it is yet *time*. In fact, I have a kind of notion to write a book about it. . . . Fraternity, liberty, &c., I want to explain, is not the remedy at all; but true *government* by the wise, true, and noble-minded of the foolish, perverse, and dark, with or *against* their consent. . . .'

Saint Thomas was only one of several who sympathised. Many letters remain to show that perhaps nobody was more cordially in agreement with him than the husband of the Lady Harriet, Mr. Bingham Baring, who was to become this May Lord Ashburton and one of the richest men in England, by his father's death and no fault of his own. The friendship uniting him and Carlyle grew into warm affection which never abated.

On 24.3.48, while Carlyle was writing to "Saint Thomas," the American Ambassador George Bancroft, the historian, was writing to James Buchanan, the future President.—[10]

'Am I never again to have a letter from you? Is the country rousing itself for sound principles? Has the echo of American Democracy which you now hear from France, and Austria, and Prussia, and all old Germany, no power to stir up the hearts of the American people to new achievements? . . .

'Here the aristocracy are overwhelmed with gloom. In the court circle I alone am the one to speak and think of the French Republic with hope, with subdued exultation, with

[10] *Life and Letters of George Bancroft*, by M. A. D. Howe, II, p. 33.

trust. The Queen was greatly agitated. If France succeeds, there will not be a crown left in Europe in twenty years, except in Russia, and perhaps England. . . .'

Carlyle was sharing neither the hopes of Leigh Hunt and Bancroft nor the gloom of the governing classes. In *Past and Present* (III and IX) he had said that abolishing the Corn Laws would give the English "room to breathe" and "time to bethink ourselves, to repent and consider." So he could now agree with Peel who was boasting that he had done that. When the news of revolution in Paris reached the House of Commons, Cobden had said to Hume,—"Go and tell Sir Robert Peel." When Hume told him, Peel pointed to the Protectionists and said, "That is what would have happened here if these gentlemen had had their way." Many years afterwards Mr. Gladstone said,—"If the repeal of the Corn Laws had been defeated, or even retarded, we should have had a revolution." Even with the Corn Laws repealed, Charles Kingsley and his associates apprehended a revolution this April.[11]

About this time when the French were preparing for a general election, there appeared among them 'an address to the electors which caused a considerable sensation,' says Espinasse.[12] 'It advised them to give their suffrages to none but plain honest men who would make all the better deputies if they were uneducated, or had very little to do with "the alphabet." Carlyle warmly approved of the tone and tenor of this address, but some time afterwards, when it turned out that it was the handiwork of George Sand, he just as warmly condemned it.'—Which seemed to Espinasse an illustration of Carlyle's 'liability to have his judgments affected by his prejudices.' But it is only in such matters as mathematics and science that the value of words does not depend on the character of the speaker. In morals and politics a voice which is only a voice is seldom of much account. When English journalists begin to sign their articles, they may begin to—come into their own. Meanwhile it is surely likely that an address to the electors, which might seem wise and praiseworthy if put forth by a responsible person or committee, might be ridiculous or a nuisance if published anonymously by Mrs. Dudevant.

Amid sounds more ominous than thunder, "excursions

[11] *Collections and Recollections*, by G. W. E. Russell, p. 142.
[12] *Literary Recollections*, by F. Espinasse, p. 171.

and alarms" as if it were the day of judgment, there was another bit of farce in the current news from France.[13]—

'April 17 (1848).—Lord Brougham, in coming back to England, not only had much of his baggage stopped as he came out of Lyons, as being too much for a good citizen, but three times between there and Paris was forced out of his carriage to salute "trees of Liberty." Conceive his face under the last operation.' They should have made him kneel!

Next day (18.4.48) the *Times* had a better joke,[14] which set the world laughing. Henry Lord Brougham at Paris had applied on 7 and 10.4.48 to the Minister of Justice for a peculiar kind of naturalisation, to be made Citizen Brougham in France and eligible for election to its Parliament, while retaining in England all his rights as a British Peer and his pension as an ex-Lord Chancellor. "Political Bigamy" the French called it. An Irish politician had once told the Speaker that "a man could not be in two places at once, unless he is a bird"; but not even an Irish political joker could think that possible for Brougham.

[13] *Life of Bishop Wilberforce*, by A. R. Ashwell, II, pp. 10–11.
[14] *Life of Lord Brougham*, by John Lord Campbell, pp. 550–6. *The Lives of the Lord Chancellors*, Vol. VIII, pp. 550–6.

IX

JOSEPH NEUBERG INTRODUCED

(1848)

WHEN lecturing at Nottingham in winter Emerson had been the guest of Joseph Neuberg, a man of forty-three, and a cosmopolitan. Originally from near Würzburg, Neuberg had long been a prosperous manufacturer at Nottingham, and was thinking now of retiring from business. His wife had died, he was childless, and he was feeling one had something else to do as well as money-making.[1] What else? It is the sphinx riddle of life.

In taking Emerson about, to Newstead Abbey and elsewhere,[2] Neuberg may have disclosed the modest thought he afterwards told to the Discussion Society[3] he had started, that a man of business who lets himself go into making more and more can only satisfy the "meaner half" of his being, and failing to provide for the "spiritual life," becomes "blinded, dwarfed, stupefied" in soul and little better than the Helots described by "our master Carlyle." In plainer words, he remains more ignorant and stupid than he need have been.

Emerson discovered Neuberg's feelings towards Carlyle, and said to Miss Neuberg, who kept house for her brother,—"I am surprised the acquaintance is confined to writing." She answered,—"I do believe my brother would give his little finger to know Carlyle." To which Emerson warmly responded,—"I shall not leave England without bringing the two together."[4] And so about Saturday, 1.4.48, he took Neuberg with him to Cheyne Row. Emerson wrote

[1] *Nottingham Review*, 5.10.1849, p. 2.

[2] *R. W. Emerson*, by A. Ireland, pp. 165–9 and 203.

[3] Address to the Discussion Society at Nottingham, by Joseph Neuberg, p. 6.

[4] For this and the letter following, see *Macmillans Magazine*, August, 1884, p. 280. The nephew of Mr. Neuberg, to whom we owe it and the documents already quoted, certifies that the article was by Dr. Sadler and authentic.

PLATE II

JOSEPH NEUBERG

From a photo which hung in the bedroom of Carlyle many years and was there when he died.

[*face p.* 32

to his wife this month[5] that he found Carlyle ill with 'an inflamed sore throat,' whereby 'I certainly obtained a fairer share of the conversation.'

Both Carlyle and his wife took to Neuberg from the first. 'A welcome, wise kind of man,' Carlyle called him in a letter to Emerson. 'Come and see us whenever you are in London,' wrote Mrs. Carlyle to him a few weeks later, and he must have been confiding his afflictions to her, for she added :—'That a man have a great and an enduring sorrow is enough always to make me his friend—provided that he do not weakly suffer it to master him. It is only the sorrowing that I can understand and sympathise with. The people who are "at ease in Zion" surpass my comprehension. So it was that I never could *get up* the least interest or affection for Emerson ; for all so amiable as he is.'

They had also chess in common, and in years to come had many a game together ; but it was always her husband he really came to see. As he afterwards explained to Friedrich Althaus,[6] speaking of Carlyle,—"We were drawn together immediately. We agreed about everything and parted in hopes of meeting again. The revolutions were making both of us then look for the rebirth of the German people, and many a time I have heard him repeat, 'Long live the German Fatherland!'"

They had both the enthusiasm if not the hopes of youth, and said to each other that the hereditary Hohenzollern might do the same things "wisely, valiantly, justly, which Democracy was blindly and insanely striving for." They soon saw they were hoping too much, and were both disappointed by the squalid upshot. They had other topics, such as Goethe. It was Neuberg who first made known to Carlyle that Goethe's father's father was a tailor who came from the north,—"from between the Thuringian Forest and the Harz Mountains"[7]—to push his fortune in Frankfurt, and married there an innkeeper's daughter, and grew rich by the inn. Neuberg had many questions to answer about that to satisfy Carlyle's curiosity. Biographers agree his story was true.

Neuberg was a man of five feet eight or nine inches, big and strong ; fair hair, and grey-blue eyes looking straight and steadily at you ; lips tightly compressed, the under one

[5] *Mem. of R. W. Emerson*, by J. E. Cabot, II, p. 155.
[6] *Friedrich Althaus*, in *Unsere Zeit.*, Leipzig, 1881, No. 6, p. 827.
[7] *Life of Goethe*, by A. Bielschowsky, English translation, I, p. 11.

slightly projecting; chin strong but not obtrusive. No wonder Nottingham was loath to lose him. Of all the services Emerson rendered to Carlyle, the introduction of Joseph Neuberg was far the greatest, for of all Carlyle's first-class disciples, so to speak, meaning the like of Emerson himself, Gavan Duffy and Tyndall, Masson and Espinasse, there was none so thoroughgoing, and none who was able to help him as Neuberg was to do yet,—the magnificently disinterested man.

X

LEWES, CAVAIGNAC, AND CHOPIN

(1848)

A DAY or two after Emerson brought Neuberg, Mrs. Carlyle went to stay with Lady Harriet at Addiscombe, to complete her convalescence after the winter's colds. Carlyle reported to them what he saw of the Chartists' tenth of April, describing Piccadilly as deserted by the usual frequenters,—'not a gentleman to be seen,'—while 'Wellington had his iron blinds all accurately down.' The Green Park was shut. So were the big gates of Constitution Hill, and a score of mounted guardsmen were 'privately drawn up under the arch.' The Chartists had been allowed to meet at Kennington Common, but they had quietly dispersed, when bidden by Feargus O'Connor.

Two days later Espinasse was calling, and describing what had been seen by himself and other reporters.[1] He tells us that 'Carlyle was beginning to compute how many persons in the vast assembly could have heard' O'Connor's voice, when Lewes came in, the same who afterwards wrote a good life of Goethe and lived with "George Eliot." She used to call him her "miniature Mirabeau," because he was ugly, almost monkey-faced, pock-marked and also small, and yet intelligent, if not altogether inspired. Mrs. Carlyle called him "the Ape" at first, but afterwards, "poor dear Lewes."

Espinasse was glad to meet a fellow-journalist of distinction, and says that he had expressive features which a smile made agreeable, and that he was transparently frank. He was not interested in Chartists. He had sent Carlyle a copy of his last new novel, and come to hear what he thought of it; and Espinasse was amused to watch how Carlyle 'fenced with the anxious enquirer,' soothing him without a fib, and comforting him with the news that Mrs. Carlyle had taken the book with her to the country, to be read there not only by herself, but also by "a very high

[1] *Literary Recollections*, by F. Espinasse, pp. 278–82.

lady," meaning Lady Harriet. He censured in general terms the amount of love-making in modern novels. Lewes referred to *Wilhelm Meister*. Carlyle :—" There is no more of that sort of thing in *Wilhelm* than the flirtation which goes on in ordinary life. I would rather have written that book than a cartload of others," and he went on to speak of Goethe's " Olympian Silence " and other high qualities.

There was a pause when he ended, and then Lewes began again about his own novel, asking Carlyle with a boyish air of frank simplicity,—" Were not the gaming scenes to be commended ? " ' Instead of answering that Carlyle launched into a description of a gaming-house,' which he had seen in Paris in 1824, and said nothing about Lewes's book, whereupon Lewes ' spoke of a Life of Robespierre he had then on the anvil ' as well as one of Goethe. Observing the wonder on the face of Espinasse, Carlyle said to him ' genially,'— " Lewes is not afraid of any amount of work."

The two journalists stayed till eleven, and departed together, keeping company as far as their roads allowed and talking of their trade. " Who is at the head of our literature ? " asked Espinasse. " Macaulay, undoubtedly," replied the other.

Meanwhile Carlyle was writing to his wife :—' Oh, my dear, be sorry for me ! I have been in a tempest of twaddle.' He told about Espinasse and Lewes, and said,—' No wonder I am surly at people.' Yet Espinasse certifies,—" There was no trace of surliness in his manner that evening." To see ourselves as others see us would sometimes be a pleasant surprise.

Mrs. Carlyle was enjoying fine weather at Addiscombe in Lady Harriet's company. She improved so quickly that in the first week she was successfully teaching the housekeeper the mystery of making marmalade. Before the end of the month she was back in London, where even the fribbles of fashion were talking politics. Louis-Philippe stayed in the shade ; but the runaway Prince of Prussia, alias " Prince Cartridge," was decorating the dinner-table of the Prussian Embassy in London till it was safe to go home. He lived to return and become by the grace of Bismarck the first Kaiser of the new German Empire. His grandson was the runaway Will of 1918 ; and was only following his grandfather's example in saving his people from any tepmtation to regicide by running away.

Few of the gentry in London needed to be told what

Carlyle was telling his mother this summer, that the General Cavaignac keeping order in Paris was brother of his deceased friend Godefroi Cavaignac.—'His poor old mother still lives; has now no child but him; has a strange history to look back upon from the days of Robespierre all the way. It is very curious to me to think how the chiefs of these people, as Armand Marrast [and] Clément Thomas (late Commander of the National Guards), used to sit and smoke a pipe with me in this quiet nook some years ago; and now Louis-Philippe is out and they are in—not for ever either.' Espinasse[2] says Armand Marrast had been brought to Cheyne Row by Cavaignac, and 'sung to Carlyle rustic songs in vogue among the French peasantry.' Mrs. Carlyle was writing this summer to her cousin, Helen Welsh:[3]—'The one earthly thing that I have been getting any real satisfaction out of has been the wise and valorous conduct of General Cavaignac—and the admiration he has won from all parties. If I had been his sister I could not have watched his progress with more interest.'

Perhaps the most welcome of all the "artists" whom the February Revolution sent from Paris to London was Chopin, the prodigy of pianists and the pet of fine ladies.[4] Mrs. Carlyle heard him twice performing and wrote to her cousin,—'I never heard the piano played before, could not have believed the capabilities that be in it.' Chopin called at Cheyne Row, and Carlyle told a common friend afterwards that he could see at once that he was "an excellent, gentle, much suffering human soul," and sent him kind messages; but never said a word about the affair that caused so much gossip. For many years Chopin had been living with Mrs. Dudevant, the fictioneer George Sand, who had become almost respectable by holding on to him so long. But this year she had cast him off, and he was dying of consumption. He was her junior, only thirty-eight while she was over forty and a grandmother, and she had put him in a novel and had no more use for him. When she heard he was dying she went to see him, but was refused admittance. If she had only known he was going to die so soon, she might not have cast him off.

[2] *Ibid.*, p. 238.

[3] *Jane Welsh Carlyle, Letters, &c.*, by Leonard Huxley, pp. 309–10.

[4] *Chopin*, by J. C. Hadden, Chapter VI in particular; and see *Literary Recollections*, by F. Espinasse, p. 267.

XI

ABOUT THE IRISH

(1848)

IT was a sign of the times that the violent Chartist was an O'Connor. The common people saw no need to revolt in England or in Scotland. It was only among the Irish that there was danger. And so it was now about Ireland that Carlyle was publishing a few words of wisdom. *The Repeal of the Union* is reported to have appeared in the *Examiner* on 29.4.1848; and a fortnight later a sequel to it on *Legislation for Ireland*. Two in the *Spectator*, *Ireland and the British Chief Governor*, and *Irish Regiments of the New Æra*, are dated about the same time.[1]

The last three were full-length articles. The first was two or three times the usual length, and directly aimed to clear away confusion of thought which might lead to violence. According to many of the Irish, he explains without naming "Dan," the *Repeal of the Union* is the one thing needed to make Ireland happy. But it is impossible. Ireland is too close to England. Repealing the union would enable foreigners, French, American, and other, to interfere in English business.—

'True, the Irish have enough to complain of. We too have governing classes that do not govern, and working classes that cannot longer do without governing. But we bear our woes till they can be articulated into proposals; we do not think (that) to rush out into the street and knock men down will be the way of healing them. Considerable improvements have been made in this island; but what is remarkable, by pikes and insurrection not one of them hitherto. Our Civil War itself proceeded according to Act of Parliament. . . . So the case stands thus. Ireland is

[1] For dates, *Thomas Carlyle*, by W. H. Wylie, p. 245. All are reprinted by the Leadenhall Press, edited by P. Newberry, and named *Rescued Essays of Thomas Carlyle*.

invited to become British; to right its wrongs along with ours.'

A good Belfast doctor, Henry MacCormac, sent a protest or supplement to this article, and explained that Ireland suffered from "the abstraction of capital in every form, produce sent out to be sold to pay rents to absentees," etc. The address was odd:—

—— Carlyle,
Author of the *French Revolution*,
—— Street (name of Street forgotten),
Chelsea (if not in Chelsea to be forwarded).[2]

Carlyle wrote to the editor of the *Examiner* and did all he could, with what success does not appear, to get a hearing for MacCormac, who complained that London papers were taking no notice of a letter he had addressed to Lord John Russell!!!

In *Legislation for Ireland* Carlyle derided Lord John Russell for proposing trumpery bills for the registration of voters, and neglecting one for the sale of encumbered estates. He applauded as 'a small piece of everlasting Justice in Chancery dialect' the new Poor Law of 1834, which purported to stop death by starvation, and pointed out that the landlords and tenants were 'all in one boat now,' and that encumbered estates should be sold.

The *Spectator* article on *Ireland and the British Chief Governor* was also a demand for remedial measures for Ireland, inasmuch as 'the law of Nature itself makes us now participant of Ireland's wretchedness. *Steam-passage from Ireland is occasionally as low as fourpence a head.*' [3]

The second *Spectator* article on *Irish Regiments of the New Æra* was a plea for organizing labour in Ireland, where something of that sort was urgently needed. He dwelt on how the Irish talent for fighting had been utilised in regiments, and suggested to make use of 'another and a still better' talent, that for *digging*.—'The Irish show an indisputable talent for spade-work. Men skilled in the business testify that, with the spade, there is no defter or tougher worker than the common Irishman. . . . This delving talent brings no advantage to the possessor of it.' He is not set to work as he should be; 'and his fate at present, with nothing but "supply and demand" buzzing round

[2] Unpublished letter, South Kensington Museum.
[3] Italics added.

him, and in *his* ear the doom-summons, "Thou shalt die starved for all thy digging talent," is the hardest of any creature's, and unjustest. Much is put off till the morrow; but this, of trying to find some spade-work for the disorganic spademen, cannot be delayed much longer. Colonels of field-labour *can* be found if you search with diligence. . . .'

Carlyle referred to the parliamentary debates as 'public-speaking transacted in the hearing of twenty-seven millions, many of whom are fools.' Wherein he was saying ditto to Benjamin Franklin and Rabelais, and was no more original than if he had been quoting the multiplication table, for it is a commonplace in almost every religion and philosophy that we are all born fools, and that most of us continue so in many ways. But Press and platform were so much alike in flattering and misleading the people that he was now almost alone in saying such a thing, and it became a fashion to quote it as an eccentricity of his! Which made him repeat it and emphasize it as a commonplace; and that was the main thing that made simple persons suppose him "no better than a Tory."

On 16.5.48 he was writing to someone:—[4] "If land and the people could be brought into the true relation to one another, there need not be, at this hour, an idle man in Ireland. I think it a pity the Lord Lieutenant himself, or some other, did not call together practical Rational Persons such as you, and ask,—what can be done?"

Instead of which Lord Clarendon, the Lord Lieutenant, who had learned little but "diplomacy," was now arresting John Mitchel and Co., and about to arrest Gavan Duffy; and had no leisure to attend to anything so vulgar as organizing labour.

[4] Letter sold at Sotheby's and printed in the *Pall Mall Budget*, 10.12.1891.

XII

EMERSON IN LONDON

(1848)

EMERSON went over to Paris to see a revolution in the making. But early in June " the seraphic man " returned to London to lecture, by special request, to the gentry in Portman Square, and to the middle class in Exeter Hall.[1]

Carlyle attended, of course; and 'very soon after the delivery of the first lecture' took Espinasse with him on a visit of congratulation, which was 'embarrassing. He could get out little more than that the lecture was "very Emersonian." Then the subject was swiftly dismissed' and they talked of a common friend, and 'Carlyle laid it down as a fact that a long upper lip denoted " a certain resonance to the noble," ' which Espinasse noted as edifying, but women of sense laughed at, saying they wondered he did not postulate a moustache as well, seeing his wife had both. There is something likeable in the sage's absurdity.

He went to all the lectures, and 'elsewhere than in Emerson's presence,' according to Espinasse, called them " moonshine," and then again, " intellectual sonatas." He told Espinasse that " the high people " complained that Emerson " had little to say to them " ; and it was true that Emerson usually sat silent at the London dinner-tables. Which may be why Carlyle declared he was ' " a beautiful figure among those talking Yankees," and the ideal of an American gentleman.'

In private conversation while the lectures were in progress, Carlyle told Emerson the audience " was partly new at every lecture."[2] Carlyle had so much to say about the evil times that Emerson at first supposed he meant to start a newspaper, and he was thinking of that; but also of

[1] *Literary Recollections*, by F. Espinasse, pp. 160, 165; and the John Forster Collection, South Kensington Museum, for the special request, signed by T. C., Charles Dickens, Bulwer-Lytton, etc.

[2] *R. W. Emerson*, by J. E. Cabot, II, pp. 165–8, 170, 180, etc.

" short off-hand tracts, to follow each other rapidly, on the political questions of the day,"—the *Latter-Day Pamphlets*, in short, already in contemplation.

As Emerson wrote before long,[3]—' Thomas Carlyle is an immense talker . . . not mainly a scholar, like the most of my acquaintances, but a practical Scotchman, such as you would find in any saddler's or iron-dealer's shop, and then only accidentally, and by a surprising addition, the admirable scholar and writer he is. He has a strong religious tinge, with the utmost impatience of Christendom and Jewdom and all existing presentments of the good old story, and biding his time, meditating how to undermine and explode the whole world of nonsense which torments him. He is obviously greatly respected by all sorts of people and can see society on his own terms.' . . .

(To) ' young men, especially those holding liberal opinions, (who) admire free trade, freedom, moral suasion, freedom of the Press (etc.), he says he thinks the first thing he would do in Parliament would be to turn out the reporters, and stop all manner of mischievous speaking to Buncombe' (*alias* bunkum). '" In the Long Parliament," he says, " the only great Parliament,—they sat secret and silent, grave as an ecumenical (or world-wide church) council, and I know not what they would have done to anybody that had got in there, and attempted to tell out of doors what they did." In short, instead of general go-as-you-please, the Government should show people what to do and make them do it. " Here the Parliament gathers up six millions of pounds every year to give to the poor, and yet the people starve. I think if they would give it to me to provide the poor with labour, and with authority to make them work, or shoot them,—and I to be hanged if I did not do it,—I could find them in plenty of Indian meal." This was merely his ultra-logical way of speaking, for flogging in the last resort is always enough to make men work—as well as compulsion can make them.

' He throws himself readily on the other side,' wrote Emerson, explaining that ' if you urge free trade,' he said,— " St. John (Bolingbroke) was insulted by the Dutch ; he came home, got the law passed that foreign vessels should pay high fees, and it cut the throat of the Dutch, and made the English trade." ' He finds the sight of a great mob

[3] *Impressions of Thomas Carlyle in* 1848, by Ralph Waldo Emerson, *Scribners' Monthly*, May, 1881, pp. 89–92.

depressing. He saw once, as he told me, three or four miles of human beings, and fancied that the earth' (pronouncing *ea* in the old way like *a* in way or fate), '"was some great cheese, and these were mites." If a Tory takes heart at his hatred of stump-oratory, he replies:—"Yes, the idea of a pig-headed soldier who will obey orders, and fire on his own father at the command of his officer, is a great comfort to the aristocratic mind."

'Mere intellectual partisanship wearies him; he detects if a man stands for any cause to which he is not born and organically committed. He hates a literary trifler (such as) Guizot, nor can decorum, the idol of the Englishman, win from him obeisance. Combined with this warfare on respectabilities, and pointing all his satire, is the severity of his moral sentiment. In proportion to the peals of laughter amid which he strips the plumes of a pretender' and ridicules hypocrisy, he 'worships whatever enthusiasm, fortitude, love or other sign of good nature is in a man. There is nothing deeper in his constitution than his humour. He feels that the perfection of health is sportiveness, and will not look grave even at dullness or tragedy. His guiding genius is his moral sense; but that is a truth of character, not of catechisms.

'He says,—"there is properly no religion in England. These idle nobles at Tattersall's,—there is no work or word of serious purpose in them; they have this great lying church; and life is a humbug." He prefers Cambridge to Oxford, but he thinks Oxford and Cambridge education indurates the young men, as the Styx hardened Achilles, so that when they come forth of them, they say, "Now we are proof: we have gone through all the degrees, and are case-hardened against the veracities of the Universe; nor man nor God can penetrate us."

'Edwin Chadwick is one of his heroes, who proposes to provide every house in London with pure water. In the downfall of religions, Carlyle thinks that the only religious act which a man nowadays can securely perform is to wash himself well.

'Of course, the new French Revolution of 1848 was the best thing he had seen, and the teaching this great swindler, Louis Philippe, that there is a God's justice in the Universe after all, was a great satisfaction.' He admired Czar Nicholas because he did not run away in a funk, like the rest of the kings in danger, but the date should be noticed, 1848. It was not till 1849 that Nicholas became the Don Quixote of royalty and waged bloody war needlessly upon Hungarian Liberals, which by and by brought nemesis upon him in the shape of the Crimean war.

Meanwhile Carlyle appeared to Emerson to be 'keeping the manly attitude best of all men in England. He has stood for scholars, for the people, for the Chartist, for the pauper, intrepidly and scornfully teaching the nobles their duty. In England, where the morgue of aristocracy has very slowly admitted scholars into society,—a very few houses only in the high circles being ever opened to them,—he has carried himself erect, made himself a power confessed by all men, and taught scholars their lofty duty. He never feared the face of man.'

As to what Carlyle thought of Emerson, we are left guessing a good deal. When Espinasse praised the "high ethical ideal" of the lecturer, Carlyle said,—"Emerson's ethics consist chiefly of prohibitions."

Espinasse referred to the "striking passage" wherein he "compared man's life on earth to a bird alighting on a rock, resting for a while, and then flying away into infinite space."

Carlyle :—"Merchant, you figure well."

Espinasse :—"What do you mean ?"

Carlyle :—"A man in Dumfriesshire—where every shopkeeper is called a merchant—entered a shop and was presented with a bill he could not pay. He inspected it carefully, and finding no mistake returned it to the shopkeeper, saying in a mournful yet complimentary tone,—'Merchant, you figure well.'"

It is a curious coincidence that in the seventh century the wise men of Northumbria, comparing the Christian religion with the pagan, said the life of man was like a sparrow's passage through the hall on a winter night. Coming in from the darkness, it tarries for a moment in the light and heat of the fire, and then flying forth it disappears again in the dark. Such is our life, the whence and whither unknown to us. So they decided for the new religion, as it seemed to have some certain knowledge on these points.[4] What Emerson was gently breaking to his audiences was that we knew no more of the whence and whither than our pagan fathers, except only this,—we knew that nobody could know. No wonder Crabb Robinson declared that he had

[4] *History of the English People*, by J. R. Green, I, pp. 64–5.

delivered " the most liberal discourse that Exeter Hall had ever heard." [5]

It was remarked of Emerson that he opened out and spoke more freely at the house of the Carlyles than anywhere else, and there it was that Espinasse said he ' listened to the most copious utterance which in private I ever heard come from Emerson's lips.

' It may have been a deliverance of Emerson's own, but he professed to be only repeating what had been said to him by a friend who complained of the domination of " the alphabet." In his European travels this friend had been struck with the much that had been said and was known about " the alphabet," men who had written anything, compared with the obscurity (of) great workers and doers from the architect of Cologne Cathedral onwards. A catalogue of illustrative contrasts followed. This depreciation of literature from Emerson did seem to me singular, but was, of course, echoed sympathetically by Carlyle.

' On another evening, the conversation turning on lecturing, Carlyle bantered Emerson on the easiness of his platform-tasks, reading " from a paper before him," and its contrast with his own difficulties, " a poor fellow, set up to hold forth without any paper " to help him.

' Mrs. Carlyle was more dissatisfied than her husband with Emerson's ethics. Dilating in his high-flown optimistic way on the ultimate triumph of good over evil,' so that one should not trouble oneself, he ' went the length of saying that even in a whore-house man is still tending upwards, or words to that effect. Mrs. Carlyle's indignation at this knew no bounds, and for some time she could scarcely speak of Emerson with patience. Emerson's admiration for her abated visibly, till at last he was heard to say that " the lady " was worth cultivating, mainly because she could tell you most about the husband.'

When Emerson finished his lecturing about the end of June, he had to decide which of " the unseen spectacles of England " was to fill his few remaining days there, and he decided for Stonehenge in the company of Carlyle.

[5] *R. W. Emerson*, by Dr. R. Garnett, p. 146.

English history therein.' (Or rather, is more likely to have said—"a key to all English history.") 'He can see, as he reads, the old saint of Iona sitting there, and writing, a man to men. The *Acta Sanctorum* show plainly that the men of those times believed in God, and in the immortality of the soul, as their abbeys and cathedrals testify: now, even the Puritanism is all gone. London is pagan. He fancied that greater men had lived in England than any of her writers; and, in fact, about the time when those writers appeared, the last of these (greater men) were already gone.

'We left the mound in the twilight, with the design to return the next morning. I engaged the local antiquary, Mr. Brown, to go with us to Stonehenge, on our way (to Wilton), and show us what he knew of the "astronomical" and "sacrificial" stones. I stood on the last, and he pointed to the "astronomical," and bade me notice that its top ranged with the sky-line. "Yes." "Very well. Now, at the summer solstice, the sun rises exactly over the top of that stone, and, at the (supposed) Druidical temple at Abury, there is also an astronomical stone, in the same relative position."

'In the silence of tradition, this one relation to science becomes an important clue; but we were content to leave the problem with the rocks. . . .'

Astronomers now calculate from the change in the point of midsummer sunrise, that if the builders made no mistake in fixing the axis of their temple, their date was 1840 B.C. or about that time.[2] Emerson continued:—

'After spending half an hour on the spot, we set forth in our dog-cart over the downs for Wilton, C. not suppressing some threats and evil omens on the proprietors, for keeping these broad plains a wretched sheep-walk, when so many thousands of English men were hungry and wanted labour. We came to Wilton and to Wilton Hall, the frequent home of Sir Philip Sidney, now the property of the Earl of Pembroke, and the residence of his brother, Sidney Herbert. My friend had a letter from Mr. Herbert to his housekeeper, and the house was shown, and Carlyle, catalogue in hand, did all too much justice' to the portraits, pictures, and statuary, while Emerson admired the lawn and the gardens.

'On leaving Wilton House we took the coach for Salisbury. The Cathedral, which was finished six hundred years ago,

[2] *The Age of Stonehenge*, by C. H. Stone, *XIX Cent. Mag.*, Jany., 1922.

THOMAS CARLYLE

From the painting by John Linnell, now in the National Portrait Gallery, Edinburgh. Dated 1844.

[*face p.* 48

has a modern air. Whilst we listened to the organ, my friend remarked,—" The music is good, and yet not quite religious, but somewhat as if a monk were panting to some fine Queen of Heaven." C. was unwilling, and (so) we did not ask to have the choir shown us, but returned to our inn,' and took train to Bishopstoke, where Arthur Helps received them and took them in his carriage to his house at Bishops Waltham.

XIV

EMERSON'S PLAN FOR PEACE

(1848)

On Sunday, 9.7.48, in the house of Arthur Helps, to continue Emerson's report,[1] 'we had much discourse on a very rainy day. My friends asked whether there were any Americans—*any with an American idea*,[2]—any theory of the right future of that country? Thus challenged, I said:—

" Certainly, yes: but those who hold it are fanatics of a dream which I should hardly care to relate to your English ears, to which it might be only ridiculous,—and yet it is the only true." So I opened the dogma of no-government and non-resistance, and anticipated the objections and the fun, and procured a kind of hearing for it. I said, it is true that I have never seen in any country a man of sufficient valour to stand for this truth, and yet it is plain to me that no less valour than this can command my respect. I can easily see the bankruptcy of the vulgar musket-worship,—though great men be musket-worshippers;—and 'tis certain, as God liveth, the gun that does not need another gun, the law of love and justice alone, can effect a clean revolution. I fancied that one or two of my anecdotes made some impression on C '—which would be very " like him," for ever reverent of reality,—' and I insisted that the absurdity of the view to English feasibility could make no difference to a gentleman; the soul might quote Talleyrand '—the ancient retort: " But I must live, Sir." " *I do not see the necessity*."

This is very Emersonian indeed. *The original quip referred to the life of another*, and meant,—I do not see the need for *you* to live. It was prehistoric—the natural idea of a savage ready to kill any one not on his side. As Emerson

[1] *Emerson's Works* Vol. IV, English Traits, Chapter XVI.
[2] Italics added.

applies it, it refers to *one's own life*! It is the *opposite* of the instinct of self-preservation. Emerson continued:—

'As I had thus taken in the conversation the saint's part, when dinner was announced, Carlyle refused to go out before me,—"he was altogether too wicked." I planted my back against the wall, and' Helps in short said 'he was the wickedest and would walk out first.'

In the afternoon, on the way to Winchester, Emerson said that his friends asked him many questions about American things. What Helps remembered was that both Emerson and Carlyle showed a 'very minute knowledge of grasses.'[3]

'Just before entering Winchester, we stopped at the Church of Saint Cross, and, after looking through the quaint antiquity, we demanded a piece of bread and a draught of beer, which the founder in 1136 commanded should be given to every one who should ask it at the gate. We had both, from the old couple who take care of the church. Some twenty people every day, they said, make the same demand. This hospitality of seven hundred years' standing did not hinder C. from pronouncing a malediction on the priest who receives £2000 a year that were meant for the poor, and spends a pittance on this small beer and crumbs.'

In Winchester Cathedral 'William of Wykeham's shrine-tomb was unlocked for us, and Carlyle patted affectionately the recumbent statue's marble hands, for he rightly values the brave man who built this Cathedral and the School here,' etc. Indeed he was a great worker in his day, William of Wykeham. "Everything was done by him and nothing without him," said Froissart. Emerson concluded:—'But it was growing late. Slowly we left the old house, and parting with our host, we took the train for London.'

In their talk at the house of Helps about the abolition of war, it is as likely as not that Emerson would repeat what he was fond of telling, an anecdote of the Duke of Wellington which he had heard from Samuel Rogers.[3] A lady was expressing a passionate wish to see a great victory, and Wellington said to her,—"Madam, there is nothing so dreadful as a great victory, excepting a great defeat."

Espinasse was on the lookout, as soon as they came back to London.[4] 'I saw Carlyle immediately after his return

[3] *Emerson's Works*, Vol. VI, p. 135,—"Quotation and Originality."
[4] *Literary Recollections*, by F. Espinasse, pp. 164–5.

from the Stonehenge expedition,' he says, 'and he was full of indignant protest against Emerson's doctrine of limitless *laissez-faire*,' or let men do what they like. Carlyle declared roundly,—"if acted on, it would prevent a man from so much as rooting out a thistle."

Our reporter was diligent in enquiries. 'As far as I was able at the time to make out,' he tells us,—'Emerson (had) startled his host and fellow-guest by propounding the doctrine of *non-resistance in its extremest form*. . . .[2] (His) theory was that the wise man should have such perfect confidence in the ongoings of the universe, the development of the human race included, as to refrain from fighting with pen or tongue, not less than with sword, for the good and against the bad, and should regard even the best government and legislation as superfluous interferences with the ordained economy of things. At any time Carlyle would have rejected Emerson's spiritual Quakerism. Much more must it have been repugnant during 1848, when he was boiling over with an almost insurrectionary indignation against things in general.'

It may have been after the Stonehenge trip, but all that seems sure is that it was in 1848 that Carlyle took Emerson to see some of the shady parts of London, in order to convince him that "the Devil is still active," and in short, that if one could see below the surface, "The Gates of Hell might be found in every street."

What a lady is reported[5] to have said that Emerson told her was :—"Carlyle was very angry with me—for not believing in a devil,"—in human shape, the only kind of Devil Carlyle believed in,—"and to convert me Carlyle took me amongst all the horrors of London,—the gin shops, etc.,—and finally to the House of Commons, plying me at every turn with the question, 'Do you believe in a Devil noo?'" If the "noo" is correctly reported, the question may have been part of some good story in Scottish dialect, for it was in telling such that Carlyle was likely to say "noo."

"Emerson broached some amazing theories," said Carlyle to Gavan Duffy afterwards,[6] "about war altogether ceasing in the world, but when he was closely pressed on the method of this prodigious change, luckily for him, luncheon was announced, and he would not speak one word more" about it.

[5] *Life of George Eliot*, by J. W. Cross, pp. 136–40.
[6] *Conversations with Carlyle*, by Sir C. Gavan Duffy, p. 201.

In Paris this summer, Clough had been Emerson's "chief dependence at the dinner hour and afterwards"[7] every day for a month.[8] Clough thought Emerson what Emerson ended by thinking Clough, an improvement on Carlyle, who seemed now to Emerson merely the "ablest living writer," but a typical Englishman himself, matter-of-fact to a fault and consequently "politically a fatalist," and careless of ideas.[1] Both Clough and Emerson felt far above the like of that, and there was nothing but approval from Emerson for what Clough said to him in bidding him farewell at the Liverpool docks,[8]—"Carlyle led us out into the wilderness and left us there." They lived to know better, especially Clough, who became an intimate at Cheyne Row, and if he had not died too soon, might have justified the hopes of Carlyle who said, "I expected great things of him."[8]

Whatever critics may say about Emerson's lack of humour, nobody can deny that his behaviour a few years later gives as good cause for laughter as anything in Don Quixote,—the humour of reality is always the best. It was when the American Civil War began. Carlyle had done all he could to avert it, and pugnacious for peace as usual cursed it aloud as the "Nigger-Agony"; whereas Emerson, the ethereal apostle of universal peace, and of infinite non-resistance, even to the death, the preternatural super-Quaker, was screaming to kill as loudly as the women or any other of the non-combatants.

[7] *Memoir of R. W. Emerson*, by J. E. Cabot, II, pp. 164, 173–4.
[8] *A. H. Clough*, by J. I. Osborne, pp. 92, 159, 66 and 156.

XV

IN VANITY FAIR

(1848)

IT was mainly in the evenings that Carlyle was now reading the Acts of the Saints or other books of general interest. The revolutionary disturbances of 1848 had been like a morning bugle to him. Daily he was at his desk in his working hours. As he afterwards said of the four years following 1845,—'Much was fermenting in me, in very painful ways. Irish Repeal, etc., newspaper articles,—trifling growls, words idly flung away. In the revolutionary 1848, matters had got to a kind of boiling pitch with me, and I was becoming very wretched for want of a voice. Much MS. was accumulating on me, with which I did not know what in the world to do.' What could he do when the most friendly editors were muzzling him ?

About this time he was soliloquizing in his journal (10.8.48).—'May I mark this as the *nadir* of my spiritual course at present ? Never till now was I so low—utterly dumb this long while, barren, undecided, wretched in mind. My right hand has altogether lost its cunning. Alas ! and I have nothing other wherewith to defend myself against the world without, and keep it from overwhelming me as it often threatens to do. Many things close at hand are other than happy for me just now ; but that is no excuse.' Which shows how exacting he was to himself ; for these vague words seem to refer to his private nightmare that his wife's nervous system might give way altogether and she sink into insanity. Most men of letters would feel that that was reason enough for their right hands being numb. His soliloquy went on.—'If my own energy desert me, I am indeed deserted. . . .

'The most popular character a man can have is that which he acquires by being offensive to nobody, soft and agreeable to everybody. All men will cordially praise him, and even in some measure love him if so. A fact worth some reflection : a fact which puts the popular judgment *out of court*, in individual moral matters. People praise or blame according as they themselves have fared softly or fared hardly in their intercourse with a man. And now who are "*they*"? Cowardly egoists, greedy slaves; servants of the Devil, for the most part. Woe unto you if you treat them softly, if *they* fare well with you! Oliver Cromwell, for doing more of God's will than any man, has to lie under the curses of all men for two hundred years. Consider and remember.'

It was not till 1851, when Macready took leave of the stage, that Carlyle took leave of the theatre,[1] but assuredly it was mainly to please his wife that he went to such places. 'In the season,' says Espinasse,[1] 'his wife would sometimes drive about with him to concerts, but except in the rare case of a Chopin, he cared little for them or for any music that was not Scotch and wedded to Scotch ballads. Mrs. Carlyle played and sang them very expressively,' but she surprised Espinasse by her emphasis in refusing to sing "Auld Robin Gray." Perhaps she thought it hollow, as her husband did. It may have been in 1848 that Carlyle said to Espinasse that he had been at the first performance of *Richelieu*, which Bulwer-Lytton wrote for Macready and everybody went to see, including Queen Victoria, 'and Carlyle declared that he felt quite sorry for her, condemned to sit and see a King made as wicked, weak, and contemptible as Louis XIII in Bulwer-Lytton's play.' This may have been apropos of the performance of *The Merry Wives of Windsor* at the Haymarket in 1848 by Charles Dickens and his friends.[2] The Queen was there too, and Espinasse says that 'seeing the Carlyles in a private box, he went to it, and found them there accompanied by Captain Sterling, John Sterling's brother. When the curtain fell, Carlyle said, "A poor play," but cried, "plaudite, plaudite!"'—which may perhaps have been one of the last times that that old Latin word was heard used in that way at the Haymarket. 'Mrs. Carlyle took a good deal of interest' in the lady who played Mrs. Quickly, Mary Cowden Clarke, Shelley's daughter, and Espinasse answering her questions had the pleasure of feeling himself useful.

An additional attraction in the box where the Carlyles sat may have been Mrs. Carlyle's cousin Jeannie, who kindly kept her company this summer, and whom Carlyle described

[1] *Literary Recollections*, by F. Espinasse, p. 267.
[2] *Life of Charles Dickens*, by J. Forster, II, p. 365.

to Forster,[3] 22.8.48, in accepting an invitation to dinner and a box at the Opera on 24.8.48 :—" A cheery bright little girl,—and the only specimen I know or ever saw of the ancient Scottish *golden hair,* once very fashionable, now quite gone out,—hair the colour of a new guinea."

It is likely Mrs. Carlyle had no other companion than Jeannie at a 'morning music party' given by a friend, where she was rather displeased to see girls of sweet seventeen 'trilling and quavering with *the smile* of a consummate opera singer' . . . to a crowd of ladies and '*young marriageable Lords,* one of whom, Lord Dufferin, said to me,—" A charming way of passing a morning this !—And such a capital thing—don't you think,—for curing them of all sorts of shyness ? " Decidedly !'[4]

It was Jeannie's enjoyment of the opera on 24.8.48 which kept them all in Forster's box 'till the very finish.' The centre of attraction, Jenny Lind, was no stranger to Carlyle, who had sat beside her months ago and 'had to speak French to her all dinner,' and found her 'a nice little, innocent, clear, *thin* " bit lassie," ' modest and sensible. As he watched her now on the stage, he thought her a 'genuine little creature' with good voice and skill, but unfortunately with 'nothing but *non*-sense to sing or act,' the piece being trash. Old Wellington came in to see it ; and Thackeray was there, and Lady Blessington. Carlyle watched the audience, as he wrote to his brother, 'some three thousand *expensive*-looking fools,' indifferent to the senselessness of the show. " Depend upon it," said he to Forster, when the ladies were not listening, of course, " the Devil is busy here to-night, wherever he may be idle."

Which makes it seem possible that among the MSS. he was now writing was the essay on *The Opera,* published in a " Keepsake for 1852 " by his friend Procter, " Barry Cornwall." Of course the essay dealt with the Opera in general terms, revealing how it amounted to the waste of music and the natural gifts of the actors, for the idle amusement of insignificant moneyed people. It is an excellent essay, as amusing as a vivid report, yet as serious as the best of sermons, differing indeed from sermons mainly in this, that the writer was a preacher who meant *all* he said.

[3] John Forster Collection in South Kensington.
[4] *Jane Welsh Carlyle, Letters, &c.,* by Leonard Huxley, p. 309.

XVI

AT THE GRANGE

(1848)

THERE is a hint of what Carlyle was thinking of in his working hours in a letter to the Rev. A. Scott, once Irving's assistant. 'Your Parisian connections,' he wrote in August, 'are of a more recent date than mine,' and for that reason he begged Scott to find out for him the truth of what had been in the English newspapers, about the 'national workshops' in Paris. It was said that workmen were being sent from there into the country, and under 'severe military discipline reclaiming waste lands. The principal question,' wrote Carlyle, 'would be, do the *ouvriers* (workmen) actually earn their franc and half daily, under these conditions, or are they merely *paid* so much daily, and made very miserable in the process?'

At the end of August Jeannie Welsh went home, and Carlyle and his wife went on a five-weeks' visit to the Ashburtons at the Grange in Hampshire. Dating from there on 19.9.48,[1] Carlyle sent on the best of the reports, which Mr. Scott had been able to get for him, to Thomas Spedding, who had suggested the enquiry.—'Here is a kind of answer concerning the French Task-workers on the Sologne, the best I have yet got. The Enterprise seems much smaller than the Newspapers represented it, and I doubt it will gradually die away, and leave not even an effective reminiscence of itself.'

Describing their visit, Mrs. Carlyle wrote to Mrs. Russell that it 'was anything but a *retirement;* for in London we should not have seen half so many people,—the house being filled with company the whole time.' Carlyle's report to his mother is more explicit.—

'Charles Buller is here—a very cheerful man to have beside one. The Lady's mother (the widow Lady Sandwich) is the only woman visitor except Jane. Lady Sandwich

[1] *Cornhill Magazine,* June, 1921, p. 750.

used to live always in Paris, till she was driven home by the late Revolution; a brisk, talking, friendly, and rather entertaining character; has been very beautiful at one time. She has no other daughters left but this, and no son but one; plenty of money, and fair health; but, alas! *Nothing to do*. That is not a very easy life after all.'

Mrs. Carlyle was writing at the same time to her cousin Jeannie,[2] and saying that Lady Sandwich 'is a *very* agreeable and a good sort of woman to my notion, tho her daughter can hardly endure her.' Mrs. Carlyle and Lady Sandwich became "very thick together," and continued friends as long as they lived. Carlyle's letter to his mother went on.—

'We have a store of other Lords—Lansdowne, Auckland, Granville, with one or two official commoners. Alas! as Stephenson the engineer said, and as I often say, "If it were not for the clothes, there would be little difference."'

It may have been on this occasion that "Dicky" Milnes complained to Lady Ashburton[3]—"You are more tolerant of Charles Buller's republicanism than of mine, and you know Charles is much redder than I am." "You mean—more read," said she, and changed the subject.

The Grange had a regiment of servants and remained as complete a "Castle of Indolence" as before the Reformation, when it was a Monastery. A letter from Carlyle to his brother John reveals the way of life there, which was typical.—

'Life in this grand mansion is one of total idleness . . . an elaborate *representation*. We rise about eight. Shaving, bathing, dressing, all deliberately done, last three-quarters of an hour. One might sleep to perfection here. Sleep is one's best employment at present. Before nine we are out, most of us, I eastward into a big portico that looks over lake and hillside towards the rising sun, where I smoke sauntering up and down, joined by Jane if she can manage it, much to my satisfaction. Breakfast is at half-past nine, where are infinite flunkeys, cates, condiments—very superfluous to me, with much "making of wits," and not always a very great allowance of grave reason. That ends in about an hour. From that till two, I continue trying to keep private to my own room, but do not always succeed. To go

[2] *Jane Welsh Carlyle, Letters, &c.*, by Leonard Huxley, p. 311.
[3] *Nineteenth Century Mag.*, March, 1892, article by the Countess of Cork.

down into the drawing-room is to get into the general whirl. After luncheon, all go for exercise, the women to drive, the men to ride.'

On some such occasion as this,[4] when Carlyle was at the Grange, 'a party of gentlemen returning from a walk in the dusk' beheld what they supposed to be 'a magnificent meteor,' and, presumably at the dinner-table, described it 'in glowing colours and with much enthusiasm. Carlyle heard them in silence to the end,' but knew enough of astronomy to be sure it was no meteor they had seen, but only an ignis fatuus; and so when his 'view of the phenomenon' was wanted, he merely said:—"Ay, some sulphuretted hydrogen, I suppose, or some rubbish of that kind." Which was more scientific than polite, and made the good Henry Taylor moralise,—"he delights in knocking over any pageantry of another man's setting up."

Men were often afraid of him, but never women or children. Taylor's wife rejoiced in Lady Ashburton's approval of her triumphant rejoinder on some similar occasion. *She* had been telling some wonderful story—no matter what—and Carlyle 'flashed his blue lights across the table' and demanded,—"Will you *swear* it, Mrs. Taylor?" "Yes!" she cried, "by all that *you* believe in!"[5] Perhaps Mrs. Taylor herself was the only orthodox Christian present; but she would not be aware of that. Assuredly she felt strongly about religion; but she could never draw Carlyle into any debate about it.

Guests came and went. Carlyle looked on, content to feel a foreigner to it all, telling his brother,—'To one like me, it would be frightful to live on such terms.' His hours of idleness were filled with 'strange old *reminiscences*,' and recollections of people he had known who had passed away. In going about he was watching how working people were living in Hampshire, and reported to his mother.—

'The people here seem to me much less hard worked than in the North. They are very ill off, I believe, if their landlords did not help them; but seem to require much more to make them *well* off than Scotch people do. Their cottages are mostly very clean, with trees about them, flower bushes into the very windows, and a trim road, paved with bricks, leading out from them to the public way. The ploughmen, or farm servants generally, go about girt in

[4] *Autobiography*, by Sir Henry Taylor, I, p. 330.
[5] *Guests and Memories*, by Una Taylor, p. 149, and see pp. 69, 70, 89–91.

buckskin leggings from toe to midthigh ; rags are seen nowhere, nor, I suppose, does *want* anywhere do other than come upon the parish and have itself supplied. The gentry, I imagine, take a great deal more pains with their dependents than ours do. For the rest, the tillage is all more or less sluttish, thistles abounding, turnips sown broadcast, bad fences, abundance of waste ground, and roads and paths' which occupy '*ten* times as much ground as with us. You can *ride* in any direction at your own pleasure, and nobody dreams of finding fault with you. There are walks and rides, I think twenty miles long, in the park, and solitary, as if you were in the heart of America,' meaning the uninhabited country in the west.

The waste of land that might be used was a sight that always vexed Carlyle, and surely it is sinful for a nation to allow it when there are hordes of idle men. On this and many other such points, the owner of the Grange, Mr. Baring, now Lord Ashburton, used always to agree with Carlyle, but he contented himself with good resolutions, and let himself go 'in the general whirl.'

XVII

EDITORS AND CONTRIBUTORS

(1848)

A LETTER written at the Grange on 26.9.48 to end a little "tiff" between Espinasse and an editor in Manchester has some sentences of general interest.[1]—

'DEAR BALLANTYNE,—

'. . . This controversy I know well enough to be perpetual and universal between Editor and Contributor: no law can settle it; the best wisdom can do no better than suppress it from time to time. On Espinasse's side I will counsel patience; on your side I would say that though an editor can never wholly abandon his right to superintend, which will mean an occasional right to alter, or at least to remonstrate and propose alterations, yet it is in general wise, when, as in this case, you have got a really conscientious, accurate, and painstaking contributor, to be sparing in the exercise of the right, and to put up with various unessential things rather than *forcibly* break in to amend them. You have perhaps but a faint idea how much it distresses and disheartens such a man as I describe; nay, lames him in the practice of his art, and tends to put his conscience especially into painful abeyance. "What is the use of me?" his literary conscience says; "better for us all that I went to sleep." When a man *has* a literary conscience—which I believe is a very rare case—this result is a most sad one to bring about; hurtful not to himself only, as you may well perceive. In fact, I think a serious sincere man *cannot* very well write if he have the perpetual fear of correction before his eyes;' and, in short, should be made to feel himself 'within very wide limits his own director.'

In this connection it may be interesting to quote what Espinasse has recorded[2] of the private verbal advice Carlyle

[1] *Thomas Carlyle*, by M. D. Conway, pp. 212–3, for full text without names.

[2] *Literary Recollections*, by F. Espinasse, pp. 130–1.

had given him, when he took to journalism not long ago. Panizzi had worried him out of his employment in the British Museum, and when Espinasse told Carlyle he intended to live by writing, he received a 'most emphatic warning against literary vanity.' "In literature," said Carlyle, "a man can do nothing worth doing until he has killed his vanity." Another advice was,—"Avoid hypochondria, pride, and gloom: they are a waste of faculty." He advised him to take whatever work he could get, saying,—"A man is an indestructible fragment of the Universe, but if he wishes to live, he must not be nice." Of course there was always understood the proviso,—unless it is wrong; but "do not," said Carlyle, "mistake the shriek of self-love for the voice of conscience." What may have been a parting benediction as Espinasse was leaving for Manchester was,—"The heart that remained true to itself never yet found this big Universe finally faithless to it."

Perhaps it was because he knew so well what an editor owed to his contributors that Carlyle was beginning to drop the thought of becoming an editor himself. At any rate soon after smoothing matters for Espinasse he was inviting John Forster to dine and spend a Sunday with him for "a long talk," and said:[3]—"I hardly believe anything will ever come of the Twopenny-Trash scheme; the nature of the beast (shunning Marketplaces and the glare of light, loving Tobacco smoke, and private autocracy) forbids it; however, we shall see."

[3] John Forster MSS., South Kensington Museum, letter of 18.10.48.

XVIII

IS HELL ETERNAL?

(1848)

A WOUNDED American soldier is said to have answered some professional Christian,—"Stranger, I have no time for conundrums." That is the effect of many of Carlyle's replies to theological queries. He ignored the abuse of himself as an unbeliever, but was as ready as Voltaire or Saint Paul to respond to sincere enquirers, particularly to young people uneasy to find themselves outgrowing their creeds. The letters they drew from him would fill many volumes. Here is a good sample, now written at the Grange, and communicated by a cousin of the addressee, Miss Jane A. McIntyre, Ventnor, Isle of Wight. She lived mostly in London, and was a "fine Christian woman, very broad-minded in her later years," said her cousin; and she cherished this letter as a treasure through her long life.[1] She had asked whether Hell was eternal, a question then agitating English Christians, and was answered thus (27.9.48).—

'MY DEAR MADAM,—

'The question that perplexes you is one that no man can answer; you may console yourself by reflecting that it is by its nature *insoluble* to human creatures,—that perhaps what human creatures mainly have to do with such a question is to get it well put to rest, suppressed if not answered, that so their life and its duties may be attended to without impediment from it. Such questions in this our earthly existence are many.

'"There are two things," says the German philosopher, "that strike me dumb: the Starry Firmament (*palpably* infinite), and the Sense of Right and Wrong in man." Whoever follows out that "dumb" thought will come upon

[1] Printed without the addressee's name in *Thomas Carlyle*, by H. J. Nicoll, revised edition, 1881, pp. 139–40.

the origin of our conceptions of Heaven and Hell,—of an Infinitude of merited Happiness and an Infinitude of merited Woe,—and have much to reflect upon under an aspect considerably changed.

'Consequences good and evil, blessed and accursed, it is very clear, do follow from all our actions here below, and prolong and propagate and spread themselves into the Infinite, and beyond our calculation and conception; but whether the notion of *reward* and *penalty* be not, on the whole, rather a *human* one transferred to that immense divine fact, has been doubtful to many. Add this consideration, which the best Philosophy teaches us: that the very *consequences* (not to speak of the *penalties* at all) of *evil* actions die away, and become abolished, long before Eternity ends; that it is only the consequences of good actions that are *eternal;* for these are in harmony with the laws of this universe, and add themselves to it, and co-operate with it for ever, while all that is in *disharmony* with it must necessarily be without continuance and soon fall dead:—as perhaps you have heard in the sound of a distant chorus of voices, in the sound of a Scottish Psalm amid the mountains; the true notes alone *support* one another, all following the one true rule; the false notes, each following its own different false rule, quickly destroy one another, and the Psalm, which was discordant enough near at hand, is a perfect melody when heard from afar.

'On the whole I must account it but a morbid weak imagination that shudders over this wondrous divine universe as a place of Despair to any creature; and contrariwise a most degraded human sense, sunk down to the region of the *brutal* (however common it be), that in any case remains blind to the *infinite* difference there ever is between Right and Wrong for a human creature—or God's Law and the Devil's Law.—

'Yours very truly,

'T. CARLYLE.'

CHARLES BULLER.

[face p. 64

XIX

WILLIAM MACCALL

IN 1842 John Sterling had become acquainted with an uncommon kind of cleric, " a tall erect man " of thirty, with a " military bearing," William Maccall, from Ayrshire,[1] then vegetating at Crediton in Devonshire as a Unitarian divine. He had outgrown the orthodoxy of his church at home, but not yet turned away from Theology altogether. John Sterling gave him a letter of introduction to Carlyle, but when Maccall was next in London Carlyle was in Scotland, and it was only in 1848 that Maccall became acquainted with Carlyle. They were introduced to each other at a soiree given by Chapman in honour of Emerson. By that time Maccall had come to London with wife and child, having left his Unitarian congregation and decided to live in London by lecturing and preaching and writing for the Press. Carlyle invited him to Cheyne Row.

He came, and then delivered the letter given him long ago by John Sterling,—which " deeply moved " Carlyle.[2] Before Maccall departed, Carlyle had become acquainted with his circumstances. As Mrs. Carlyle afterwards explained,[3] Maccall 'was within sight of starvation when he first came here,' and 'Mr. C. exerted himself for him in several directions.' His friend Macready the actor being then in America, and Mrs. Macready needing a tutor for a boy of hers 'too nervous to be sent to school,' Maccall was engaged by her on Carlyle's recommendation at sixty pounds a year for three hours a day, and gave satisfaction. He was also introduced to John Parker, the publisher who then owned and edited *Fraser's Magazine*, and did for it a good article on Joseph de Maistre. In many similar ways Carlyle helped Maccall, and in this the first year of

[1] *Literary Recollections*, by F. Espinasse, pp. 247–55, amplified by what Mr. Espinasse said verbally to D. A. W.

[2] *Letter of W. Maccall*, printed in the *Pall Mall Gazette*, 19.12.84.

[3] *Letter of Mrs. Carlyle*, printed in *Pall Mall Gazette*, 26.11.84.

their acquaintance he wrote to him a long letter [4] about a MS. Maccall left with him, a translation with a Preface of Spinoza's *Tractatus Politicus.*[5] No fault was found with the translation; but the Preface was criticised severely. Instead of giving a sketch of Spinoza's life and enough about the book to attract the reader into that subterranean cavern, Maccall was writing as if to proclaim,—" I don't care tho you call me an agnostic," and to brandish his argumentative weapons,—the very method to repel instead of attracting readers. Any publisher would object to such a Preface, and there was little chance that anyone would undertake the book at all. Carlyle urged Maccall to recognise this after he had made sure of it; and it may be remarked that the book did find a publisher, but is now " rare " and " inaccessible,"[5] so that it is likely to have been unsuccessful.

Carlyle went on to say that to be prompt to recognise disagreeable facts is the way to get better knowledge of the Celestial Powers and of our terrene element, and so to discover what to do next. That is the only way to profit by experience. Discussing next Maccall's book on 'The Individuality of the Individual,' Carlyle confessed he liked it much better than the Spinoza. " To grow to all that one was meant to be " is all the law and all the prophets; but unhappily that profound truth is in Maccall's book 'wrenched from its environment' and made into a 'new religion,'—the kind of thing Carlyle could not approve. 'To found a sect' or set out as if to do so, 'seems to me like a kind of spiritual suicide for any man of geniality.' *A man should not make use of his inmost convictions as things to talk about.* He should swallow down his divine idea and let it shine forth in all he says and does, and so irradiate a little the Egyptian darkness of the world.

'You have attained to what not one in a thousand attains to,—you see the utter damnability of cant and conventions of all kinds.' That was a great achievement, and Carlyle hoped he would not stop there, but go on, in spite of Spinoza and the Socinian writers and even such as Epictetus and Antoninus. To all these one had now to say " Farewell," and emerge into the world 'where we have been too long wanted, and where our seedfield and battlefield are.'

[4] Unpublished letter, read on 30.10.1896 by D. A. W. Discussing this letter, David Masson described Maccall in the same way as Espinasse had described him.

[5] *Spinoza's Works,* translation by R. H. M. Elwes, Pref., p. xxxiii, footnote.

Carlyle went on to admonish Maccall of the contradictions and failure he would meet if he persisted in what Espinasse calls his 'aggressiveness,' and it may be added that, in the thirty or forty years that followed, Maccall discovered by experience how wise the advice was which he could not follow. The letter quoted may explain what puzzled Espinasse, to whom Carlyle introduced Maccall at another soiree at Chapman's before long. Maccall at once confided to Espinasse that Carlyle had just been telling him to—"Come out like an athlete."

He never did so in the way Carlyle intended. He threw himself into lecturing with little success; and Espinasse, who went to hear him, explains that he could never 'forget himself in his subject.' As a journalist his aggressiveness made him dangerous or dull. 'For a contemporary English author to have a literary reputation was to expose himself to be tomahawked by Maccall,' except in a few cases, such as Carlyle and John Wilson. Many a bit of his writing had to be suppressed by editors as 'too virulent,' but with all his faults he 'was one of the most honest and honourable of men, with noble qualities of head and heart.' His frugality was equal to the narrowness of his means, and he 'never lost his manly bearing,' tho poor all his life. He saw Carlyle occasionally to the end. "I have a great regard for poor Maccall," said Carlyle once to Espinasse; "there never was a man who went about with any dignity on so little money." He added that "tho everyone needs something of that individuality which Maccall preached, it is not to be 'perked up' into a doctrine for the guidance of a man's conduct through life."

Espinasse gives specimens of Maccall's invectives against Mill and Feuerbach, but the best thing he tells is this.—'Maccall is the "satirical friend of mine" whom Carlyle quotes [6] as saying,—"You may paint with a very big brush, and yet not be a great painter."' And Espinasse adds what Carlyle omits,—"It was of (the Rev.) George Gilfillan that he said it."

[6] *T. C.'s Frederick*, Book I, Chapter I.

XX

CHARLES BULLER

(1848)

THE gayest of all the talkers at the Grange this autumn, Charles Buller, was discussing Ireland, then a nightmare to all public men. He was now Chief Commissioner of the Poor Law in Lord John Russell's Government, and plainly coming to the front—respected in the Commons and popular there. He had taken in good part the rebuke of Peel in his younger days,—"If the honourable member for Liskeard will cease for a moment from making a buffoon of himself, I will, etc." His colleagues and their Lord-Lieutenant Clarendon were trying to feel happy because they had got John Mitchel convicted and sentenced to fourteen years by a packed jury and a servile judge; but even in the law-courts they were having defeats as well as victories, and however much they tried to hide the fact from English voters, the awful horrors of many-thousand-fold deaths from famine in Ireland had put them in a pillory. While red revolution was running over Europe, the most urgent question for the English was the condition of Ireland. Charles Buller was not the man to shrink from talk of it at the Grange.

It is a curious coincidence that one of the things he said should be done [1] was approved by Sir Robert Peel,—making payments to the Irish clergy. It does not appear that Buller would have had any hand in the shabby Whig deals with Dan O'Connell. He had prepared a detailed plan for better administration by organizing labour and emigration, and incidentally ending the idiotic English rule requiring a jury to be unanimous before they can come to a finding. We know that Carlyle was writing both to John Mitchel and to Lord Clarendon and receiving replies, and we may be sure that Charles Buller knew about all that. Gavan

[1] *The Greville Memoirs*, Part II, Vol. III (1848), pp. 221, 241, 249–51.

Duffy was in custody while they were at the Grange this autumn, and in October Carlyle was writing to him from Chelsea.[2]

Next month Charles Buller underwent an operation, and while still weak from it caught a fever and died (29.11.48), "without previous illness reckoned of importance till a day or two before."[3] His father had died a few months before him, his mother followed soon, and all that Carlyle's best pupil might have done for the good of England or Ireland became a might-have-been.

'He was a "Reformer" from his earliest youth,' wrote Carlyle in his obituary notice,[3] 'and never swerved from that faith, nor could swerve. His luminous sincere intellect laid bare to him in all its abject incoherency the thing that was untrue, which henceforth became for him a thing that was not tenable. What he accomplished, therefore, whether great or little, was all to be *added* to the sum of good; none of it to be deducted. There shone mildly in his whole conduct a beautiful veracity, absence of all cant, hypocrisy, and hollow pretence, not in word and act only, but in thought and instinct.

'A man of wit he indisputably was, whatever more, among the wittiest of men. To hear him, the most serious of men might think within himself, "How beautiful is human gaiety too!" Alone of wits, Buller never made wit; he could be silent or grave enough. His wit, moreover, was ever the ally of wisdom, not of folly, or unkindness, or injustice; no soul was ever hurt by it; never, we believe, never, did his wit offend justly any man, and often have we seen his ready resource relieve one ready to be offended, and light up a pausing circle all into harmony again. In truth, it was beautiful to see such clear, almost childlike, simplicity of heart, co-existing with the finished dexterities and long experiences of a man of the world.'

Lady Ashburton was in great distress and writing to Carlyle what his wife called,[4] "as sorrowful a letter as *I* could have written . . . sad as death." He was "unwearied in writing consolations and sending her books to comfort her." Thackeray told Mrs. Brookfield that "poor old Charles Buller's" fate "affects me very much, so much

[2] *Conversations with Carlyle*, by Sir Charles Gavan Duffy, pp. 31–33.
[3] *Article in the Examiner*, by T. C., 2.12.48, reprinted in *Rescued Essays of T. C.* See also *Fraser's Mag.*, Feby., 1849, and *Westminster Review*.
[4] *J. W. Carlyle, Letters*, edited by Leonard Huxley, p. 315.

that I feel as if I were making my will and getting ready to march too."[5]

Fifty years afterwards Lady Airlie told Mr. Hare.[6]—'As soon as I came out, I went with my parents to the Grange, where the first Lady Ashburton was very kind to me, and I passionately adored her. There I first saw Carlyle and Mrs. Carlyle, but he had known my Mother very well before. . . . I cannot describe what Charles Buller was. Girl as I was, I loved him, but so did every one else,—he was so very delightful. I remember as if it were to-day going into my Mother's room: all her long beautiful hair was down, and she was sobbing violently. "Oh!" she said, "Charles Buller is dead." How I longed to cry, too, but I did not dare. I only went to my own room in most bitter grief. Wherever he went, Charles Buller brought sunshine with him. He left me his "Coleridge" in his will. It surprised people that he should leave anything to a young girl like me, and when I went to the Grange again, many spoke of it. Each had something to show which had belonged to him: we all mourned together.'

He 'can be ill spared to the party and to the country,' declared Greville,[1] who was little prone to admiring anybody, but in this instance said:—'He is a great social and a great public loss; disinterested, generous, and high-minded, perhaps the most popular member of the House of Commons; an admirable speaker, full of matter, lucid, never dull; sure of an attentive and favourable audience, he would have become a very eminent man.'

[5] *Mrs. Brookfield and Her Circle*, by C. and F. Brookfield, p. 272.
[6] *The Story of My Life*, by A. J. C. Hare, VI, pp. 441–2.

XXI

IN THE DOLDRUMS

(1848–49)

A NEW edition of Cromwell Carlyle began before 1848 was out and finished next summer, but that was easy work,—like proof-correcting. He was steady every morning at his desk, puzzling over what else to do. The revolutionary rows on the Continent were like the crackling of conflagrations in adjacent streets. His Irish friends were keeping him awake to the failure of potatoes this year also,—starvation was again impending over millions in Ireland; but cholera at home and exciting foreign news were diverting the public attention. What *was* he to do?

It might be now, when Young Ireland was in prison, that Espinasse heard Carlyle remarking that "the Irish priests alone stood up persistently for the people." [1] That would be because they were Irishmen as well as priests. It was an old saying which even the priests' pet boy, Dan O'Connell, himself repeated,—"From Rome we take our religion; but politics we prefer *home-made*." [2] They would have done better with home-made religion also.

'Popery and the Papacy Carlyle held in abhorrence,' says Espinasse. 'He thought that the misfortunes of the Irish were in great part clearly traceable to their rejection of the Reformation. "The Irish peasant," he said, "if left to commune with his own soul, would feel that murder was a damnable crime, but he knows that the priest will give him absolution for it, and so he thinks little of it."' Espinasse enquired about 'the old scheme for a State endowment of the Irish Roman Catholic clergy,' which Charles Buller had been reviving; but now that Charles Buller was dead, and Carlyle was watching with loathing the dirty deals of the Whigs with O'Connell and Company, he answered grimly:—"If it were to be done at all, it would have to be done by

[1] *Literary Recollections*, by F. Espinasse, p. 198.
[2] *Life of Cardinal Manning*, by E. S. Purcell, II, p. 622.

statesmen of a much higher morality than any we have at present."

Perhaps the best commentary on all Carlyle wrote or said about Ireland is in what his friend St. Thomas (Erskine of Linlathen) wrote to him this summer :—' I have read your articles with the wish that you had some steady organ through which you might converse with the people of these countries periodically. I am sure it would be most healthful for many, and they would receive from you what they would refuse from any other. . . . Is it not altogether a most wretched delusion to suppose that a half or quarter civilised people should be legislated for and treated as if they were civilised ? England is to be blamed doubtless for selfishness in her dealings towards them in time past, *but not for the assumption of authority, which is just what they need, were it only wise.*' [3]—If only it were wise ! " Much virtue in an if ! "

About the beginning of November, 1848, Fitzgerald spent an evening with Carlyle and reported [4] :—' He lectured on without intermission for three hours : was very eloquent, looked very handsome : and I was very glad to get away. He gave an account of a Quaker who had come to remonstrate with him concerning certain doctrines about Peace, etc.—" when," (said Carlyle), " I went on with a deluge of hot matter like what I have been pouring out to you, till I almost calcined my poor Quaker—Ah me." The regret was genuine on the part of Carlyle. He shared the Quakers' love of truth and hatred of strife, but not their old-fashioned superstitions about other worlds, " where all is made right that so puzzles us here." As John Sterling had explained to Caroline Fox,[5] when she was delighted and surprised by the discovery that Carlyle remembered her,—" Oh, he's interested about you ; he likes your healthy mode of Quakerism ; it's the sort of thing with which he can sympathize more than any other." The friendship that followed showed Sterling was right.

' Carlyle gave me an American pamphlet on Capital Punishment, with some of his own characteristic notes in the margin,' writes the new St. Caroline, who goes on to describe his ' famous laughs, hearty and bodily,' with so

[3] Italics added. *Letters of T. Erskine*, II, p. 60.

[4] *Some New Letters of Edward Fitzgerald*, by F. R. Barton, pp. 164–5.

[5] *Memories of Old Friends, Journals and Letters of Caroline Fox*, I, pp. 203, 244, 295–6, 324.

much sympathy that it seems plain she joined in laughing at the pamphleteer, so 'oddly inconsistent' in his feeling for the value of human life, inasmuch as he was 'in favour of going to war with England, thus willing to sacrifice thousands of brave fellows, while he would save the life of a miserable rascal who cut his wife into pieces.'

St. Caroline could laugh with Carlyle, yet pleaded that 'God could bear with the criminal' tho 'man could not,' to which Carlyle replied:—"Why, there are many things in this world which God bears with. He bears with many a dreary morass and waste, yet He gives to man the will and the power to drain and to till it and to make oats grow out of it. But you'll make no oats grow out of men's corpses," he admitted, and our St. Caroline, as true a reporter as ever handled a pen, assures us that 'Carlyle does not like Capital punishment, because he wishes men to live as much and as long as possible; he rejoices in the increasing feeling that it is a right solemn thing for one man to say to another, "Give over living!"'

The death of Charles Buller in November would make useless much of what Carlyle had been writing on politics, for with Buller disappeared the hope of any good being done by the Government of Lord John Russell, which was drifting in the usual way, its members incapable of thinking of anything but holding on,—like monkeys on a raft. Before 1848 was out, the French voters put Napoleon the Little atop, and Bismarck was finding the Prussian peasantry loyal to kings, the royal "rope-dancers," as one of their own ministers called them in talking with Bismarck. Even the Bomba blackguards were coming back! The futility of the fighting to follow was palpable. Carlyle was sick at the sight of horrors he could not hinder. As a Persian officer said after dinner, according to Herodotus (ix., 16), when their big defeat at Plataea was impending,—"The bitterest of sorrows is to know much, but be unable to act accordingly."

About Christmas week Erasmus Darwin, in his pawky way, put a poser to Mrs. Carlyle, which she repeated to her husband,—"Who will write Carlyle's life?" Carlyle, in his simplicity, did not realise that this was partly chaff, but moralised in his journal with delicious absurdity (29.12.48).—'The word reported to me set me thinking how *impossible* it was, and would for ever remain, for any creature to write my "life." The *chief* elements of my little destiny have all along lain deep below view or surmise, and never will or can be known to any son of Adam. I would say to my biographer, if any fool undertook such a task, "Forbear, poor fool! Let no life of *me* be written; let me and my bewildered wrestlings lie buried here and be forgotten swiftly of all the world. If thou write, it will be mere delusions and hallucination. The confused world never understood, nor will understand, me and my poor affairs; not even the persons nearest to me could guess at them;—nor was it found indispensable; nor is it *now* (for any but an idle purpose) profitable, were it even possible. Silence, and go thy ways elsewhither."'

Which comes to nothing more than what is a proverb in the East, that nobody can ever know the thoughts or the feelings of any other. Men pass each other on the streets, mysterious as the stars.

When by and by Joseph Neuberg was assisting Carlyle to turn over his heaps of MSS., 'on nearly every page,' wrote Neuberg to his sister,[6] 'there are marginal notes which have nothing to do with the text, and in which he seems to be talking with himself by the way. Here are some of them:—"Alas, no use continuing in this manner!" . . . "2nd Jan., 1849. To-day is the second of the year. Already the year contains but 364 days; how are days wasted!" "3rd Jan. Alas, alas, a day to be wasted again; are all days to be wasted then? Good Heavens!"'

Most of the marginalia are undated but assignable to 1849, such as these:—"Ach Gott! This is mere rubbish." "No getting the steam up." "Enough of that; ach!" In writing of a clergyman, he scribbled on the margin, as if feeling for a word,—"Rev. Cambric Muslin." "Seraphic Loose-locks." "Smart Fellow of College." "Macassar Oil." Etc., etc.

Good Arthur Helps was going abroad for his health, and it seems to have been towards the end of 1848, or early in 1849,[7] that in writing to ask Carlyle to call at his house when riding in Hampshire, and let him know how the children looked, he went on to suggest that if he himself were not to come back,—"it would be a very good-natured

[6] *Carlyle and Neuberg, Macmillan's Mag.*, August, 1884, pp. 281–3.

[7] Dated 1844, at page 391 of the *Correspondence of Sir Arthur Helps*, apparently by mistake. It reads like a letter not very long before the next in order, dated 18.9.1849. Cp. pp. 76–8, etc. Internal evidence seems clear for 1848 or early in 1849.

thing in you to redeem my promise for me and give the world a second volume of the Conquerors" of the New World, *a history intended to help up the negroes by showing exactly how they came to be slaves in America.* This suggestion is interesting because Helps was sure to know well how Carlyle felt towards the negroes.

XXII

THE BRITISH MUSEUM LIBRARY

(1849)

ON 8.2.49 Carlyle was examined by the Commissioners appointed to enquire into the British Museum.[1] He had helped to procure the enquiry by joining in 1847 [2] in the complaints against the preposterous Panizzi, who had now been "Keeper of the Printed Books" for a dozen years.[3] One of Panizzi's subordinates became his biographer, and the pious faith in the infallibility and general perfection of the meritorious and peppery Italian refugee, which was becoming and convenient to his subordinate, appears at times unintentionally funny in the biography. Thus it is written :—

'In 1835 the Natural History Departments engrossed the principal attention of the investigating body' (a Select Committee of the Commons).[3] 'The Library escaped with comparatively slight notice. Twelve years had now' (in 1847), 'elapsed, during eleven of which Panizzi had been "Keeper of the Printed Books." There could, perhaps, hardly be a better proof of the energy of his administration than the immensely elevated ideal of a public Library which *it* [4] had produced. He was tried by *a standard created by himself*,[4] and which but for *him* [4] would have had no existence. The men of letters who had been silent in 1836 were now clamorous for the realization *of an ideal which they owed to him*,[4] and the severity of their attacks was in truth the best testimony to *his* [4] deserts.' It is not easy to realise that this is meant seriously. It is unadulterated impudence. No Italian Pope was ever more preposterous.

'In the minute of July 13th, 1839,' Panizzi was ordered

[1] *Report of the Commissioners . . . with Minutes of Evidence*, pp. 272–85. H.M. Stat. Office, 1850.

[2] *Carlyle on Cromwell and Others*, Book XV, Chap. XI, p. 372.

[3] *Life of Sir Anthony Panizzi*, by L. Fagan, I, pp. 146, 255–65, etc.

[4] Italics added.

by the Trustees 'to have the catalogue ready in press by December, 1844.' As to 'whether the Catalogue ought to be printed at all,—the opinion of the literary witnesses unconnected with the Museum was naturally strongly in favour of a printed Catalogue. The opinion of Panizzi may be gathered from the verbal replies he had already given to questions put to him by the Library Committee of the Trustees on March 6th, 1847.

'"The Catalogue might be completed by the end of 1854 of all the books which the Museum will contain up to that period. It would take to 1860 to prepare such Catalogue in such a state of revision as might be fit for the press. It would occupy seventy volumes. It would require one year to correct the press of two volumes. It would, therefore, require thirty-five years to pass the Catalogue through the press, and, when completed in 1895, it would represent the state of the Library in 1854."'

If the "Trustees" had not been hopelessly incompetent, it should not have taken them a day longer to decide, when Panizzi had thus delivered himself into their hands, that somebody else must replace Mr. Panizzi in the management of the Library. With a much-reduced salary he should have been set to some subordinate employment. But he was a smart fellow in his way, and had taken the measure of the noodles above him. If they had been capable men, he would have tried no humbug, but have had the Catalogue finished and printed by 1844—the five years allowed for it at first should have been ample. As they were noodles, he had his way, and made believe that the Catalogue of such a Library required immense elaboration, and that he and the other officials employed upon so sublime a work must be left to take their own time in the performance of their mysteries.

The Commissioners of 1847–49, who reported in 1850, were a little, but only a little, better than the Trustees upon whom they had to pass judgment. The majority were taken in by Panizzi's humbug, and agreed that the Catalogue should not be printed. The only suggestion they made to meet the wishes of Mr. Carlyle and the other literary witnesses was ignored by the perfect Panizzi. Let his partial biographer have the telling of it,[3] to show how Panizzi has prevented serious students from finding the Library as serviceable as it should be.—Not only was the Catalogue never printed and never up to date,—it was also a clumsy thing. 'One most important recommendation they (the Commissioners) made, which unfortunately was not acted upon—viz. the provision of means for *the compilation of an index of subjects* [4] to the Catalogue, to proceed *pari passu* with the alphabetical titles of the latter. This would have doubled the value of the Catalogue; but thirty years have passed, and the Catalogue is still destitute of this inestimable auxiliary. The suggestion may still be carried into effect at any moment, as regards accessions for the future; but the lost ground will be regained with difficulty.'

Perhaps, before the Report is destroyed as waste paper, which most of it now is, the evidence of Carlyle may be reprinted. Conscientious librarians may find it useful, especially what he says about Cataloguing. Even the part of his evidence which the Commissioners seem to have considered nonsensical shows him, what he always was, a pioneer in proclaiming the usefulness of public libraries and the need for them.[1]

He said there should be " more libraries in London than at present " . . .

Question :—" You think it of great importance that . . . a printed catalogue . . . should be distributed to the great provincial libraries ? "

Answer :—" If there is to be any real studying in England, yes. The object of such distribution of the catalogue is to encourage that. If there is not going to be any real study in England, there is, of course, little use in distributing catalogues,—there is little use in keeping up the library at all. But I hope the time is coming when there will be a public library in every county,—when no Englishman will be born who will not have a chance of getting books out of the public libraries. I am sorry to believe that we, of this country, are worse supplied with books than almost any other people of the civilised world. I have seen it stated that in the island of Iceland a man has a better chance of getting books out of the public resources than we have. I believe every Icelander, when he comes to Kiekianik to sell his year's produce of stock-fish or whatever else, gets a number of books, by order of the King of Denmark, out of the library there, and carries them home to read in his own house in the winter-time; a privilege that no Englishman has at all. This, as far as I understand, is the only public library we have."

A little later Viscount Canning, one of the Commissioners,

recurred to the surprising suggestion " that the people of all other countries were better supplied with books than the people of this country," and asked him :—" Do you speak with reference to the accommodation which the public libraries give, or to the cheapness of books ? "

" I speak with reference to the public libraries ; to the books accessible to the public, which the public may read. I believe there are in Germany some 400 great libraries which are free to the public. I do not know whether they are entirely open or not, but I understand them to be virtually open : they are supported by the various countries ; but we have only one library—the one in the British Museum —and yet this is the richest and largest empire in the world. That, I consider, entitles me very decidedly to say, that we are considerably worse off in that respect than the Germans are."

He told plainly how the British Museum Collection of books on the French Revolution had been made useless to him by the lack of catalogues and access. " For all practical purposes this Collection of ours might as well have been locked up in water-tight chests and sunk on the Dogger-bank, as put into the British Museum. That is my experience about it." The fine collection of works on the Civil War in England, given by George III and known as the King's Pamphlets, had a catalogue in MS. prepared by some purchaser of the books, but the Museum Trustees had not yet printed even that !

Careless of the feelings of Panizzi, he contrasted the Library to its disadvantage with the Advocates' Library in Edinburgh and the Bibliothèque Royale in Paris, where one had only to name a book and the Librarian went and sought for it.—" I would have a total abrogation of that arrangement by which a man is obliged to seek for a book himself. I consider that entirely unreasonable. Like a haberdasher requiring me, if I went into his shop and asked for a yard of green ribbon, to tell him in what drawer the ribbon was lying. Drawer ? I should naturally answer : I want such a ribbon ! I tell you what I want, and *you* must know in what drawer the ribbon is. . . ."

About the Bibliothèque Royale, Question :—" Did you furnish the officer with the titles of the books that you wanted ? "

Answer :—" I told him the nature of the book by such a description as suffices a man in ordinary life. If I want to specify a man, I do not begin by defining all his qualities and scientific attributes; I call him by the name of John Thomson, and he is easily to be found by any man who is willing to find him. On mentioning a book, the librarian said that he would seek it for me."

It made Panizzi furious to be likened to a haberdasher; but the metaphor made the meaning very plain, and Carlyle was fond of it. He used it in talk long afterwards;[5] and now he explained how the Museum rule caused a great waste of time to the readers,—more than half an hour sometimes wasted in getting all the needless details from the catalogue about a book. "I do not remember," he said, "that I ever asked for a book at the Library, during the period I have been here,—above twenty-four years now,—that required me to look at the description in the catalogue for the purpose of specifying it. I knew the book, and could give such a description of it out of books and resources which I have at home, as was perfectly sufficient to describe it to the attendant."

"I wish to understand," said Lord Seymour, "under what system you wish the Library of the British Museum to be managed?"

"I have not formed any system for the management of the Library," he replied. "It is not my business. My business at the Library was to try to get a little task of my own worked out; I accomplished that; and I am now endeavouring to give the Commissioners the benefit of any experience I have had. I have formed no scheme for the management of the Library: but I should say that if a man came with an ingenuous and honest purpose to investigate English history, he ought to have a fair chance of trying the resources the establishment affords. *And he cannot do that now, for it is in perfect confusion.*"

The great defect of the Library, to which most of Carlyle's evidence was directed, was the lack of catalogues. But he answered very freely about everything he was asked.

As for the old reading-room then in use, he said in reply to questions, "There is need of a great deal more space, if there is to be any opportunity of people really studying. . . . It has very bad ventilation; the atmosphere is very bad. . . . I have gone into that room when it has been quite crowded, and there has been no seat vacant, and I have been obliged to sit on the step of a ladder: and there are such a bustle

[5] *Life of T. Carlyle*, by R. H. Shepherd, II, p. 66, footnote.

and confusion that I never do enter the room without getting a headache—what I call the Museum headache—and therefore I avoid the room till the last extremity. . . . For a long time the only use I have made of the library was to consult some particular books that had a bearing upon the subject I was studying, by turning up a page or two. . . .

"There are several persons in a state of imbecility who come to read in the British Museum, sent there by their friends to pass away their time. I remember there was one gentleman who used to blow his nose very loudly every half hour."

When asked for advice about the selection of books to be purchased, he rather astonished the Commissioners by insisting on the need of keeping out any book "decidedly bad."

Question :—"Do not you consider that the books ought to be a selection to suit all classes of opinion ?"

Answer :—"Yes : and I should be very catholic ; much more so perhaps than you expect. Where I found any kind of human intellect exercised, even tho the man were a blockhead, if he were trying to do his best, I would not reject his book. But where a man was a *quack*, and his work was decidedly bad, I should consider I was doing God service, and the poor man himself service, in extinguishing such a book ; and, in short, that it was necessary to be *select* in choosing books out of the whole world."

Perhaps the most sensational and significant thing said on this occasion was the quietest in appearance. For a dozen years the preposterous Panizzi, one of the most truculent flunkies then alive, had been eagerly seeking a public quarrel with him, aware how much a serious row with Carlyle would add to his importance, and how little love could be felt by the *rabble* of the Tories for the vindicator of the French Revolution and of Oliver Cromwell. "Dicky" Milnes was one of the Commissioners, and it was he who saw his chance and popped the awful question :—"Who was the librarian with whom you state you were not acquainted ?"

"Mr. Panizzi ; the same gentleman who is now librarian."

It may be needful to add that Panizzi bore a life-long grudge against Milnes, who had opposed the appointment of Panizzi to the post he held, on the ground that such an official ought to be an Englishman.[6]

[6] *Life of R. M. Milnes, Lord Houghton*, by T. W. Reid, II, pp. 277–9 and 404.

In giving his evidence Carlyle had not dissembled how "the Librarian" had hampered instead of helping his researches, but did not name Panizzi till directly asked to do so, and then avoided further mention of him. He praised by name Mr. Watts, a member of the staff; and in reply to questions told the Commissioners, to the joy of the staff, something more than they asked.—

'The general conduct of the attendants, I should say, according to all my experience, has been quite exemplary, worthy of all commendation, civil and prompt, and in every way proper. . . .

'I wish to bear my testimony to the intelligence, serviceableness, and methodic accuracy of all the servants that I see about the reading-room. No better class of men have I seen anywhere; many of them have come to me, and volunteered to help me through the difficulties that beset my path. There was a man, who is since dead, of the name of Scott, who was well known for his obliging disposition: in the reading-room he has repeatedly come and helped me to find out a book; he has taken all kinds of trouble: he was not acquainted with books, except on the outside; but by dint of exercising his observation, he could afford great help to readers in finding books. So far as I have seen, every servant in the reading-room seems to be a worthy person, anxious to assist the readers: and if I had any suggestion to make, I should say that they ought to be better paid; they seem to be rather poor-looking men, and I should say that they were deserving of more than they now get.'

XXIII

MACAULAY AND THE STUARTS, &c.

(1849)

IN February Carlyle and his wife stayed a while at Headly Grove, Epsom, as the guests of Captain Anthony Sterling, and writing to John Forster from there[1] (19.2.49), Carlyle described his solitary rides, 'amid the beautiful chalk hills,'—yesterday to Reigate, the day before to Dorking, the day before that on Epsom race-course,—and said,—'I find the sermon which this old Earth preaches to me, when she has the opportunity, worth all other sermons.' Macaulay's History was the sensation of the season; and Carlyle confessed to Forster that it had disappointed him, tho he had expected little.—'Flat: without a ray of genius . . . and as for story, there *is* no story, and the Devil himself couldn't make one! Stuart Kings and their fetid canaille (or stinking doggery), what story is in them or ever can be? Oblivion, zero, and eternal silence, that is *their* story. . . .'

When Neuberg called on Monday, 12.3.49, he reported to his sister[2] that Mrs. Carlyle was out, but that he had 'a very pleasant evening. I had him all to myself. We made tea together, and he told me many things that I desired to know. He was in a very good humour, and is the tenderest of mankind when one can look somewhat into the depths of his nature.'

Soon after then Carlyle was writing what was printed as an article in the *Spectator* of 14.4.49, denouncing the hopeless methods of Lord John Russell's government in Ireland, and proving the need there for common-sense in command and—Sir Robert Peel. He told his sister that what made him write was 'real *conscience*. . . . I really ought to stick to my paper; and work away till I get heated: part of my big monstrous meaning, which everybody would be apt to shriek over, might then perhaps be got uttered soon.'

[1] John Forster MSS., S. Kensington Museum, letter of 19.2.49.
[2] *Carlyle and Neuberg, Macmillan's Mag.*, Aug., 1884, pp. 281–3.

XXIV

INDIAN MEAL OR MAIZE

(1849)

THE failure of potatoes had now made maize or Indian meal from America a common food in Europe. But why, Carlyle enquired of Emerson, is there a *bitter* final taste which makes the throat smart? Emerson consulted his brother-in-law, Dr. Jackson, "our best chemist," and reported (23.1.49) that the bitterness was due to the corn being kiln-dried before it was sent. This was done to make it less likely to turn musty on the voyage, but it hindered some of the starch becoming sugar. So all that was needed to get the corn at its best was to get it without kiln-drying. To let Carlyle make sure of that, Emerson sent him a barrel of fresh corn. Lord Ashburton took charge of the grinding, and the flour tasted 'sweeter than wheat or any other grain, with an excellent rich taste, something like that of nuts.' To finish his share of the enterprise, Carlyle then wrote an account of it, which appeared in *Fraser's Magazine* for May,[1] explaining, for the benefit of all, the way to 'get Indian meal such as our American cousins get, that we may eat it with thanks to Heaven, as they do.'

'This grain seems likely henceforth to be the staff of life for overcrowded Europe; capable not only of replacing the deceased potato, but of infinitely surpassing' it. In short a man could support life on it for little more than a penny a day, and there was no danger, 'for unlimited periods yet, of its becoming dearer. . . . In the valley of the Mississippi there could Indian corn enough be grown to support the whole posterity of Adam now alive: let the disconsolate Malthusian fling his "geometrical series" into the corner; assist wisely in the "Free-trade movement"; and dry up his tears.'

In thanking Emerson Carlyle assured him,—"It is really a small contribution towards world-History, this act of yours and ours."

[1] Reprinted in the *Scottish Review*, 28.2.1907; and see *Literary Recollections*, by F. Espinasse, pp. 165–8.

XXV

A USE FOR LATIN AND GREEK

(1849)

JOHN STUART BLACKIE the Latin Professor at Aberdeen was now a man of forty; but fifteen years ago he had put *Faust* into English verse, and he always talked and wrote as a disciple of Carlyle,—a "windy disciple," Carlyle once called him,—and now he was meditating a translation of the Greek Æschylus to which Carlyle gave his blessing, writing to him on 16.4.49[1]:—'Æschylus beyond doubt is a good book to try. A Body of Greek Literature (small rigorously selected body), Body of Greek Dramatists first of all, is what the world now emphatically demands of the Scholar-Guild. . . . Not learned babblement about Greek Heroes and Myths, but wise speech . . . a kind of real Heathen Greek Bible (or set of small select books we can read) we do expect from our expensive Professors of Classicality,—terribly expensive if we compute *all* they have cost us!—and for this object I think they will never get a better model than the Divine Hebrew Bible,' plain prose, in short.

However, in the multitude of counsellors there is folly as well as wisdom, and Professor Aytoun persuaded Blackie to put the choruses into rhyme, which did not hinder Carlyle from helping him, later in the year, 'to find the right publisher for this canonical book of the "Heathen Bible."' He praised the blank verse and even the 'rhythmic matter . . . the grimmer is my protest against your having gone into song at all with the business.'

Carlyle's affection for our old Bible made it his lifelong opinion that it was the best model for any translator, and surely he is right. It seems to have been the model of the best of the later translators into English of the "Heathen Bible."

[1] *John Stuart Blackie*, by A. M. Stoddart, I, pp. 245–6.

XXVI

THE CROMWELL STATUE AT ST. IVES

(1849)

WHEN Carlyle was questioned about the New Houses of Parliament, "Shall Cromwell have a statue there?" he answered doubtfully:—"Cromwell? Side by side with a sacred Charles the Second, sacred George the Fourth, and the other sacred Charleses, Jameses, Georges, and Defenders of the Faith,—I am afraid he wouldn't like it! Let us decide provisionally, No."

The question was now being raised again and a "People's Statue" proposed 'at London, Huntingdon, St. Ives, or Naseby Field.' One of the promoters of the claims of St. Ives, the Rev. I. K. Holland, asked Carlyle to help them, and received a reply (16.4.49) which has been preserved and repeatedly printed.[1]

Carlyle began by saying plainly how unworthy we were to-day to set up a statue to the like of Cromwell. 'Nevertheless I have privately resolved, if such a thing do go on, to subscribe my little mite to it on occasion, and to wish privately that it may prosper. . . . You and your townsmen have sure ground to stand upon; ground that is sure, and will carry such an enterprise in all times, even in the Hudson, Dundas, and Brazen Duke of York times,' (alluding to the Piccadilly pillar.) 'St. Ives wishes to claim the honour of having once been Oliver Cromwell's place of abode, an honour likely to be its most peculiar one for a thousand years.

'Proper, good every way, and right on the part of St. Ives: while you keep within these limits, the soul of Oliver himself, if he looked down upon you, could not disapprove.'

He ended by recommending the market-place of St. Ives as the most suitable spot for the proposed memorial, and there the statue of Cromwell was at last set up in 1901.

[1] S. C. Lomas's edition of *T. C.'s O. C.'s Letters and Speeches, Introduction,* by C. H. Firth, pages xxxiv to xxxvi, and footnote.

XXVII

LOUIS BLANC

(1849)

LOUIS BLANC had become famous in 1840 by a fine work on the Organization of Labour,—it may have been from him that Carlyle had learned that phrase. His exposure of the rascality of King Louis-Philippe had helped to cause the revolution last year, and he had been a leading member of the Provisional Government at Paris. John Robertson brought him to Cheyne Row this spring, and excited Mrs. Carlyle by telling her,—[1] "It was in *his* arms that Godefroi Cavaignac died. He talks of him as a Divinity."

On 26.4.49 Carlyle was writing in his journal:—'Louis Blanc was here twice—a pretty little miniature of a man, well shaped, long black head, brown skin; every way French aspect; quick, twinkling, earnest black eyes; a smallish melodious voice, which rather quavers in its tones; free, lively, ingenious utterance, full of friendliness, transparency, logical definiteness, and seeming good faith; not much vanity either; a good little creature, to whom, deeply as I dissented from him, I could not help wishing heartily well.'

He could abundantly satisfy Carlyle's curiosity about the "national workshops," and was sure of his approval for the last thing he had been doing,—his "solemn warning" to his countrymen about the end of 1848 not to have any President elected by universal suffrage.[2] He thought General Cavaignac a "very inferior" person to the General's brother Godefroi; and the election of Napoleon the Little made him prefer to live in London.

[1] *J. W. Carlyle, Letters, &c.*, by Leonard Huxley, p. 320.
[2] *Autobiography of Moncure D. Conway*, II, p. 240.

XXVIII

CHARLES DICKENS'S DINNER-PARTY

(1849)

ON Saturday, 12.5.49, there was a dinner-party at the house of Charles Dickens, who was still under forty and just beginning *David Copperfield*, which was coming out serially. Both Thackeray and old Rogers came, Mrs. Gaskell and Kenyon, the witty Douglas Jerrold and Hablot Browne alias Phiz, a Rev. Mr. Tagart and his wife, and the two Carlyles accompanied by young David Masson, who felt it promotion to get into such company. He remembered it so well that forty-seven years afterwards he could talk of it as if it had been the day before.[1]

'Carlyle,' he said, 'was, as usual at parties, dressed well but unobtrusively, with the utmost plainness, whilst to-night he showed his respect for the occasion by wearing a fine waistcoat. It was chiefly by their waistcoats that gentlemen in those days had room to show their taste.' What dwelt the best in Masson's memory was the unusual cordiality of Dickens, who seemed particularly rejoiced at the sight of them and hurried to greet Carlyle, and shook him very warmly by the hand, saying several times how glad he was to see him, and putting many questions in a filial way about his health, till at last Carlyle laughed and replied, in the very words of Mrs. Gummidge in the third chapter of *David Copperfield* :—" I know what I am. I know that I am a lone lorn creetur', and not only that everythink goes contrairy with me, but that I go contrairy with everybody." The pat quotation made Dickens entirely happy, he laughed and laughed,—it was a treat to see him, as John Forster also tells, for he too overheard this.

Tho Dickens had to turn to receive another guest, he was always 'edging to be within hearing' of Carlyle,—it

[1] On 16.12.96 he gave D. A. W. verbally a minute description. See also the *Carlyle Letters*, especially those of *Mrs. C.*, edited by Leonard Huxley, pp. 326–7, and see *The Life of Charles Dickens*, by John Forster, II, pp. 438–9.

was easy to see who was the hero of the evening to *him*. In fact it was too easy to be agreeable to " old Rogers," who pointed to a chair beside him and said to Mrs. Carlyle,— " Sit down, my dear. I want to ask you,—is your husband as much infatuated as ever with Lady Ashburton ? " " Oh, of course," she said, laughing, " why shouldn't he ? " " Now do *you* like her ? " he asked. " Tell me honestly, is she kind to *you*—as kind as she is to your husband ? "

" Why, you know, it is impossible for *me* to know how kind she is to my husband ; but I *can* say she is extremely kind to *me*, and I should be stupid and ungrateful if I did *not* like her."

" Humph ! " (disappointedly).—" Well, it is very good of you to like her when she takes away all your husband's company from you—he is always there, isn't he ? "

" Oh, good gracious, no ! " cried Mrs. Carlyle, laughing. " He writes and reads a great deal in his own study."

" But he spends all his evenings with her, I am told ? "

" No, not all,—for example you see he is here this evening."

" Yes," he said in a tone of vexation, " I *see* he is here *this* evening, and *hear* him too, for he has done nothing but talk across the room since he came in." Which made Mrs. Carlyle tell her cousin that Rogers was ' ill-natured ' and a ' devilish old man . . . who ought to have been buried long ago.' It would never occur to her that anybody should be displeased at playing second fiddle to her husband.

Happily Rogers was not near her at table and there was a novelty, interesting to a woman, to describe to her cousin.— ' The dinner was served up in the new fashion—not placed on the table at all, but handed round,—only the dessert on the table and quantities of *artificial* flowers. Mrs. Gaskell I had already seen at my own house,—a natural unassuming woman whom they have been doing their best to spoil by making a lioness of her.'

John Forster was not the only one who heard with alarm at the dinner-table above the tumult of tongues ' the good Mr. Tagart,' who sat next Carlyle, ' launching at him various metaphysical questions in regard to Heaven and such-like.' To the ' great relief ' of everybody, according to Forster, Thackeray dexterously ' introduced, with quaint whimsicality, a story, which he and I had heard Macready relate, of a country actor who had supported himself for six months on his judicious treatment of the tag to the Castle Spectre.

In the original it stands that you are to do away with suspicion, banish vile mistrust, and, almost in the words we had just heard from the minister to the philosopher, " Believe there is a Heaven, nor doubt that Heaven is just ! " In place of which Macready's friend, observing that the drop fell for the most part quite coldly, substituted one night the more telling appeal, " And give us your applause, for that IS ALWAYS JUST ! " which brought down the house with rapture.'

After this there was no more post-obit palaver, but plenty of harmonious heat " to get the steam up " naturally, and make it as happy an evening as Masson ever knew. He *saw,* he said, a long talk going on between Carlyle and Rogers ; but tho Rogers was eighty-six, he could hear so well that one did not raise one's voice in speaking to him, and so Masson could not follow the talk, but only see that Rogers was as happy as a fish in water, being indeed an old-fashioned republican, like Thackeray and the most of the company. He had been a friend of Horne Tooke, and when a boy he had flung up his cap at his father's bidding and hurrahed for the American victory of Bunker's Hill.[2] A gentleman once complained of the open seats in churches now taking the place of private pews. " You might find yourself sitting next your coachman," sighed the snob. " So you might in Heaven," replied old Rogers.[2]

[2] *Rogers and his Contemporaries,* by P. W. Clayden, II, pp. 223 and 266.

XXIX

"A VERY PLEASANT EVENING"

(1849)

ON 14.5.49 Neuberg called at Cheyne Row and found Miss Bölte and Dr. John in possession; but 'after a little while the master put on his coat with the velvet collar, and we went off together,' wrote Neuberg to his sister.[1] 'He walks rather like a Catholic priest, his long thin body somewhat shambling. He was in a serious and tender mood, and spoke earnestly and finely the whole way. At Lord Ashburton's we had a very friendly reception.'

A month earlier Carlyle had taken Neuberg there by appointment;[2] but this seems to have been a random call. 'My lord and lady,' the letter went on, 'were in the drawing-room, which is the richest room I have seen anywhere—Würzburg and Munich royal palaces not excepted. Later, other gentlemen came in, among them the Russian ambassador. Carlyle's unrestrained conversation with these people is very amusing. The general tone of the company was cultivated and simple. Not once did I hear the words "My Lord" or "My Lady." At half-past eleven we left, and I accompanied Carlyle a part of the way home.'

When afterwards asked about his notes of such conversations, Neuberg 'replied with emotion, putting his hand on his breast, "They are here."'

[1] *Carlyle and Neuberg,* by Dr. Sadler, *Macmillan's Mag.*, Aug., 1884 pp. 281–97.

[2] Letter from T. C. to J. N., unpublished.

XXX

CURRENT NEWS, ITALY, &c.

(1849)

At this time Mazzini was conspicuous in all the newspapers, for Napoleon the Little had sent a French army to conquer the Roman republic and restore to power the Pope who had run away, and Mazzini was one of the three leaders of the republicans. Many are the reports of what Carlyle said in reply to questions about his friend. An entry in his journal gives the gist of them all, 17.5.49.—

'Mazzini busy at Rome resisting the French, resisting all people that attack his "Republica Romana," standing on his guard against all the world. Poor Mazzini! If he *could* stand there in Rome, in sight of all Italy, and practically defy the whole world for a while, and fight till Rome was ashes and ruin, and end by blowing himself and his assailants up in the last strong post, and so yielding only with life, he might rouse the whole Italian nation into such a rage as it has not known for many centuries; and this might be the means of shaking out of the Italian mind a very foul precipitate indeed. Perhaps that is really what he was worth in this world. Strange, providential-looking, and leading to many thoughts. . . . Whatsoever good we have, the Gods know it well, and will know what to make of it in due season.

'Mazzini came much about us here for many years, patronised by my wife; to me very wearisome, with his incoherent Jacobinisms, George-Sandisms, in spite of all my love and regard for him; a beautiful little man, full of sensibilities, of melodies, of clear intelligence, and noble virtues. He had found Volney, etc., in a drawer in his father's library while a boy, and had read and read, recognising a whole new promised land illuminated with suns and volcanoes. Father was a physician in Genoa. He, forced to be a lawyer, turned himself into Young Italy, and, after many sad adventures, is *there*. What *will* become of him? we ask daily with a real interest. A small, square-headed, bright-eyed, swift, yet still, Ligurian figure; beautiful, and merciful, and fierce; as pretty a little man when I first saw him, eight or nine years ago, as had ever come before me. True as steel, the word, the thought of him pure and limpid as water; by nature a little lyrical poet; plenty of quiet fun in him, too, and wild emotion, rising to the *shrill* key, with all that lies between these two extremes. His trade, however, was not to write verses. Shall we ever see him more?'

Then Carlyle in his journal let his pen run on to English news about George Hudson, the leading railway speculator.—

'King Hudson flung utterly prostrate, detected "cooking accounts"; everybody kicking him through the mire. To me and to quiet onlookers he has not changed at all. He is merely detected to be what we always understood he was. The rage of fellow-gamblers, now when he has merely lost the game for them, and ceased to swindle with impunity, seems to us a very baseless thing. One sordid, hungry *canaille* are they all. Why should this, the chief terrier among them, be set upon by all the dog fraternity? One feels a real human pity for the ugly Hudson.

'Thomas Spedding the other night was describing to us the late figure of Hudson's private life, as Spedding himself and others had observed it. Overwhelmed with business, yet superadding to it ostentatious and high-flown amusements, balls at great country houses fifty miles off, etc., etc. With early morning he was gone from Newby Park, and his guests off by express trains over all the island; returned weary on the edge of dinner, then first met his guests, drank largely of champagne, with other wines; "ate nothing at all, hardly an ounce of solid food"; then tumbled into bed, worn out with business and madness. That was the late daily history of the man. Oh, Mammon! art thou not a hard god? It is now doubtful whether poor Hudson will even have any money left. Perhaps that would be a real benefit to him. His brother-in-law has drowned himself at York. What a world this ever is! Full of Nemesis, ruled by the Supreme, rebelled in by the Infernal, with prophetic tragedies as of old. Murderer Rush, Jermy's natural brother!' (This referred to the case of a landowner, Jermy, shot by his tenant Rush.) 'To pious men, he too might have seemed one of the fated. No son of Atreus had more authentically a doom of the Gods. The old laws are still alive. Even railway scrip is subject to them.'

Thus in the current criminal news Carlyle recognised Eternal Justice and Fate, seeing it clearly through the diabolical darkness of law-courts and exchanges,—like the Sun shining through a London winter fog.

In April his friend Charles Gavan Duffy had been brought to trial in Dublin for the last time, and when once more the trial ended without a conviction, Lord Clarendon's men had to let him go. Whereupon he at once began to plan how to revive his *Nation* newspaper, and presently came over to London for 'a few weeks, and saw much of Carlyle, Mrs. Carlyle, and their closest friends,' especially John Forster of the *Examiner*, who took to Duffy at once and advised and helped him well, and continued to do so all his life.[1]

As soon as Carlyle's work on the last important edition of Cromwell was plainly going to be finished in two weeks, he wrote to Gavan Duffy, now home in Dublin (29.5.49).—'Dear Duffy, There has risen a speculation in me of coming over to have a deliberate walk in Ireland, and to look at the strange doings of the Powers there with my own eyes for a little. . . . Ireland seems to me the notablest of all spots in the world at present. "There is your problem—yours, too, my friend," I will say to myself. "There, see what you will make of that." William Edward Forster, the young Quaker whom you have seen, offers to attend me. . . .' Then followed details of preparations, and in particular the books about Ireland he was reading, including 'the life of St. Patrick—Jocelyn's absurd legend; the dreary commentaries of poor Bollandists; and St. Patrick's own *Confessio* (which I believe to be genuinely his, tho unfortunately it is typical, not biographical); and one of the few places where I yet clearly aim to be is on the top of Croagh Patrick. . . . The famishing' Poor Law 'Unions I of course want especially to see. . . .'

It was now that James Spedding, biographer of Bacon, brought James Anthony Froude to Cheyne Row, and Froude tells us what is abundantly corroborated:—'Gavan Duffy had been a guest in Cheyne Row; and the story which he had to tell of cabins torn down by crowbars, and shivering families, turned out of their miserable homes, dying in the ditches by the roadside, had touched Carlyle to the very

[1] *Conversations with Carlyle*, by Sir C. Gavan Duffy, pp. 33–7, etc.; and *My Life in Two Hemispheres*, by the same, II, pp. 95, 110, etc.

heart. He was furious at the economical commonplaces with which England was consoling itself. He regarded Ireland, "that ragged body of a diseased soul," as "the breaking-point of the huge suppuration which all British and all European Society then was."'

When James Spedding and Froude arrived, they found Carlyle at Jocelyn's St. Patrick in the *Acta Sanctorum*, and were told he had just been reading how an Irish robber had "stolen a goat and eaten it, and the saint had convicted him by making the goat bleat in his stomach. He spoke of it with rough disgust; and then we talked of Ireland, of which I had some local knowledge."

"He treated me," said Froude, who got leave to call again, "shortly and sternly." Which may be explained by a note[2] Carlyle had sent to John Forster not long ago about *The Nemesis of Faith* lately published :—'Froude's book is not,—except for wretched people, strangling in white neckcloth and Semitic thrums,—worth its paper and ink. What on earth is the use of a wretched mortal's vomiting up all his interior crudities, dubitations, and spiritual agonising belly-aches, into the view of the public, and howling tragically, "See!" Let him, in the Devil's name, pass them, by the downward or other method, in his own water-closet, and say nothing whatever! Epictetus's sheep, intending at least to grow good wool, was a gentleman in comparison. . . .'

It was long before Carlyle gave a second thought to Froude. He was now preoccupied about the condition of Ireland and England, and had just written to his mother :—'I do not expect to find much new knowledge in Ireland if I go; but much that I have lying in me to say might perhaps get nearer to some way of utterance if I were looking face to face upon the ruin and wretchedness that is prevalent there.' In his journal there is a curious entry: 'Often in my sleep I have made long passages and screeds of composition in the most excellent approved commonplace style. I wish I could do it awake; I could then write many things—fill all newspapers with my writing. The dream seems to say the talent is in me; but the knack is wanting, and will perhaps for ever be.' Which recalls what Huxley wrote,[3]—"As anyone knows who ever heard Carlyle talk, the style natural to him

[2] In the John Forster Collection of MSS. in South Kensington Museum, a letter dated only "Chelsea, Wednesday," from T. C. to John Forster. The conjectural date assigned is 21.3.1849.

[3] *Professor Tyndall*, by T. H. Huxley, *Nineteenth Century Magazine*, January, 1894, p. 4.

was that of *The Diamond Necklace*. If he is chargeable with affectation at all (and I do not think he is) it is rather when he writes the classical English."

Writing to Gavan Duffy on 8.6.49 to accept an offer to be his guide in Ireland if not taken into custody again on 12.7.49, when his bail terminated, Carlyle used words that seemed to Duffy an inspiration, and which he treasured all his life.[4]—

'Fear nothing for the "12th of July" . . . you *have* passed through that most dangerous experiment, and a new and clearer course will henceforth open for you, not to terminate without results that all wise men will rejoice at. You have an Ireland ready to be taught by you, readier by you just now than by any other man; and God knows it needs teaching in all provinces of its affairs, in regard to all matters human and divine! Consider yourself as a brand snatched from the burning, a *providential* man, saved by the beneficent gods for doing a *man's* work yet, in this noisy bewildered, quack-ridden and devil-ridden world; and let it, this thought, in your modest ingenuous heart, rather give you fear and pious anxiety than exultation or rash self-confidence—as I know it will.'

Then he went on to discuss the details of their tour, in which the only fixed point was that he must see the "famine districts." His wife was delighted to see him prepare to go to Ireland. For herself she had already arranged a round of pleasant visits this season. She was about to revisit Scotland, which she had never seen since her mother died, and also her native Haddington, which she had not seen for twenty years.

[4] *Conversations with Carlyle*, by Sir C. Gavan Duffy, pp. 38–9.

BOOK XVII

TOURING IN IRELAND

1849

I

TO DUBLIN BY SEA

(1849)

ON 24.6.49 Carlyle was writing his final arrangements to Gavan Duffy, and said that the chief attraction of going by steamer was that he might be 'for two days *entirely alone*. Alone, and very miserable, it will beseem me to be, a good deal, in this the most original of my "tours."'[1] Which was a good resolution he was not able to keep, and it needs to be explained. He was sometimes prone to try to regulate his feelings, and in this instance was reminding himself that he *ought* to be miserable, because he feared to be too much the reverse!—Like the old lawyer Edwards who confessed:—"You are a philosopher, Dr. Johnson. I have tried, too, in my time to be a philosopher; but, I don't know how, cheerfulness was always breaking in." Carlyle was about to escape from proofs and drudgery and London smoke and dirt and noise into the fresh air he always enjoyed. He was naturally anxious not to show untimely good spirits when in the company of persecuted men, whose friends had lately been ruined according to law, or when visiting a people decimated and degraded by famine, and distracted by misgovernment and many mischances.

On 'a close damp-sunny'[2] Saturday morning, 30.6.49, he boarded the Chelsea steamer at 'Cadogan Pier; left my poor Wife gazing sorrowfully after me, and was wafted swiftly down the river.'[2] As this and many another passage like it has been misunderstood, it should be explained that Carlyle was much addicted to the Scottish fashion of using the word *poor* as a term of endearment. According to the dictionaries, it is sometimes so used in America also.[3] Assuredly Mrs. Carlyle was more to be envied than pitied, and seemed so to herself and all who knew her. A few

[1] *Conversations with Carlyle*, by Sir C. Gavan Duffy, pp. 41–2.
[2] *Reminiscences of My Irish Journey in* 1849, by T. Carlyle, pp. 1–38.
[3] *Standard Dictionary*, meaning No. 6, 1895 edition.

hours after watching his departure, she was driving out with Lady Ashburton to Addiscombe, to spend a long week-end there in very jolly company.

Perhaps it should be said here that the *Reminiscences of My Irish Journey in* 1849, now quoted, were private notes, never meant for publication and never given away, but stolen, in a way to be explained by and by. The Preface of 1882 is all wrong.

Meanwhile Carlyle was conveyed in a boat from the river steamer terminus, the floating platform above London Bridge, to the *Athlone* at Alderman Stairs. He noticed the 'hurried toilsome eyes' of the 'ragged, lean, greasy, sooty creature,' his boatman, who 'whisked his way like a needle through innumerable impediments,' and when paid double his proper fee, asked more, and then 'splashed away again about his business.'

The *Athlone* was lying all 'as if in a kind of greasy sleep.' He paid his fare and studied his fellow-voyagers, mostly Irish. At ten o'clock, with unexpected precision, a bell rang 'and we jumbled forth on our way,' but paused at Gravesend to pick up Irish soldiers, recruits and invalids from India, many of them drunk. The boat that brought the corporal in charge of them having drifted past the ladder, the corporal stepped into one of the pilot-boats hooked behind the steamer, 'cool he amid the tumult of noises and splashing of spray; and twisted gallantly aloft over the stern; dashed the spray from self and papers, and with a brisk calmness' Carlyle could not but admire, stepped smiling forward to his place, the foredeck. Smoking a cigar on the bridge beside the Captain, 'an excellent, civil, able, old Welshman,' Carlyle was watching the sea of Irish faces on board, and the 'wild expanse of shoals and channels' at the mouth of the Thames. The light-boats were 'bobbing and capering in the wild surf,' as the steamer passed near, and they seemed to him 'the dreariest objects in this world.' He was thinking of the two men on each with no function whatever but to keep a light burning at night, and how 'narrow' a 'share of this Universe' was theirs.

He came on deck at seven on Sunday, a beautiful sunny morning, and 'looked intently with many thoughts' at Ventnor,—houses and gardens 'hung out there against the morning sun,—and one of them had been John Sterling's last dwelling.' Which reminded him that John Forster would just be arriving at adjoining Bonchurch, 'little dreaming of my whereabouts.' Scanning the coast intently with a glass, he could not see a living figure, whereby he discovered it was farther away than it seemed. His fellow-voyagers had much to tell him. A half-pay Sergt.-Major seemed the best worth remembering, 'a most healthy practical man,' who told of soldiering in India, 'mainly economics—what you could *get*, and pocket or swallow' was his theme; and then his 'pensions, promotions, appointment now' to some military job about Falmouth. 'Soldiering like working, in such men,' the listener reflected, 'strong both ways, as native oak: the strongest kind of men.' Indeed, it is only the exceptional man who can continue healthy in the British Army, especially in India, where it has been called the Almighty's incinerator for white rubbish. Yet the material is often very fine,—it is the conditions of life that are hideously wrong.

After breakfast the Captain told Carlyle that a man had been lost overboard last night,—one of the Irish "Invalids" less lucky than the Sergt.-Major,—he had drowned his sorrows in alcohol and needed nothing more now. Carlyle had helped to pacify the man when he was rowdy on the Saturday, and he remembered now the "angry-bewildered" expression on his face, as of one who had "lost his way" among conditions he deemed unfair. It is not, however, a peculiarly Irish expression, tho in those famine years more often seen in Ireland than in England. That "angry-bewildered" look has been seen [4] on faces of many colours, black and white, brown and yellow, and perhaps it is nowhere more common than among Europeans in India. Thus the only other sample Carlyle remarked now was another invalid from India, a man with drooping eyebrows, nose and mouth, and 'eyes full of sorrow and rage,' whom he overheard declaring, "I have a right to be here, sir, I want my ration." Angry bewilderment congealed is the key to much in Kipling and to Lyall's Land of Regrets.—

> 'What lured him to life in the tropic?
>   Did he venture for fame or for pelf?
> Did he seek a career philanthropic?
>   Or simply to better himself?
> But whate'er the temptation that brought him,
>   Whether piety, dullness or debts,
> He is thine for a price, thou hast bought him,
>   O Land of Regrets!'

[4] By D. A. W.

By Sunday night they were in Plymouth harbour, where more passengers came aboard. This gave new hearers to a talkative Irishman, who had competed for Carlyle's attention yesterday, but left him now as a monopoly to the Sergt.-Major, who was glad to tell him about the pilchard-boats they saw cutting about, and do the honours of the gnarled rocky coast as far as Falmouth, where he landed at noon.

Before dark they had rounded Land's End and headed north; but the wind was westerly, and the Atlantic waves kept them exceedingly unsteady through the night. It was not till after breakfast-time on Tuesday that they were in the lee of the Emerald Isle and smoother water. Meanwhile Carlyle had been assisting the attendant of a passenger going to Dublin for surgery, fixing his umbrella over the invalid, and also making himself useful to two Misses Hewit, poor Irish maidens no longer young, who had come on board at Plymouth, and looked as if they wanted to be spoken to. When the ship was in stormy water and they were sick and neglected by the stewardess, they sent him for their basket, and he retrieved it for them, tho the stewardess would not find it till the Captain jogged her memory. Then Carlyle assisted her and used his 'soothing eloquence' upon her. She might have pleaded that the Misses Hewit had an unusual amount of boxes. They had intended to emigrate to Australia, but finding the free passage promised them to be a passage among paupers, they shrieked at the notion of it and were returning to Ennis in Clare. Which explains what happened on the quay at Dublin on Tuesday afternoon, 3.7.49, when the *Athlone* arrived there. The Misses Hewit directed Carlyle to stay by the luggage they had landed, till they came back with the rest of it: which he duly did, and only after dispatching them with all their luggage safe, did he get int a cab and go to the 'Imperial Hotel' where he was expected.

II

CARLYLE IN AN INN
(1849)

THE 'Imperial Hotel people brightened up into enthusiastic smiles of welcome at sound of my name,' wrote Carlyle in his notes when his travels were over.[1] The reason was that the Hotel belonged to Miss Purcell, aunt of Edward Fitzgerald, who had told her to expect Carlyle, and, indeed, had told everybody else he knew who could be useful to such a visitor. 'All was done for me,' the notes continue, 'that human waiterage could do; I had a brisk-eyed deft Irish youth by way of special attendant, really a clever, active, punctual youth, who seemed as if he would have run to the world's end for me at lifting of my finger: he got me' everything I wanted, in short, 'attended to my letters, clothes, messages, waited on me like a familiar fairy. . . . Bedroom the quietest they had. . . . Could they have got me into a room really "quiet," where I might have really slept, *all* had been well there. But that was not possible; not there, nor anywhere else in inns. One's "powers of observation" act under sad conditions, if the nerves are to be continually in a shatter with want of sleep and what it brings! Under that sad condition, as of a gloomy pressure of waking nightmare, were all my Irish operations transacted; no escape from it; therefore *say* nothing more of it, but do the best you may under it as under a law of fate.'

This was always Carlyle's experience, in England and Scotland, France and Germany, as well as in Ireland; and according to the best expert opinions the reason was not in the inns but in himself. He was suffering from hearing morbidly acute by reason of nervous weakness. The trouble was begun by overstudy in his early years, and abated during the country life at Craigenputtock; but work in London brought it back upon him worse than ever,

[1] *Reminiscences of My Irish Journey in* 1849, by T. Carlyle, pp. 38–9.

and the nervousness of his wife, for whose pleasure he remained in London against his will, reacted upon him in many ways.

In July, 1849, he may have been worse than usual, because of the excitements and disappointments of 1848 and 1849; but what mainly affected him now and also in his German tours was that he was by no means open to take his ease in his inn,—he was not touring for pleasure or amusement but working at high pressure, intently looking at realities. This has often been remarked about the tours in Germany. In Ireland he was even more intent, and also deeply moved by his "ruling passion" of pity. The mere sight of the miseries of the "distressful country," demoralised by long-continued famine, kept him awake at nights, as he groped for a word in season that might give light or peace. Which explains why, instead of accepting the Clarendons' invitation to dinner on Saturday, he went to Howth that day for a swim in the sea, and a quiet evening and sound sleep at the house of Mr. Hutton near there. It also explains why Duffy and he arranged their movements so as to let him have a few nights here and there in quiet houses.

III

DUBLIN AND GLASNEVIN SCHOOL

(1849)

IT was about ten o'clock on the night of arrival that John O'Hagan found Carlyle at the hotel writing letters, and told him,—" Duffy will be here in half an hour." Then Duffy came and told him how to deliver next day his letters of introduction to people in Dublin, and took the rest of the letters home with him, to scheme out their route.[1]

In delivering his letters on Wednesday, 4.7.49, Carlyle made no secret of Duffy being his adviser and companion, which gave a mild shock to the local " men in buckram." [2] Perhaps it made him all the more welcome to the energetic, squinting Dr. Stokes, the 'son of a United Irishman,' who booked him for dinner on Thursday, while Sir Duncan MacGregor, the Chief Commissioner of Police, 'an excellent old Scotchman, soldierly, open, genial, sagacious,' engaged him to dinner on Friday and kindly relieved him of the rest of his military letters. This left him free to be a good while in the house of Dr. Callan, where Duffy and his wife were, Mrs. Callan being Mrs. Duffy's sister and one of the many ladies whom Carlyle beheld "decorating Ireland." [3] The day was ended by dinner at the house of Dr. Evory Kennedy, where Carlyle met Cooke Taylor, an Irish man-of-letters pensioned by Government, fighting with the pen for his patron, Lord Clarendon, and talking, too, but not to the admiration of Carlyle, who wrote,—' I pitied but could not love him, with his semi-deceitful and self-deceiving speech, thought and action.'

On Thursday, 5.7.49, there was a 'whirlpool' of cards and callers, messages and invitations. In the afternoon Sir

[1] *Reminiscences of My Irish Journey in* 1849, by T. Carlyle, pp. 39–60.
[2] Told by Sir Charles Gavan Duffy to D. A. W.
[3] *Conversations with Carlyle*, by Sir C. Gavan Duffy, p. 37 and footnote, and *Life in Two Hemispheres*, by Sir C. G. D., I, p. 72 and footnote, p. 286, etc.

Philip Crampton, the Surgeon-General, drove Carlyle out to Phœnix Park, to call on the Lord-Lieutenant, Clarendon, who was out, however. When Carlyle wrote his name in the visitors' book, a servant produced her Ladyship's book also and was told,—" I haven't the honour to know her Ladyship." An invitation to dinner on the Saturday followed this call. To it he was able to answer that he was to quit Dublin that evening and could not come. Then a ' new very polite note came from Lord Clarendon, offering me introductions, etc. ; for which I wrote a second note,—" Not needed, thousand thanks." ' What is remarkable is the friendliness of Carlyle's relations with both " The Castle " and the opposition.

At Stokes's dinner on this Thursday night the talk was to the tune of Irish-versus-English, in spite of all that Carlyle could do to divert it. He would not affect any interest in old quarrels, and did not hide that he had no respect for Ireland as it was and had been recently. Let bygones be bygone, and quarrels stop. Dr. Stokes was distracted by his divided duty,—as a host, and as an hereditary patriot. He grew gloomy and contradictory, while his wife did not conceal her dudgeon. Carlyle confessed to himself that he had been bored by her talk ' to excess, but I did not give way to that ; had difficulty, however, in resisting it,' and perhaps was not so successful as he supposed in not letting her see his feelings.

The treat of the evening to him was talk about Irish antiquarian matters with a Rev. Dr. Todd, ' Dean or something, a little round-faced, dark-complexioned, squat, good-humoured and knowing man,' and with " dear old Petrie," a landscape-painter and antiquarian, ' a thin, wrinkly, half-ridiculous, yet mildly dignified man, speaks with a *panting* manner,'—the reverse of glib, tho full of ' real knowledge ' about Irish antiquities, and with a soul so free from snobbery that at an early stage of the banquet he set the contagious example of preferring punch to wine. Perhaps such vulgarity helped to disgust ' foolish Mrs. Stokes, a dim Glasgow lady.' " Dear old Petrie " went part of the way home with Carlyle, and was to meet him again on Saturday at the Museum of the Royal Irish Academy. Carlyle was impatient of political animosities and patter about the rows of 1798, but intensely interested in real knowledge of antiquity.

On Friday he was at a breakfast at John O'Hagan's,

19 Talbot Street, where there was no escape from politics, for the intellectual patriots would talk of nothing but Irish-versus-English, and the majority of them, including even the oldest, the Maynooth Theology Professor, Dr. Murray, a big, burly, red-faced man, seemed too 'full of fiery Irish zeal' to consider the matter rationally. Carlyle said as little as possible, and that he parted on friendly terms with Dr. Murray is pleasantly proved by this, that two or three years later Dr. Murray sought and obtained his help to get admission to the *Edinburgh Review*.[4] But what Carlyle was trying to convey to the patriots was a great surprise to them :—"England does not hate you at all, nor love you at all ; merely values and will pay you according to the work you can do."

Duffy was one of this party, and also 'the Laureate of '98,' a young 'Fellow of Trinity College' called John K. Ingram, to whom we owe what may outlive his songs,—the history of how the breakfast party ended.[5]

A vinegary 'pale, shrill logician,' and 'intolerable' . . . according to Carlyle, joined the party *after* breakfast, and 'drove me out to smoke.' How he did it was what Ingram delighted to tell with laughter for a generation afterwards. 'Ralph,' for that was his name, 'came in late in a hurried rapid way, and at once addressed Carlyle :—"Well, Mr. Carlyle, so you've come over to learn the truth about Ireland for yourself. Well, there are two methods of approaching Truth, the Synthetic Method and the Analytic Method. You are a geometer, Mr. Carlyle, and I need not explain these methods to you and how they differ."

'So he went on and on, all the rest reduced to silence. Carlyle, across the table, listened grimly, and at length, when opportunity offered, said :—"Sir, I have lived long enough to appreciate the value of time ; and have lairned to drad the *fluent man* far more than the stutterer."'[5]

It is only fair to add that of the seven Irish intellectuals met by Carlyle this Friday morning, all were young but Dr. Murray, and both Ingram and another seemed 'Irish-rational,' while a third, young Mr. Hutton, took no side. He was a neighbour of O'Hagan, and his main concern was to persuade Carlyle to accept an offer of hospitality from

[4] *Conversations with Carlyle*, by Sir C. Gavan Duffy, pp. 175–8.
[5] Letter of T. W. Lyster in the *Times Lit. Supplmt.*, 16.9.20. What the mis-spellings seem to mean is that he pronounced learned with the sound of *a* in *say*, and dread with the sound of *a* in *had*. It is old-fashioned.

his father, who lived near Howth. On Wednesday Carlyle had been speaking of going to Howth for a swim in the sea. Why not go on Saturday and sleep the night there ? It was a most kind offer, and thankfully accepted.

Meanwhile, on Friday, after breakfast, the young men took Carlyle to see the University and its Library and Museum. Duffy presented to him Isaac Butt, a politician and lawyer who had defended him lately, and was by and by to start the Home Rule party, which Parnell carried far. 'A terrible black burly son of earth,' Butt seemed to Carlyle now,—'talent visible in him, but still more animalism ; big bison-head, black, not *quite* unbrutal : glad when he went off. . . .'

He belonged as a Home-Ruler to the generation to come. Sir Alexander MacDonnell, Chief Commissioner of Education, who claimed attention next, was like Stokes the "son of a United Irishman" of a generation past. MacDonnell now came by appointment with his car, and conveyed Carlyle to the Glasnevin suburb, and showed him at work there a combination of Teachers' Training School and Model Farm, which pleased him better than anything else he saw in Ireland, appearing liker a realisation of his own and Goethe's ideal of education than anything he ever saw anywhere. He spoke of it often, as long as he lived [6] ; and here is what he wrote about it when it was fresh in mind.—

'Modest slated buildings, house, school and offices, for real use and fit for that. Slow-spoken, heavy-browed schoolmaster croaks out sensible pertinent speech about his affairs : an Ulster man—from Larne, I think ; name forgotten,—has 45 pupils, from 17 to 21 years ; they are working about, dibbling, sorting dungheaps, sweeping yards. Mac. speaks to several : coarse rough-haired lads, from all sides of Ireland, intelligent well-doing looks through them all. Schooling alternates with this husbandry work. Will become National schoolmasters,—probably factors of estates, if they excel and have luck. Clearly, wherever they go, they will be practical missionaries of good order and wise husbandry, these poor lads ; *anti*chaos missionaries these : good luck go with them, more power to their elbow ! Such were my reflexions, expressed partly in some such words. Our heavy-browed croaking-voiced friend has some 30 cows ; immense

[6] *Shooting Niagara : and After ?*, end of Chap. VIII ; and W. Allingham, *A Diary*, p. 172, etc., etc.

pains to preserve all manure, it is upon this that his husbandry turns. A few pigs, first-rate health in their air. Some 30 acres of ground in all; wholly like a garden for cultivation: best hay, best barley; best everything. I left him and his rough boys, wishing there were 1,000 such establishments in Ireland: alas, I saw no other in the least equal to it; doubt if there is another. Mac. talking confidentially and with good insight too of Archbishop Whately, &c., set me down at the hotel, to meet again at dinner.'

The dinner was at the house of Sir Duncan MacGregor, who sent a car to fetch Carlyle, and handed to him as he departed a general missive to the Police Stations,—" Be serviceable if you ever can to this Traveller"; which was needed once and found to avail.

What Carlyle remarked about Dublin was its over-supply of animosities and lack of work. It was not now the real "Capital" of Ireland, less so, perhaps, than either Glasgow or Liverpool. It was not the home of lords of any kind. 'Not even the sham-lords with their land-revenues come hither now. The place has no manufactures to speak of; except of ale and whisky, and a little poplin-work, none that I could hear of.' It lived on litigation 'and the sham of Government. . . . Alas, *when* will there any real aristocracy arise (here or elsewhere) to need a Capital for residing in!'

IV

A SATISFACTORY SATURDAY

(1849)

ON Saturday morning, 7.7.49, " dear old Petrie " came for him and they walked together to a breakfast at the Zoo.[1] The only record of the talk there is a trifle explained to him afterwards by Duffy,[2] and datable here. Carlyle remarked :—" Shelley is a poor creature, who has said or done nothing worth a serious man being at the trouble of remembering." Duffy did not make a note of all he said ; but it is easy to guess the drift of it. He was writing to Browning soon after this about Browning's essay on Shelley :—' I am not sure but you would excommunicate me if I told you all I thought of Shelley ! Poor soul, he has always seemed to me an extremely weak creature ; a poor, thin, spasmodic, hectic shrill and pallid being. . . . The very voice of him (his style, &c.), shrill, shrieky, to my ear has too much of the ghost ! ' Which recalls what " Dicky " Milnes has reported he said [3] :—" Shelley is always mistaking spasmodic violence for strength, I know no more *urned* books than his." That is to say, his books are like the cinders and ashes of cremated bodies ready to be put into sepulchral urns. The report ran on :—" It is like the writing of a ghost, uttering infinite wail into the night, unable to help itself or anyone else."

Now there was present young D. F. MacCarthy, one of the Young Ireland poets, familiar to readers of the *Nation*, and an enthusiastic " Shelleyite," the same who twenty years later became one of Shelley's biographers. His tastes were known to many now at table, who rather admired him for remaining silent, ' out of respect for the laws of hospitality.' Not so old Carleton, author of *Traits and Stories of the Irish Peasantry* and much else, a man of fifty-five, who

[1] *Reminiscences of My Irish Journey*, by T. C., pp. 60–6.
[2] *Conversations with Carlyle*, by Sir C. G. Duffy, pp. 63–4.
[3] *Life of R. M. Milnes, Lord Houghton*, by T. Wemyss Reid, I, pp. 435–6.

had received a Civil List Pension last year. He now with emphasis said ditto to Carlyle, declaring,—" This is what I've long been saying to these young men, but they won't listen to me."

MacCarthy :—" Surely, Carleton, you would not disparage Shelley's masterpiece, *Sartor Resartus* ? "

There was a ripple of laughter, but Carleton escaped the trap and answered :—" Ah, my young friend, it would be well for Shelley if he could write a book like *Sartor Resartus*."

After breakfast and a look at the animals, the visitor was taken to the Academy, and Petrie did the honours of its Museum with enthusiasm, assisted well by the Secretary. Its rare antiquities were 'really interesting' to Carlyle, and dwelt in his memory, 'for everything has a certain *authenticity*, as well as national or other significance, too often wanting in such places.'

Then after settling at his hotel, he spent an hour and a half at the Board of Works, examining maps and statistics with Colonel Larcom, the head of the Ordnance Survey. He was particularly interested in a very ingenious new coloured map, with figures referring you to tables, which Larcom had made 'for behoof of the Poor Law Commissioners, a really meritorious and most valuable work.'

Colonel Larcom came to the hotel door with him, where Ingram and another were waiting to 'bowl him off' to the Howth railway. He had a bathe at Howth, tho the tide was out, and saw the sights around, remarking for himself that the fishing boats in the bay were pilchard boats from Cornwall. To the ruins of a 'big old Abbey, overgrown with thistles, nettles, burdocks and squalor,' he got access 'through dark cabins by the *back windows*,' and departed 'leaving a few coppers amid hallelujahs of thanks.' Then came a quiet evening in the house of Mr. Hutton, whose four beautiful daughters placidly sat sewing, while their Mother entertained the stranger till the time came for him to go to bed, where he enjoyed the first sound sleep he had had in Ireland ; for in Mr. Hutton's house, when he retired to rest, he heard no sound but the soothing voice of the everlasting sea.

V

KILDARE AND GLENDALOUGH

(1849)

ON Sunday morning he returned to Dublin [1] and took train to Kildare, on the way to Kilcullen, where Edward Fitzgerald's relatives were expecting him. He was to be the guest for two nights of the widow of the poet's "Uncle Peter" Purcell. [2] Purcell was the name of the poet's father and of the poet himself when a boy, till it was changed to the more fashionable name of his mother, Fitzgerald.[2] Let curious readers see Thackeray's description [3] of the home of this good Uncle Peter as it was in 1842, for the H—— of Thackeray means Halverstown near Kilcullen, where Carlyle was now to stay, and his Mr. P—— was Peter Purcell. "Such people," wrote Thackeray,[4] "are not to be met with more than a few times in a man's life." "Uncle Peter" was now dead. It was his widow who received Carlyle.

Duffy in the meantime had gone to Kilkenny, where Carlyle was not due till Tuesday night. The attraction of Kildare was antiquarian mainly, as appears from one of his letters from London before he started:—'Kildare town and then to Glendalough through Wicklow (Gap) is figuring in my imagination. Kildare for St. Bridget's sake—Bridekirk, her kirk I suppose, was almost the place of my birth; and Bridget herself, under the oaks 1400 years ago, is for her own sake beautiful to me.' She had founded four nunneries, whereof the chief was Kildare.

So when he landed at Kildare this Sunday about noon, he at once enquired, but discovered nobody who knew anything, about 'St. Bridget's "Fire Tower-House,"' of long ago. The bishop had abolished her sacred fire

[1] *Reminiscences of My Irish Journey*, by T. Carlyle, pp. 67–81.
[2] *Life of Ed. Fitzgerald*, by Thomas Wright, I, pp. 29, 30, 165, 233.
[3] *Thackeray's Irish Sketch Book*, Chap. II.
[4] *Works of W. M. Thackeray, with Biog. Introdn.*, Vol. V, p. xxvii.

many centuries ago; but in old histories she and Columba and Patrick are the three leading Irish saints, and his guess was right about Bridekirk too,—she was the tutelary saint of the Douglases on the Scottish Borders. Bridekirk meant Bridget's church.

From Kildare station to Kilcullen his road lay through the village of Kildare, and there he was met by a carriage sent by his hostess. He sat in it smoking, and while the friends who came in it made a call, he was observing such a sight as he had never seen before. Knots of worshippers coming from church were hanging about the streets, 'and everywhere round them hovered a harpy-swarm of clamorous mendicants, men, women, children:—a village *winged*' (in rags), 'as if a flight of harpies had alighted in it! In Dublin I had seen winged groups, but not *much* worse than some Irish groups in London that year: here for the first time was "Irish beggary" itself!'

The rag-winged swarm, receiving nothing from him, departed, 'all but two, young fellows, cowering nearly naked on opposite sides of me twenty yards off. "Take this groat and divide it between you,"' he said at length, and with an "explosion" of thanks they also went round the corner.

Back came one,—"Ach, yer honor! He won't give me the twopence."

"Then why don't you lick him, you blockhead, till he either die or give it you?"

'Two citizens within hearing burst into a laugh,' wrote Carlyle. But it would have been wiser to say plainly as his own father would have said,—"I do not believe you." Violence is like fire, too dangerous to play with. In Burma about 1904 a man owed half a rupee to each of two men for some slight service; and having no change, gave a rupee to one and said,—"Divide it." The receiver promised the other,—"I'll pay your share when I get change"; but spent it all, and the other struck him when he was asleep and killed him. For which he was convicted of murder, but sentenced to penal servitude for life only, not to death, because of the provocation.[5]

On Monday Carlyle went through Wicklow Gap to Glendalough and back. The black boggy hills and a lead-mine resembled Galloway and the Leadhills of Scotland; and a man galloped past them, only pausing to say he was

[5] D. A. W. was the judge who tried the case.

going for a surgeon and a priest,—a miner had just been killed; and from the other side of the valley they heard the piercing cries of some woman bereaved, 'in wild rage of lamentation.'

Glendalough was grim. The seven churches built to pray in were all damp mouldering ruins now. Bare hills were standing round the old ruins and the graves both old and new,—'many burials *still* here,' he remarked,—and right and left, on every hand, wherever one turned, there was one sound only, that of tattered wretchedness in every figure howling, "*Lave* a penny for the love of God!"

It seemed a fair guess that 'the central fact' of Glendalough was its "patterun" or patron saint, Kevin, and that the kings of old days, who had dedicated chapels and had themselves buried there, had done so in the hope of a 'straight road to Heaven' or post-obit fire insurance. Carlyle took away with him from Glendalough some heath and ivy, and sent it to Edward Fitzgerald next day, with a letter praising the Irish race in general as truly social, and Fitzgerald's kindred in particular, who had welcomed him like a Brother.[6] There is no sign that he regretted his pilgrimage. But like many another pilgrim, he found that what he had come to see was a trifle compared to what he saw on the way, and especially near Kilcullen, as he looked around him.

He had been bred on a farm and knew much of science, and was an amazingly good observer. Peter Purcell had employed 110 persons cultivating 400 acres well and prosperously; and a Scotch farmer who seems to have been carrying on his work took Carlyle walking in the potato field, as Mr. Purcell had taken Thackeray, and both had the same story to tell about the reclamation of the Common by the peasantry themselves, with no help or advice from the Government but rather the contrary,—occasional imprisonment.[3]

Carlyle had already noticed for himself the abundance of lime everywhere, and of good ground needing only to be drained; and what he saw and heard at Kilcullen went far to confirm his conclusion, soon amounting to a conviction, that what Ireland needed most was to subordinate landlordism to the public interest and set the people to work on the land. Thus in driving him to the railway this (Tuesday)

[6] Fitzgerald MSS., Trinity College, Cambridge, letter of 10.7.1849.

afternoon, Mrs. Purcell showed him the ' Curragh of Kildare, a sea of beautiful green land,' offering ' *work* for about 10,000 people if they were set to it instead of left to beg.'

There was no train here seven years ago when Thackeray passed this way, but now Carlyle took train as far as Bagenalstown, and went thence by road, on a ' dusty dusky evening,' to Kilkenny.

VI

KILKENNY

(1849)

At Kilkenny Carlyle was to stay at the house of the Mayor, Dr. Cane, 'lately in prison for "Repale," now free and a Mayor again.'[1] In honour of the occasion Mrs. Cane had asked to dinner to meet him three Poor Law Inspectors, O'Shaughnessy and two others, besides Duffy, and he found them all waiting when he arrived after eight, and listened to the immense amount of things they had to tell him. He had sprained his foot in the potato field this morning, and Dr. Cane bandaged it so well that, as he said,—'it didn't trouble me above another day.'

Mrs. Cane was that best of all good things, an 'excellent mother and wife,' and a motherly hostess. She not only made him sure of two good nights' sleep, but even discovered his writing-case needed a canvas cover and quickly provided one. The doctor deserved such a mate,—'a tall, straight man,' wrote Carlyle, 'grey eyes, black head; deep bass voice, speaks slowly as if preaching. Irish moral Grandison—touch of that in him; sympathy with all that is good and manly, however, and continual effort towards that. Likes me, is hospitably kind to me, and I am grateful to him.'

On Wednesday O'Shaughnessy, whom also Carlyle liked, took him to see the poor-houses. He had to cater for 8000 paupers: 'huge arrangements for eating, baking, stacks of Indian meal stirabout; 1000 or 2000 men lying piled up within brick walls, in such a country, on such a day! Did a greater violence to the Law of Nature ever before present itself to sight? . . . Hospital: haggard ghastliness of some looks,—literally, their eyes grown "colourless," as Mahomet describes the horror of the Day of Judgment. . . . No hope but of stirabout; swine's meat, swine's *destiny*: right glad to get away.'

Duffy and he set out together for Waterford on the Thursday.

[1] *Reminiscences of My Irish Journey*, by T. Carlyle, pp. 81–7.

VII

CARLYLE AND GAVAN DUFFY

(1849)

IN going from Kilkenny to Waterford on Thursday, 12.7.49, Carlyle and Duffy had the railway for about a third of the way. The rest was not made yet, so that they had to go by the road, walking where it was steep, and most of the way sitting chatting on a " private car,"—" Duffy keeping me busy at *talk!* " [1] noted Carlyle.

'Our talk was at first of the scenes in the (Kilkenny) workhouse,' wrote Duffy.[2] 'The house was full of men fit for active industry, and women, vigorous and healthy, squatting on the floor like negroes in a slaveship. Carlyle was vehement in his indignation' and said:—" I look at many things in Ireland with silent pity, but the workhouse where no one works is unutterably despicable. Consider the absurdity of shutting up thousands of forlorn creatures to be fed at the cost of beggars like themselves. Why not regiment these unfortunate wretches, and thrash them, if it proved needful, into habits of industry on some lands at home or in the colonies? Try them for a couple of years, I would say, and if they cannot feed and clothe themselves, they ought to be put out of the world."

To which of course Duffy replied at once that the poor people would be delighted to work, but were the serfs of a Parliament which made them swelter in idleness. The rest of their talk, he says, was mostly 'of eminent men whom he had known. When I named a man, he spoke of him. When I named another, he took up the second'; and so on; and whatever seemed memorable was written 'daily, and finally offered to him to read.' Carlyle 'playfully excused himself, but tacitly sanctioned the practice.' Duffy was not imitating Boswell. He says he was writing simply for 'my personal instruction,' and thought of destroying the notes when they had 'answered their original purpose.' It was

[1] *Reminiscences of My Irish Journey*, by T. Carlyle, pp. 87–92.
[2] *Conversations with Carlyle*, by Sir C. Gavan Duffy, pp. 73–4, 46–53.

for that purpose that he had arranged them according to the topics, and sometimes leaves us doubtful about the dates. He was not thinking of any others ever seeing what he had written, and happily the dates do not matter.

Carlyle was now fifty-three years of age. He commonly wore 'a dark suit, a black stock, a deep folding linen collar, and a wide-brimmed hat.' Duffy goes on to describe[2] him as a man of 'strong, well-knit frame, a dark, ruddy complexion, piercing blue eyes, close-drawn lips, and an air of silent composure and authority,' looking in short like one 'who had filled some important employment. There was not a shade of discontent or impatience discernible in his countenance.' He stood quite straight and was nearly six feet tall, with thick, bushy, darkbrown hair, and the shaven chin, which projected a little if you looked close, was in keeping with the big forehead. On one point there is a conflict of evidence. According to Froude, "his eyes were a deep violet, with fire burning at the bottom of them, which flashed out at the least excitement." Which the other witnesses[3] deny. They corroborate Duffy; and the photographer, whom Carlyle declared the most successful of those who took his photo, agreed with the other witnesses in saying :[4]—"The eyes were very deepset and clear, dark blue—with plenty of bright white round the pupils, and he always looked straight at you. That is what people would mean by talking of 'flashing' or 'devouring' eyes. When he asked me questions, I felt as if the eyes darted out towards me."

After describing how Carlyle appeared to strangers, Duffy continued.[1]—'But I must speak of his relation to his fellow-traveller. If you want to know a man, says the proverb, make a solitary journey with him. We travelled for six weeks on a stretch, nearly always *tête-à-tête*. If I be a man who has entitled himself to be believed, I ask those who have come to regard Carlyle as exacting and domineering among associates, to accept as the simple truth my testimony that, during those weeks of close and constant intercourse, there was not one word or act of his to the young man who was his travelling companion unworthy of an indulgent father. Of arrogance or impatience not a shade. In debating the arrangements of the journey, and

[3] Friends, relatives, and servants, and David Masson and J. Patrick, photographer.

[4] Mr. Patrick to D. A. W.

all the questions in which fellow-travellers have a joint interest, instead of exercising the authority to which his age and character entitled him, he gave and took with complaisance and good-fellowship.'

Describing their conversations, Duffy said:—'He did not declaim but conversed,' and in replying to questions about people gave 'his actual estimate of the person in question. It has been said of him that he had a habit of looking down upon his contemporaries, but it was from a real, not an imaginary eminence. He insisted on a high standard of duty in the men whom he discussed; but it was a standard he lived up to himself, and it only became chimerical when applied to all above the crowd. His own life was habitually spent in work, and belonged to a moral world almost as far apart from the world in which the daily business of life is transacted as the phantom land of the *Pilgrim's Progress*. . . .

'His talk was a clear rippling stream that flowed on without interruption, except when he acted the scene he was describing, or mimicked the person he was citing. With the play of hands and head he was not a bad mimic, but his countenance and voice, which expressed wrath or authority with singular power, were clumsy instruments for badinage. His attempts, however, were more enjoyable than skilful acting; he entered so frankly into the farce himself, laughing cordially. Tho he commonly spoke the ordinary tongue of educated Englishmen, if he was moved, especially if he was moved by indignation or contempt, he was apt to fall into what Mrs. Carlyle called "very decided Annandale."'

VIII

WHO IS THE BEST TALKER IN LONDON?

(1849)

'THE casual mention of Edmund Burke,' wrote Duffy,[1] 'induced me to ask Carlyle who was the best talker in London?' Carlyle replied:—" When I first met Wordsworth I had been assured that he talked better than any man in England. On that occasion he kept discoursing on how far you could get carried out of London on this side and on that for sixpence. When I knew him better, I found that no man gave you so faithful and vivid a picture of any person or thing which he had seen with his own eyes."

Duffy:—" May I assume that Wordsworth came up to this description of him as the best talker in England?"

Carlyle:—" Well, you would get more meaning out of what Wordsworth had to say to you than from anybody else. Leigh Hunt would emit more pretty, pleasant, ingenious flashes in an hour than Wordsworth in a day. But in the end you would find that you had been drinking perfumed water in one case, and in the other you got the sense of a deep, earnest man. There was one exception to your satisfaction with the man (Wordsworth). When he spoke of poetry he harangued about metres and so forth, and one could not be at the pains of listening to him. But on all other subjects he had more sense of a sound and instructive sort than any other literary man in England."

Duffy suggested that Wordsworth might consider what he had to say very instructive, as he had wrought a revolution in English poetry. " No, not so," said Carlyle. " All he had got to say in that way was like a few driblets from the great ocean of German speculation. Coleridge brought it over, and they translated Teutonic thought into a poor, disjointed, whity-brown sort of English, and that was nearly all. But tho Wordsworth was the man of most practical mind of any of the persons connected with literature

[1] *Conversations with Carlyle*, by Sir C. G. Duffy, pp. 53–6.

whom I have encountered, his pastoral pipings are far from being of the importance his admirers imagine. He is essentially a cold, hard, silent, practical man, who, if he had not fallen into poetry, would have done effectual work of some sort in the world. This is the impression one gets of him as he looks out of his stern blue eyes, superior to men and circumstances."

Duffy said he 'had expected to hear of a man of softer mood, more sympathetic and less taciturn. Carlyle said: "No, not at all; he is a man quite other than that; a man of immense head and great jaws like a crocodile's, cast in a mould designed for prodigious work."

'After a pause he resumed.—"As far as talk might be regarded as simply a recreation, not an enquiry after truth and sense, Jeffrey said more brilliant and interesting things than any man I have met in the world. He is a bright-eyed, lively, ingenuous little fellow, with something fascinating and radiant in him when he gets into his drawing-room tribune. He is not a great teacher nor a man of solid sense like Wordsworth, but his talk is lively and graphic, tho not in any remarkable degree instructive or profitable. It is pleasant and titillating, like the odorous perfume of a pastille."'

Duffy remarking,—"I started in life with the traditional estimate of Jeffrey as the king of critics, and found his articles in the *Edinburgh Review* thin and disappointing," Carlyle replied.—"Yes, his speculations and cogitations in literature were meagre enough. His critical faculty was small, and he had no true insight into the nature of things; but the *Edinburgh Review* had been of use in its time, too. When a truth found it hard to get a hearing elsewhere, it was often heard there. At present the great *Review* is considerably eclipsed, and (its) influence is quite gone."

IX

BROWNING AND COLERIDGE

(1849)

GAVAN DUFFY writes,[1]—'I begged him to tell me something of the author of *Bells and Pomegranates*, in which I took great delight.' He quoted and described it. Carlyle heard him out and replied :—" Robert Browning has a powerful intellect, and among the men engaged in literature in England just now is one of the few from whom it is possible to expect something. He is somewhat uncertain about his career, and I myself have perhaps contributed to the trouble by assuring him that poetry is no longer a field where any true or worthy success can be won or deserved. If a man has anything to say entitled to the attention of rational creatures, all mortals will come to recognise after a little that there is a more effectual way of saying it than in metrical numbers. Poetry used to be regarded as the natural, and even the essential, language of feeling, but it is not at all so ; there is not a sentiment in the gamut of human passion which cannot be adequately expressed in prose. Browning's earliest works have been loudly applauded by undiscerning people, but he is now heartily ashamed of them, and hopes in the end to do something altogether different from 'Sordello' and 'Paracelsus.'"

Then Carlyle told of his first meeting with Browning and the true story of the courtship of Miss Barrett, concluding,—" They married and are living together in Italy, like the hero and heroine of a medieval romance."

Duffy presently quoted a letter from a friend to whom he had lent 'Sordello,' enquiring whether it might be the sacred book of the Irvingite Church, written in their unknown tongue ? And asking why poetry should be more abstruse than mathematics ? Meanwhile he quoted a poem of Coleridge's to show its " most astonishing resemblance to one of Browning's various styles," such as " in a smaller man would suggest palpable imitation."

[1] *Conversations with Carlyle*, by Sir C. Gavan Duffy, pp. 56–62.

Carlyle replied :—" Browning is an original man, and by no means a person who would consciously imitate any one. There is nothing very admirable in the performance, likely to tempt a man into imitation. It will be seen by and by that Browning is the stronger man of the two, and has no need to go marauding in that quarter."

Duffy said :—" I think the stronger man will find it hard to match 'Christabel,' or 'The Ancient Mariner,' or to influence men's lives as they have been influenced by 'The Friend' or 'The Lay Sermon' in their day."

" Not so," said Carlyle. " Whatever Coleridge has written is vague and purposeless, and intrinsically cowardly, and for the most part is quite forgotten in these times. He had reconciled himself to believe in the Church of England long after it had become a dream to him." Then he spoke about Coleridge to the same effect as he was soon to write in *John Sterling*, concluding,—" When all is said, Coleridge was a poor, greedy, sensual creature, who could not keep from his laudanum bottle, tho he knew it would destroy him."

After a pause Carlyle added,—" One of the products of his system was Hartley Coleridge," whom he described,—the drunken son of the great Coleridge, and another son not named but described :—" a Protestant priest, a smooth, sleek, sonorous fellow. He has the management of some model High Church schools at Chelsea, and quacks away there, pouring out huge floods of the sort of rhetoric that class of persons deal in, which he tries to persuade himself he believes."

Duffy's rejoinder was to quote the best of Coleridge's shorter poems, which he declared worthy of Milton, etc.

> " How seldom, Friend ! a great good man inherits
> Honour or wealth, with all his worth and pains !
> *It sounds like stories from the land of spirits,*
> *If any man obtain that which he merits,*
> *Or any merit that which he obtains.*
> For shame, dear Friend ! . . . Greatness and goodness
> are not means but ends . . ." and so on.

" Yes," said Carlyle, " there are bits of Coleridge fanciful and musical enough, but the theory and practice of his life as he lived it, and his doctrines as he practised them, was a result not pleasant to contemplate."

X

WALTER SAVAGE LANDOR

(1849)

WHEN Duffy mentioned Savage Landor, Carlyle said :[1]—" Landor is a man of real capacity for literary work of some sort, but he has fallen into an extravagant method of stating his opinions, which makes any serious acceptance of them altogether impossible. If he encountered anywhere an honest man doing his duty, he announced that here was a phenomenal mortal, a new and authentic emanation of the Deity. This was a sort of talk to which silence was to be preferred. Landor had not come to discern the actual relation of things in this world ; very far from it. But there was something honourable and elevated, too, in his views. He was sincere and altogether persuaded for the time that the wild fancies he paraded were verities. But the personal impression he left, on those who (met) him, was that of a wild creature with fierce eyes and boisterous attitudes, uttering prodigious exaggerations on every topic that turned up, followed by a guffaw of laughter that was not exhilarating ; rather otherwise, indeed."

Duffy said,—" He dropped his paragons as abruptly as he took them up," and illustrated this by the instances of Bolivar and Sir Thomas Wilson, about whom he quoted what John Forster had just been telling him of Landor's present opinions.

" Yes," replied Carlyle. " That was his method. He was not inflexible in his opinions, but in his determination to be right, which was the more manful and honourable method."

Then Duffy discussing Landor's " Imaginary Conversations " urged that they ' had the dramatic form without the dramatic spirit,' and quoted many instances. Carlyle admitted he was right,—" the ' Conversations ' are all more or less Landor," and tho superior in width of interest,

[1] *Conversations with Carlyle*, by Sir C. Gavan Duffy, pp. 64–7.

they were inferior in dramatic quality to the "windy rollicking *Noctes*" of John Wilson.

"Is not Literature merely Landor's pastime, taken up by fits and starts?" was Duffy's next enquiry. The answer was:—"Landor has been drawn into literature by ambition. He found it did not altogether succeed with him. His merits were far from being acknowledged by all mankind, which soured him in dealing with his fellow-creatures."

After a pause, Carlyle went on.—"When Landor was young, he went to Italy, believing that England was too base a place for a man of honour to dwell in; but he soon came to discover that Italy was intrinsically baser. For the last ten years he lived near Bath, coming rarely to London, which he professed to hate and despise. He had left his wife in Italy, giving her all his income except a couple of hundred pounds. She was not a wise or docile woman, and he could not live with her any longer. He was about to remove his children that they might be properly educated; but the eldest son snatched up a gun, and declared that by God he would shoot any one who attempted to separate his mother and her children. So Landor had to leave them where they were."

"Is his wife the Ianthe to whom so many of his poems are addressed?" was the next question.

"I think not," said Carlyle. "Ianthe is probably a young girl at Bath, whom Landor counts the model of all perfection, and whom he gets a good deal rallied about in London."

It was at Lady Blessington's that Carlyle had met old Landor, who had the honour of having drawn out her brightest stroke of wit. As Henry Chorley testified, on one occasion Landor was 'more petulant and paradoxical than ever' in Lady Blessington's drawing-room, making pious M. Rio wince by attacking the Psalms of David, till Lady Blessington put a stop to that by saying 'in her arch inimitable way, "*Do* write something better, Mr. Landor!"'[2]

[2] *Henry F. Chorley, Autobiog., &c.*, by H. G. Hewlett, II, pp. 192–3.

XI

DICKENS AND THACKERAY

(1849)

DUFFY was unable to share the popular admiration of Dickens, and begged Carlyle to speak about him. Admitting that his humour was irresistible, he enquired,—"Is there a character in his books, except Mrs. Nickleby, whom one met in actual life?"

"Dickens," said Carlyle,[1] "is a good little fellow, one of the most cheery, innocent natures I have ever encountered, and maintains something of his old reporter independence." But "his theory of life is entirely wrong. He thinks men ought to be buttered up, and the world made soft and accommodating for them, and all sorts of fellows have turkey for their Christmas dinner. Commanding and controlling and punishing them he would give up without any misgivings, in order to *coax and soothe and delude them into doing right*. But it is not in this manner the eternal laws operate, but quite otherwise. Dickens has not written anything which will be found of much use in solving the problems of life. But he is worth something; worth a penny to read of an evening before going to bed."

Duffy suggested,—"The difference between his men and women and Thackeray's seems to me like the difference between Sinbad the Sailor and Robinson Crusoe."

"Yes," said Carlyle, "Thackeray has more reality in him, and would cut up into a dozen Dickenses. They are altogether different at bottom. Dickens is doing the best in him, and goes on smiling in perennial good humour; but Thackeray despises himself for his work, and on that account cannot always do it even moderately well. He is essentially a man of grim, silent, stern nature, but lately he has circulated among fashionable people, dining out every day, and he covers this native disposition with a varnish of smooth,

[1] *Conversations with Carlyle*, by Sir C. Gavan Duffy, pp. 74–6.

smiling complacency," which in short "is not salutary discipline for work of any sort."

Thackeray himself felt that. 'Bayard Taylor told me,' reports the Rev. Moncure Conway,[2] 'that he once visited the studio of Baron Marochetti with Thackeray,' who pointed to a sculpture of St. George and the Dragon, and said,—"Every man has his dragon; mine is dining out; what's yours?" "The same," said Taylor.

[2] *Autobiography of Moncure D. Conway*, II, p. 4.

XII

SMALL TALK

(1849)

DROPPING into small talk, Carlyle remarked a discovery he had made in Ireland.[1] The Irish called the tenpenny piece once current a "hog," and that made sense of the proverbial expression, going the whole hog. An Irishman who began to give a friend a treat in a frugal spirit might warm to the business and say he'd go the whole hog. In the common meaning of hog, the words were hopeless nonsense. Duffy matched this with his discovery newly made that plasterers call a mortar-board a "hawk," and he thought that that was the key to Hamlet's phrase about himself, "I know a hawk from a handsaw." But Carlyle would not agree, preferring the usual explanation of handsaw meaning a heron.

When he mentioned Mazzini's blunder of calling paupers "poors," a much funnier sample of the same kind of mistake was told by Duffy. A friend of his had just been visiting the great Munich Professor Döllinger and said to him,—"There is a prodigious multitude of infidels in Germany, I fear." "Yes," replied Döllinger, "infidels are numerous, but there are a good many fiddles (fidels) too."

When they were not talking on the way to Waterford, Thursday, 12.7.49, Duffy was *humming* tunes and Carlyle was watching the 'squalid hamlets' and cottages they passed, 'with their lean goats and vermin.'[2] A farm was pointed out to him about a mile from the road where sixteen or eighteen policemen[3] 'seizing for tithes were set upon and all killed some eighteen or more years ago.'[2] Then they came to where the road was broken, and Duffy hoped it was from "Repale Insurrection," but Carlyle, a mason's son, was able to make sure it was from bad masonry.[2]

[1] *Conversations with Carlyle*, by Sir C. Gavan Duffy, pp. 67–9.
[2] *Reminiscences of My Irish Journey*, by T. Carlyle, pp. 88–9.
[3] *Irish Sketch Book*, by Thackeray, Chap. III.

XIII

WATERFORD

(1849)

ONE of the few talks Carlyle has noted was this Thursday afternoon, when he wrote,[1]—'I argued with Duffy about Smith O'Brien, I infinitely vilipending, he hotly eulogizing the said Smith.' This may have been just before they 'rattled over' the 'long wooden bridge' that led them to 'the bright trim-looking quay' of Waterford harbour.

Their hotel which faced the quay was 'rather in an encumbered state,' for, like Thackeray seven years ago, they had come at 'Assize time.'[2] Letters were awaiting them, and a new discovery at dinner, that the London soles were Waterford fish. Then they walked about to see things and people. The convicted patriot Meagher (Mar) had lived in a street abutting their hotel. His father was there still. The failure of the potato had ruined Waterford's trade in bacon and butter. They decided to depart the next day, Friday, 13.7.49, and want of sleep in the crowded hotel made Carlyle accept thankfully offers of hospitality on the road to Cork.

They breakfasted with two priests, and Carlyle was particularly pleased with the younger "Father," a 'clever man this, black-eyed florid man of thirty, not ill-informed, and appears to have an element of real zeal in him, which is rare among these people.' The appreciation seems to have been mutual, for the younger priest came back with him to the hotel. It was a hot and dusty but also a pleasant and breezy afternoon, as they drove away to the west through what Thackeray called 'a country blue, hilly and bare,' and Carlyle called 'scrubby' and 'ill-cultivated.'

[1] *Reminiscences of My Irish Journey*, by T. Carlyle, pp. 89–94.
[2] *Irish Sketch Book*, by Thackeray, Chap. IV.

XIV

SIR JAMES STEPHEN AND SIR HENRY TAYLOR

(1849)

WHEN Duffy wanted details of what was amiss, he was told what he could not deny,—" Not one fence in 500 will *turn* the cattle. These hedges are mostly gorse and not attended to." The first town they reached was Kilmacthomas,[1] where Duffy was recognised with general enthusiasm, even shared by the policeman. " I would like to give a cheer for that gent," the driver whispered to Carlyle, who answered,—" Don't, it will do him no good." Next they came to Dungarvan and then to Cappoquin, where Duffy stayed at the hotel, while Carlyle took a car to Dromana, the house of Lord Stuart. Duffy was to go on Saturday direct to Cork, where he had much business, and Carlyle was to arrive there on the Monday.

It seems to have been on this Friday's journey that Duffy enquired about Sir James Stephen,[2] whose essays on Hildebrand and other subjects he had much admired.

" He is a man of good brains," said Carlyle. " He was placed early in the Colonial Office, and had got trained in official life till he obtained a complete command of its formulas and agencies; and it was found, whoever was Colonial Minister, Stephen was the real governor of the colonies. He bowed to every suggestion of the Minister, and was as smooth as silk, but somehow the thing he did not like was found never to be done at all. Charles Buller named him Mr. Mother-country.

" His biographies of saints was a dilettante kind of task, which he took up on account of the quantity of eloquent writing that could be got out of it, not from any love of the subject. He had no notion of living a life in any way resembling the lives of these men. He could talk about them, and inspect their doings with curious eyes, but doing like

[1] *Reminiscences of My Irish Journey*, by T. Carlyle, pp. 94–7.
[2] *Conversations with Carlyle*, by Sir C. Gavan Duffy, pp. 78–82.

them was no part of his purpose; quite otherwise, indeed. Stephen had recommended these subjects to me before he took them up himself, but I could not discern a vestige of human interest in them.

"Latterly Stephen retired from official life on account of the death of his son in Germany, and got knighted. Terribly shattered (by the son's death), he retired to his family to try to knit up silently the ravelled sleeve of life. He lives at Windsor, and seldom comes to London now. Stephen is a clever man in his strange official way. He is one of the Clapham people; and tho he professes to apply their creed to human affairs generally, he has small belief in its potency by this time, one can see."

Then Duffy praised "Philip van Artevelde" and said he would like to hear something of the author. Carlyle said:—"Henry Taylor is an official under Stephen in the Colonial Office, but not at all a man of the same intellectual girth and stature. But a notable person too—a sagacious, vigilant, exact sort of man. Philip van Artevelde is his idea of himself; but he is altogether a different person from that. He is cold and silent for the most part, and rather wearisome from the formal way he states his opinions. He has been a sailor, and had he stuck by the ship he would have made a serviceable officer; for he has inflexible valour, and that silent persistency which is the main thing which makes England what it is.

"He is engaged just now on a comedy—a hopeless project—there is not the smallest particle of humour in the man. He may be said to be a steadfast student, tho he reads in all only half a dozen books; but he reads them a page a day. Bacon is one of them, and his great light on all subjects."

"If I may judge by my own feelings," said Duffy, who was aware that what had been said about Browning and poetry had a moral for him too,—"Mr. Taylor is living evidence that there is much to be said in poetry for which prose has no substitute, or at any rate that there are men to whom poetry is more natural. I find his chief drama a constant enjoyment, but his prose has not the smallest attraction. There is ability and abundant experience in 'The Statesman,' for example, but I think the style heavy, the ideal of a Minister of State low, and the motif (or idea) poor, and even immoral."

Carlyle replied:—"Charges of that kind have been made

against the book, but unjustly, as I judge. Taylor expresses the highest ideal he has conceived of the thing he has been working among, in the unprofitable racket of the Colonial Office. It is the result of his actual experience, one may see—a plea for a juster allowance for the many impediments which have to be encountered in working public affairs. He has a great reverence for whatever is standing erect, and thinks we are bound to accept it cheerfully because it is able to stand, overlooking the fact that there is a question behind all that—an altogether fundamental question—on which our reverence strictly depends."

This is interesting as it reveals the inner conviction of Carlyle, that men should *not revere* a human institution unless it is just. Nature makes no mistakes, but men are always making them. He went on :—

"Taylor has a high opinion of his own class, and a silent anger, one can perceive, at my unaccountable contempt for officialities. You may be interested to know that he has married a charming little countrywoman of yours, a daughter of Spring Rice, and lives out of town. He has got his office into such a perfect system that he could work it by attending a couple of hours a day."

Duffy laughed and answered :—"I make no doubt that the whole Civil Service would be willing to work their offices in the same way if they were allowed."

XV

JOHN FORSTER

(1849)

"IT is impossible not to like John Forster as a man," said Duffy.[1] "His literary papers are often pleasant, but I can make nothing of his political articles in the *Examiner*, which seem to have no settled purpose."

"For the most part," replied Carlyle, "Forster advocates the theory of human affairs prevalent in fashionable Whig circles, if any one wants to hear that sort of thing. He is a sincere, energetic, vehement fellow, who undertakes any amount of labour to do service to one. Jane got the bulky MS. of a novel from Miss Jewsbury, a scraggy little woman, with nothing beautiful or attractive about her, but with agreeable talk; and he read it through, cut objectionable things out of it, prepared it with much pains, as one could see, for the Press, and it got read and talked about in London drawing-rooms. He is a man who likes to live among people who mean honestly, and, on the whole, chooses his company with tolerable success. If he gets hold of any opinion that he comes to believe, he makes all manner of noise and vehement clatter over it, and forwards it by every means he can devise; but if it falls into disrepute and other people desert it, he just leaves it there and seeks out some other fancy to fondle in place of it. He is not a man who has any serious truth to proclaim, or any purpose in life which he lays to heart, but he is infinitely friendly and entirely sincere in his attachments. A good, upright man, one might confidently say."

[1] *Conversations with Carlyle*, by Sir C. Gavan Duffy, pp. 83–4.

XVI

ALBANY FONBLANQUE

(1849)

DUFFY ran down Albany Fonblanque,[1] who had been a radical journalist and editor of the *Examiner* till 1847, and then taken an office under the Board of Trade. Said Duffy now :—" I asked Forster who was writing feeble imitations of Fonblanque in the *Examiner*, and was surprised to learn the writer was Fonblanque himself. The philosophical Radicals proclaim him the greatest journalist in England ; but he seems to want seriousness. His articles are pleasant, but Jeremy Bentham and Jonathan Wild do not always amalgamate naturally, and public interests cannot be successfully treated in the spirit of an opera-bouffe " (or farce).

" Fonblanque is a better man than you suppose," replied Carlyle,—" a serious-looking man, with fire in his eyes. He seems to consider that his task in the world is to expose fallacies of all sorts, which in fact he does with considerable adroitness and skill."

" His paper was the organ of the educated Radicals in the Reform era," rejoined Duffy. " It has shifted round and become a Government organ." What was taken for granted as a known fact, but may need to be mentioned here, was that Fonblanque as a proprietor of the *Examiner* had still a general control of it. Carlyle replied :—" Fonblanque has changed under the influence of circumstances, but not at all with conscious dishonesty. Lord Durham when he came home," meaning from Canada in 1838, " asked him to dinner and he began to circulate up and down in society yonder in London, and so came to look at Government from another point of view. Philosophical Radicalism is intrinsically barren. Fonblanque has said all that is in him to say on that."

[1] *Conversations with Carlyle*, by Sir C. Gavan Duffy, pp. 84–5.

XVII

RINTOUL AND CAPTAIN STERLING

(1849)

DUFFY'S mention of "the greatest journalist in England" may have suggested what Carlyle said next, after a pause.[1]—"Among newspaper men, Rintoul, a Scotch printer who owns the *Spectator*, is a man of deeper insight than any of them—a man altogether free from romantic or visionary babblement or the ordinary echoes of parliamentary palaver. He was the first man in England who openly declared his complete disbelief in Reform and the Whigs, and now it is everywhere seen that his opinions are sound. He writes the literary papers in his journal. There is nothing very deep in them, but neither are they ever mere wind. He speculates on literature in a very natural manner. But he believes in nothing, and has but a poor barren theory of life, one may perceive. (Yet) he is essentially a diligent and upright man, and he turns out a newspaper which, on the whole, is the best article of that kind to be found anywhere in England just now." This was the same Rintoul who founded the *Dundee Advertiser* and then the *Spectator*, and made a success of both.

What was said of his disbelief in the Whigs recalled the similar change in the *Times*, and Duffy asked about Sterling, commonly called the "Thunderer of the *Times*." He was told what can be read in Chapter V of *John Sterling*, and Carlyle now added :—"It was rumoured up and down, in the trivial talk of London, that the *Times* was paid for this change, but that was altogether a mistake. Sterling had acted on his knowledge and convictions, and they soon came to be the convictions of his employers. Since his death, people missed his writings considerably, which is by no means wonderful when one considers the despicable makeshifts and inane trivialities which form the bulk of what is called newspaper literature."

[1] *Conversations with Carlyle*, by Sir C. Gavan Duffy, pp. 84–8.

XVIII

THE NETHER DARKNESS, &c.

(1849)

DUFFY told how much he had been disappointed by the dramas of Talfourd, and declared,—" I can never get over the conviction that his reputation is the result of unduly favourable criticism by his literary associates of two generations."

Carlyle said [1] :—" Not so in any sinister sense. He has lived among literary people from the time of Charles Lamb and Leigh Hunt, has probably done them many kindnesses, and kept coquetting with letters. So they took an interest in him and praised his plays—over-praised them probably ; but Talfourd had not stimulated or invited this sort of notice. It is quite true, however, that his reputation is entirely undeserved. There is no potency in him ; nothing beyond the common, unless it is a sort of pathetic loyalty to his earliest associates. He had learned something of Charles Lamb's fantastic method of looking at things.

" Lamb had no practical sense in him, and in conversation was accustomed to turn into quips and jests whatever turned up—an ill example to younger men, who had to live their lives in a world which was altogether serious, and where it behoved them to consider their position in a spirit quite other than jocose ; for a wrong path led to the Nether Darkness."

This " Nether Darkness " is a sample of Carlyle's way of using words and phrases current among religious people. Hell was what they meant by it, the " Prince of Darkness " being Satan ; but Duffy did not need to be told that Carlyle meant nothing of that sort, but only moral ruin and its consequences. Discussing this and similar passages Duffy said in extreme old age,[2]—" The future life is a mere Perhaps to me as it was to Rabelais. Before 1849 I had outgrown Christianity, but, like Carlyle, tabooed the topic."

[1] *Conversations with Carlyle*, by Sir C. Gavan Duffy, p. 86.
[2] To D. A. W.

XIX

FATHER O'SHEA AND EMERSON, &c.

(1849)

CARLYLE told Duffy of the letter from Cork written by Father O'Shea in 1834 about *Sartor*,[1] and Duffy promised to arrange for him to meet Father O'Shea,—"nothing is easier." This led to reminiscences, and Duffy enquired about the letter from the "Bookseller's Taster" in the Appendix to *Sartor*, and was told [2]:—

"Certainly it is genuine. It was the verdict of one of Murray's critics; Lockhart is believed to be the man. His opinion was more favourable than the writers of the Athenæum and the like pronounced on the book when it was published. I have not found literature a primrose path; quite otherwise, indeed. My earliest experiments failed altogether to find acceptance from able editors, and when at length I came to be recognised as a writer who had something to say, editors were still alarmed at the unheard-of opinions I promulgated, and probably because I did not wear the recognised literary livery of the period. I have tried for some permanent place in life with little avail, and have commonly eaten bread as hardly earned as any man's bread in England. I can testify that the literary profession, as it is called, has not been to me by any means a land flowing with milk and honey. I may say, were it of any moment at all, that tho I have a certain faculty of work in me, the woman who manufactures the last sensational novel has probably got more money for a couple of her strange ventures than I have been paid by the whole bookselling craft from the beginning to this hour."

Duffy suggested that the critics may have misinterpreted him, and he admitted,—"Criticism in general has become the idlest babble"; but he said,—"Thackeray, John Sterling and John Mill have written of my work in various

[1] *Carlyle to the French Revolution*, p. 366. (Book X, Chap. XV.)
[2] *Conversations with Carlyle*, by Sir C. Gavan Duffy, pp. 88–94.

quarters with appreciation and more than sufficient applause," and in the *Revue des Deux Mondes* lately there were some essays on Cromwell by a French writer, M. Montégut, which " contain a deeper and truer estimate of my theory of life and human interests than I have met anywhere in a review before."

He also told of Emerson who had been as prompt to appreciate *Sartor* as Father O'Shea. " Can Emerson's ideas be regarded as original ? " asked Duffy, and was answered :—" Emerson took his system out of *Sartor* and my other writings in the first instance, but he worked it out in a way of his own. It is based on truth, undoubtedly ; but Emerson constantly forgets that one truth may require to be modified by a precisely opposite truth. His writings want consistency and a decisive intelligible result. One is constantly disappointed at their suddenly stopping short and leading to nothing. They are full of beauties—diamonds, or at times, bits of painted glass, strung on a thread,—which have no necessary connection with each other. He frequently hits upon isolated truths, but they remain isolated—they nowhere combine into an intelligible theory of life."

" Did you find more in the man than in his writings ? " was Duffy's next question. " No," said Carlyle. " When we come to talk with each other, our opinions are constantly found to clash. Emerson believes that every man's self-will ought to be cultivated, that men will grow virtuous and submissive to just authority, need no coercion and all that sort of thing. He knows that there are men up and down the world fit to govern the rest ; but he conceives that when such a man is found, instead of being put in authority, he ought to be restrained with fetters, as a thing dangerous and destructive. However, Emerson bears with great good humour the utter negation and contradiction of his theories. He has a sharp, perking little face, and he keeps bobbing it up and down with 'Yissir, yissir,' (*mimicking*), in answer to objections."

It is pleasant to add that Carlyle told Duffy fully of Emerson's visit to him at Craigenputtock, and of how Emerson got money for him in America by publishing *Sartor* there and other books, taking the risk himself, and sending Carlyle the profits.

XX

CARLYLE INSPECTS THE TRAPPISTS

(1849)

ABOUT nine o'clock on Friday night Carlyle was welcomed to Dromana House by Lord Stuart de Decies, and after a bath and refreshments soon went to rest in a big bedroom, 'looking out on woody precipices that overhang the Blackwater,—begirt with mere silence! I slept,' he wrote, 'and again slept, a heavy sleep; still remembered with thankfulness.' The Blackwater is the Irish river that seemed to Thackeray "as fine as the Rhine,"[1] and the sound sleep and the surroundings made his Saturday here seem to Carlyle 'the pleasantest morning and day of all my tour.'[2]

Perhaps it should be explained that letters from Lord Monteagle, ex-Mr. Spring-Rice, secured Carlyle a welcome from Lord Stuart and others of the Irish Aristocracy. The family was all away except Lord Stuart and a step-daughter, who was the wife of a German officer 'now fighting against the Hungarians.' As they took breakfast Carlyle was as happy as a schoolboy to find the tea to his taste,—'hot, as you rarely find it in a great house.' Letters came, and they all three had 'a nice quiet hour or two,' the lady 'zealously' demonstrating how entirely righteousness was on the side on which her husband was fighting. Her stepfather, Lord Stuart himself, was a man of fifty with smallish black eyes, full cheeks, and the good-natured candid-*drawling*-dialect that reminds you of England. He seemed a man of good natural faculty, sensibility to fun, and 'the most perfect politeness.' For a morning ride he took Carlyle through gardens and woods to Dromana village, a clean and slated hamlet founded by his predecessor for weaving seventy or eighty years ago. The weavers came from Ulster, and now that weaving was ended here, their posterity were living by country labour, 'reasonably well, you would say.'

[1] *Irish Sketch Book*, by W. M. Thackeray, Chap. IV.
[2] *Reminiscences of My Irish Journey*, by T. Carlyle, pp. 96–104.

After luncheon Lord Stuart took Carlyle a drive in the direction of the Knockmeildown Mountains to the Mount Melleray Monastery, where they arrived after two. The monks were Trappists, most ascetic of the Christian kind, resembling the strictest Buddhists. The differences are slight. The Trappists are vowed to absolute silence, whereas the Buddhist can talk to other men or monks; but a Trappist would kill a louse without a blush, and feel no shame for taking life,—which a Buddhist would deem wicked; and the straw mattress of the Trappist might seem to the other demoralising self-indulgence. Both are greatly addicted to prayers and conscious meditation. The Trappists also profess to do manual labour, and it was on the supposition they did it that Thackeray cracked jokes when passing here seven years ago; but he only looked at their buildings from Cappoquin, and Carlyle's description shows how little their manual labour amounted to.

'Hooded monks;—in brown coarse woollen sacks that reach to the knee, with funnel-shaped hood that can be thrown back;—Irish physiognomy in a new guise! Labourers working in the field at hay, etc.; *country* people they, I observe, *presided* over by a monk.—Entrance, squalid hordes of beggars sit waiting; Irish *accent* from beneath the hood, as a "brother" admits us; learning the Lordship's *quality* he hastens off for "the Prior,"'—(it is likely that he was not himself one of the few allowed to speak to strangers. The Prior was—) 'a tallish, lean, not very prepossessing Irishman of forty,' and 'conducts us thenceforth.

'Banished from Mount Meilleraye in France about 1830 for quasi-political reasons, the first of these Irishmen arrive penniless at Cork, knowing not what to do. A Protestant Sir Something gives them "waste land," wild craggy moor on this upland of the Knockmeildowns. Charitable Catholics intervene with other help: they struggle, prosper, and are now as we see. Good bit of ground cleared, drained, and productive; more in clear progress thereto. Big simple square of buildings, etc. Chapel very grand, all the decorations done by monks. Dormitory very large, wholly wooden and clean. Bakehouse, poor library, nasty *tubs* of cold stirabout, coarsest I ever saw, for beggars; *silence; each monk, when bidden do anything, does it, folds hands over breast, and disappears with a* LARGE *smile and a low bow;—curious enough to look upon indeed!*

'Garden rather weedy, a few monks poking about in it; work rather make-believe, I feared. Offices in the rear; extensive peat-stack, mill; haymakers, one or two young monks actually making hay.

'Rise at 2 a.m. to their devotions; have really to go through a great deal of drill-exercise through the day, independently of work. One poor fellow in the library has been dabbling a bit in the elements of geometry,—elemental yet ingenious.' Apparently it would be the Prior who said:—' "The other night a lead spout has been torn off from our cow-house there; a new thing, theft from *us*." Excellent brown bread, milk, and butter, is offered for viaticum; Lord Stuart, I see, smuggles some gift of money; and with blessings we are rolled away.

'The new "Monastery" must have accumulated several thousand pounds of *property* in these seventeen years, in spite of its continual charities to beggars; but this must be very much the result of public charity, Catholic Ireland much approving of them; and I confess the whole business had, lurking under it for me at this year of grace, a certain *dramatic* character, as if they were "doing it."—Inevitable at this year of grace, I fear! *Hard work I didn't see monks doing, except it were the one young fellow who was actually forking hay.* Food, Glory, dim notion of getting to Heaven, too,—I suppose these are motive enough for a man of average Irish insight? The saddest fact I heard about these poor monks was, that the Prior had discovered some of them surveying the Youghal-and-Cappoquin steamer, watching its arrival from their high moor as the event of *their* day; and had reprovingly taken away their telescope: ah, me!'

How delicious is the humour of reality! The Prior as he told this would be feeling that he was impressing on his visitors how fine a Prior he was, and how superior his establishment; whereas in fact he was revealing it to be a place whose discipline made men worse, not better, and stifled natural curiosity, the mainspring of knowledge and spiritual life, the feeling that best makes life to-day worth living. "Ah, me!" Thus it was that in spite of all Carlyle's sympathy for things medieval, he had now to go away with a sigh and a thought not unlike Thackeray's, that if the Mount Melleray monks were consistent, they would "take to a wild-beast life at once."[1]

At dinner at Dromana that night Lord Stuart's agent,

Sir Somebody Shaw, an Ayrshire man and a hearty and hoary old Peninsula soldier, 'rattled pleasantly away, plainly chaffing Carlyle that he would never do for a soldier, telling,—" Napier used to say, if you would be a soldier, learn to *sleep!*" He added apparently, 'few can do it; Napoleon could. Snatch sleep whenever and wherever there is a chance.' About ten o'clock Carlyle reluctantly tore himself away from such pleasant company, and was driven to Lismore, where Mr. Currey, the Duke of Devonshire's agent, was awaiting him and had quiet quarters ready, where Carlyle was soon 'dissolved in grateful sleep, be-murmured by the Blackwater.'

XXI

TO CORK

(1849)

IT had been the sight of the Blackwater river at Lismore and the castle there that made Thackeray match it with the Rhine,[1] and even Carlyle who hated talk of the picturesque confessed to himself that it was 'very beautiful,' and in parts 'fantastic-pretty.' Assuredly the Sunday following his night at Lismore was almost as pleasant as the preceding day and even more instructive.[2]

Never was there 'a more assiduous host than this Mr. Currey' of Lismore, nor one better able to reply to difficult questions. His principal, the Duke of Devonshire, owned land extending to the peak of the highest Knockmeildown, and Mr. Currey began the day by a drive towards the mountains, through 'well-shaded country, up the clearest of little rivers' to a schoolhouse, which is 'to be developed into an *Agricultural* school by "the Duke"'; but of course on a Sunday only the buildings could be shown. Carlyle observed that Currey had learned to speak to the natives in their own Irish. They met many of them 'coming from Chapel.' In returning Currey showed him the park of 'an *anarchic* squire' who 'had been shot at.' Then he drove to the banks of the Blackwater, where a boat was waiting for them, and Currey taking the oars and Carlyle the helm, they moved for some miles on a river 'fine enough,' and then came home to dinner.

After dinner Currey drove his guest down the west bank of the Blackwater, looking across at Dromana, and arriving at Youghal, where it mingled with the sea; and 'much talk' they had by the way. 'Well, courteously, wisely' did Currey reply to many questions about things in general, and agriculture in particular, and the confusion of leases, and the Duke's endeavours to deepen Youghal harbour, and

[1] *Irish Sketch Book*, by W. M. Thackeray, Chap. IV.
[2] *Reminiscences of My Irish Journey*, by T. Carlyle, pp. 104–17.

how he borrowed Government money to embank the marsh (there), and employ the Youghal poor in the famine year; which still goes on,—good speed to it!' This was one of the few sensible "relief" works Carlyle discovered in progress in Ireland.

In Youghal town he was shown in passing the house that once had been Sir Walter Raleigh's, 'now a Quaker's,' and 'with a right hearty good night' to Currey, he found himself in quiet sleeping quarters.

Next morning the wife of the Caretaker of the mansion where Carlyle had slept tried hard to get him to subscribe to "Methodist Missions in Ireland"; but the intended victim has left it on record,—"I won't." He never would subscribe to that sort of thing, and doubtless did what could be done to content her in some other way. Her son took down his luggage to the coach, while he walked through the town, the name of which had been made familiar to him long ago by his brother Alick's singing a song of "Yoogal Harbour." "Yawal" he found the people calling it now, as he walked about and watched the 'dingy semi-savage population, rough, fierce-faced, ragged, in the market-place.'

Then he took the coach, and went west. At Killeagh a woman who entered there and sat beside Carlyle was soon weeping and telling him,—"My son was driving me last time I was here, and is buried now in that churchyard." Bethinking her of "God's will," or reminded of it, she 'gradually quieted herself.' Then came Castle Martyr and Middleton, and then the 'long irregular Firth' of Cork Harbour. Duffy was dining out when Carlyle reached the hotel, so he took an after-dinner walk in Cork, and has recorded phonetically the loud chant of a blind beggar he stopped to hear on the bridge over the river Lee. One seems to hear it yet.—"Oah Kehristins may the Lard protect you from the dangers av the night, and guide yer sowls, etc., etc., and may ye never know what it is—forever dark and have no eyes—and for Kehroist's sake, leave a penny for the blind that can never see again!"

In the hotel near eleven o'clock he had a most welcome but unexpected caller, "Father O'Shea,"—'a little, grey-haired, intelligent-and-bred looking man with much gesticulation, boundless loyal welcome, *red* with dinner and some wine, engages that we are to meet to-morrow,—and again with explosion of welcome, goes his way.'

XXII

CORK

(1849)

THE forenoon of Tuesday, 17.7.49, was filled by letters and a walk in the streets and market-place of Cork. At two o'clock Duffy introduced his friend Denny Lane, with whom they were to dine that evening in his cottage by the sea,—' a fine brown Irish figure, Denny,' wrote Carlyle,[1] a distiller by trade, but lately, like Duffy, a prisoner for his ' repale ' politics ;[2] ' frank, hearty, honest air, a little like Alfred Tennyson.' At four o'clock Carlyle joined Duffy and the rest of their company on the deck of a steamer, and as it moved down the Firth admired the ' beautiful white city ' of Cork, ' at the foot of its steep woody slope.'

On the way to Denny's cottage, Carlyle called for Father O'Shea and was kept waiting for some time, because the servant was unwilling to disturb the holy man doing his devotions in the garden,[3] where he looked in the distance like a living statue. The usual devotions done, ' statue Shea becomes live Shea, and cordially greets me again,' and in a few minutes they are facing each other at the dinner-table of Denny Lane, with Lane's old mother on the one hand of Carlyle, and Father O'Sullivan on the other, a cheery man of fifty with a *brick*-complexion and a yellow wig, the wittiest of O'Shea's curates. Duffy was there too, and editor Barry, and three or four others. But the priests did best. O'Shea revealed himself to Carlyle's admiration, ' didactic, loud-spoken,' yet ' courteous, good every way, a true gentleman and priest in the Irish style ; ' and as the punch went round the wit of O'Sullivan kept them laughing merrily all the time.

The sun had set when they came out, but eastward across the water lay the seaport of Cork on the " Great

[1] *Reminiscences of My Irish Journey*, by T. Carlyle, pp. 117–23.
[2] *Conversations with Carlyle*, by Sir C. Gavan Duffy, pp. 95–6.
[3] *Thomas Carlyle*, by Moncure Conway, p. 72.

Island" in the harbour,—Cove it was called then, and afterwards Queenstown. They took a boat and rowed over to it in the beautiful still summer twilight, and walking about the seaport, came upon a group of the natives round a modern Homer, in straw hat and rags; and Denny Lane wondered to behold Carlyle also soon intently listening. His song was a ballad of a modern Irish Hercules, whose all-conquering weapon was his "blackthorn stick." That was the burden of the ballad. "Sure the craithurs are sick," he once began. Then followed babble Carlyle could not follow, but everything was cleared and cured by the "blackthorn stick!" 'Sootiest piece of nonsense I ever heard,' thought Carlyle. Ashamed of it at last, Denny Lane pulled him away to their boat. There was light still on the sea, tho it was growing dark ashore, and as they rowed to the mainland again, O'Sullivan at the helm, editor Barry and another sang songs. One of them was a sailor's song of love, with the chorus, "In hopes to harbour in thy arms!" It ended with a marriage amid a round of applause, the reverend steersman O'Sullivan remarking confidentially,—"tho joining faintly in the chorus, in the name of the Church I beg leave to protest!"

They returned to Cork by road,—it was two o'clock in the morning when the car with Carlyle and O'Shea in it arrived at his hotel door, where they parted, and saw each other no more. Carlyle was glad to hear from Duffy and others how "good" a man O'Shea was, and how he 'labours diligently among a large poor flock, (has) three or four curates, and tho nothing of a bigot, seems truly a serious man.'

XXIII

"BY KILLARNEY'S LAKES AND FELLS"

(1849)

SHINE LALOR of Castle Lough, who "had barely escaped imprisonment in the late troubles," according to Duffy,[1] wished to show Carlyle his place and the other beauties of Killarney. So on the morning of Wednesday, 18.7.49, Carlyle and Duffy together took the coach for there. The last thing seen in Cork was a long row of idle men 'sitting against the walls of houses on the quay at the bridge end; very ugly in their lazzaroni aspect under the sunshine.'[2]

The coach went north by the famous Castle of *Blarney*, and over the watershed to *Mallow* on the Blackwater, the Mallow renowned for rakes in song, tho there were few there now but the poor soldiers, the wretched "monks of the Devil," as Thackeray would say. Barracks were dotted over all Ireland in those years, like pustules on a body diseased. From Mallow they went west up the river, towards Macgillicuddy's Reeks, whose saw-like ridges are "the highest land in Ireland." At Millstreet, where they paused to dine, the passengers on another coach that passed flung coppers to the crowd of beggars, who 'ran at them like rabid dogs,' male and female, old and young. Carlyle remarked 'one oldish fellow *beating* a boy, to keep *him* at least out of the competition.'

As they left there the rain drove Duffy inside, and in furious bursts continued till near the end of the journey. Carlyle remained outside, his fellow-passengers there telling anything they thought might be interesting,—naming Mangerton mountain, and Macgillicuddy's Reeks, Lord Kenmare's house, and at last,—"This is Killarney town." The hotel was on the side of the Lake, and driving to it from the town they overtook a funeral and heard the "Irish howl."

[1] *Conversations with Carlyle*, by Sir C. Gavan Duffy, p. 96.
[2] *Reminiscences of My Irish Journey*, by T. Carlyle, pp. 123–43.

It was a great disappointment, 'there was no sorrow whatever in the tone of it. A pack of idle women, mounted on the hearse as many as could, and the rest walking, were hoh-hoh-ing with a grief quite evidently hired and not worth hiring.' Carlyle did not need to be told this was not specially Irish, but a widely spread and ancient custom, surviving in Egypt and many other places, and familiar in the Palestine of Jesus as the way of their ancestors.

Shine Lalor's 'beautiful little place' was near the hotel, and he joined them at breakfast next day, Thursday, 19.7.49, and brought them to his house. He was 'a quick, intelligent little fellow, with little bead-eyes and features and *repale* feelings, Irish altogether.' It was quickly settled he was to go with Carlyle over the Gap of Dunloe, and that they would meet at the head of the uppermost lake his younger brother, an embryo-doctor, with a boat, and a friend, the 'Rev. Dr. Moor, Principal of Oscot, high heavy man in black catholic gaiters, Catholic Harmonious Blacksmith, really very like Whewell,' the Harmonious Blacksmith of Trinity College, Cambridge.

Shine Lalor, Duffy and Carlyle set out together, and first beheld the Workhouse,—'3000 strong, the old *abominable* aspect of "human swinery".' Which done, another Lalor kept Duffy company at Castle Lough, while Carlyle and Shine Lalor drove away, and when they were alone together, Shine confided his affairs to his companion, and delighted him by agreeing with him that 'any Parliament in these times is a mere talking machine,' and 'that "Parliament in College Green," even if it could be had, is moonshine.' Meanwhile he took Carlyle over a farm of his, where the farmer's business was tending forty head of cows, and showed him a "National School" and an "Out-door relief" station, where the visitor admired Shine's 'frank, swift talk to the squalid crowd, full of a noisy hum expressing greed, suspicion, and *incarnated nonsense* of various kinds.'

Their way led at first past 'ragged wet hedges, weedy ditches, spongy-looking flat country,—like a *drunk* country fallen down to sleep amid the mud.' But as they went higher they came into moors like Galloway and Craigenputtock; and then to misty glens and hills and 'high rugged black cliffs,' as they walked on through the "Gap," having dismissed their car. They came to a dark cottage where two women sat with 'a dirty table and bench,' and pressed upon them "the dainty of the country, whisky and goat's milk." The younger of the two, Carlyle remarked, 'if lifted from her squalor, might be a handsome woman.' He tasted and paid for the "dainty," tho he did not like it, and soon they reached their boat.

The boatmen rowed and sang, and they went merrily through the lakes, landing occasionally. Carlyle recognised the arbutus which decorates the islands and the hillsides, and saw what any visitor can see there in July, as good a mixture of the sublime and the beautiful as any natural scenery can show. There were many fine little houses on the shores, and interesting ruins, too, but nothing more welcome than Shine Lalor's dwelling, when at last they arrived there again in the evening with good appetites.

They sat down to dinner about a dozen, including Mrs. Lalor and her sister. Carlyle enjoyed the "noisy-Irish" dinner-party, merry and wise, so much that it was only at a late hour that he and Duffy departed, emerging into a 'pitch-dark night,' and were escorted to their inn through the woods.

XXIV

THE MOST WRETCHED PEOPLE IN IRELAND

(1849)

FOR a week after they met in Cork, on 16.7.49, Duffy could not get Carlyle to say a word about literature, and tells us,—" The land question was a constant topic." [1] Carlyle's contempt for " repale " and concern about the land and economic questions began to be found contagious. Even in beautiful Killarney, Shine Lalor was delighted to talk of nothing else. When they left for Limerick on Friday, 20.7.49, driving north-east towards King William's Town as their first stage, they had to go for ' some fifteen dreary miles, over ' a scandalous wide moor ' with no productive industry to be seen but a single limework and a little cutting of peat. Carlyle had seemed to Duffy too ' disposed to insist that difference of religion made the people unduly suspicious of Irish landlords.' So Duffy now told him that Lord Kenmare who owned this land wăs a Roman Catholic like his tenants, and suggested a look into the houses his Lordship provided for his fellow-Catholics.

Observing how the people working ' looked hungry in their rags, and hopeless, (with an) air as of creatures sunk beyond hope,' Carlyle complied, and has noted :—' Look into one of their huts under pretence of asking for water ; dark, narrow, *two* women nursing, other young woman on foot as if for work ; but it is narrow, dark, as if the people and their life were covered under a tub, or " tied in a sack " ; all things smeared over too with a liquid *green* ; the cow has her habitation here withal. No water ; the poor young woman produces butter-milk ; in real pity I give her a shilling. Duffy had done the like in the adjoining cottage. Ditto, ditto,' elsewhere, ' with the addition that a man lay in fever. These were the wretchedest population I saw in Ireland. " Live, sir ? The Lord knows ; (on) what we can beg and rob," ' (meaning *scrape up*). ' Lord Kenmare's

[1] *Conversations with Carlyle*, by Sir C. Gavan Duffy, pp. 96–8.

people, he never looks after them. . . . Bog all reclaimable, lime everywhere in it ; swift exit to Lord Kenmare and the leases, or whatever the accursed *incubus* is. The people, as I surmise, do *live* by " butter-milk " ; wretched produce of a lean cow here and there, still alive upon the bog ; pound or two of butter—precious stuff it must be in these huts ! Indian meal, and there is sour milk over and above.'

As they drove away from these horrid slums on the moor, Carlyle said to Duffy [1] :—" I often think how like Ireland is to the Irish horse Larry, which I had at Craigenputtock. Larry sometimes broke into insubordination, but on the whole he was one of the most generous, kindly, and affectionate fellows that one could anywhere encounter. Mrs. Carlyle became dissatisfied with her mount one day when we were riding on the moors, and proposed to try Larry. Up to that moment Larry had been skittish and intractable, but after Jane got on his back he behaved himself like a gentleman. He was on honour, and conducted himself accordingly."

" Larry *was* like his countrymen," answered Duffy. " He knew when he was well treated, and had a decided objection to perpetual whip and spur."

Another thing that struck Carlyle and alone went far to justify his impatience with the existing land laws, was how a landlord ' " prints his image " here on the face of the earth ; and you have beauty alternating with sordid disordered ugliness, abrupt as squares on a chessboard, all over Ireland.' [2] This Friday, for example, the very road they were travelling on grew better as they came nearer to King William's Town ; and on arriving there they beheld ' slated cottages ' and ' hedges and fields with crops and cabbages in them, a blessed change indeed.'

While they were still at dinner, ' a jolly, effectual-looking man of fifty, Mr. Boyne,' came to wait upon them and show them everything. Thus they were not only able to behold this earthly paradise in Ireland, but to learn how it had been made.

[2] *Reminiscences of My Irish Journey*, by T. Carlyle, pp. 143–7, and 171.

XXV

AN IRISH TRIPTOLEMUS

(1849)

ABOUT eighteen years ago a tract of waste extending to many miles, about King William's Town and the sources of the Blackwater river, had lapsed to Government by the expiry of long leases, and instead of leasing it again for a trifling rent as useless moor, Mr. Griffith of the Irish Board of Works had got sanction to improve it, and had put Mr. Boyne on the work of reclamation.

Mr. Boyne had proved a capital " Colonel of Spademen," and had already turned more than a square mile of the waste into 'a country beautiful to eye and mind,' wrote Carlyle.[1] 750 acres were now yielding good crops. There were many small farms, and Mr. Boyne's own farm ran to some hundreds of acres, with thirty or forty cottagers. 'His dairy,' wrote Carlyle, 'was the *best*—or practically equal to the best—I ever saw. Excellent rye,—" walk through it, gentlemen, you won't hurt it," ' said Boyne,—' as high as one's chin,' declared Carlyle, 'thick, clean and regular.' There were oats also, 'bright, copious green grass and 100 head of " specimen cattle " among others;' and his cottagers, 'as we saw them at their labours, looked healthy, hearty, swift and brisk, and even joyful,—decidedly the pleasantest aspect, or the only " pleasant " one, I can remember in Ireland.'

The Government outlay had been £24,000; but, as Boyne explained, there were roads to Kanturk and other places made out of that for the benefit of the whole countryside, and the rents of the farms go to the Government. He told many details which made the result seem very satisfactory. At the same time he candidly admitted that if he had been a landowner, he would not have taken the same method of reclamation, but got good farmers and let the land with improving leases. " But," asked Carlyle, " if you had 2000

[1] *Reminiscences of My Irish Journey*, by T. Carlyle, pp. 147–54.

labourers, already fed and clothed to your hand, such as sit in the Killarney workhouse idle at this moment?" Boyne's eyes sparkled; but,—'his practical solid soul refused to admit so transcendent a speculation, and he did not dwell on that outlook.'

What nobody, and least of all Duffy, could deny was that there was lying hereabouts enough of idle moor to give useful spadework to all the paupers in Cork County for half a century to come. As they returned to the house, where Mrs. Boyne had tea ready for them, her husband explained how the "Land Improvement Society" had ended in bankruptcy,—by paying £30 for a bull worth £8, and other such doings. "Remarkable Triptolemus, this Boyne," concluded Carlyle on reflection, applying to modest Boyne the name of the Greek Hero who was credited with being the first to use the plough and sow corn and start civilisation, the legendary favourite of the Goddess of Mother Earth.

'Heavy broad man, fat big cheeks, grey beard well shaven,' he wrote. 'Clean enough; smallish but honest kindly intelligent hazel-eyes, and nice brows to his big round head, which he flings slightly back in speaking, and rather droops his eyelids; Irish accent, . . . a Meath man, Land-surveyor's son, . . . copious bubbling speech in querulous-genial tone, wholly *narrative* in character. Simplicity, energy, eupepticity; a right healthy thick-sided Irish soul; would one knew of 1000 such! Catholic, I should think, but we didn't ask. Wife, a timidly-polite, yet sufficiently energetic-looking rather beautiful woman of the due age; was recorded—by Boyne, with oblique politeness—as admiring Duffy; had excellent scones, tea, cream and butter;—which ended, we, really with emotion and admiration, quitted Boyne-dom. Police-Sergeant was there, who brought up our car for us.'—It was here that he had used Sir Duncan McGregor's general missive. He was careful to give the Sergeant only "many thanks," as Duffy had told him,—"Money will insult."

From there they took Mr. Boyne's new road through Newmarket to Kanturk, where Carlyle observed that Duffy, 'loyal soul as always, yielded me by far the best room' in the hotel.

XXVI

"SHAKESPEARE'S JULIET" AS A WIFE

(1849)

ON the morning of Saturday, 21.7.49, after looking round Kanturk and making enquiries, they settled that Duffy was to drive to Mallow Railway Station, and on the way drop Carlyle at the gate of Sir William Becher's house and go on alone. They were to meet in Limerick at the chief hotel. Carlyle had a letter to Sir William Becher from Lord Monteagle, and one to Lady Becher from Major Sterling. So Lady Becher welcomed him 'handsomely.' She had rare jewels round her as they sat down to lunch, two of her three handsome sons and two fair daughters, 'fine-featured people all.'[1] Yet tho her politeness was perfect, her talk was 'stinted-practical,' and the visitor felt uncomfortably that she did not like him, 'peering at me through her cold blue eyes, half-shut with anxious scrutiny. I could not contrive to like her,' he confessed to Duffy, meaning especially at first.

He could not help contrasting her with her picture. Conspicuous in the drawing-room hung 'the big picture' of her as Juliet, engravings of which Carlyle remembered from his boyhood. That would be when she was the actress Miss O'Neill,—"a great actress," said Macready, resembling Rachel, with "a narrow range of character, yet each perfect in her own sphere."[2] He thought her "Shakespeare's Juliet" indeed,—a beautiful embodiment of genius, grace, and virtue.[3] She was luckier far than Juliet in the play. In 1819 she was married to Becher and was likened by Macready to a star, which had excited the wonder of the world by its shining, and then gone out of sight for ever suddenly,[3]—a rare phenomenon in astronomy, tho familiar in theatrical constellations. Her husband bought the

[1] *Conversations with Carlyle*, by Sir C. Gavan Duffy, pp. 98–9, and *Reminiscences of My Irish Journey*, by T. Carlyle, pp. 154–64.

[2] *Macready as I Knew Him*, by Lady Pollock, p. 29, and pp. 33–4.

[3] *Macready's Reminiscences, &c.*, edited by Sir F. Pollock, I, pp. 97–8, 180–1.

picture, and as he seems to have been, like his present visitor, a happy hen-pecked man, it may be that he had never noticed what the visitor saw at once,—how little of the attraction of the fair Juliet of the picture survived in Lady Becher. Thirty years makes a big difference in any woman.

Perhaps there was more in her yet than she would let this visitor see on a sudden. Some years after this Macready was delighted to find " beauty and grace in her still, tho I had been told it was all gone." [2] There was some excuse for her shyness to Carlyle when he arrived, considering what a notorious rebel had dropped him at their gate! She knew nothing else about him except that he was heterodox, whereas she was " perfect Church of England " and zealous in her creed.

She went walking with him after lunch and began to tolerate him. As there was no train to Limerick on Sunday, he had to stay till Monday, and he came to know his hostess better. She was 'a tall stately leanish figure of fifty-five; of strict, hard aspect, high cheek bones, and small blue eyes, expression of vigour, energy, honesty. House and grounds beautiful; school, cottages, peasants, all in perfect order. All things trim and nice. A strict religionist (is) Lady Becher, really wholesome and worthy, easy enough to talk with, nor quite unproductive; her *boudoir* by the side of the hall, father and mother's portraits in it, and all manner of lady-elegancies; people meeting her " mylady-ing " &c.; everything has been subdued to herself, I find, and carries the image of her own strict methodic vigorous character.' She did not omit to tell him of her son in Canada, soldiering. The two at lunch were going into the law for a living and to-day setting out for Killarney.

Then came a walk with Mr. Wrixon, Sir William's brother and man of business, who was a gentleman-farmer there. " Wrixon " was 'the original name, " Becher " was adopted for heritable reasons.' At dinner-time, half-past six, Sir William himself appeared, 'much lamed by some fall from his horse; fine, mildly dignified old gentleman, reminds me of Johnstone of Grange.' After dinner one of the young ladies played to Carlyle innumerable Jacobite tunes, while the rest of the party were at whist, and Lady Becher ended by singing to him " Bonnie Prince Charlie."

While others drove to church, Mr. Wrixon and Carlyle walked there on the Sunday, talking economics. Carlyle remarked a change in passing a hedge as they went along the highway,—ground untilled, thistles, docks, dilapidated cottages, ragged men. " What is this ? " Mr. Wrixon told him,—" Lord Limerick's estate." There had been an eviction there, as a sequel to " two years' troublous insolvency. Here is one of them. I will just set him going for you. Turn the spigot, and he will run all day." The note-book of Carlyle lets us overhear.—

'Middle-aged farmer-peasant accordingly takes off his hat, salutes low (and) walks hat in hand, (the) wind blowing his long thick hair, black with a streak of grey, (as he talks of) his woes (and) bad usages. I distinguish little but at all turns " tham vagobonds " ! He has been fellow-sub-lessee of lands along with various other " vagobonds " ; he paid always on the nail, they not ; all are now turned out into the road together, the innocent along with the guilty. (A) kind neighbour has taken him in with wife and children. (He seems) a reasonably good kind of man, and in the truest perplexity, with laws of the truest injustice. " And have you any notion what you are to do now ? " " Not a ha'porth, your honour." Mr. Wrixon can give no work, wishes he could. The poor man will write to the agent at Cork, begging (a) passage to America,' and in short Mr. Wrixon is to vouch for his respectability.

As they walked on, the 'sad contrast' continued. The cottages and lands 'all gone to savagery,' Mr. Wrixon frankly explained to be the result of 'Lord Limerick's method, and his father's before him.' He naturally complained a great deal about the injustice of tying 'a Becher to a Limerick in this way ; not left to swim the gulf of pauperism separately, but obliged to do it together!' Carlyle most cordially sympathised,—'a universal complaint,' he noted, 'quite tragic to see the justice of, everywhere.'

The parson who " performed " at the church reappeared at the dinner-table ; but the best of the Sunday evening was Lady Becher's side talk, 'now quite softened to me,' especially when he suggested to her to write her autobiography. She talked about her life as an actress at length, but 'like one quite above all accidents of that kind—as a sovereign might speak of some incident of her early life in exile.'

Sir William and his brother both together drove with Carlyle to Mallow Station on Monday.

XXVII

HISTORY AND POLITICS

(1849)

CARLYLE arrived in Limerick by train in time to see the town in Duffy's company.[1] 'An old London acquaintance, busy here in Poor-law,' named Richard Bourke, hailed Carlyle soon after arrival, and persuaded him to come to his father's house at Lisnagry near-by the following evening. This fitted well into Duffy's plans, as he wanted to go ahead to Galway the next afternoon.

Duffy's most urgent business at this time was arranging the revival of his *Nation* newspaper, and nothing was allowed to interfere with that. The Galway editor he went to see was Edward Butler,—one of the best of his friends and helpers. In the Limerick hotel, he read aloud to Carlyle some choice Irish Ballads, which failed to delight him. Carlyle declined to sympathize with anything that seemed to glorify mere strife. Without obtruding it unpleasantly, he was teaching Gavan Duffy and other leaders of the Irish people that fighting was out of date,—it was time to think of working. But Duffy tried literature again. He much admired the new epic of *Festus* then popular, as Tennyson and others also did, and he asked Carlyle 'if he knew anything' about it. But Carlyle 'had never read' Bailey's *Festus*, 'understood it was a sort of shadow of Faust. The poem made a great sensation in New England, and might have merits of which he was not aware.' Then brushing aside politely the babble about books, Carlyle talked to some purpose on Irish politics, reiterating and reinforcing his opinions as often as required in the days that followed.[2]—

"It is inconceivable how Irishmen fight futile and forgotten battles over again. Petrie is still in a rage against

[1] *Reminiscences of My Irish Journey*, by T. Carlyle, pp. 164–70.

[2] *Conversations with Carlyle*, by Sir C. Gavan Duffy, pp. 101–107. At page 107 the talk turns to a book by Mr. Buckle, published in 1857 and 1861.

Bryan Boru for having upset the ancient constitution of Ireland—not a very serious calamity, one may surmise. It was working well, it seems,—or seems to Petrie, at any rate—till Bryan conquered and brought into subjection the subordinate princes. Bryan pleased the immortal Gods, but the other parties pleased Petrie. Bryan Boru, his friends and enemies, his conquests over Celts and Danes, present to one's mind only interminable confusion and chaos; or if there may be, as your headshaking implies, a ground-plan more or less intelligible, it is not worth searching for. But there is a period of Irish history really impressive and worthy to be remembered, when the island undoubtedly sent missionaries throughout all the world then known to mankind, when she was a sort of model school for the nations, and in verity an island of saints. A book worthy to be written by some large-minded Irishman is one on that period, accompanied by another, which unhappily would be a tragic contrast, on the present and future of the country."

The justice of the opening remark, and the need for it, are both comically proved by an anecdote John Morley has told of his experience at Dublin Castle.[3] 'One day (1893) there happened to be a considerable faction-fight in Cork. I asked at the Castle what it was about. "Oh, it was the old quarrel between the two earls in the time of Queen Elizabeth."—Here was the fatality of history indeed! What the special quarrel was I had not time to identify then or since.'

As for the suggestion of a history of the early Christian days of Ireland, it was exactly the same sort of thing as Dr. Johnson suggested on 19.5.1777 to the venerable and learned antiquary, Charles O'Connor. But O'Connor was too old to do it, and Duffy was too busy with the things of the day,—it awaits some other. If Carlyle had remembered Dr. Johnson's suggestion, he would have been likely to mention it. The many-volumed *Acts of the Saints* he had been reading was probably what made him think of it. Meanwhile Duffy answered:—"It is an Irish 'Past and Present' you desire, but I think there is more need of an Irish 'Chartism,' a vehement protest against the wickedness of ignorant and persistent misgovernment."

"There is misgovernment enough in Ireland," he admitted, "and in England too, but there it is encountered

[3] *Recollections*, by John (Viscount) Morley, I, p. 344.

in an altogether different spirit. This longing after Bryan Boru is not a salutary appetite. There is scarcely a man, I should say, among the whole catalogue of Bryan Borus, worth the trouble of recalling."

"They will compare favourably," said Duffy, "with the English Kings from Henry VIII to George IV, both august personages included."

About George IV Carlyle was eloquently silent. But he astonished Duffy by taking up his challenge about Henry, and said :—"When one comes to consider the circumstances Henry had to deal with, he will be seen to be one of the best kings England ever had. He had the right stuff in him for a king, he knew his own mind; a patient, resolute, decisive man, one can see, who understood what he wanted, which is the first condition of success in any enterprise, and by what methods to bring it about. He saw what was going on in ecclesiastical circles at that time in England, and perceived that it could not continue without results very tragical for the kingdom he was appointed to rule, and he overhauled them effectually. He had greedy, mutinous, unveracious opponents, and to chastise them was forced to do many things which in these sentimental times an enlightened public opinion"—(laughing as he spoke)—"would altogether condemn. But when one looks into the matter a little, it is seen that Henry for the most part was right."

"Among the things he wanted and knew how to get," answered Duffy, "was as long a roll of wives as the grand Turk."—Which shows how little Duffy knew of Grand Turks. He went on.—"It would have been a more humane method to have taken them, like that potentate, simultaneously (rather) than successively,—he would have been saved the need of killing one to make room for another, and then requiring Parliament to disgrace itself by sanctioning the transaction."

Carlyle said quietly :—"This method of looking at King Henry's life does not help much to the understanding of it. He was a true ruler at a time when the will of the Lord's anointed counted for something, and it is likely that he didn't regard himself as doing wrong in any of those things over which modern sentimentality grows so impatient."

It was by developing Carlyle's idea of Henry, making a fancy picture of it, that Mr. Froude made a great hit in history-writing, and a great deal of fame and money; but that was long after 1849, and Duffy was slow to admit that any such view was possible, and raised many objections he could not afterwards remember; but there was one thing in the argument which dwelt in his memory. "A friend of mine," he said, "finds in your philosophy two theories which cannot be reconciled. One is that a man without a purpose in life is no better than carrion. The other is that a man who affirms that he has a purpose is a manifest quack and imposter. I myself have a similar difficulty I would like to have cleared up. You teach that a man of genius is commonly quite unconscious of it, and you despise as a cheat anyone professing to be so endowed. Suppose I ask you,—are you a man of genius? If you say No, how am I to accept that as a satisfactory answer? If you say Yes, consider on your own theory what consequence follows."

After laughing, Carlyle explained.—"All this will be found in perfect harmony, with proper deductions for the practical purpose in view on each occasion. As to myself, a forlorn and heavy-laden mortal, with many miseries to abolish or subdue into silence, I make no claim to preternatural endowments of any sort, few mortals less. As for genius, *genius* is in some senses strict vigilance, veracity, and fidelity to fact, which every mortal must cherish, if his life is not to have a tragic issue."

Then followed a long pause of silent meditation. Duffy said nothing. At last Carlyle went on.—"One has to accept the manifest facts. How else? Not one man in a million speaks the truth in these times, or acts it, and hence the condition of things,—thousands of wretches in the poor-house, and hundreds busy fox-hunting or foreign touring in complete indifference to them. A man of the *rascal* species, who set up a bank of lies as his capital and equipment in life, could not have existed before the last century; but now you find a man of that class wherever you turn up and down the world. Plain dealing and frank speaking seem to have vanished. Every year it is harder and harder to get an honest article of any fabric—a thing which is what it purports to be and not something shamefully the reverse. Our (present) forlorn time might be called the age of shoddy. The inevitable end and net result of this sort of thing is one which I need not be at the trouble of specifying."

"A lively young man of my acquaintance," said Duffy,

" insists that there is something to be said for shoddy." Then followed a defence of it in the original sense of the word, meaning cloth which is inferior because it is made from wool which has been used before. If that is sold for what it is, there is nothing to be said against it, of course; but " the shoddy " Carlyle was cursing was any *sham*, any false pretence, anything sold as *different* from what it was. It is curious that Carlyle did not point that out, but it was like him not to argue. All he said was,—" Yes, there is always a Devil's Advocate, who has a good word for his distinguished client; but the less men traffick in that sort of commodity, the better it will be for them in the long run."

XXVIII

"O'BRIEN BRANDY-FACE & CO."

(1849)

AS the evening wore on two priests and an editor came to them in the hotel, and the talk that followed over tea was more copious than pleasant to Carlyle. For tho he had all along been earnest in dissuading big John Mitchel from violence, he had liked the man; and the senior of these priests, as Carlyle had doubtless learned from Duffy, was 'he that roused the (Limerick) mob against Mitchel last year, a brandy-faced, pock-marked, very ugly man, of Irish' features, and 'a baddish kind of priest.'[1] At a Nationalist soiree at Limerick in 1848 this fellow had been able to make the rabble run to stone John Mitchel, apparently because of his hostility to Dan O'Connell.[2] As soon as possible Carlyle had an urgent call to pay which took him out, and he only returned in time to say Good Night on the stairs to 'O'Brien Brandy-face & Co.'

Next morning, or maybe a day or two later, he recurred to Mitchel and enquired of Duffy:[3]—"Was difference of policy the main cause of your separation?"

"Certainly it was," replied Duffy. "He wanted to advise the people not to pay poor-rate, poor-rate being the poor man's rent, and to prepare for immediate insurrection, when famine was everywhere and the French Revolution had not revived the national spirit." Thus far Carlyle was on Duffy's side, but Duffy went on.—"You are accountable for another difference. You taught Mitchel to oppose the liberation of the negroes and the emancipation of the Jews. He wanted to preach these opinions in the *Nation*, but I could not permit this to be done, (as) my own convictions were altogether different."

According to Duffy's report, Carlyle replied:—"Mitchel

[1] *Reminiscences of My Irish Journey*, by T. Carlyle, pp. 167–72.
[2] *My Life in Two Hemispheres*, by Sir C. Gavan Duffy, I, pp. 270–1.
[3] *Conversations with Carlyle*, by Sir C. Gavan Duffy, pp. 116–7.

will be found to be right in the end. The black man cannot be emancipated from the Laws of Nature, which have pronounced a very decided decree on the question, and neither can the Jew." It need hardly be added that Carlyle was far from a partisan attitude on either of these topics, as his writings show, and Duffy never denied.

Since last year much had changed. Mitchel's martyrdom had sanctified him in the eyes of Limerick. Priest "O'Brien Brandy-face" was no longer proud of the row he had stirred. In the forenoon of Tuesday Carlyle was going about in the town with Duffy, and after Duffy departed at noon, "Young Limerick,"—no connection with the Lord of that name,—'ciceroned him through the streets and showed him the locality' of Mitchel's 'tragi-comedy.' At four o'clock he departed in the gig Richard Bourke had provided for the house of his father, Sir Richard Bourke.

XXIX

SIR RICHARD BOURKE

(1849)

SIR RICHARD BOURKE was 'a fine old soldier' and a retired official of seventy-two.[1] He had been one of the men of brains in the British Army, and had had a chance of showing himself fit for something more than to be food for powder. His long career had ended handsomely in the administration of New South Wales from 1831 to 1837, where he minimised strife and organised emigration, and is remembered still as one of the best of their governors, in the days when nominal governors were not mere figure-heads. Such a man was all the more worth going to see because he had found occupation in retirement by improving 'a black bare bog,'[2] which he had bought near Limerick. 'Beautifully improved' Carlyle found it to be,—'shaded with good wood, neat little house and offices, neat walks, sunk fences,' *alias* ditches, 'drains and flourishing fields; again "the stamp of a man's image."' On the reclamation work the local labourers were 'doing very well.'

The old man becomes like an old acquaintance in Carlyle's notes.—He is 'lean, (and has a) clean face hacked with scars,' not duel smudges but honourable scars. In 1798 Richard Bourke was a young ensign and was shot through the jaws at the battle of Bergen.[1] His head is 'snow-white' now, but his 'grey bead-eyes inextinguishably lively.' He is 'low-voiced, (and) steady, methodic and practical intelligence looks through his existence here.'[2] He 'rises at six, but is not visible' in working hours of the morning, leaving visitors to entertain themselves or talk with the ladies.

On Wednesday afternoon he took the reins himself, in driving to the grounds of a rich neighbour, and apparently

[1] *Dict. of Nat. Biog.*, article *Sir Richard Bourke*, and book there quoted, Braim's *Hist. of New South Wales*.

[2] *Reminiscences of My Irish Journey*, by T. Carlyle, pp. 172–6.

entertained Carlyle, who was sitting on the box beside him, with the family history of the man and of his father and grandfather,—the best kind of country talk. At home in the evening he had much to tell of what he had seen abroad.

Every morning a 'group of ragged solicitants hung about the front door, in silence, for many hours, waiting "a word with his honour"; tattery women, young and old; one ragged able man; his Honour safe within doors, they silent, sitting or standing without, waiting his Honour's time, tacit bargain that no servant was to take notice of them, they not of him. Similar expectants in small numbers I had seen about Sir William Becher's: probably they wait about most gentlemen's houses in Ireland in this sad time.' But resident landlords like Becher and Bourke were few. One of the most surprising of Carlyle's conclusions was that 'the *English* Absentee generally far surpasses the native resident as an owner of land; and that all (sides) *admit* the fact.' [3] However that may be, another thing has to be admitted,—that men of such quality as this Bourke are too good to be "typical" of any class or kind.

[3] *Reminiscences of My Irish Journey*, by T. Carlyle, p. 109.

XXX

BY GALWAY BAY

(1849)

ON Thursday afternoon, 26.7.49, young Bourke who had contrived the visit conveyed Carlyle to Gort, where he could see an insolvent union, and also catch the Galway coach next day, and on the way see all the country well. First they went up the Shannon to Killaloe, and saw the south end of Lough Derg, looking over the water to the green high hills on the eastern side and the great slate quarries there, with the hills of Clare on their left as they bent through Scarriff to the west and north, bare, high hills, 'black-fretted, and with spots of culture.' It was a stony country, but much of it reclaimable, 'a country that *might* all be very beautiful, but is not so, is bare, gnarled (and) craggy, (so that it) speaks to you of sloth and insolvency.' It reminded him of how the Irish describe the beginning of time,—"When every place was no place, and Dublin was a shaking bog." [1]

Among the hills beyond Scarriff Carlyle saw a girl at the door of a solitary cottage '*dripping* a potful of boiled reeking greens,—(she) has picked out one as we pass, and is zealously eating it; bad food, great appetite,—extremity of hunger, likely, not unknown here.'

They reached Gort too late to go inside the union, but in time for tea and a talk with a friend, Poor-law Inspector Horsley. Bourke stayed with him. Carlyle slept at the inn, and caught the early morning coach on Friday. So he arrived in Galway early, after seeing on the way 'fifteen miles of the stoniest, barest barrenness I have ever yet seen, in some places almost like a continuous grey flagged floor.'

It was well that he was in time enough to see the town without staying overnight; for the assize had filled the hotel, and 'the town was one vortex of lawyers.' The letters waiting for him did not detain him long,—he was

[1] *Reminiscences of My Irish Journey*, by T. Carlyle, pp. 178–95.

'incredibly quick as a reader' say many eye-witnesses. Yet there was something in the letter from his wife worth reading again, now when without rudeness we may look over his shoulder. Writing on 20.7.49, she described how she had been on the platform at a political meeting when she was the guest of W. E. Forster.—

'I suppose Forster has sent you a Bradford paper containing the report of our meeting. It went off very successfully. . . . The Bradford men, filling the hall to suffocation, were a sight to see!—to cry over, "if one liked,"—such ardent, earnest, half-intelligent, half-bewildered countenances, as made me, for the time being, almost into a friend of the species and advocate for *fusion de biens*,' (Pooling of all property—the St. Simonian recipe). 'And I must tell you "I aye thocht meikle o' you," but that night "I thocht mair o' you than ever."'

That was what was said of John Brown in 1685, by his widow, when Claverhouse had murdered him in cold blood. The letter runs on.—

'A man of the people mounted the platform and spoke;—a youngish intelligent-looking man, who alone, of all the speakers, seemed to understand the question, and to have feelings as well as notions about it. He spoke with a heart-eloquence that "left me warm." I never was more affected by public speaking. When he ceased, I did not throw myself on his neck, but started to my feet and shook hands with him. Then "a sudden thought" struck me: this man would like to know you; I would give him my address in London. I borrowed a pencil and piece of paper and handed him my address. When he looked at it, he started as if I had sent a bullet into him—caught my hand again, almost squeezed it to "immortal smash," and said,—"Oh, it is your husband! Mr. Carlyle has been my teacher and master! I have owed everything to him for years and years!" I felt it a credit to you really to have had a hand in turning out this man;—was prouder of that heart-tribute to your genius than any amount of reviewer praises, or aristocratic invitations to dinner. Forster had him to breakfast next morning. I shall have plenty of things to tell you when we meet at leisure, if I can only keep them in mind. . . . God bless you, dear. . . . All to be said worth the saying lies in that.

'Your affectionate JANE W.C.'

By the time Carlyle had finished reading this and his other letters, Duffy and the local editor, Edward Butler, had a car ready, and they three went to look at the sights of Galway, so as to be ready for the afternoon four o'clock coach for Tuam.

'On the streets of Galway,' Duffy has written,[2] 'we saw crowds of creatures more debased than the Yahoos of Swift—creatures having only a distant and hideous resemblance to human beings. Grey-headed old men, whose idiotic faces had hardened into a settled lear of mendicancy, and women filthier and more frightful than the harpies, who at the jingle of a coin on the pavement swarmed in myriads from unseen places; struggling, screaming, *shrieking* for their prey, like some monstrous and unclean animals.'

As a relief to such horrors, Carlyle was taken to the suburb of Claddagh, 'inhabited only by fishermen, who exclude all strangers from their society.' He found 'a kind of charm in that poor savage freedom; kind of wild Irish community; or savage poor republic trying still to subsist on fishing here. . . . Claddagh (is) as like Madagascar as England. . . . Priests and reverence for priests abound. . . . Dark, deep-sunk people, but not naturally bad.' Which should remind us that these notes of his were never meant for publication, and that 'not naturally bad' was an old Scottish way of saying—fairly good. No wonder he enjoyed the sight of the Claddagh. The diligent and independent fishermen there were like an oasis in the deserts of beggary all round. He inspected their school, and pronounced it as 'good as any he saw'; and then he went into many of the huts in the company of the 'priestly schoolmaster, a brisk, frank, clever kind of man,' who spoke Gaelic, and seemed 'to be free of them all. Net-weaving is going on: husbands all out at the fishing.'

Then followed 'hospitable luncheon' from the 'good editor,' Edward Butler, 'a burly, thick-necked, sharp-eyed man,' whose company it is plain that Carlyle enjoyed. He gathered, no doubt from Butler's talk, that he had been a Maynooth student who 'couldn't be a priest,' and in private despised and disliked and even 'counterworked' the great "John of Chume," *alias* John MacHale, Roman Catholic Archbishop of Tuam. This "John of Chume" was the most popular and "patriotic" of the prelates then, and one

[2] *Conversations with Carlyle*, by Sir C. Gavan Duffy, pp. 121 and 111–12.

who believed in his native Irish tongue perhaps as much as in Christianity. Of course Butler never departed from external adherence to the church of his fathers. As Duffy said long afterwards,[3] explaining himself as well as Butler:—"The proud persecution of Roman Catholics as inferior beings by the English in Ireland has made every man of the right sort who is born among the Roman Catholics feel it a duty to stick by them, however much he laughs inside at the hocus-pocus of the priests, and even if he no more believes in their religion than in Jupiter."

It may have been at this luncheon that a curious talk about Lynch Law took place, one of the derivations of the word Lynch being the name of a Galway Mayor, who hanged his own son to make sure he would not be rescued. On this occasion Carlyle reprobated as intolerable some outrages by artisans,—involving murder, it may be explained. He compared them to "the ugly gambols of Lynch Law beyond the Atlantic." Duffy says [2] that he suggested:—"Something may be said for Lynch Law. It is the only chivalry of the old type left in the world, which righted wrongs and chastised evil-doers for the simple love of Justice. Its officials may be regarded by imaginative persons as the knight-errants of the Nineteenth Century."

Carlyle laughed aloud and said:—"They are knights worthy of the century, blind, passionate, ignorant, and intolerably self-confident in their ignorance. Lynch Law is the invention of a people given to loud talk and self-exhibition, who have done nothing considerable in the world that ever I have heard of."

After lunch Carlyle discovered that one of the lawyers who had been enquiring after him was a "Chambers Walker" of Sligo, a man he knew, and a friend of Petrie and Major Sterling. Mr. Walker warmly invited both him and Duffy to stay with him in Sligo, and mounted along with them into the coach for Tuam. At the same time Carlyle was amused to see what Duffy had not noticed till afterwards, that at the moment of mounting, Duffy almost 'rubbed shoulders with Attorney General Monahan, a rather sinister polite gentleman in very clean linen, who strove hard to have got him hanged lately, but couldn't.'

There was enthusiasm at Tuam when the people knew that Duffy had come in the coach.—"Yer hanar's wilcome to Chume!" was the cry, and a crowd began to gather, and

[3] To D. A. W.

a brass band would have been performing if he had lingered long in the street.

There was time to look at the two cathedrals in the summer evening before they went to bed,—the Roman Catholic and the Protestant Episcopal. Part of an ancient cross was in the Protestant cathedral, and the rest of it, the root or basis of it, in the other. "Judgment of Solomon has not answered for these two mothers,"[4] said Carlyle with a laugh, in which it cannot be denied that Walker and Duffy joined.

[4] 1 Kings iii. 16–28.

XXXI

THE PLAIN-SPOKEN BRIDE

(1849)

SOMEWHERE between Galway and Sligo, seemingly at an early part of the way, a honeymooning couple were with Carlyle and Duffy among the inside passengers.[1] 'The bride was charming,' says Duffy, who had known her at Belfast when he lived there some years ago, and he goes on to tell us :—'Carlyle courteously talked to her about sight-seeing and the pleasures of travelling, mounting at times to higher themes, like a man who had never had a care.'

Great was the amazement of Gavan Duffy, all the greater because he had been unable for many days to get Carlyle to think of anything but the Irish Land and Labour question. So when Carlyle got out of the coach for a moment at a roadside station and the bride immediately exclaimed,—"Who is that twaddling old Scotchman who won't let anybody utter a word but himself ?" Duffy was so tickled that he 'burst into a guffaw of laughter which was not easily extinguished.' He was able to control himself in time to let the young lady know she had been honoured, so that when Carlyle came in again, she was more demure and charming to him than ever. But in the evening Carlyle enquired of Duffy,—"What were you laughing at so boisterously ?"

'I told him,' he has written, 'expecting him to be as much amused as I was. But he was as much disconcerted as a beau of four-and-twenty. The absurdity of her judgment he refused to see, and was disposed to insist that she was merely a charming embodiment of the voice of the people, for undoubtedly he was an old Scotchman, and probably he twaddled a good deal to no purpose.'

[1] *Conversations with Carlyle*, by Sir C. Gavan Duffy, pp. 112–3, supplemented verbally.

XXXII

WESTPORT AND CASTLEBAR

(1849)

IT may have been apropos of the plain-spoken bride that Duffy told Carlyle that, when in London lately, he had heard people laughing at the idea of him impressed on a Whig official. When Carlyle was mentioned at a dinner-table, the official looking puzzled asked his neighbour,—"Isn't that the man who wrote the 'French Revolution' with a Scotch accent?"[1]

Carlyle laughed heartily and mimicked him by various foolish phrases, always ending with the Scotch accent. Duffy suggested,—"He would have made an epigram instead of speaking foolishly if he had enquired whether the Mr. Carlyle in question was not the man who wrote all his speculations about Ireland with a decidedly Scotch accent." Whereat Carlyle only laughed again, and told of the Scottish Judge Lord Braxfield, whose leading maxim was "Hang a thief when he is young and he'll not steal when he is old." Addressing a prisoner once he is reported to have said,—"Ye're a vera clever chiel, man, (very clever fellow, sir,) but ye would be none the worse of a hanging."

At Tuam they parted from Mr. Walker, to meet again at Sligo, while Duffy and Carlyle went by Castlebar to Westport, through storms of wind and rain. Carlyle remained on the outside of the coach the better to see the drains and other improvements, reported to them as a set-off to some of the evictions.[2] A 'gigantic drain' he did not fail to see and a 'first-rate new farmstead,' which seemed to him a 'most weighty consideration in favour' of the evicting landlord, inasmuch as now 'for peasants that will work there is employment here.' But Carlyle did not need to be told that landlords left at large are worse than wolves, and he was greatly struck by the 'systematic suppression of

[1] *Conversations with Carlyle*, by Sir C. Gavan Duffy, pp. 114–22.

[2] *Reminiscences of My Irish Journey*, by T. Carlyle, pp. 195–207. And *letters*, of course.

the peasantry by the landlords,' in the West of Ireland where they were travelling now, and where the newly made ruins of cabins and houses, in all directions, caused the countryside to look like a land which soldiers had been deliberately making desolate.

At Westport they found that most of the people to whom they had letters had gone away, but two were left, an Englishman who conducted them to the workhouse, and an excellent Dean Bourke, who joined them there and could tell them anything they wanted. This Catholic Dean was a 'middle-aged, middle-sized figure, rustyish black coat, Hessian boots, white stockings, good-humoured, loud-speaking face, frequent Lundy-foot snuff.'

In the workhouse, 'human swinery' had reached its worst,—'30,000 paupers in this union, population supposed to be about 60,000. 3 or 400 big fellows tumbling about with spades, picks and barrows, "levelling" the end of their workhouse hill; at first glance you would think them all working; look nearer, in each shovel there is some ounce or two of mould, and it is all make-believe; (and there are) 5 or 600 boys and lads pretending to break stones. Can it be a *charity* to keep men alive on these terms? In face of all the twaddle of the earth, shoot a man rather than train him, with heavy expense to his neighbours, to be a deceptive human *swine*.'

Duffy did not deny that the poor fellows were only "making believe to work," but he insisted that the blame was to be laid on men in London, "the Parliament having negatived the proposal to turn these huge buildings into factories, where useful industries might be taught to young men and women, while the able-bodied were employed in raising the food they consumed."

Here and now is as likely as any other occasion to have been when Carlyle made a famous reply to the question,—"What is to be done?" The good Dean Bourke and the friendly Englishman who guided them to the workhouse would be as eager to hear a reply to that as anybody, and Duffy had asked it more than once. It may have been after one of Duffy's cursings of the Parliament that Carlyle said,—"*Blacklead* these two million idle beggars, and sell them in Brazil as Niggers,—perhaps Parliament, on sweet constraint, will allow you to advance them to be Niggers!"

Confessing this to Emerson afterwards, Carlyle explained:—'Such masses of chaotic ruin everywhere fronted me, the general fruit of long-continued universal falsity and folly; and such mountains of delusion yet possessing all hearts and tongues: I could do little except *admire* in silence the general "Bankruptcy of Imposture," as one there sees it. . . . God is great; all Lies do now, as from the first, travel incessantly towards Chaos, and there at length lodge!' Or to quote the *Latter-Day Pamphlets* he was about to write,—"Not an idle sham lounging about Creation upon false pretences, upon means which he has not earned, upon theories which he does not practise, but yields his share of Pauperism somewhere or other."

Meanwhile a mad pauper woman was shrieking to get at the Dean. The keepers seized her and bore her off shrieking. 'Dean, poor fellow,' noted Carlyle, 'has to take it "asy," I find.' When they all came out together from the workhouse, 'ragged cohorts are in waiting for him, persecute him with their begging. "Get along wid ye," cries he impatiently, yet without ferocity:—"Doun't ye see I'm speaking wi' the gintlemen?" Wherever he shows face, some scores of wretches beset him, soon waxing to be hundreds.' . . . '"Go, I don't *keer* if ye were dead," he says to them, and doesn't affect any sensibility he cannot feel.' . . . 'He confesses he dare not stir out except on horseback, or with some fenced park to take refuge in,—poor Dean Bourke!'

'In Westport,' wrote Duffy in his diary, 'the sight of the priest on the street gathered an entire pauper population, thick as a village market, swarming round him for relief. Beggar children, beggar adults, beggars in white hair, girls with faces grey and shrivelled; women with the more touching and tragic aspect of lingering shame and self-respect not yet effaced; and among these terrible realities, imposture shaking in pretended fits to add the last touch of horrible grotesqueness to the picture!'

As they came away, Carlyle said:—"The Irish problem is to make a beginning in checking pauperism. This is the first task a sensible man would desire to see taken in hand. I will not attempt to show the way, not being familiar with practical business; but I am sure there is a way. Peel has great advantages, from his mastery over the details of business, knowing what this axle and that wheel are fit for. If he were only thirty years of age (and) with his present experience, he would do some notable work before he died."

Croagh Patrick mountain was only four miles away, and Carlyle had looked forward to seeing it for St. Patrick's sake. Dean Bourke enquired now sympathetically,—"Won't ye go to it?" and told of the beautiful prospects in Clew Bay. But Duffy had wished to stop at Castlebar, because of the bad weather, and Carlyle consented now to return there with him after lunch.

Meanwhile he found time to write at Westport a letter to his brother Dr. John, in which he mentioned that it, the 'poorest of all the Poor Unions in Ireland, has already spent of British cash, £133,000; needs £1100 per week, and *did* gather last week for Poor-rate £28, (and) the week before, zero!' It may have been here that, as Duffy reports,[1] 'we were shown the mansion of a baronet who spent in London a rental of £30,000 a year drawn from his Irish tenantry; he had ejected 320 persons within a few months, and was in arrears with his poor-rate.'

At Castlebar in the evening Carlyle went to call on a Captain Farrar, a Poor-law Inspector, for whom he had a letter; and found him an intelligent man of good strong character, about thirty years of age, and able to illuminate many things by details worth knowing. Duffy had been speaking of the Irish poor-rates as the poor man's rent. Captain Farrar had to tell:—"Westport Union has £1100 a-week from Government; Castlebar has £800." He named a third with £1300, etc., explaining that that was how they had to live from week to week, the local rates being small in proportion and generally not 'collectible.' There are 'no rents, little or no *stock* left, little cultivation. . . . We hear of landlords "living on the rabbits of their own park."'

As Carlyle walked home through the streets of Castlebar, where people not in rags were making their Saturday markets, he came to a grim conclusion,—which Duffy could not deny:—'Society is at an *end* here, with the land uncultivated, and every second soul a pauper. "Society" here would have to eat itself, and end by cannibalism in a week, if it were not held up by the rest of our empire still standing afoot!'

Next morning, Sunday, 29.7.49, he breakfasted with Captain Farrar; and as he and Duffy were starting for Ballina, they were joined on their pilgrimage by William Edward Forster,—another fine young man about thirty,—eager to be with Carlyle and learn from him as much as possible. On the preceding Wednesday he had escorted Mrs. Carlyle to Morpeth, and seen her safe into her train for Haddington. The news of her he brought made him doubly welcome. They three had the public car all to themselves as they rolled north towards Ballina over 'wide stony moorlands,' with 'gloomy hulks of mountains' on the west, and 'in sight of the desolate expanses of Lough Conn.'

XXXIII

'BABBLING OF "LITERATURE"' AGAIN

(1849)

AFTER leaving Westport for Castlebar and on the way to Ballina next day, Sunday, 29.7.49, there was more of what Carlyle called 'babbling of "Literature,"' at Duffy's instance, Carlyle indulging him with an effort.[1]

The authorship of the Letters of Junius was a problem that had seemed of perennial importance to two generations and was still interesting to Duffy. Carlyle said at once,—"In my opinion it does not matter a brass farthing to any human being who was the author of Junius." Duffy rejoined:—"One cannot well be indifferent to a question which is alleged to touch the honour of either Burke, Chatham, Gibbon, or Grattan. There is a library of controversy on the question—books, pamphlets, letters, and articles,—the writers of which must have set a considerable value on the solution of the problem."

"It probably does not concern the honour of Burke and the rest in the slightest degree," replied Carlyle. "Persons who concern themselves with questions of this nature seem to be of opinion, if anyone cares to know, that Philip Francis was the man."

"If I am sure of anything," cried Duffy, "it is that Francis was *not* the man." So Carlyle had to hear a tedious demonstration that Francis was *not* Junius, just as on 21.3.50 following he had to endure Macaulay perorating to prove that he was.[2] In both cases he said plainly it did not matter a brass farthing to anybody, and then endured the talk he could not avoid; and doubtless Macaulay might have written as Duffy wrote,—"Carlyle made no answer, and proceeded to speak of other things."

In 1845 Duffy had been travelling in the same part of Ireland in the company of John Mitchel and John O'Hagan.[3]

[1] *Conversations with Carlyle*, by Sir C. Gavan Duffy, pp. 114–16 and 122.
[2] *Life of Lord Macaulay*, by G. O. Trevelyan, Chap. XI, p. 480, footnote.
[3] For details not in the *Conversations with Carlyle* refer to Gavan Duffy's *Young Ireland*, pp. 736–7.

He now told how they were all together in an inn one evening and O'Hagan read aloud to the other two a chapter of *Sartor*. While they were so engaged 'a dapper little cockney commercial traveller' was ushered into the same sitting-room, and sat drinking brandy and water at another table, listening in mute amazement to what was being read till he could stand it no longer and cried:—" Forgive me, gentlemen, for interrupting you, but you don't mean to say that all that blessed nonsense is printed in that book?" O'Hagan assured him that it was a genuine book he was reading, and written by Thomas Carlyle.

" Carlyle!" he exclaimed. I " am not astonished at anything that fellow would publish. I saw his shop in Fleet Street, with a bishop in one window and the devil in another." O'Hagan told him that Thomas Carlyle was as different a person from Richard Carlile as Solomon the wise king from Solomon the old-clothes-man. But he refused to believe it. " Why, sir," said he, " I saw with my own eyes his shop in Fleet Street, with the bishop and the devil side by side."

Carlyle said:—" The bagman was better informed than his class, since he knew enough to construct an hypothesis of his own on the subject. Opinions and criticisms about myself are things I hear with little satisfaction. They are for the most part unutterably trivial and worthless. I am known in some small degree to a few men whom I know in turn, and that is all that is needful or salutary."

Arriving once at an hotel, when Duffy told him that a clever student begged a line in his handwriting, a guiding maxim, if he might choose, Carlyle wrote on a scrap of paper and handed to him,—" Fais ton fait," do what you should, the thing you are here to do.

XXXIV

" JOHN OF CHUME," &c.

(1849)

ON the way from Castlebar to Ballina Carlyle cast longing eyes on a 'ruined cottage in a *nook*, belongs to Lord Lucan, treeless yet screened from winds, nestled among the rocks, and (with the) big lake,' (Lough Conn), 'close by. Why couldn't *I* get it for a hermitage!'[1]—Observe the punctuation,—this was not a question even to himself, it was only an exclamation!

The cottage would have been sold or leased cheap, but Carlyle never spoke of it even to Duffy. Mrs. Carlyle would have shrieked at the suggestion, and it is only fair to her to quote more of his notes.

'Inexpressible solitude, unexampled desolation; bare grey continent of crags, clear sea of fresh water,—and *across* the lake, some farms and tufts of wood visible far off, (and) one mournful ruined-looking place, which was said to be a burying-ground and monastic ruin. Clear blue sky, black showery tempests brewing occasionally among the hills.

'Brother car meets us, (and there is) brief dialogue among the crags. (A) little pugnosed Irish figure in Sunday clothes, (who) had been escorting a comrade (in the car that meets us), mounts now beside Duffy, (and) proves to be a tailor, I think. (An) account (is given) by him of certain neighbouring localities. "Archbishop McHale," "John of Chume," was born hereabouts, peasant-farmer's son.' . . . 'We passed his birthplace to-day (29.7.49); a wild grim patch of farm by the shore of (the) big desolate lake among the wilderness of stony moors and mountains: a place to nurse a man of some talent into a priest of much fanaticism,—poor "John of Chume," cursing with bell, book and candle, according to his trade. . . . Given a vivacious greedy soul, with this grim outlook vacant of all but the

[1] *Reminiscences of My Irish Journey*, by T. Carlyle, pp. 208–9, and *Letters*.

eternal crags and skies, and for reading of life's huge riddle, an Irish mass-book only,—one has a kind of glimpse of "John of Chume";—poor devil after all!'

It does not appear whether Carlyle was ever aware that "John of Chume" translated part of the Bible and of Homer into his beloved Gaelic. Such a work of merit would surely have turned the pardon into praise. "John" lived to ninety, which alone is a certificate of good character.

XXXV

BALLINA AND SLIGO

(1849)

ARRIVING at Ballina on the Sunday, 29.7.49, Carlyle was conducted to the workhouses by an Inspector, 'Captain Hamilton, an Ulster man; big cheeks and black *bead*-eyes; Calvinist-philanthropist; a really good, but also (a) really stupid man.' [1] At one of the workhouses a discharged soldier who had been drilling the boys begged for something of the nature of "shoes." '"There is Cobden, you see!" said poor bead-eyed Hamilton (to Carlyle); "discharged that man, and now he comes upon *us*!" Kindness à la Exeter Hall; this, with strict Calvinism for life-theory, is Hamilton's style.'

At his own house in the evening Captain Hamilton appeared a 'good and hospitable man'; but he started to 'convince me of philanthropy,' wrote Carlyle, tho in fact Captain Hamilton may have been merely making the natural mistake of supposing him already convinced. Captain Hamilton could see for himself Carlyle's sympathy with the suffering and famished people, and is not likely to have known anything else about him except, vaguely, that he had written about the French Revolution and vindicated Cromwell, and on Wednesday next was to be the guest of Lord George Hill, the foremost of good Protestant "improvers" in Ireland. If Hamilton had looked at any of Carlyle's writings on hearing he was coming, it would be at the Cromwell, for Cromwell was, even more than King William, the hero of Protestant Ireland, and of people like Captain Hamilton.

Whatever he began saying to Carlyle, he soon was horror-struck at the responses he was receiving, and privately enquired of Duffy, who appeared at least a Christian tho a Catholic,—"Is Mr. Carlyle an Atheist or what?" "No, not that, but neither Calvinist nor Catholic," was the only

[1] *Reminiscences of My Irish Journey*, by T. Carlyle, pp. 209–24.

answer possible. Captain Hamilton was sufficiently reassured to undertake to conduct them through a " country of evictions " the next day.

When he punctually appeared, next morning at breakfast, Monday, 30.7.49, it was only Forster who settled to go with him and look at the " country of evictions " ; but Carlyle went again to the workhouse, and ' looked into the areas ' with him, and then, ' for his sake and my own, decline to go farther (and) return to (our) inn.'

In going through the town, Carlyle explored the street-market of Ballina, and discovered there an absurdity worthier of a comic paper than of real life even in Ireland. A poor huckster from Belmullet, forty-two miles to the west, had brought a cartload of dulse he had gathered there, and sold in the market in Ballina for two shillings. Eighty-four miles driving a horse and cart, and some hours spent in gathering the dulse and then again in selling it, for two shillings ! The horse fed as it could on the wayside. But how was the man to feed ? ' Was such industry ever heard of before in this world ? ' Carlyle was asking himself, and it was not the poor huckster he was blaming,—' Oh Heavens, innumerable mortals are to blame for it ; which quack of us is *not* to blame for it ? '

Another sight he saw was ' Col. Somebody riding into town, a great " Exterminator " hereabouts, and a great improver ; stubborn, uncultivated, big red-haired face, and solid military figure, from 50 to 60 ;—not the worst of Ballina men, *he*,'—was the conclusion.

Leaving Forster to be enlightened by Captain Hamilton and Duffy to be entertained by his friends the Dillons, and both to rejoin him in Sligo the next day, Carlyle alone took the coach for Sligo, where Mr. Walker was expecting him ; and heard all the sins of the cruel Col. Exterminator from a groom who was his fellow-passenger on the first part of the way,—' long ghastly series of roofless cottages visible enough. . . . Flat waste of moor ' made most of the landscape, with ' patches ' of cultivation. ' Poor cottier digging his little plot of potatoes, three or four little children eagerly " gathering " for him : pathetic to look upon.'

The coach at last descended into Sligo, ' beautiful town and region altogether.' Sligo Bay and the sea and the mountains, he admired them all, and—what was equally satisfactory in another sense—' Mr. Walker with servant and nice neat car is waiting. How charitable (this is) to the dusty pilgrim! No host can do a kinder thing, than *deliver* a poor wretch in these circumstances, save him from porters, inn-waiters, and the fatal predatory brotherhood!' He soon was happy for the night in Mr. Walker's 'neat little country house.'

Next day Forster and Duffy were punctual, and they saw the Sligo workhouse and relief works were like what they had seen elsewhere, but the countryside was unusually delightful, especially the fine Lough Gill. Tuesday ended pleasantly with a dinner-party at Mr. Walker's.

On Wednesday, 1.8.49, 'kind hospitable Walker' deposited Carlyle 'at the car stand in Sligo before six of the sunny morning,' and took farewell. Awaiting his companions, Carlyle stood watching the busy beggars,—the 'only industry (then) really followed by the Irish people.' Perceiving him an unprotected stranger, perhaps supposing him a cleric, for he was sometimes said to look like one, the beggars crowded round him, as the Westport beggars did to good Dean Bourke. "For the love of God, yer hanar!" was their cry. They hushed when he began to speak to them, and this was what they heard:—"Wouldn't it be worth your consideration, whether you hadn't better drown or hang yourselves, than live a dog's life in this way?"

The crowd of beggars withdrew from him unanimously. The car he was to travel in was 'full to overflowing. (A) fat gross fellow, some bacon-dealer, I suppose,' he has written, 'a Sligo wit,' got in beside him; and may have seen how the beggars were scattered by him, and felt inspired to do likewise. At any rate he did adjure someone in the crowd—in the mind's ear one seems to hear him yet—"Go home and shave yourself!" The answer came at once,—"Sure I'm not so ugly as you, shaved or not!"

The coach moved slowly away towards Donegal, the horses hardly equal to the unusual load,—in steep places the passengers got out and walked,—that 'fine calm morning,' with 'Sligo Bay and the bright sea, and moory mountainous capes in front of us, and the Donegal mountains blue-black' farther away.

XXXVI

PARTING FROM GAVAN DUFFY

(1849)

THROUGH Bundoran and Ballyshannon, they drove to Donegal, and saw no sign of life in the 'dingy, desolate' country across Donegal Bay but Killybegs town and a coastguard station.[1] Meanwhile Carlyle was hearing the life history of a fellow-passenger, an old 'cleanly peasant,' who had been a coastguardsman and 'for 30 years seems to have done nothing else but merely "look out."' A single adventure with a smuggler many years ago appeared to be 'the one peopled point in his old memory'; but as he talked the listener could learn 'particulars of coastguard discipline and ways; well-done excise,' was the conclusion, and,—'when a thing is to *be* done, it can be done.' This is one of Carlyle's leading thoughts, and familiar as a kind of key to much of his writing. In administering public business, in particular, the great thing needful is to get men to see that it *has to be done*. Once that is seen aright, men find or make a way to do it easily enough, and can organise labour when needful as well as excise.

A lagoon embanked to reclaim the land was the most remarkable thing they saw on the road to Donegal, and Forster stayed behind there to enquire into it further, arranging to meet Carlyle at Gweedore the next day, Thursday, 2.8.49. Meanwhile Carlyle found time at Donegal to 'run across to see the sumptuous old castle there, which had been extended in Queen Elizabeth's time.'

From Donegal Carlyle and Duffy travelled towards Stranorlar over high dark moors, with 'here and there a speck reclaimed into bright green,—and the poor cottier oftenest gone.' Duffy was going now to Dublin to revive his newspaper the *Nation*, which Lord Clarendon had stopped for about a year; and on this, the last day of their tour together, he was speaking to Carlyle confidentially and without any

[1] *Reminiscences of My Irish Journey*, by T. Carlyle, pp. 224–8.

reserve, as to a father,[2] and Carlyle noted afterwards,—'Duffy earnestly talking, consulting, questioning; pathetic, as looking to the speedy *end* now.' Descending at last from the edge of the moor into the welcome green of the pleasant valley of Stranorlar, while still some miles from the town, Carlyle beheld a 'fat heavy figure, in grey coarse woollen,' running alongside the coach, waving to him and crying,—"All r-right!" The coach picked up the stranger. It was Plattnauer, an old acquaintance, now a tutor in the family of Lord George Hill, and sent to meet Carlyle, as Mr. Walker had met him at Sligo, and convey him to Hill's house, about twenty miles from Stranorlar.

Nobody could be more delighted to go on such an errand, for tho, as Mazzini phrased it, Plattnauer was "losing the human curve" by good living at noble tables, he was under deep obligations to Carlyle and his wife and was glad to do anything he could in return. He was a "political refugee" nobleman from Prussia, who came to London long ago, and was succoured in distress by the Carlyles, and recommended to suitable employment. He now relieved Carlyle of travelling cares, when they descended at the coach-stand in Stranorlar street, and Gavan Duffy, stretching out his hand with silent, sorrowful face, said Farewell.

Tho much has been written of this tour by both Duffy and Carlyle, and many have debated how far it helped to turn political agitation in Ireland into economics, what is best worth telling about it remains to be told for the first time now. Gavan Duffy was then the embodiment of Irish opposition to the Castle and Downing Street, a rebel who could be neither removed nor bullied nor bribed. "Respectable people" were expected to look askance at him, and at this crisis such countenance as Carlyle's company and friendship gave him was "invaluable," he said. Half a century afterwards he flushed with joy and seemed to become suddenly young again, and spoke of it with pride and gratitude,[2] saying:—"It was a rare good thing for him to go about with me as he did, and what nobody else who counted so much would ever have dreamed of doing. The Castle resented it. He showed me a letter of private remonstrance he received from the Lord Lieutenant, Clarendon. It made no difference at all,—he stood by me steadily, and merely by doing so, did me immense good."

[2] Verbal statements by Sir C. Gavan Duffy to D. A. W., with express leave to use them.

XXXVII

LORD GEORGE HILL

(1849)

FOR fourteen miles Plattnauer conveyed Carlyle through 'greenish country, mostly tilled, not deficient here and there in wood, and with gnarled crags,'[1] and then about six or seven o'clock up the long ascent of the broad main street of Letterkenny, to the hotel, where Lord George Hill's own car was waiting to finish their journey to his house at Bally-arr.[2] When Hill stepped out himself to welcome them on arrival, this famous improver of Irish bog was seen to be a 'handsome, grave-smiling man of fifty or more; thick grizzled hair, *elegant* club nose, low cooing voice, military composure and absence of loquacity; a man you love at first sight.'

Indoors an elderly lady was seen and some children were still afoot, so that there was time for the men to take a walk after tea, 'with pleasant familiar talk,' as if between old acquaintances. Carlyle was shown not only potatoes and turnips, but also "Egyptian wheat"—grown from wheat found in a mummy case,—growing on what had been waste Irish bog till lately. 'For supper after our return' Hill ordered as a compliment to the stranger—'Irish stirabout, a frightful parody of "Scotch porridge," like hot dough, which I would not eat and even durst not, except in *semblance*.' This was all a mistake. The stirabout was porridge, but badly made by an English cook. Carlyle pretended to have a stomach equal to it, in order that Lord George Hill might not be disappointed by seeing that what he meant for a treat was not appreciated. Such hypocrisy received its proper punishment. Lord George provided the same for Thursday, too, which seems to have forced Carlyle into frankly confessing that it was useless to him. At any rate it was not mentioned on Friday.

[1] *Reminiscences of My Irish Journey*, by T. Carlyle, pp. 228–53.

[2] According to a map, north of Letterkenny, and between Ramelton on the east and Kilmacrenan on the west.

On Thursday morning, 2.8.49, Carlyle enjoyed the fatherly wit of Hill with his children, in English, German, and French. Plattnauer was going with Hill and himself to Gweedore, which made Plattnauer happy and gave the youngsters a holiday. Gweedore was the centre of the big estate on the coast and reaching to Mount Errigal, which Lord George had been improving for the last seventeen years. It was a few miles south of the Bloody Foreland, which is the North-West corner of Ireland; and every week for seventeen years, it is said, Lord George had gone to it along the road by which he now drove Carlyle,—the most bleak and dismal twenty-two miles of road that Carlyle had ever travelled.

The visitor's knowledge of country life and work was plain to everybody. He noticed the ill-regulated little farms. One of the sights on their way was the dunghill on one of them, and Lord George had to say,—"I have admonished him (the farmer) *not* to let it run to waste so, but he does not mind." Then they came to a National School on the moor, which Carlyle inspected and found bad; and a 'ghastly staring "New Catholic Chapel"' there, which he called a true "Irish Joss-house"; and what seemed to him "a scandal to behold" was that pack-horses were being used instead of carts for the peat. But they saw Lough Beagh, too, "the prettiest of all the Donegal lakes," and Lough-na-Cung, the head of which was like a '*Cumberland* pass,' and the 'beautiful and conspicuous' white peak of Mount Errigal, '*roof*-shaped and therefore conical from some points of view,' to say nothing of the other mountains standing round about, and the abiding beauty of the ever-lasting sea, changing but aye the same.

Drains in various directions showed that Lord George Hill was not the only improver. Many good landlords with well-filled purses were following his example. Perhaps the pleasantest thing was the goodwill that plainly abounded here. At the Halfway House where they watered the horse, a good-humoured woman declared she "*will* have a drop of Poteen" for you when you return. Carlyle has noted:—'Lord George knows all these people; speaks kindly,' some words in Gaelic or otherwise, 'to every one of them. Excellent, polite, pious-hearted, healthy man; talk plentiful, sympathy with all good in this Lord George, candid openness to it; fine voice, excellent little *whistle* through his teeth as he drove us,—horse performing admirably.' At the head of Lough-na-Cung, after fifteen miles of continuous 'black desolation,' came a pretty patch of improvement to delight the eye,—bright as emerald, 'both grass and woods,' like 'a tidy fairy-garden, fine trim little house with incipient farms and fields adjoining'; and soon after then as they came upon the lands of Lord George Hill himself, "A hundred thousand welcomes!" said he in Gaelic with a smile. At Gweedore Inn, which had been built by him, they found W. E. Forster waiting according to yesterday's arrangement. He was kindly welcomed by Hill.

The 'signal-staff flag' was now run up to proclaim that the landlord was present and accessible. The rain had ceased, and they walked about to see what could be seen. They mounted the hillside and looked across the river Clady, which runs from Lough-na-Cung through Gweedore to the sea.

One of the first things Lord George Hill had done was to stop the "rundale system" of letting the land, from which he is credited with helping to deliver Ireland, and a "work of merit" indeed that was. Here is one of its iniquities which even a modern Legislature could hardly match.—A large area of land was let in one lot to a number of farmers, who were not partners but separate farmers, and yet were each held liable for the total collective rent! That was what had ruined the poor man on Lord Limerick's estate, who had lately been introduced to Carlyle by Mr. Wrixon, the brother and agent of Sir William Becher. But even that was only one of the system's absurdities. As if to ensure bad farming, the farmers did not get their holdings all in one place, but each had to make the best he could of many detached pieces, scattered here and there.

On his own ground Lord George Hill could alter this at once, and did so, but he could not alter all at once the slovenly habits that went along with it. There was more than the bog to be improved!

Many dry-stone fences were in a chronic condition of being half-done, tho stones were plentiful and the landlord said all he could. There was no rent paid in the famine year, and ever since then it had been uncertain, and trifling even when paid, for rents were not being raised. '7s. 6d. was no uncommon rent, and 30s. about the highest,' noted Carlyle.

At dinner at the inn, Carlyle enquired of Hill's 'chief-manager, a hook-nosed, lean, slow-spoken man' of forty-five from Aberdeen,—"What do you think of these people?"

"Oah-h! a whean deluidit craiturs, Sir; but just—ye see——." Carlyle walked with him after dinner to see the new farm-house, which the Aberdonian was getting built for himself, and the new fields he was subduing from the moor, presumably on such an "improving lease" as Triptolemus Boyne had said would be the best way for a landlord to "improve." The land was all "pure peat," but lime was "abundant everywhere,"—he seemed sure to succeed. And so did about half a dozen others, Aberdeen and Ulster men; but the natives, "lazy, superstitious, poor and hungry," appeared as sure to fail. "There is no hope for these men as masters," said Carlyle roundly more than once to Lord George Hill, remembering, perhaps, what Boyne had shown him at King William's Town. "Their one *true* station in the universe is *servants*, slaves if you will; and never can they know a right day till they attain that."

The evening talk in the inn was interesting. Carlyle and Forster were told 'how these people conspired to throw down Lord George's fences; how they threatened to pay no rent, at first, but to *shoot* the agent if compelled to pay, and got their priest to say so; (and) how they had no notion of work by the day. (They) came from 8 to 11 a.m., and shrieked over the hook-nosed Aberdonian when on Saturday night he produced his book, and insisted on paying them by the *hour*. In brief, they are dark barbarians, not intrinsically of ill dispositions.'

After buying the estate, Lord George Hill had paid, for the sake of peace, sums of several hundred pounds for various alleged rights, 'right of fishing,' 'right of keeping an inn,' and so on. There was abundance of fish; but the people had never "fished" the waters well, and neither would nor could. In vain he gave them lobster pots and tried to teach them. At last he brought a fisherman from Aberdeen, who was now doing well and was 'the only clear immediate source of revenue' on that side of the estate.

The talk on such things lasted till bed-time on Thursday. On Friday morning they explored the rest of the estate, as far as the mouth of the river, and then along the coast. They interviewed both a priest and a parson, with little satisfaction in either case. Perhaps the most typical sight shown Carlyle was a man in rags breaking stones on the road, who had refused to work some months before, and only took the job when his cousin, on whom he was sponging, had no more potatoes left. "May the Devil pity him!"

said Carlyle, who seems to have been persuaded by this and other such " modern instances " credibly told him that ' the people,' meaning the Irish natives, will not do a day's work for wages as long as they have potatoes or anything else to feed upon. So he repeated to Lord George what he had said already :—" Yours is the largest attempt at benevolence and beneficence on the modern system ever seen by me or like to be seen,—the emancipation, all-for-liberty, abolition-of-capital-punishment, roast-goose-at-Christmas system. Alas, how can it prosper ?—Except to the soul of the noble man himself, who earnestly tries it and works at it, making himself a ' slave ' to it these seventeen years ! " Lord George appeared to acquiesce,—which seems to reveal his character to us.

They lunched at the hotel and drove home that afternoon ; but they walked much of the way, and they had the pleasure of seeing the eagles that dwell on the ' black, rocky ' mountain called Muckish. They reached home late and went soon to bed.

On Saturday morning (4.8.49) Lord George took him to call on a peasant farmer who was rich, and as they were returning home, he saw Lady A., ' a delicate, pious, high and simple lady with the children in the garden,—sister of Lord George's former wife.' Then the coach was yoked and Lord George took the reins, Carlyle on the box beside him, Plattnauer and Forster behind, and away they drove by pleasant fields and agreeable roads. They passed Ramelton and went seawards through pleasant country to Rathmullen, whereabouts Lord George put his guests upon the ferry across Lough Swilly, and he and Plattnauer took ' a really pathetic and polite farewell.' Carlyle confessed to himself in his note-book, which was never intended for other eyes than his own, that he had nowhere lately seen such a ' beautiful soul ' as Lord George Hill.

He did not conceal his sentiments from Forster, who was with him and soon was writing : [3]—' I doubt whether a man could be found more possessed with a sense of duty and active benevolence than Lord George, and yet with a stern resolve and patient determination, which no difficulty can daunt or tire. The tone and the manner of fatherly love with which he spoke in sympathy and encouragement to every one he met, knowing the names and circumstances of every cottier, were most beautiful to witness. Any

[3] *Life of W. E. Forster*, by T. Wemyss Reid, p. 140.

chance, however, of his driving industry into the present generation of his tenantry seems but hopeless. Everything in his house is very complete, and there is the elegance of high breeding beaming over a most well-ordered household; but the utmost simplicity, not to say economy, which I fear his benevolence compels him to exercise. Breakfast at eight, dinner at one, and the like. His effectiveness, his happy blending of love and justice, and his utter absence of all cant, make him a man after Carlyle's heart, and he is in raptures with him. I am glad he should meet so good a specimen of the high evangelical school.'

XXXVIII

THE PARTING BENEDICTION, &c.

(1849)

IT was 'a bright windy afternoon' as the 'red-haired ferryman' took Forster and Carlyle across Lough Swilly.[1] There lay in front of them then a '*bare* country as before, as *always* in this island, but with a Scotch aspect rather than Irish, beggary and rags having now become quite subordinate.' It seemed 'too populous' for the visible means of subsistence, however. There were many 'clusters of cottages, slated here, but visibly *hungry*'-looking. Only some 'attorneys' country-seats' seemed prosperous. After seven miles they turned a corner and suddenly saw Londonderry, 'rising *red* and beautiful' on its bluff or hill, the Foyle running 'broad and clear past the farther side of it, moderately supplied with ships. (It is) the prettiest-looking town I have seen in Ireland.'

In their hotel they soon received a call from 'the most influential (Presbyterian) layman in Ulster,' James McKnight, now editing the *Derry Standard*.[2] He had heard from Duffy that Carlyle was coming; and it may be added that this was the same "Dr. McKnight" who next year, 1850, was to preside at the Dublin Conference which Duffy was contriving, and which started the Tenant League. At present his task was to take Carlyle and his companion through Derry and show them the historical old cannon and the other sights of the town. He answered questions frankly, telling all he knew, and unconsciously revealed the animosities raging then and there,—London Companies *versus* Derry Town, and so on. Carlyle could see he was 'an honest kind of man,' with 'a kind little orderly polite wife,' and pleased them both by accepting their invitation to breakfast on Monday, to meet some Notables of Derry.

By 1849 Dr. McKnight had been for some years the

[1] *Reminiscences of My Irish Journey*, by T. Carlyle, pp. 253–62.

[2] *My Life in Two Hemispheres*, by Sir C. Gavan Duffy, I, pp. 203–05, II, pp. 29–38, etc.

secretary of the Tenant Protection Society in Ulster, and he and Duffy were earnestly agreed in trying to get North and South to join in working for economic reforms, and in particular reform of the land law. What they wanted made law was something like the rules which seemed to Gladstone impossible in 1880, and which were enacted in the Land Act of 1881,[3]—Fair Rent, Fixity of Tenure, and Free Sale of Tenant Right,—in short, something similar to the *practice* of the good Christian landlord, Lord George Hill.

On Sunday (5.8.49) Carlyle wrote a polite letter of farewell to Clarendon, the Lord Lieutenant, that he was not returning by Dublin but sailing from Derry. Then a Captain of Engineers surveying there, to whom he had a letter, conducted him and Forster to Templemoyle, an agricultural school some miles from the town, and on the east of the Foyle,—which let them see the town and the landscape from the other side. In the course of the day they also heard the London agent of one of the Companies who were landowners there explaining what he thought of the Irish as payers of rent. With a nominal rental of £4000, he could not get £1500 for his Company, and he had not prospered as well as he would have liked in buying out the tenants or getting them to emigrate. "If," said he, "I had an Irish estate, I would sell it; if I couldn't, I would give it away."

Carlyle observed that in Derry the mills were not as usual in Ireland, all corn mills,—'one linen or flax mill at least visible'; but the town had not escaped the general slump in business. 'Trade terribly gone, all say,—much poverty,' was the sad conclusion this Sunday night.

Monday, 6.8.49, was a sunny hot morning. In breakfasting at McKnight's Carlyle felt stifled, and with the lady's permission succeeded, with an effort, in lifting the window and letting in fresh air. Which seemed typical of his message! The guests included a 'big Derry Protestant clergyman, ex-Mayor Haslett,' and other 'weighty men,' all eager to hear what his "remedy for Ireland" was, and plying him with many questions to draw that out. There was no set speech, nor continuous long talk, but he felt he had been too emphatic, which shows the weighty gentlemen had succeeded in getting him to speak out pretty plainly. One would have liked to know what they said of it all afterwards among themselves. The gist of what he said to them was this,—'The remedy for Ireland is to cease generally

[3] *Life of W. E. Gladstone*, by John Morley, III, pp. 54–7.

from following the Devil, there is no other remedy that I know of! There has been one general life-element of humbug these two centuries; and now it has fallen *bankrupt*. This Universe, my worthy brothers, *has* its laws, terrible as Death and Judgment, if we "cant" ourselves away from following them.

'What *is* a landlord, at this moment, in any country, if Rhadamanthus looked at him? What is an Archbishop? Alas, what is a Queen? What is a British specimen of the Genus *Homo* in these generations? A bundle of *hearsays* and authentic appetites; a *canaille* whom the Gods are about to chastise, and to extinguish if he cannot alter himself!' And so on, expatiating on what remained steadily Carlyle's opinion, first expressed to Duffy and Dean Bourke at Westport, that '*the Irish problem is to make a beginning in checking pauperism*,' an opinion in which men of sense in Derry were likely to agree. It is likely, but nowhere on record, that he would go on to express as he had done to Duffy his confidence in Peel as the man for the crisis.

Whatever he said, the Derry Notables took it all very well, and saw him and Forster off in their Glasgow steamer about one o'clock in the afternoon.

XXXIX

TO SCOTLAND

(1849)

TWELVE hours after leaving Derry, the steamer was approaching Glasgow, and by 2 a.m. Carlyle and Forster were at ease in their inn near the quay. Next morning his old friend David Hope took them to his house and did the honours of the 'Commercial Capital of Britain,' while Carlyle thanked Heaven 'for the sight of real human industry with human fruits from it once more.'

On Wednesday, 8.8.49, they took leave of Hope and went by train together to Ecclefechan station, where the faithful Forster parted from him. Then he drove to Scotsbrig, where his mother still lived and was eagerly looking for him. Besides his brother the farmer who lived there always, his brother Dr. John seems to have been there too at this time on a visit, and letters were awaiting him from his wife, who was at Auchtertool in Fifeshire, on a long visit to her cousin there, the Rev. Walter Welsh.

Carlyle was as happy as a schoolboy, tho, as usual, he did not think of that at the time. What he recorded two months later of these days was this :—'The sight of fenced fields, weeded crops, and human creatures with whole clothes on their backs,—it was as if one had got into spring water out of dunghill-puddles ; the feeling lasted with me for several days.' [1]

On 13.8.49 he wrote to Emerson.—'By all laws I owe you a letter. . . . Your *second* Barrel of Indian Corn arrived perfectly fresh and admirable . . . seven good weeks ago,' when in short I was 'on the wing for a "tour in Ireland." I hoped somewhere in my Irish wayfarings to fling you off a letter ; but finding nowhere half a minute left to me . . . it is my *earliest* leisure, after all, that I employ in this purpose. I have been terribly knocked about too,—jolted in Irish cars, bothered almost to madness with Irish balderdash,

[1] *Reminiscences of My Irish Journey*, by T. Carlyle, pp. 261–3.

above all kept on dreadfully short allowance of sleep;—so that now first, when fairly down to rest, all aches and bruises begin to be fairly sensible; and my clearest feeling is the uncomfortable one "that I am not Caliban, but a Cramp." What the other results of this Irish tour are to be for me I cannot in the least specify. For one thing, I seem to be farther from *speech* on any subject than ever.'

XL

RURAL RESTING

(1849)

FOR two or three weeks Carlyle was ruminating at Scotsbrig. In the potato fields he was thinking of the poor Irish as he was watching 'the miserable roots getting daily spotted more and more, yet without that murrain rapidity of '46,' as he told Duffy; and he comforted himself with the reflection,—'Anyway, there cannot now be any "famine" as in '46, poor-rates being everywhere established.' . . .

In the last week of August he joined his wife at Auchtertool, and convoyed her to the house of his friend "Saint Thomas" Erskine of Linlathen, some miles from Dundee. We can get a glimpse of him there on Wednesday, 29.8.49, through the eyes of the local great man, the Rev. George Gilfillan, who gladly came and spent that forenoon with them.—

They walked to the shore, where Gilfillan and Carlyle bathed in the sea. Carlyle 'seems in high health and good spirits,' wrote Gilfillan,[1] 'and is as usual full of talk. We enjoyed the morning much. He spoke with no enthusiasm of Glamis,' tho he 'had been' there. 'I do not think he cares much for scenery,'—does not care to talk about it at any rate. On another day Gilfillan reports what seems to refer to the same occasion.[2] 'I spent a forenoon lately with Thomas Erskine and Thomas Carlyle, walking on the brink of the German Ocean. It was fine to find their deep and eternal dissimilarities mellowed and softened into harmony, and to hear the concert formed between the meek low voice of the one and the strong, yet still and melancholy, accents of the other. I could not thoroughly sympathize with either, but I loved and—shall I add?—pitied both. I suspect I was repaid in kind,' concludes Gilfillan.

[1] *George Gilfillan*, by R. A. and E. S. Watson, p. 181.
[2] *Ibid.*, p. 77; but the date 1850 seems a mistake for 1849.

XLI

IN THE HIGHLANDS AND ELSEWHERE

(1849)

ON 1.9.49, the Saturday following, Carlyle went by Perth to the summer quarters of the Ashburtons, whom he had promised to visit, Glen Truim House. It was not far away,—just over the watershed of the adjacent Grampians, near the line of the railway to-day from Perth to Inverness; but the railway had not been all made in 1849, and Carlyle had to complete his journey by coach. It was the afternoon before he was set down on the roadside, in sight of his destination,—'a rather foolish-looking, turretted, diminutive, pretentious, gray-granite sort of a place, half a mile off,' and which on arrival he found about the size of two Craigenputtocks and badly planned, decidedly dear at £500 for two months, which he was told was the rent of it.

Happily the open upland moors around and the fresh air were also like Craigenputtock; and the only drawbacks were the dullness of the company,—some Lords who could only babble about killing birds, mere bloody poulterers, so to speak, and women sketching,—and the want of room, the house being '*crowded* to the ridge-tile, (with) nearly twice as many people as are good for it.' But Milnes was due in a day or two, and 'the departure of one Peer of the Realm makes an immensity of room: so many flunkeys, lady's maids, etc., are in his train.'

Writing to his wife the morning after he came, Carlyle described to her the journey up through Dunkeld, where he had recognised the 'fat old landlord' of the hotel, grey-haired to-day, and 'much broader' than he used to be in 1823. 'A still olive-coloured mist hung over all the country. Kinnaird and the *old* house which was my sleeping-place when I used to write to you,' and wrote Schiller and translated Wilhelm Meister, he might have added, 'were greyly discernible across the river amid their trees. I thought of the water-hen you have heard me mention, of the pony I used to ride, of the whole world that then lived, dead now mostly, fallen silent for evermore, even as the poor Bullers are, and as we shall shortly be. Such reflections, when they do not issue pusillanimously, are as good as the sight of Michael Angelo's *Last Judgment*, and deserve their place from time to time.'

Another set of reflections arose as he looked around him in the 'shooting Paradise,' that the attraction of such places was as a change from monotonous luxury and idleness,—'weary are the lives of rich men that require such a change.' One of his ways of humouring his wife—a thing worth learning—was to take every excuse to praise her. So now as she had advised him not to go to the Highlands, he summed up his description to her thus:—'It is, in fact, such a scene of *folly* as no sane man could wish to continue in or return to. Oh, my wise little Goody! What a blessing in comparison with all the Peerage books and Eldorados in the world is a little solid sense derived from Heaven!'

'Poor Lord Ashburton looks rustic and healthy, but seems more absent and oblivious than ever,' he told her, and added, 'a few reasonable words with me seem as if suddenly to awaken him to surprised remembrance.' On Tuesday, 4.9.49, Ashburton drove him to Loch Ericht for 'fishing,' and on the way said that 'the present adventure costs him about £1200. He admitted that it was a very stupid business,—"except in respect of health."' In reply Carlyle suggested:—"Men really desirous of 'hunting' ought to go to Africa with its lions, to America with its bears and boas, to some place where wild animals really are and stand in need of hunting; whereas here, except it be the catching of rats, there is really no legitimate field for the 'hunter,' and his era is quite done!" 'All this was mildly taken,' and they had a great deal of serious talk that day, and Ashburton made a new set of good resolutions; but the only thing worth adding is that during the three or four hours of the 'fishing,' Carlyle took no share in the sport, and lay among the heather all alone.

A few days later Carlyle caught a little colic by too violent exercise, he believed, Lord Ashburton and he riding 'over stock and stone on highland ponies.' The patient keeping to his room, Lady Ashburton was alarmed, as there was much cholera about, and sent her house doctor in to see him. The doctor soon came out again and said :—" Carlyle received me with invectives against myself and my profession, saying that 'of all the sons of Adam they were the most eminently unprofitable, and that a man might as well pour his sorrows into the long hairy ear of a jackass.' "[1] Which reassured the hostess.

Meanwhile Mrs. Carlyle was at Scotsbrig, and as she afterwards wrote from Cheyne Row to her husband's mother, old Mrs. Carlyle,—" My visit to Scotsbrig was the one in which I had most unmixed satisfaction ; for, along with my pleasure at Haddington and Edinburgh, there was almost more pain than I could bear. But you were all so kind to me (at Scotsbrig), and then you were little changed, and in short, in finding so much to please me at Scotsbrig, I missed nothing I had ever possessed there. In the other places it was far otherwise." What remained for years, and maybe for ever, a secret from her husband, must now be told.

Forty-six years afterwards a son of Carlyle's brother James, " old John Carlyle," a farmer at Langholm, was describing this visit,[2] saying he had been a boy at the time and remembered it well, especially the happy evenings when the work was all done and everybody came together, servants and children and grown-ups. This visit which lasted a week or so was the first time he had seen *much* of his aunt, Mrs. Thomas Carlyle, so as to feel he knew her. " She was always fragile and delicate," he said. " I recollect one night my grandmother was in great spirits and started some game for us all, which set us romping, I forget what it was—maybe blind-man's-buff,—but I was close by and saw well something I will never forget. Grandmother came up quietly unobserved behind my aunt, and, placing her fingers in my aunt's armpits, began to tickle her. They both laughed a great deal and we were all laughing, when suddenly my aunt became as white as paper and sank down on the floor as if she were dead. My grandmother was in a terrible fright, and it was some time before my aunt recovered. It was heart-disease." Dr. John was soon in attendance, and " we were all warned, servants and all," said his namesake and nephew, John Carlyle, our witness, " that it was never to be spoken of, lest Uncle Tom should hear of it and be

[1] *Autobiography of Henry Taylor*, I, pp. 331–2.

[2] To D. A. W. at his own house in Langholm, first on 31.12.1895, and then on 25.7.1896.

uneasy." Before the middle of the month, Mrs. Carlyle went on to her uncle's house in Liverpool.

From Glen Truim House Carlyle came to Edinburgh, and on Friday, 14.9.49, in breakfasting at Jeffrey's with Jeffrey's daughter and her husband Empson and the children, he learned the sad news that his old friend and his wife were both suffering from the effects of a fall on the shore at Newhaven. Lady Jeffrey was confined to her room; but, as Carlyle recorded in 1867,—' Jeffrey I did see, after some delay, and we talked and strolled slowly some hours together. Jeffrey was very kind to me, but sadly weak; much worn away in body, and in mind more thin and sensitive than ever. He talked a good deal; was friendly (and) good, but tremulous (and) thin, (which was) almost affecting in (its) contrast with old times. Grown *Lunar* now, not Solar any more! He took me, baggage and all, in his carriage to the railway station, Mrs. Empson escorting; and there said Farewell,—for the last time.'

Carlyle's destination was Scotsbrig again, and there he stayed about ten days more, till his wife had done the last of her visits and was ready to receive him at home. They had been corresponding like lovers all the time they were apart; and Mrs. Carlyle had resumed her old relations with her friends in Scotland, which her husband and doctors had long been wishing to see her do. Describing her visit to her father's three sisters in Edinburgh, Elizabeth, Anne and Grace Welsh, who all lived together, and gave her a much warmer welcome than she expected, she had written to her husband (5.9.49):—' It was a great comfort to me to be so received. My heart was opened by their kindness to tell them that it was nothing but apprehension of their bothering me about my soul which had estranged me from them so entirely. Anne's reply, given with an arch look and tone, was very nice,—" Indeed, Jeannie, you need not have been afraid of our setting ourselves to reform you; it is plain enough that nothing short of God's own grace can do that, but I won't despair that a time may come, tho I am not such a fool as to think that I can hasten it." '

Her father and mother's "old servant" Betty, Mrs. Braid, was in Edinburgh now, and received her with open arms. She was little older than Mrs. Carlyle,—they had grown up together. This is the Betty quoted in a letter from Liverpool, dated 14.9.49, to Carlyle at Scotsbrig:—

' Oh, my dear, my dear! How thankful I may be that

I knew nothing of that colic till it was over! A colic in these cholera times would have alarmed me in any circumstances; but there—remembering, as I still do, "rather exquisitely," my own sore throat transacted at Alverstoke three winters ago, and other little attacks of my own, under the same regime—how could I have stayed in my skin, with no certainty that you would be able to get so much as a cup of bad tea, never to speak of hot water to your feet, or human sympathy? You were not, it would seem, so wholly left to Providence as I was; still it is a great mercy that you were not long laid up in that house, or any other of their houses. As my aunt Grace told me very often during my bad day: "There is mercy mixed up with all our afflictions! It is a great comfort to think you are in better hands than ours—I mean in Jesus Christ's."

'"Oh, ay," said dear Betty, "Christ has care of my bairn a'wheres (everywhere), even on the railway! And a great comfort that is for me to think, now that she gangs sae muckle be them!" (goes so much by them). But of all that, some quiet evening in Chelsea.'

In the last week of September, they were at home together at Cheyne Row, with many a good story to tell each other.

XLII

EXHORTING DUFFY, &c.

(1849)

ON arriving home, Carlyle found waiting a letter from Duffy and answered it at once at great length, incidentally mentioning he had already on the same day 'written two letters, all on Ireland.' He had received the first numbers of the revived newspaper the *Nation*, and wrote (29.9.49) : [1]—

'I like the new *Nation* very well, especially No. 3 of it. I seem to see there a beam of real star-fire and manful insight and endeavour, shooting forth from amid the old too-smoky and fuliginous elements ; and destined yet, by Heaven's blessing, to subdue them all to itself, and beam clearer and clearer. . . . Better or worse, yours is the only voice I hear in Ireland entitled to any considerable regard from me—the one human voice there amid the infinite barking and howling. May you truly *love* wisdom, and regard all other things, popularities, nationalities, &c., &c., as mere noise and nonsense in comparison. Him that is loyal to wisdom, wisdom *will* reward and him only ; he shall "acquire strength by going," for all the universe is on *his* side, and his light, in the darkest of nights, even in Ireland's night of 1849, "shall shine more and more unto the perfect day." Your temptations, and open and disguised impediments, I discern too well, will be many ; but the task is great, and, if you front them well, the prize, too, is great. Courage, patience, the eye to see and the heart to endure and do, may these be yours, and all that follows from them !'

Then he discussed the potato rot of this year, and told of 'a farmer in the Perth region, who had gained £2000 by his potatoes alone last year,' which Carlyle lamented as demoralising, 'making agriculture a kind of gambling.' He went on to curse the land-laws.—

'You are surely right in what you argue about the state

[1] *Conversations with Carlyle*, by Sir C. Gavan Duffy, pp. 127–32.

of the land: that it is a covenant of iniquity, clean contrary to God Almighty's law, and conformable only to my Lord Chancellor's law, that now gives a ploughing man access to Irish soil (and you may add Scottish and English and European if you like); a terrible solecism—alas! alas! the outcome of a million other silent and spoken solecisms . . . and contraventions of the everlasting Acts of Heaven's Parliament! . . .

'You are sure of my sympathy and of all good men's in any feasible attempt to improve even a little that misery of miseries. In "land tenure" itself some considerable improvement might by express law be brought about; but I have no clear notion' of the Act of Parliament needful. 'If you have, explain it publicly, but not till you have studied it well, and talked with lawyers, political economists, and all such classes upon it. . . . On the whole be practical, be *feasible*, that is the one condition; support in abundance awaits you here if that be complied with. More power to your elbow. . . . 'T. CARLYLE.'

A postscript followed which is interesting now as it tells of Francis Espinasse, then seeking employment as a journalist.—'Espinasse, a young Edinburgh man,' (French father, but bred in Edinburgh, and apparently with a Scotch mother), 'is a kind of hero, and is now threatened with changing into a kind of Scotch *Rousseau*, so unpropitious are the elements to him. An excellent scholar, especially in German, &c., full of exact information on all manner of subjects, discernment sharp as a hawk's—especially on the satirical side; in all ways an honourable, proudly veracious, anti-humbug little fellow, and very much to be relied on for doing whatsoever he undertakes to do. Honest to the bone, if you can believe me, who have known him for several years. Of late he has once or twice taken to the imitation of me, which looks absurd, but he can write in other styles than that, and used to do literary &c. articles for the Manchester *Examiner* very well indeed.'

Espinasse lived to have the pleasure of reading this more than forty years afterwards, when Duffy published it, and has written in English one of the best lives of Voltaire in any language,[2] to say nothing of the Carlyliana in his Literary Recollections.

[2] *Life of Voltaire*, by Francis Espinasse, Great Writers Series, Walter Scott publisher.

XLIII

TIP-TOP JOURNALISM

(1849)

DUFFY was suffering from lack of help in producing his revived paper, the *Nation*, tho the help he needed was not such as Espinasse could supply. As he has explained,[1] —'All my colleagues in the earlier *Nation* were either dead, exiled, suffering the penalties of treason, or in a very few cases disheartened by failure. I aimed to enlist recruits to fill their places, but I did not conceal from such new-comers the hard terms the service of Ireland imposed, or that the work to be done would be slow and obscure. They were no longer invited to share in literary projects. Our ship was a wreck. Whoever could help would be welcome.' So Duffy wrote an appeal which he reprinted in 1892 in his *Conversations with Carlyle*. Here is what may suffice to show its drift.—

'WANTED, A FEW WORKMEN.

'Ireland has urgent need of workmen, able and willing to work—of men who will gradually create about them, each in his own city, hamlet, or narrow corner, a circle of light and vital warmth, where there is now ignorance and lethargy. . . . If there be practical sagacity anywhere in this country, it never had a more favourable field in the world. The very offices of Government are vacant—nearly as vacant as if a revolution had given up Dublin Castle to the people. Not the official uniform, and the salary indeed; but the power to create and guide operations, and get work done—the true essence of authority.

'The places are vacant,' but in short competent candidates are few. 'Spouting, speechifying, and operations of that sort can be performed by a large proportion of the adult population of this island. The faculty of writing

[1] *Conversations with Carlyle*, by Sir C. Gavan Duffy, pp. 134–50.

sonorous and swelling sentences is nearly as common. O'Connell made a guerilla of ruthless speechifiers, and Young Ireland created " a mob of gentlemen who write with ease." But there is no country in Europe where there is so little *practical* genius, practical skill or fruitful practical knowledge, as in Ireland. The smallest official trained in the petty routine of public business, the dullest commissioner who does " jobs " for the Executive, has generally more administrative capacity than some of the best of our public men. . . .

'Let such young men as feel honestly called to help us in this design send us their names, and they will be enrolled in a company from which we predict substantial and permanent services to Ireland. But it is workmen we want. With idle politicians, amateur politicians, trading politicians, we propose to transact no business. One hour from the man who gives ten to his own proper pursuits will be precious, (or) ten hours from the student. . . . But no magic can turn the jaded hacks of politics, or the fops of literature, into men fit for this company. The fitness of candidates will be tested by the work they can accomplish. . . .

'When Napoleon turned administrator, he proclaimed as the issue of his task that not one pauper should remain in all France; and' in short he would have done it but that 'the clash of arms called him away. . . . This is work for barely one generation. In one generation the Electorate of Brandenburg grew into the powerful, populous kingdom of Prussia. . . . If they (our men) will be wise and resolute, a great thinker has foretold their victory. " Even the casualties of life," he says, " seem to bow to the spirit that will *not* bow to them; and yield to subserve a design which they threatened to frustrate." Ireland wants a few workmen of this calibre.'

The words quoted at the end were of course Carlyle's. He wrote as soon as he read the article (2.10.49) :—' Capital article, dear Duffy, that in last *Nation*: " Wanted, a few Workmen ! " To every word and tone of that I say, Amen. Stand by that; that is the real text to preach innumerable sermons from, the one result to be striven for. *I call this the best article I ever read on Ireland;* a noble " eloquence " in this, the eloquence of sorrow, indignation, and belief. Cart is not put *before* horse in these utterances of yours, the first time I have ever seen that condition observed—that I can remember—by any patriotic Irish writer or speaker whatsoever.

'Steady, steady! Hold on in that course, which will spread out wide as the world for you, and you will do immense good; *ut fiat*!' (So may it be!) 'In great haste,

'Yours, T. CARLYLE.'

It is pleasant for preachers in Press and pulpit alike that the effect of their exhortations is generally as immeasurable as that of gas let into the air, or liquid spilt in the sea. Thus they cannot be confounded like the Welshman who told Hotspur,—"I can call spirits from the vasty deep," and was answered, "So can I, or so can any man: But will they come when you do call for them?"

In this instance Duffy says that recruits responded, and that,—'Out of these speculations on the duty of Irishmen came the Tenant League of 1850, and the commencement of a land war not yet finished, and the first Parliamentary party of independent opposition.'

Meanwhile Carlyle was finishing his share of their tour in Ireland. Long ago he had formed the habit of thinking out and recording soon whatever he learned in travelling. Perhaps what led him into this was a remark of Rousseau that he was sorry he had not done so. Accordingly as soon as Carlyle was fairly settled at home, he read again the letters he had written from Ireland to his wife and kindred, and from the 4th to the 16th October he was occupied in writing the notes, which were afterwards stolen, and published only after his death as *Reminiscences of My Irish Journey*.

Next month, November, 1849, he sent Duffy an article for his newspaper on "Trees of Liberty." It was printed "anon" as directed, but spotted at once for Carlyle's by Mr. Rintoul of the *Spectator*. It suggested that when 'every patriotic Irishman, that is, almost every Irishman now alive,' would say he would die for his country, he might be advised to plant a tree for it. Once upon a time, 'as the old chroniclers write, "a squirrel could have run from Cape Clear to the Giant's Causeway without once touching the ground"'; but now the land lay bare. It needed many things, and nothing more than trees.

With unintended humour, Duffy tells us:[1]—'I probably wrote him, what it would have been discourteous to print, that his pleasant little paper betrayed a fundamental unacquaintance with Irish affairs. It was hopeless to reforest a country where, if a tenant planted his seed or sapling and tended it until it became a mature tree, the law declared it to be the property of the landlord, without a scrap of compensation to the man who reared it.'

Which only shows how the political strife had confused one of the clearest heads in the country, and hidden from him in his editorial haste the inward meaning of what Carlyle had written. It was not for personal profit but for " Ould Ireland's " sake that men were to plant the trees! Duffy did not think of that at the time, preoccupied as he was about the urgency of land law reform ; and in old age he could only smile at the recollection. Carlyle never hurt his feelings by pointing it out. About two thousand years before, a wise man had said, presuming that the land laws were all as they should be, that there were few actions more unselfish on the part of a man no longer young than planting a tree, so seldom can it happen that the benefit of the tree can come to him that plants it.

BOOK XVIII

CONTEMPORARIES

1849

I

A "VOLUNTEER SECRETARY"

(1849)

AFTER Carlyle had finished the notes of his tour in Ireland, "What next?" he asked himself. To write on politics seemed the obvious answer. It was partly to quicken his utterance on politics that he had gone to Ireland; but what he had seen there of the result of English inefficiency in administration confirmed the grimmest of his conclusions, yet left him more than ever perplexed where to begin. The current dogma of *laissez-faire* or let-alone,—let Government do nothing,—seemed to sanctify the silly supposition that any fool could do the work of Government. Carlyle was turning over his bundles of unpublished MSS. with little exhilaration; and writing on 6.11.49 to his old friend William Graham,[1] commissioning him to buy a carpet for his mother, he dropped a few remarks which seem to prepare us for what was soon to follow.

He told him he was trying to work, but felt as if clearing away mud before beginning to build.—'London is getting populous again. Absurd "Peace Meetings" with quantities of empty balderdash talked in Exeter Hall,' such things and criminal trials are the talk. 'A thoroughly anarchic Europe, after vain attempts at "reformation" by parliamentary eloquence and street barricades, settling lazily into the old malodorous slough-of-despond again, *not* to lie long there.... One sits rather, looking silent at all that.'

While thus meditating politics in working hours, Carlyle was never neglecting outdoor exercise. One afternoon this November the painter Gambardella brought a 'great, sprawling' double 'velocipede' or bicycle, and Carlyle and he, like a pair of boys, pedalled 'along the highways three hours,' to Wimbledon and back, together.[2]

In the meantime Mrs. Carlyle had been entertaining her

[1] Unpublished letter.
[2] *Letters of J. W. Carlyle*, edited by L. Huxley, p. 337.

husband as usual with picturesque descriptions of her own adventures during her round of visits, and in particular a four-days' visit to Joseph Neuberg and "his dear little sister" at Nottingham.[3] Neuberg had then confided to her that he was retiring from business, and bent on an intellectual life. He meant to spend a while at Bonn. "But," said he, "what I would really like best would be to serve Carlyle as a volunteer secretary."

In September he was taking leave of his Nottingham friends,[4] and by November he was in London, on the way to Germany but willing to stay awhile if wanted. Carlyle wrote to him on Saturday, 10.11.49.[1]—

'DEAR SIR,—

'Jane tells me you at one time thought of offering yourself to me as "volunteer secretary," by way of having a generous employment in this world!—How that may have been I know not; but if you really have leisure and heart for a little of that kind of work, then sure enough I at present stand much in need of such a service as that were on your part. A mass of embroiled papers written last year, and tied up in batches; which have been repeatedly on the edge of the *fire*, which I think *is* their ultimate just destination, but to which I grudge to commit them indiscriminately just yet, till a better search have been made whether there be not some fractions of *in*combustible perhaps in the melancholy imbroglio. The help of one like you might really be valuable in this small case. For there needs not only a Copyist, able and willing to decipher my blottings, and reduce them to clear legibility; but there needs also a man of decisive judgment and insight, who could completely appreciate what he read, know in some measure what might be worth something, and what was clearly worth nothing, reduce the confused matter to heads, and thus help essentially to disentangle the living part of these Papers from the dead. Copyists I have had of the required kind, and could perhaps again get (though not without some trouble), but a Copying *Editor*, of that sort, I should in vain apply for by aid of money and the labour market. In the meanwhile, to do the service myself, I find, on repeated attempts, is difficult on many accounts, and, I suppose, will prove impossible, with the *fire* so near at hand. That is the

[3] *Macmillan's Magazine*, Aug., 1884, pp. 281–4.
[4] *Nottingham Review*, 5.10.1849, p. 2, col. 1.

real state of the matter; to which, if what my wife reports was serious and not (as is more likely) jest, and if you have done with your Nottingham affairs, and are really *free* to volunteer for what you like, I thought I might as well call your attention in passing.

'After all, I fear it is but one other cowardly instinctive artifice on my part to *shirk* the real difficulty; for the truth is, I have got something to write again, in these times, an *un*written insupportable something, towards which these Papers were an attempt evidently futile as such;—and I suppose there will be no way of determining what to write and what to keep silent, or how at all to proceed in the matter except—except, alas, getting into that dreadful paroxysm of clairvoyance which is usual to me in writing Books, but which I shudder to contemplate as inevitable again!

'So that, on the whole, it is perhaps really no vital matter whether you say No to all this, or even say Nothing; but let it all evaporate, as a cloud, into the vague blue, and matters take their course as if it had not been. You will forgive me at any rate; and consider this a thing not to be spoken of except to myself. . . . Come and see us some evening soon. . . .

'T. CARLYLE.'

Next day, Sunday, 11.11.49, Carlyle was writing in his journal. After noting his summer whereabouts, he went on:—'To Annandale a second time, and thence home, leaving my poor mother ill. The last glimpses of her at the door, whither she had followed me, contrary to bargain; these are things that lie beyond speech. How lonely I am now grown in the world; how hard, as if made of stone. All the old tremulous affection lies in me, but it is as if frozen. . . . The general history of man? Somewhat, I suppose, and yet not wholly. Words cannot express the love and sorrow of my old memories, chiefly out of boyhood, as they occasionally rise upon me, and I have now no voice for them at all. . . . God help me. God soften me again; or rather let me pray for *wisdom*, for silent capability to manage this huge haggard world—at once celestial and infernal, which has been given me to inhabit for a time and to rule over as I can. No lonelier soul, I do believe, lies under the sky at this moment than myself.

'Masses of written stuff which I grudge a little to burn, and trying to sort something out of them for magazine articles, series of pamphlets . . . does not yet succeed with me. . . . All these paper bundles were written last summer, and are wrongish, every word of them. Might serve as introduction or accompaniment to the unnameable book I have to write. In dissent from all the world; in black contradiction, deep as the bases of my life, to all the philanthropic, emancipatory, constitutional, and other anarchic revolutionary jargon, with which the world . . . is now full. Alas! and the governors of the world are as anarchic as anybody; not pleasing at all to be in a minority of one in regard to everything. The worst is, however, I am not yet true to myself; I cannot yet call in my wandering truant being, and bid it wholly set to the work fit for *it* in this hour. Oh, let me persist, persist—may the Heavens grant me power to persist in that till I do succeed in it!'

Next day, Monday, he was assured of Neuberg's readiness. On Tuesday Neuberg was with him; and by the Friday Carlyle was entering in his journal,—'Papers on the "Negro Question," fraction of said rubbish, coming out in the next *Fraser*' (December's). It is often described as the first of the *Latter-Day Pamphlets*, which were soon to follow; and might seem to simple eyes the ancient miracle of an answered prayer. But the miracle of these writings does not depend on any such coincidence,—they are the most truthful political utterances in recent history.

THE "Negro Question" was what this prelim
pamphlet was called in *Fraser* (December, 184
in reprinting it Carlyle changed Negro into "N
which was his only reply to the vituperation it
John Mill was one of those that wrote to co
saying in private,—" Carlyle turned against all h
Moncure Conway [1] has explained that Mill, et
posed Carlyle believed in democracy as they di
simply mistaken about him. Even the lik
Robinson, who should have known better, wa
Mrs. Austin: [2]—" Carlyle has been led by va
grade himself more than any man of our age by
defence of Slavery as an institution."—" By van
he,—revealing the kind of motive that might
fluenced—Crabb Robinson.

Far from defending slavery "as an institution
was holding the mirror up to nature for the most
said plainly that the 'buying of Black war-ca
Africa, and bringing them over to the sugar islands
again,' was 'a contradiction of the Laws of this Un
which we should 'heartily pray Heaven to end,' and a
'help Heaven to end it wherever the opportunity is given.
But tho he expressly said he did not wish to see the me
emancipated made slaves again, still he did not join th
chorus of English writers and speakers glorifying themselves as better than Americans, because a few years ag
the English Parliament had paid twenty millions to slave-
holders in the West Indies, and stopped slavery.

There were few men better acquainted than he with th
result of that expensive performance. Besides the paper
and books that were open to everybody, he had heard a

[1] *Autobiography of Moncure D. Conway*, II, p. 103.

[2] *Three Generations of Englishwomen*, by Mrs. Ross, I, p. 239, correctin
Nov. to Dec.

great deal from the Sterlings and many others with direct knowledge, to say nothing of Sir James Stephen and Henry Taylor of the Colonial Office, who were sure to be frank with him and knew all that could be known officially.[3] Carlyle was so plainly serious and discreet, and so reliable not to misuse whatever was told him, that all sorts of people were continually talking to him confidentially all his life, and nobody ever regretted it.

Thus it happened that he was and even was known to be acquainted with the facts, and the sensations may be imagined of the politicians and journalists who saw him ... the flapdoodle, wherewith they had been humbug... people, winking at each other. He explained that ...as not such an evil thing, in itself, that the English ...d acted wisely and nobly in paying twenty million ...end it suddenly in the West Indies. Our public ...orted from our own poor labouring men, had been ...wasted, with no better result than to ruin the ...s, ' the fruitfulest region of the earth going back ...while the emancipated slaves were guzzling ...d rotting in idleness. For this result of " Exeter-...thropy," our Social Science had no remedy but ... of " Let-alone " and " Supply and demand," ...e circumstances meant—importing more niggers ...ins grew dear, ' and black men there, like white ... are forced by hunger to labour for their living. ... be a consummation,'—to have turned the West ...o ' an Ireland, and Black ! ' Such ' Social Science ' ...cal Economy he called a ' Dismal Science,' and the ...s stuck to it ever since, and ' Exeter-Hallery and ...ragic Tomfoolery,' *alias* the Dismal Science, are ...nked together grotesquely.

Insisting that the thing to do was to consider what it is ...hat Fact and Nature demand of us, he maintained that ' the everlasting duty of all men, black or white, is to do ...ompetent work, to labour honestly according to the ability ...iven them.' So the black man should not get any land to ...row pumpkins unless on condition that he worked. The ...ardships and injustices of slavery, ' the old Demerara ...ethod ' as he called it, had to be avoided, ' for injustice is ...*orever* accursed : and precisely our unfairness towards the ...nslaved Black man has,—by inevitable revulsion and fated ...urn of the wheel,—brought about these present confusions.'

[3] Compare the *Greville Memoirs*, P. I, V. II, pp. 348–9, 359–60.

How to abolish the abuses of slavery could not be seen in a hurry,—would take generations, perhaps centuries, to discover aright; but he suggested that there 'ought to be in every Slave State, a fixed legal sum, on paying which any Black man was entitled to demand his freedom.' He pointed also to the 'Dutch Blacks in Java,' who were fixed to the land, and to the 'Serfs of the Middle Ages,' who were allowed to marry and live a family life. But what most of all astonished the pundits of the Dismal Science was his insistence on a right principle which took the ugliness out of slavery, when arranged on reasonable conditions,—'That in every human relation, from that of husband and wife down to that of master and servant, nomadism is the bad plan, and continuance the good.'

III

RIGHT PRINCIPLES IN POLITICS

(1849)

THE right principle which took the ugliness out of slavery,—that in every human relation, nomadism is the bad plan, and continuance the good,—was not the only novelty in the essay called 'The Nigger Question.'

What provoked the politicians was that he would not play their game and join in humbugging the people. He had been the first to raise the 'Condition of England Question,' and now he kept it ever in the background, as if it dwarfed in importance even the absurdities being done in the West Indies. He said plainly that it was for the white women in England, starved into prostitution, 'that my heart bleeds and my soul is heavy. . . . Look at that group of *un*sold, unbought, unmarketable Irish "free" citizens, dying there in the ditch, whither my Lord of Rack-rent and the constitutional sheriffs have evicted them; or at those "divine missionaries" of the same free country, now traversing, with rags on back, and child on each arm, the principal thoroughfares of London.'

Here is the stroke of humour that set men cackling, and literally reverberated round the globe.—'Certainly, by any ballot-box, Jesus Christ goes just as far as Judas Iscariot; and with reason, according to the New Gospels, Talmuds and Dismal Sciences of these days. Judas looks him in the face; asks proudly, "Am not I as good as thou? Better, perhaps!" slapping his breeches-pocket, in which is audible the cheerful jingle of thirty pieces of silver. "Thirty of them here, thou cowering pauper!" My philanthropic friends, if there be a state of matters under the stars which deserves the name of damnable and damned, this I perceive is it!'

The "Hickory Buckskins" of the Slave States in America reprinted this article;[1] but were dismayed to find on study of it that it gave ammunition to the Abolitionists, for the

[1] *Autobiography of Moncure D. Conway*, I, p. 54.

justice which Carlyle required, to make the condition of their slaves endurable, was precisely what the Hickory Buckskins were declining to allow. Theodore Parker of Boston, their sternest critic and the negroes' friend, was inspired to his best argument against them by this passage about Judas. "We know what judges can be made to do," said Selden, and politicians are no better. So the politicians and judges in America, "in the interest" of the slave-drivers, had made a "law" to secure the recapture of runaway slaves in other states, and were trying to make people obey it because it was a "law"! Whereas in truth all law enacted depends for its force on the presumption that it is right and just. The "flunkey jurisprudents" of England in the nineteenth century occasionally forgot that, poor fellows, and perpetrated a great deal of piffle in consequence; but even they might have admitted it in words, and assuredly that presumption is the true part of the Stoic doctrine on the Law of Nature, and the Christian on the Law of God. Any part of any "law" which is contrary to good conscience, enlightened and cultivated conscience, is the most loathsome form of iniquity; and any "authority," be it King or Congress or any other, enforcing "law" which is wrong or unjust, is like a thief or murderer in the uniform of a policeman.

Here is how Theodore Parker dealt with the plain-dealing scoundrels in Washington, politicians and judges and their servants, standing up for "law" against conscience. He told them in effect that Judas Iscariot would have done what they wanted,—they must be like him!—

He 'took his "thirty pieces of silver"—about fifteen dollars; a Yankee is to do it for ten, having fewer prejudices to conquer—it was his legal fee, for value received. True, the Christians thought it was "the wages of iniquity," and even the Pharisees—who commonly made the commandment of God of none effect by their traditions—dared not defile the temple with this "price of blood"; but it was honest money. It was as honest a fee as any American commissioner or deputy will ever get for a similar service. How mistaken we are! Judas Iscariot was not a traitor; he was a great patriot; he conquered his "prejudices," performed "a disagreeable duty" as an office of "high morals and high principle"; he kept the "law," and the "Constitution," and did all he could to "save the Union"; nay, he was a saint, "not a whit behind the very chiefest

IV

MYSTIFYING THE MASTER

(1849)

On Tuesday, 4.12.49, when Carlyle was fifty-four, Neuberg reported to his sister the good news that he had seen him feeding the cat and laughing at the pup from Manchester, new arrivals both. Mrs. Carlyle had made these additions to the family without consulting her husband, as she feared he might not want them, and was glad to see him reconcile himself to their company.

Neuberg and she had gone into town this morning together and bought a card-case for a birthday present, and put it into a used envelope. Neuberg stayed to dinner, and was still present when there was a postman's knock at the front door, which the maid had been told to give to "mystify the master." In she came with the present in her hand as if she had just received it from the postman, and handed it to Carlyle, who was lying on the sofa.

He looked at the envelope and said:—"Another letter from Espinasse! I had one from him this morning, and this is his handwriting. What in the world is there in it? H—m, a card-case! That's good, however,—just the thing I wanted. Mine does not fit my new cards, which they always change in size. Quite providential! Ha, ha, ha! Just the thing I wanted. But how in the world did little Espinasse get to know that I wanted a card-case?"

"'Tis your birthday, too," said Mrs. Carlyle.

"Ah, how did he get to know that?"

She made no answer. Carlyle rose from the sofa, and taking a pocket-comb from his pocket, smoothed his wife's hair with it and said,—"Ah, I know now it is your doing. You told Espinasse to send it?"

"I declare upon my honour I did no such thing."

"It is your doing, however," he said. She answered,—"I assure you I never wrote a word to Espinasse about it," and so on. Neuberg tells no more. Maybe he discreetly departed and left them debating.[1]

[1] *Macmillan's Mag.*, Aug., 1884, p. 282, letter from J. Neuberg to his sister, 4. and 5.12.49.

V

SYDNEY DOBELL HAS AN INTERVIEW

(1849)

EARLY in December, 1849, Sydney Dobell came to Carlyle with a letter of introduction from the Rev. George Gilfillan.[1] He was an amiable young man of only twenty-five and married, but already on his travels in search of the health he was never to enjoy. He often told in years to come how he 'was at first somewhat stunned and bewildered by the tremendous eloquence poured forth—the point of which appeared to be to urge him to adopt any handicraft rather than literature as his occupation in life'; but he made an 'appeal to Carlyle's own practice, which was received with the kindliest good humour.' Carlyle had mistaken him for a young man coming to town to live by writing; and changed his tune on learning he was going elsewhere in search of health, and had some 'independent means.'

Reporting on 12.12.49 his 'hour's conversation' to Gilfillan, Mr. Dobell said he found Carlyle 'loveable,' and added,—" If there be divinity in movement, then is Carlyle divine. Body, hands, eyes, lips, eyebrows,—almost cheeks, for even they seemed mutable,—did you ever see such a personification of motion? We had a long talk—he was very kind to me,—and if I had been blindfold and heard it in the street, I could have sworn at once to the speaker. But it made me melancholy to see how hopeless—no affectation of despair, but heartfelt black hopelessness—he is of himself and all mankind. We had a tough argument whether it were better to have learned to make shoes or to have written *Sartor Resartus*. He delighted me at parting with a promise to come" and, in short, visit the Dobells in the country, whenever Mr. Dobell was well enough to stay steadily at home, which never happened.

[1] *Life and Letters of Sydney Dobell*, by E. J., I, pp. 110–13.

VI

THE GOSPEL OF SILENCE, &c.

(1849)

ONE of the reasons why *The Nigger Question* and the *Latter-Day Pamphlets* commanded attention was that Carlyle was known to be as serious as any practical man could be. His visit to the Model Prison in London, for example, described in the second pamphlet, was what everybody would expect before he wrote about it. His inspection about the end of this year, 1849, was as complete as that of a Royal Commission or paid Inspecting Officer would have been, and it was probably about the same time and at the Ashburtons' that he met the third Earl Grey, then Secretary of State for the Colonies, and was as downright as if speaking from the Front Opposition Bench in Parliament,[1] and more sincere.

The topic was emigration. In *Sartor* Carlyle had mocked at Malthus, and ten years ago in *Chartism* shown in detail how easy it would be to organise emigration to Canada and Australia,—'with war-ships rotting idle, which might bridge all oceans. With trained men, Barristers, Clergy, Scholars, in passionate want of work;—with as many Half-pay Officers of both Services, wearing themselves down in wretched tedium, as might lead an emigrant host larger than Xerxes' was!' In *Past and Present* also he had demanded 'a free bridge for emigrants: we should then be on a par with America itself, the most favoured of all lands that have no government.' . . . Nothing had been done, because the Cabinet feared to offend the manufacturers, and the one thing sure about emigration was that it would tend to raise wages. Carlyle declared that "A fair day's wages for a fair day's work" was 'the everlasting right of man.' But the men of money who dominated the Government were not of that opinion, and in Press and Parliament

[1] *Literary Recollections*, by F. Espinasse, pp. 200–03.

scoffed at Carlyle, comparing the overflowing hosts of unemployed to 'the bursting of a Wen.'[2] Even the *Quarterly Review*, a Tory organ, was "little-Englander" then, and derided the notion that the people who were going to America or Australia with 'nothing but the animal craving for food and money . . . can generate a nation.'[2] Carlyle told Earl Grey,—"I would do in a single year all that needs to be done for emigration, tho officialism pronounces it impossible in any number of years." He told Espinasse afterwards that Grey "blushed," which shows he had more conscience than was usual among politicians.

Having said his say about Emigration, Carlyle did not need to go on about it, and Espinasse is curiously mistaken in saying that he 'cooled very considerably about' it. On the contrary, he never missed a chance of doing or saying anything he could to further it,—as will be seen in 1868.[3]

Education was another national need on which Carlyle insisted in *Sartor*, as well as in his later political writings, and Espinasse admits he was 'faithful to the cause of education, tho I heard him once at least speak doubtfully of the value of an extension of education if it (only) enabled the multitude to indulge more freely than before in what he called "Eliza Cookery." Eliza Cook was a popular poetess and editress who advocated "social progress" in the most sentimental, sugary, and flowery style.'

When the Lancashire Public School Association was formed to set up schools in that county, Carlyle wrote to encourage its promoters, and Espinasse, who became its secretary, quotes the letter.—'No man, no generation of men, has a right to pass through this world, and leave his children in a state of ignorance which could have been avoided; and if many generations among us English have already too much done so, it is a sadder case for England now, and the more pressing is the call for this generation of Englishmen. In all times and places it is man's solemn duty whether done or not, and, if in any time or place, I should say it was in Lancashire, in England, in these years that are now passing over us.'

'After great opposition,' reports Espinasse,[1] 'a "great" public meeting, or "demonstration" to further the Association's object was to be held (at Manchester) in the Free

[2] *Quarterly Review*, quoted in *T. Carlyle*, by E. P. Hood, p. 364.
[3] *Conversations with Carlyle*, by Sir C. Gavan Duffy, pp. 233–4, etc.

Trade Hall,'—on 12.12.49, and 'Carlyle was invited to address it. He was evidently not disinclined to come, when he wrote to me asking what I thought of the matter. Probably from over-fastidiousness on his account, I did not think that his appearance on such a stage would be desirable for him. On the other hand, it would have been a clear dereliction of duty on my part to advise him not to come. So I carried out his favourite doctrine of silence, (and) left his letter unanswered,' and so he did not come.

"Why did you not come?" Miss Jewsbury indignantly wrote to Neuberg. "Carlyle behaved very—shabbily I was going to say but I suppose that would be treason—only I cannot understand how a man fully convinced—as he professes to be—of the importance of an object allowing a natural disinclination to trouble to stand in the way of his exerting himself in the least—there never was an occasion on which he might have done so much good with so little trouble."

"Never," moralised poor Espinasse, presumably because he found Carlyle did not praise his practice of silence on this occasion, "never did any man less practise what he preached than Carlyle in this matter of speech and silence." Which is certainly not relevant to the occasion, to say the least. Espinasse was not practising at all the gospel of silence, but shirking a difficulty.

On 1.12.49 Carlyle had written to his mother about the Manchester meeting, saying,—'I really have some notion' of making the speech they want, 'for it might do good, and would be to myself a real relief.'

This confirms the guess of Espinasse that he would have come if encouraged. What Espinasse should have done was to give information only, not advice; and if it became clear that advice was wanted, to mention that he was Secretary. On the other hand, Carlyle was really practising aright the gospel of silence, inasmuch as he seems to have abstained from fault-finding when he discovered what had happened. In short, the gospel of silence is to be silent at the right time, which means and includes tabooing self-praise and smut and every sort of utterance that gives needless pain to another, particularly fault-finding, the besetting sin of teachers by trade,—like Carlyle himself. But there is a time to speak. As Carlyle once noted in his journal, 'Speech is human, silence is divine, yet also brutish and dead: therefore we must learn both arts.' All which had been taught by precept and example by many long ago, including Confucius, five hundred years before Christ, to say nothing of Christ himself, and the best of our saints and sages for the last two thousand years. Carlyle's gospel of silence is too true to be a new discovery.

VII

JAMES DODDS

THE same James Dodds, whom Carlyle had persuaded to stick to the law for a living instead of going into journalism, had come to London in 1846 when he was thirty-three, and had prospered well,—it was a rush of Scottish railway business that had brought him to work as a Parliamentary agent; and he continued to be a frequent caller at Carlyle's till some time in the fifties.[1] He could, and did, boast that 'he had heard from Mr. Carlyle's lips the substance of many of *The Latter-Day Pamphlets* before they were published.'

Before he came to London his spiritual evolution was complete. He never escaped from the cage of the Bible, and after fluttering about a bit, settled on his perch, an evangelical Christian, tho more like an old Scotch Covenanter than a modern Englishman.

At Cheyne Row, as among sensible people in Scotland for many generations, the rule was silence about religion in the presence of believers; and Dodds made many friends there, —John Carlyle and Procter, Craik and Lewes. He became a champion of Mazzini, and a friend and unpaid legal adviser of Leigh Hunt. In short, the prosperous lawyer remembered well the dreams of his youth, and gave his leisure to lecturing and writing at large, doing *Lays of the Covenanters* in answer to Aytoun's *Lays of the Scottish Cavaliers*, both famous then and now forgotten, and lecturing often and well on The Fifty Years' Struggle of the Scottish Covenanters. He made a book of that title out of his lectures, and it ran to many editions; but what is most interesting here is this description of Carlyle at home, which he wrote for the *Dumfries Courier*.

'The tongue has the "sough" of Annandale, an echo of the Solway. A keen, sharp, singing voice, in the genuine

[1] *Memoir of James Dodds*, by the Rev. James Dodds, in the 1880 edition of the *Lays of the Covenanters*, pp. 75–83, 49–55.

Border key, and tranquil and sedate withal, neighbourly and frank, and always in unison with what is uttered. In his conversation he sees the very thing he speaks; it breathes and moves palpable to him, and hence his words form a picture. When you come from him the impression is like having seen a great brilliant panorama, everything has been made visible and naked to your sight; but, more and better far than that, you bear home with you an indelible feeling of love for the man, deep as the heart, long as life. No man has ever inspired more of this personal affection. Not to love Carlyle when you know him is something unnatural; as if we should say we did not love the breeze that fans our cheek, or the vine-tree which has refreshed us both with its leafy shade and its exuberant juices. He abounds himself in love and good works. His life, " not only of books," but as a man amongst his fellows, has been a continual shower of benefits. As to the young men, more especially, to whom he has been the Good Samaritan, pouring oil upon their wounds, and binding up their bruised limbs, and putting them in the way of recovery of health and youthful energy, the number of them can scarcely be told, and will never be known till the great day of account.'

Undoubtedly Dodds would have included himself among such, tho never in " doctrine " a disciple. As his business grew more and his leisure less, his visits became fewer. His friendship became more distant by degrees, but it was never clouded.

VIII

A LIVE PROPHET

According to Espinasse,[1]—'Carlyle's talk astonished all who heard it. Wise or half-wise or unwise, it was always striking, never commonplace. Dialogue too often became monologue. But in the society of two or three friends, he could be calm and reasonable (tho) emphatic, take as well as give, and listen patiently to the expression of opinions opposite to his own. In such a gathering he was most satisfactory, if not most astonishing. He possessed one gift, that of oral narration, in a more remarkable degree than any man of his generation. I have heard of a distinguished dinner-party,' where in short the diners stopped eating 'to listen with rapt attention, while Carlyle gave a very vivid account of John Sobieski's defence of Vienna against the Turks.' Somebody else had started it. This sort of thing goes far to explain the popular verdict on London's after-dinner talkers,—"Carlyle first, and all the rest nowhere."

What prevented Macaulay being named in comparison was the lack of humour, in which Carlyle excelled, and Carlyle's definition of it, as 'a genial sympathy with the under side,' applied to himself. His laughter was never at other people's expense and always without a tinge of malice, or even that miniature malice occasionally called chaff. 'There was no trace in his language or manner,' testified Venables [2] who knew him well, 'of the intolerance in his diary,' which was a private document, and impersonal in its way, like arithmetic. 'Friends or acquaintances,' said Venables,[2] 'had no rebuff or sarcasm to fear. When his equanimity was disturbed by injudicious contradiction or want of tact on the part of others, he took refuge in silence. During an intercourse of many years, I never experienced

[1] *Literary Recollections*, by F. Espinasse, pp. 90, 111, 130–31, 204–210.
[2] *Carlyle in Society and At Home*, by G. S. Venables, *Fortnightly Review*, May, 1883, p. 639.

from Carlyle a single interruption of perfect courtesy and good humour.'

During one of Venables' ' many evening visits ' to Cheyne Row,[2] Carlyle had been as usual declaiming on some interesting subject for a considerable time, when Mrs. Carlyle broke in with a long rigmarole about her coal-scuttle or something of that sort. 'As her animation seemed disproportionate to the subject matter,' reports handsome Venables, with due solemnity, ' I was a little surprised, and Carlyle said in mild remonstrance,—" How can you suppose that Venables will care for your coal-scuttle ? " " I don't suppose," she replied, " that he will care for my coal-scuttle. I don't want him to care for my coal-scuttle. But you have been talking without stopping for two hours, and I am determined to say something myself." ' Whereat 'he laughed.'

For his perfect enjoyment of society, Venables admits [3] that Carlyle ' perhaps ' required to be ' allowed to take more than his share of the conversation.' This was palpable, beyond the need for a ' perhaps,' when he was in the company of juveniles or disciples. His early habits of teaching seemed then to revive, and Espinasse [1] tells us :—

' It seemed a necessity of his nature to be always either speaking or writing. If Carlyle read, it was pencil in hand. The volumes which he borrowed from the London Library might alone furnish a mass of interesting marginalia.' But on scrutiny [4] it appeared that most of Carlyle's pencillings were to indicate dates or localities, or distances or references welcome to any reader in the lack of an index.[5] " Lecky used to say," said Dr. Hagberg Wright, the Librarian,[6] " that when he disagreed with the author, he would draw little asses' ears on the margin," but so far only one such drawing has been discovered,—it was on a German history,[7] —a small pencil drawing of a donkey's head, with exaggerated ears.

' If you came upon him,' continued Espinasse, ' when he was taking his walks, you saw his lips moving and knew that he was muttering to himself. At home he would some-

[3] *Carlyle's Life in London*, by G. S. Venables, *Fortnightly Review*, Nov., 1884, p. 595.
[4] By D. A. W., 11. and 15.6.1925, the library staff kindly helping.
[5] E.g. *Œuvres of Frederick* and *Tempelhof's Geschichte*.
[6] In *Times*, article on 20.5.1925.
[7] Von Raumer's *Frederick the Second*, p. 195.

times, rather than be silent, recite a favourite passage of an English poet, notably Milton's lines ' beginning,[8]—

"Hail, holy Light!
Offspring of Heaven, first-born!"

Once when the talk ran dry, ' he entertained me,' said Espinasse, ' with an account of the evolution of the Arabic numerals, 2, 3, &c. up to 9, by the addition of strokes and curves to the straight line 1.' This may be pleasantly paralleled by what was reported in the nineties at Langholm by John Carlyle,[9] who in 1849 was a boy at Scotsbrig, son of Carlyle's youngest brother James.—' In the evening at Scotsbrig when the talking came to an end, Uncle Tom said :—" Let us be learning something." So I started reading aloud one of his lectures on Heroes, and when I finished he told me that he had noticed that I understood what I was reading.'

Among the best things told by Espinasse [1] were the bits of private advice he received from time to time during the years that followed the loss of his job in the British Museum. He said,—' Carlyle practically aided me to start on my enforced journey into the wilderness. One of his most emphatic warnings was,—" In literature a man can do nothing worth doing until he has killed his vanity."

' As an illustration of literary magnanimity and superiority to personal feeling, he told me at full length an anecdote of Diderot. Visited by one of the out-at-elbows authors, Diderot asked him if he had anything to show of his composition in print or MS. After a good deal of very natural hesitation the visitor produced from his pocket a MS. which turned out to be a lampoon on Diderot himself. Instead of being offended, the generous Diderot looked it over, corrected it, and wrote for it a dedication to the then Duke of Orleans —father of *Egalité* Orleans—who, as it happened, was *dévot*, and therefore anything but friendly to *philosophes* of Diderot's way of thinking. The result was the purchase of the MS. by a bookseller, and twenty-four gold Louis in the pocket of the starveling scribbler.

' More appropriate than warnings against vanity,'—from which Espinasse was sure he was in no danger!—' was an admonition,—" Avoid hypochondria, pride, and gloom:

[8] *Paradise Lost*, Book III, ll. 1–55.
[9] To D. A. W.

they are a waste of faculty." On over-fastidiousness in regard to the literary employment offered to a beginner, he expressed himself forcibly: "A man is an indestructible fragment of the universe, but, if he wishes to live, he must not be nice."

'Of deeper import and more lasting value was the wise advice not to mistake "the shriek of self-love" for the "voice of conscience." And so I sallied forth into the wide world, fortified by Carlyle's oral monitions, who added these written words of encouragement:—"The heart that remained true to itself never yet found this big Universe finally faithless to it."'

By 1849 and 1850 Espinasse was back in London, and was one of several who could say that they had heard by word of mouth the 'substance' of the *Latter-Day Pamphlets* before they were published. Carlyle had advocated and openly rejoiced over the Repeal of the Corn Laws as a respite from violence. He now plainly intimated but refused to rejoice over the democracy impending, foretelling the confusion that inevitably followed anarchy, and pointing to the only road out of it, efficient administration by competent men, while scoffing at the shibboleths of modern 'Society', which seemed to have become 'wholly a bag of wind, ballasted by guineas,' and at the typical contemporary Englishman as a 'wretched mortal, stumbling about in a God's Temple, and thinking it a brutal Cookery-shop!' Never, perhaps, since Jesus was executed for libelling the highest authorities and Chief Priests, and the last inspired prophet of the Hebrews was silenced, never before had a respectable generation with money in its pocket had to endure so much plain-speaking. The incompetence of the governing gentry was the theme of the *Latter-Day Pamphlets*, and not merely actual incompetence, but incurable worthlessness as a sole or main recruiting ground for good governors. 'The vulgarest vulgar, I often find, are not those in ragged coats at this day; but those in fine, superfine, and superfinest;—the more is the pity!' So it was needful to find competent men among the common people. They did not abound in palaces and the houses of the rich,—men from such places had been tried in the balance and found wanting too long,—'poor commonplace creatures, helping themselves along in the way of make-shift from year to year, have no resource but to ensconce themselves in a safe world of habitudes, traditions, avoiding the general daylight of common-sense,' in short, they were hopelessly stupid.

Perhaps the nastiest home-truth Carlyle rubbed in was that the noodles so long in place and power had next to nothing to their credit in history. The *working* people had made the prosperity of the country and the empire. The ruling classes had staggered from blunder to blunder, and from one foolish war into another. Our twenty-three years' war against France (1792–1815) was one long mistake, and a failure in the long run in spite of Waterloo. Its expense in lives and money was the penalty we had to suffer for our national stupidity in enduring an imbecile king and incompetent ministry.

The point of the Pamphlets and of much of Carlyle's talk was the urgent need to get better men, and the danger of delay. Democracy was impending and anarchy in sight. Lord John Russell and Company were as hopeless noodles as any of their predecessors. All witnesses agree about the utter sincerity of Carlyle's distress and almost despair. Talking once to Espinasse of the sure downfall of "great masses of humbug," he ended by saying,—"You may live to see it ; I hope that I shall not."

Such was the spirit in which he admonished his contemporaries,—not seeking to stir strife, but to abate the need for it by manifesting righteousness, like many a good divine in corners where Christianity still survived, dealing faithfully with his people,—the spirit seen best of all in Christ Himself.

The late Keir Hardie, who founded the Labour Party, said that he was inspired by the teaching of Carlyle, and especially by the *Latter-Day Pamphlets*.

IX

HENRY REEVE COMES ATHWART CARLYLE

(1849)

BY the end of 1849 " Society " was feeling safe again, and its tribes of bores and bored agreed to say as little as possible about disturbances. Thus the earnestness of Carlyle in dwelling on social injustice, particularly in Ireland, was resented in all directions. Even Fitzgerald had complained of his " foaming " about it,[1] and even Espinasse [2] thought him " wearisome and monotonous."

On 19.12.49 one of the great men then, Henry Reeve, was making a note in his diary : [3]—" 19th.—Dinner at Procter's, with Harriet Martineau, Carlyle and his wife, Thackeray and Kinglake." They were all old acquaintances. Reeve had met Carlyle in 1832 at William Godwin's, when he was only nineteen years of age and merely a big and handsome nephew of Mrs. Austin. As he was going to Germany he received from Carlyle a letter of introduction to Goethe. In 1837 he had got a well-paid clerkship in the Privy Council Court by the help of his aunt and the favour of Lord Lansdowne, and thus provided for, he was able to devote himself to social intercourse and leader-writing in the *Times*,—his specialty being foreign affairs.

" He was eminently a man of the world," wrote his friend Mr. Lecky. " Probably few men of his time have been so much and so variously consulted. He always spoke with confidence and authority, and his clear, keen-cut, decisive sentences " were delivered with " a certain stateliness of manner which did not so much claim as assume ascendancy." This report of a friend assists us to imagine the scene of 19.12.49, which makes him memorable now. The only other thing to tell about him is that he edited the *Greville Memoirs*.

[1] *Letters of E. Fitzgerald*, 1894, Macmillan, I, p. 239 ; and *Some New Letters of E. F.*, by F. R. Barton, p. 134.
[2] *Literary Recollections*, by F. Espinasse, p. 204.
[3] *Memoirs of Henry Reeve*, I, pp. 216–7, and II, p. 404.

Charles Dickens seems to have been of the party.[4] At any rate, the best account of what happened is what Dickens told to Edmund Yates. The topic was likely to have been politics and most likely Ireland.—" A question of some moment having been started, it was promptly disposed of by a certain pompous gentleman," (Henry Reeve, it may be respectfully whispered,) " who took hold of it in his usual style, made it into a small parcel, and laid it away on the shelf, not to be moved thence any more. After the oracle had delivered himself, there was a dead silence, in the midst of which Carlyle, who had been blankly gazing at the great personage opposite to him, said in a truly absent manner, but perfectly audible,"—let us hope that Harriet Martineau did not need to turn her ear-trumpet to a neighbour to have Carlyle's words repeated, as she would be sure to do if she did not catch them, for this is what he said,—" ' Eh, but you're a poor creature,—a poor, wretched meeserable creature ! ' and then (he) went on with his dinner," concluded Dickens. " Carlyle was so offensive I never made it up with him," wrote Reeve in his diary.

[4] *Edmund Yates, His Recollections and Experiences*, p. 349 ; and for Dickens's friendship with the Procters, Forster's *Charles Dickens*, II, p. 436, and III, p. 7, etc.

X

CARLYLE'S IMITATION OF CHRIST

(1849–50)

EVER since Tuesday, 13.11.49, Carlyle and Neuberg had been busy among the heaps of unpublished MSS. at Cheyne Row, copying and burning, arranging and finishing. What had been "fermenting" in Carlyle "during four years of silence" was now being distilled into fiery waters. The outcry on *The Nigger Question* seems to have frightened editors. Not even the *Times* would take the rest for nothing. But publishers were willing. Chapman proposed a series of pamphlets; and one cold windy Sunday, apparently 30.12.49, he might have been seen walking in the company of Carlyle and John Forster towards his house in the Strand. He had the MS. of the first two *Latter-Day Pamphlets* in his pocket, to come out on the first of February and March next. There were to be two more in April, on the first and fifteenth of the month, and the remaining four on the first days of the months following, May, June, July, and August,—only eight in all, tho twelve were at first intended.

Since the letters of Junius, nothing so sensational in politics had been printed in England, but there was nothing personal or nasty about them. "Carlyle has taken to whisky," grinned fashionable London then; but he only laughed at that.[1] The critics compared the writer to a Hebrew prophet. It might be relevant to quote the Sermon on the Mount in a Law-court to-day. So it may be permissible as it is true to call these pamphlets Carlyle's imitation of Christ.

About Friday, 11.1.50, before the first was published, Neuberg wrote to his sister in Germany, reporting something Carlyle said of the Bible:[2]—"It is a wonderful Book, that. Some years ago I read the four Gospels through, and I wept a great deal over it. It is full of sincerities and everlasting truths. I did not find Christ that pound-of-fresh-butter character, which people have made of him. On the contrary,

[1] David Masson's verbal report to D. A. W.
[2] *Macmillan's Mag.*, Aug., 1884, pp. 283–4.

he is a man with a great deal of anger in him ; but the anger all on the right side. He always has a sharp word to return to the Pharisees. When one who has kept the ten commandments asks him whether that is not enough, he tells him,—' No, leave all thy riches and follow after me.' He goes to the Temple, and becomes indignant at the buyers and sellers there, and upsets their stalls with a kick of his foot, and takes a scourge and drives the money-dealers out of the holy place ! I thought if anybody in our days should go into our Court of Chancery and do the like there, people would give him a different character from that of a pound-of-fresh-butter ! And he was full of pity too. He wept over the holy city : ' Jerusalem, Jerusalem, thou that killest the prophets and stonest them which are sent unto thee, how often would I have gathered thy children together, even as a hen gathereth her chickens under her wings, and ye would not.' ' Daughters of Jerusalem, weep not for me, but for yourselves and your children.'

" Ah, it is a great business. And it is curious too how the Almighty has permitted it to develop itself in the way it has. Those times, too, were very much like our own ; and *there is no telling what may be preparing for us in these present centuries.*"

Next day, Saturday, 12.1.50, Neuberg had another ' very pleasant evening at Carlyle's. Master, Mrs. and the doctor were there,' he wrote to his sister,—' no one else.'

' At tea Madam narrated a strange history,' he said. Then the men went to smoke in the garden. Perhaps Mrs. Carlyle wanted to keep Neuberg for chess. " I am sure," she said, " he can't smoke a pipe." He lit nothing but a cigarette, but he went to the garden.

" Where did she get hold of that ? " enquired the doctor about the strange history. " Oh," mumbled Carlyle, " surely she has been at her book. She keeps a book with all sorts of distracted things in it, to which she goes now and then for spiritual food,"—a roundabout way of saying she collected and read up anecdotes to retail them, a habit commoner then than now.

" Indifference towards high-minded men " being mentioned, Carlyle declared :—" If Jesus Christ were to come to-day, people would not even crucify him. They would ask him to dinner, and hear what he had to say, and make fun of it." Speaking of " the moneyed people," he said to Neuberg :—" Hans Sachs, your Nuremberg shoemaker, sitting with his long white beard under his apple tree, was an infinitely nobler figure than any of the millionaires of our day. People say to me,—'It is very easy for you not to care for money—you have no children to provide for.' And I always think of Luther, poor fellow. He had some £24 a year, and his friends advised him to seek a larger income on account of his children, but he said, 'I see no duty to leave my children money; the Grace of God is better than money.'"

This suggests that, so far as conscious imitation went, or taking example, it was rather to Luther that Carlyle was looking; but Jesus, inspired by sublime 'anger all on the right side,' was the great exemplar of both him and Luther, and in one particular the similarity of the three was remarkable. "I never work better," said Luther,[3] "than when I am inspired by anger. When I am angry, I can write, pray, and preach well, for then my whole temperament is quickened, my understanding sharpened, and all mundane vexations and temptations depart." Which reminds one of the beautiful legend of Jonah, whom the Lord asked,—"Doest thou well to be angry?" And he said,—"I do well." And the answer was approved.

In the way of righteous 'anger all on the right side,' Carlyle was never more Christ-like than in the *Latter-Day Pamphlets*, which were very like what his talk used to be. Yet maybe nothing in them reveals him better than some hurried words he wrote to Gavan Duffy now, 13.2.1850.[4] '. . . The *Nation* does not yield me much that I entirely approve of, except your own articles. . . . Do not let that patriot abuse poor Clarendon and his cigars any more! His lordship is not a crapulous man by any means, or in any sense: he learned to smoke in Spain . . . really the style of that censure is canine, not by any means above the vice-regal phantasm of a government, but below it, and incapable of mending it. Also, don't rejoice over the "Breaking up of the British Empire"; the British Empire is nothing like broken up yet, nor like to be for a thousand years to come, I may prophesy. Nor is it *dis*honourable to you to be an Englishman, but honourable, if you had even been born a Roman or Spartan, withal. Believe me——'. There the paper failed, and he added no more but a few words of greeting.

[3] *Table-talk of Martin Luther*, CCCXIX.
[4] *Conversations with Carlyle*, by Sir C. Gavan Duffy, pp. 152–3.

XI

THE PRESENT TIME

(1850)

THE first *Latter-Day Pamphlet,* 'The Present Time,'—was a plea for the organization of labour as the thing most needful. But instead of pleasing fashionable folk by letting bygones be bygones, Carlyle laid bare the meaning of recent events in a style somewhat like that of Daniel to the King in presence of the Lords of Babylon, without any false pretence of lamentation, saying,—"God hath numbered thy kingdom and finished it. Thou art weighed in the balance, and art found wanting." He used verbally to quote these very words, and emphasize *found,* meaning *found out.*

He told how 'a good country priest' elected Pope had decided to be honest on the throne,—and so in his simplicity started rebellion in Sicily, and that made the French explode.

'Close following which, as if by sympathetic, subterranean electricities, all Europe exploded, and we had the year 1848, one of the most humiliating the European world ever saw. Kings everywhere, and reigning persons, started in sudden horror, and, what was peculiar and notable in this year for the first time, the Kings all made haste to go, as if exclaiming, "Don't kill us; we couldn't help it!" Not one of them turned round, and stood upon his Kingship, as upon a right he could afford to risk his skin upon. Democracy, on this new occasion, finds all Kings *conscious* that they are but Playactors. The miserable mortals, enacting their High Life Below Stairs. They fled precipitately in terror of the treadmill or worse. Such was the history, from Baltic to Mediterranean, in Italy, France, Prussia, Austria, from end to end of Europe, in those March days of 1848. Since the destruction of the old Roman Empire by inroad of the Northern Barbarians, I have known nothing similar.

'And so there remained in Europe no King except the Public Haranguer, haranguing on barrel-head, in leading article; or getting himself aggregated into a National Palaver to harangue. In city after city, street-barricades are piled, and insurrection begins; populace after populace rises, King after King capitulates or absconds; and from end to end of Europe, Democracy has blazed up explosive, much higher, more irresistible and less resisted than ever before. . . .

'This mad state of matters will of course before long allay itself, the ordinary necessities of men's daily existence will have their way. Some temporary remounting of the old machine will probably ensue soon in most countries. But there is now no hope that such arrangements can be permanent. For universal *Democracy* has declared itself as an inevitable fact of the days in which we live. Ever since the grand or *First* French Revolution, that fact has been terribly announced to all the world. Democracy is here, and in England, tho we object to insurrectionary pikes, the tramp of its million feet is on all streets and thoroughfares, the sound of its bewildered, thousandfold voice is in all writings and speakings, in all thinkings and modes and activities of men. . . .

'What is Democracy, this universal revolt of the European populations?' He calls it 'a universal *Bankruptcy of Imposture*,' so that 'we are not permitted to regret' even the anarchy, because 'at all costs it is to be prayed by all men that Shams may cease, especially Sham-Kings.'

Then the argument took a turn as offensive in England as anything Jesus said was in Jerusalem. Instead of flattering his countrymen, for being steady politically in the midst of upheavals, and praising their panacea of a Parliament which other nations were copying, he told how much even their cultivated classes failed to hate shams as they should, and how they supposed there was salvation 'in deliberate long-established lying,' while the Parliaments they were so proud of were preposterous, when taken as a sole recipe for governing nations.

It only made the offence the greater that he was able to appeal to history, and to right principles as plain as the postulates of geometry. No nation had ever subsisted on democracy. Men competent to steer the ship of state could not be selected by universal suffrage. The ancient Republics were aristocratic, not democratic concerns, and even America is only an apparent exception. 'Sure enough, America is a great and a blessed and hopeful phenomenon,' but not a 'Model Republic.' Its 'continents of fertile waste land' had enabled people there to prosper awhile without any real or skilful administration; but they would need it yet,—'long before the waste lands are full.' Then followed a famous expression first heard in his talk with Cobden, who was "an inspired bagman" said Carlyle to 'Dicky Milnes,'[1] and "always praising America to me." It seems best here to stick to what was plainly printed as the talk of 'Smelfungus,' a name for Carlyle himself. Speaking of what our American cousins have done, he said:—"They have doubled their population every twenty years. They have begotten, with a rapidity beyond recorded example, Eighteen Millions of the greatest *bores* ever seen in this world before,—that hitherto is their feat in History!" 'And so we cannot predict the success of Democracy on this side of the Atlantic from their example.'

The leading idea of the Pamphlets appeared thus in the very first, when he was arguing that what men and states have always to do is to discover and comply with 'the Everlasting Laws of Nature.'—

'Unanimity of voting' does nothing by itself. 'Your ship cannot double Cape Horn by its excellent plans of voting. The ship may vote this, and that, above decks and below,—in the most harmonious exquisitely constitutional manner: the ship, to get round Cape Horn, will find a set of conditions already voted for, and fixed with adamantine rigour by the ancient Elemental Powers, who are entirely careless how you vote. If you can ascertain these conditions, and conform to them, you will get round the Cape: if you cannot, you will never get round. Ships accordingly do not use the ballot-box at all; and reject the Phantasm species of Captains: one wishes much some other Entities,—*since all entities lie under the same rigorous set of laws*[2]—could be brought to show as much wisdom, and sense at least of self-preservation, the *first* command of Nature.'

He plainly implied that we had 'a Government tumbling and drifting on the whirlpools and mud-deluges, floating atop in a conspicuous manner, no-whither,—*like the carcase of a drowned ass*.'[2] No wonder Lord John Russell whimpered in the Commons about these pamphlets, calling Carlyle "a clever but whimsical writer."[3]

'Between our Black West Indies and our White Ireland,

[1] *Life of R. M. Milnes, Lord Houghton*, by T. W. Reid, I, p. 436.
[2] Italics added.
[3] *Literary Recollections*, by F. Espinasse, p. 182.

what a world have we made of it, with our fierce Mammon-worships, and our benevolent philanderings, and idle godless nonsenses of one kind and another. Thirty thousand outcast needlewomen (in London) working themselves swiftly to death; three million paupers rotting in forced idleness, these are but items in the sad ledger of despair.'

It is noteworthy how the host of starving needlewomen haunted Carlyle's imagination. In a Christmas number of *Punch* six years ago had been published Thomas Hood's immortal Song of the Shirt.—

> 'With fingers weary and worn,
> With eyelids heavy and red,
> A woman sat, in unwomanly rags,
> Plying her needle and thread—
> Stitch! Stitch! Stitch!
> In poverty, hunger, and dirt,
> And still with a voice of dolorous pitch
> She sang the "Song of the Shirt." . . .'

'When,' demanded Carlyle, 'when shall we have done with all this of British Liberty, Voluntary Principle, Dangers of Centralisation, and the like? It is really getting too bad. For British Liberty, it seems, the people cannot be taught to read. *British Liberty, shuddering to interfere with the rights of capital, takes six or eight millions of money annually to feed the idle labourer whom it dare not employ.*[2] For British Liberty we live over poisonous cess-pools, gully-drains, and detestable abominations; and omnipotent London cannot sweep the dirt out of itself. British Liberty produces—what? Floods of Hansard Debates and apparently little else. . . . We are fast growing one of the most absurd populations the Sun looks down upon.'

As for the English Parliament, it was no longer the effective gathering of ruling men it used to be, and in its altered shape was not likely to 'continue seaworthy' long. The Peers had 'become mere big Capitalists, Railway Directors, gigantic Hucksters, Kings of Scrip, *without* lordly quality or other virtue except cash.' In short, the old methods being 'quite worn out, England must herself again "learn how to live," '—by choosing better leaders, he meant.

There were Captains of Industry and many others fit for command in England, and millions needing to be commanded, and so Carlyle led up to his great conclusion,—the '"Organization of Labour" is the universal vital Problem of the world.'

XII

"BOREAS" AND "AGRIPPINA"

(1850)

THE first Pamphlet was dated 1.2.50, but it was out on 29.1.50, and on 30.1.50 reached the Grange in Hampshire, where Carlyle was spending a few days with the Ashburtons. Delane of the *Times* had been a fellow-guest, and Robert Lowe, the honest albino politician just returned from Australia to make a new career at home, remembered now for the epitaph by "Anon"—the greatest of all poets.—

> 'Here lie the bones of Robert Lowe:
> Where he's gone, I do not know;
> If to the realms of peace and love,
> Farewell to happiness above;
> If to a place of lower level,
> I can't congratulate the Devil.'

Lowe was soon to become a regular leader-writer on the *Times*, and he and Delane appear to have gone back to town together, leaving 'Dicky Milnes' and Carlyle the only guests. 'A pleasant wise kind of night' they and the Ashburtons had, on 30.1.50, able to talk with less reserve than on preceding evenings; and Carlyle's talk was so breezy that the lady archly called him "Boreas," and when they were all returning to town next day together, she and Milnes in the railway carriage were reading the first Pamphlet, and doubtless seeing in it a likeness to the talk of the night before.

On 1.2.50 Carlyle was at work again and as his wife was soon telling her cousin,[1] "very busy with his Pamphlets all the forenoons, and in the evenings generally at Bath House or elsewhere." She herself had a great affliction in February. The "dog-thieves of London" deprived her for some days of the company of her pet dog Nero, over which she lamented so much that Lady Ashburton called her "Agrippina," the mother of Nero, which was not taken amiss.

[1] *J. W. Carlyle: Letters to her Family*, by L. Huxley, p. 339.

XIII

MODEL PRISONS

(1850)

THE second Pamphlet in March was on Model Prisons and can be put into a nutshell. The criminals were being put to school and petted like naughty children instead of being punished. In a matter-of-fact way Carlyle exposed the absurdity of treating them better than honest workers, and his exposure has been so convincing that it takes an effort now to realise how very bold and original he was at the time of writing. The cant of religion in the thing was what he derided most, abhorring it as he did every kind of confusion between right and wrong.—

'Justice, Justice: woe betides us everywhere when, for this reason or for that, we fail to do justice! No beneficence, benevolence, or other virtuous contribution will make good the want. There is but one thing needed for the world; but that one is indispensable. Justice, Justice, in the name of Heaven; give us Justice, and we live; give us only counterfeits of it, or succedanea for it, and we die!

'O this universal syllabub of philanthropic twaddle! My friend, it is very sad, now when Christianity is as good as extinct in all hearts, to meet this ghastly Phantasm of Christianity parading through almost all. The worst, it is written, comes from corruption of the best.'

Carlyle did not shrink from coming into frank collision with the sentimental slush then popular about the wickedness of revenge, which he plainly justified as 'the natural hatred of scoundrels, and the ineradicable tendency to pay them what they have merited: this is intrinsically a correct, and even a divine feeling, in the mind of every man. Only the excess of it is diabolic; the essence is manlike, and even godlike,—a monition sent to poor man by the Maker himself. . . . This same sacred glow of divine wrath,' he insists, is 'the foundation of all Criminal Law, and except upon a basis of even such rigour, inexorable as Destiny and Doom, there is no true pity possible. The pity possible without that basis is cowardly effeminacy, maudlin laxity of heart, grounded on blinkard dimness of head,—contemptible as a drunkard's tears.' Well might the Bishops as well as the politicians feel that Carlyle taught them as one having authority, and not as the scribes! 'One of the saddest sights,' he said, 'is that of poor creatures making and unmaking "Laws"; in whose soul, full of mere vacant hearsay and windy babble, is and was no image of Heaven's Law; whom it never struck that Heaven had a Law, or that the Earth could not have what kind of Law you pleased!'

The most interesting part of the second Pamphlet now is a fragment of autobiography. The scene was in some garden. The Law-dignitary, who was not named, may be left as a problem to the Inns of Court.

'"Really, one of the most difficult questions this we have in these times, What to do with our criminals?" blandly observed a certain Law-dignitary in my hearing once, taking the cigar from his mouth, and pensively smiling over a group of us under the summer beech-tree, as Favonius (the West Wind) carried off the tobacco-smoke; and the group said nothing, only smiled and nodded, answering by new tobacco-clouds. "What to do with our criminals?" asked the official Law-dignitary again, as if entirely at a loss. "I suppose," said one'—Carlyle,—'"the plan would be to treat them according to the real law of the case; to make the Law of England, in respect of them, correspond to the Law of the Universe . . . in a word, try to do justice towards them." "I'll thank you for a definition of Justice?" sneered the official person, in a cheerily scornful and triumphant manner, backed by a laugh which irritated the other.—"Well, I have no pocket-definition of Justice," said he, "to give your Lordship. It has not been quite my trade to look for such a definition; I could rather fancy it had been your Lordship's trade, sitting on your high place this long while. But one thing I can tell you: Justice always *is*, whether we define it or not. Everything done, suffered or proposed, in Parliament or out of it, *is* either just or else unjust; either is accepted by the gods and eternal facts or is rejected by them. Your Lordship and I, with or without definition, do a little know Justice, I will hope; if we don't both know it and do it, we are hourly travelling down towards—Heavens, must I name such a place! That is the place we are bound to, with all our trading-pack, and the small or extensive budgets of human business laid on us; and there, if we *don't know* Justice, we, and all our budgets and Acts of Parliament, shall find lodging when the day is done!" The official person, a polite man otherwise, grinned as he best could, some semblance of a laugh, mirthful as that of an ass eating thistles, and ended in "Hah, oh, ah!"'

None of the Pamphlets made so immediate a hit as this. Within a few years Carlyle's friend Frederick J. Foxton was writing to him:[1]—'I have been amusing myself for some time past in tracing the influence of your writings on current events as I find them exhibited in the *Times* and other periodicals, and I think I may congratulate you that very little of your philosophy falls to the ground, and that few of your prophetic warnings are unfulfilled. The doctrine of your "Model Prisons" is being daily diluted in all newspapers and magazines, and every sound-minded man is gradually awakening to the unspeakable folly and stupidity of our criminal legislation. Reams of "Carlyle and water" are appearing daily in the shape of letters and leaders, and spouted from all platforms.'

[1] *T. Carlyle and T. Spedding*, by A. Carlyle, *Cornhill*, June, 1921, p. 753.

XIV

NOT QUITE ALONE

(1850)

NEUBERG was with Carlyle in January, 1850,[1] when they met " old Samuel Rogers," as London had called him for the last twenty years. He was to be eighty-seven this year, but still was ' stumping about most wonderfully,' according to ' Dicky Milnes.'[2] His pate was as bald as an Alpine peak, the skin all snowy white, and the big blue eyes glittering like ice, while his ' rapid shelf chin ' beneath his pincer lips was punctuating his contemptuous criticism of Macaulay's History. Neuberg was listening, and Carlyle concurring, and Rogers concluded,—" You must set Macaulay right." But Carlyle replied :—" What is the use of speaking about that scandalous period at all ? It is no history that was transacting then. It had better be forgotten very quickly. If your ancestors were hung, what business have you to talk of ropes ? "—a sentiment sure to tickle the sardonic old man.

On 5.2.50, the Tuesday after the first Latter-Day Pamphlet came out, Carlyle went to Hampstead, and sat smoking with Neuberg ' the whole afternoon.—Puff ! puff ! Such clouds ! ' wrote Neuberg next day. ' And between them he poured out lamentations over the wretchedness of human life,' which show how little his thoughts had changed since he wrote *Sartor*. Here is Neuberg's report.—

' " There is a desire in the heart of man which nothing in this life can satisfy. I want everything, and it is best, perhaps, that I should have nothing. If you give me the whole solar system, then I would say, there is the star Sirius, I want that too. Indeed, a man can do very well without happiness. When I go to bed of a night, it matters not whether I have been happy or not during the day ; it matters only whether I have done some useful thing. The

[1] *Macmillan's Mag.*, Aug., 1884, p. 283 ; and see *Rogers and his Contemps.*, by P. W. Clayden.

[2] *R. M. Milnes, Lord Houghton*, by T. Wemyss Reid, I, p. 440.

unhappiness of a man lies around him as so much work to do—so many devils to be subdued, and order and beauty to be created out of it. If a man tells me he is happy, I am inclined to say to him,—' You scoundrel, do you think you were created for nothing but to loll on sofas, and to enjoy yourself in the midst of such a sad reality as this world is ? '

' " I believe the existence of the Gods themselves is a grand infinite sadness," and so on. Puff ! Puff ! I accompanied him home in the evening, and proposed to him to go to Germany with me. He seemed not at all disinclined,' concluded Neuberg, rejoicing over this in his letter to his sister.

Two days later, 7.2.50, Carlyle was writing in his Journal : —' Trying to write my *Latter-Day Pamphlets*, twelve, if I can but get them written at all. No. 1 came out a week ago ; yields me a most confused response. Little save *abuse* hitherto, and the sale reported to be *vigorous*. . . . Among other very poor attacks on it was one in *Fraser* from John Mill. He has neither told me nor reminded me of anything that I did not very well know beforehand. No use in writing that kind of criticism. For some years back Mill, who once volunteered a close constant intimacy for a long time, has volunteered a complete withdrawal of himself ; and now, instead of reverent discipleship, which he aspired to, seems to have taken the function of getting up to contradict whatever I say. Curious enough. But poor Mill's fate in various ways has been very tragic. His misery, when I chance to see him in the street or otherwise (for we never had a word of quarrel), appeals to my pity if any anger was rising. The Pamphlets are all as bad as need be. If I could but get my meaning explained at all, I should care little in what style it was. But my state of health and heart is highly unfavourable.'

The sale continued good, and the outcry did not hurt the sale of his other books.[3] He heeded it little, and his wife was ' much amused,' he said afterwards, ' by the outside pother, and glad to see me getting delivered of my black electricities and consuming fires in that way. Strange letters came to us, during these nine months of pamphleteering ; strange visitors, who had been each wearing himself half-mad on some *one* of the public scandals I was denouncing. She went along with me in everything, *counselling* a

[3] David Masson told D. A. W. he asked T. C. and made sure of this.

little here and there,' and was careless of any consequences of 'this evident *speaking of the truth.*' By not looking at the Press, Carlyle and she escaped being worried by its 'hostility.' 'Neuberg helped me zealously,' concluded Carlyle, 'as volunteer amanuensis, etc., through all this business; but I know not that even he approved it all, or any of it *to the bottom.* In the whole world I had one complete approver; in that, as in other cases, *one*; and it worth all.'

In February, when the reviews were uniting 'in a howl of execration' against the first Pamphlet, and the second was going to press and Carlyle was writing the third, the Aberdeen students set him up as a candidate for their Lord Rectorship against the Duke of Argyll. Carlyle confessed to his brother John that this tickled him, and he added,—"His Grace I suppose stands for the Free Kirk; I for some German neologistic element and Progress of the human mind; and so the poor boys, in their red cloakies, go running about like hens with egg." While Jane was insisting that if elected he would have to go and deliver the usual speech, Carlyle was rightly anticipating that the election would go in favour of "the Lord their God, his Grace." When Espinasse enquired about 'the Rectorship, he said:[4]—"It is nothing in itself, but it is thought to be something here."'

Meanwhile Mrs. Carlyle was complaining[4] to Espinasse, "Nobody comes to the house now but a few followers of mine." Her husband, however, did not doubt of her complete approval, and in the midst of cursing 'idle pauperism, Poor-Law Relief, charitable dole-giving and the rest of it,' he recalled "one of the drollest things that ever came from Dickens." He told how 'on the occasion of Mr. Dombey's second marriage he enters the church in a new blue coat, fawn-coloured pantaloons and lilac waistcoat. Mr. Toots, surveying the scene from the gallery, informs his neighbour and friend The Chicken that this is the bridegroom. The pugilist hoarsely whispers in reply that Mr. Dombey is "as stiff a cove as ever he see, but that it is within the resources of science to double him up, with one blow in the waistcoat." Carlyle boasted that fashionable and complacent as was the Philanthropy of the day, it was within the resources of his science to "double it up,"'—which does not seem so unreasonable now as it seemed at the time.

In discussing some new "improvement" being made in

[4] *Literary Recollections*, by F. Espinasse, pp. 179–83 and 220.

Factory Legislation, Carlyle impatiently said,—" Why can't the operatives make their own bargain with the mill-owners ? " Remembering how he had praised Lord Ashley, ' the Earl of Shaftesbury that was to be, in *Past and Present*,' Espinasse took up the cudgels, and Carlyle at once ' admitted that Factory Legislation was indispensable for the protection of women and children. When I asked him whether he did not think that Lord Ashley was sincere, he would only reply,—" He is not consciously insincere," and added,— " What he is doing will come out in a way which he little expects." '[4]

Another surprise to Espinasse was Carlyle's ' abrupt and chilling reply ' to praise to himself for making German literature known in England. " It only increased the confusion," said he now.[4]

In March, an eighteen-year-old student at a college for Congregational clergy, William Hale White or " Mark Rutherford," wrote to Carlyle as a young man who " owed much to him " to assure him that " there was at least one person who believed in him " ;[5] and received this reply, which he treasured for more than sixty years, and then gave to the Carlyle House Museum.—

' CHELSEA,
' *9th March*, 1850.

' MY GOOD YOUNG FRIEND,—

' I am much obliged by the regard you entertain for me ; and do not blame your enthusiasm, which well enough beseems your young years. If my Books teach you anything, don't mind in the least whether other people believe it or not ; but do you for your own behoof lay it to heart as a real acquisition you have made, more properly, as a real message left with you, which *you* must set about fulfilling, whatever others do ! This is really all the counsel I can give you about what you read in my Books or those of others : *practise* what you learn there ; instantly, and in all ways begin turning the belief into a fact, and continue at that— till you get more and ever more beliefs, with which also do the like. It is idle work otherwise to write Books, or to read them.

' And be not surprised that " people have no sympathy with you " ; that is an accompaniment that will attend you all your days if you mean to lead an earnest life. The " people " could not save you with their " sympathy " if

[5] *Pages from a Journal*, by Mark Rutherford, pp. 2–4.

they had never so much of it to give: a man can and must save himself, with or without their sympathy, as it may chance.

'And may all good be with you, my kind young friend, and a heart stout enough for this adventure you are upon; that is the best "good" of all.

'I remain,

'yours very sincerely,

'T. CARLYLE.'

Next day, Sunday, 10.3.50, Carlyle went to Neuberg's house at Hampstead, and sat smoking with him, and drank 'three glasses of Stein wine.'

'I accompanied him back through the fields,' wrote Neuberg to his sister,[6] 'which pleased him very much and made him quite cheerful,' adding that he said:—"Who knows for how many ages these paths have been trodden? The marks of numberless generations are upon them; far back to the beginning of time, to the beginning of England."

When writing of 'The Odin Religion' afterwards, Neuberg mentioned that one of these paths,—'The road to Henton, across Hampstead Heath, is a piece of the ancient Watling Street. No wonder it makes such a hollow into the sand-rock, considering what travelling there must have been over it!'[7]

We know from Espinasse[4] that Carlyle was reading about this time the works of Andrew Fletcher of Saltoun, M.P. for the Lothians in Scotland's Parliament, and one of the best and wisest men that ever touched politics. But for wholesale bribery by rogues, the Union of 1707 would have been what Fletcher advocated, a federative one, and Scotland would have had what it still suffers from the lack of,—such independence in domestic affairs as every State has in the United States of America, in short—Home Rule.

What is also worth knowing is that Carlyle's views on slavery may have been influenced by Fletcher, and certainly his proposal for Industrial Regiments was practically Fletcher's, and was only a slight development of what had been the law and the intermittent, partial practice of Scotland for nearly a century, from the Reformation till 1660. Then came that Restoration Carlyle detested, which placed in control of Scotland two men of foreign blood, Charles

[6] Letter of 14.3.50, in *Macmillan's Mag.*, Aug., 1884, p. 284.

[7] *Westminster Review*, Oct., 1854, p. 331, footnote.

Stuart and his brother, and a handful of the worst scoundrels in the country.

'If you ever go to the British Museum, here is an enquiry for Mr. Watts and you,' wrote Carlyle to Espinasse, 19.3.50. The reference was to Thomas Watts, a member of the British Museum staff, and for many years useful and obliging to Carlyle in his researches.[8]—'In one of Byron's works, I think the Age of Bronze, at its first appearance about twenty-five years ago, I read, among some bitter abuse of Lord Castlereagh and Company (how Castlereagh had "opened his carotid artery," not cut his throat, "bless their learning," with more of the like sort), a decided eulogy on Peel, B.'s old schoolfellow. Byron testified to this effect:—"There is one man of real talent among them, and I never will believe but *he* one day will see through all that d—d nonsense, and come out of their squad."

'Now I want a copy of these words: they are not given in Murray's late edition of the works; nor perhaps anywhere except in the first or early editions? I am very sure of having read said words about the time I mention. . . .'

It remains a guess that the quotation was verified, and maybe quoted to Peel by Carlyle. All we know for sure is that some weeks later Carlyle mentioned Byron to Peel, who at once began talking kindly of the days of long ago, when "Birron" and he were boys together at school.

Meanwhile the third and fourth Pamphlets, on Downing Street as it was and as it should be, were being put into final shape, and both were published in April.

[8] Unpublished letter, copied in Mr. Gridley's *Cuttings*.

XV

DOWNING STREET

(1850)

THE third Pamphlet began :—' From all corners of the wide British Dominion there rises one complaint against the ineffectuality of what are nicknamed our " red-tape " establishments, our Government Offices, Colonial Office, Foreign Office, and the others, in Downing Street and the neighbourhood.' As for the Colonial Office, its performances were bad and its functions a mystery, while the other offices, Home and Foreign, escaped the same unanimity of cursing only by escaping notice. The Home Office, by ignoring the need to organise labour now, when the starving Irish were crowding in upon us, was ' more deficient and behind the wants of the Age than the Colonial,' while the Foreign Office had made Britain a public nuisance,—a ' Hercules-Harlequin, the Attorney Triumphant, the World's Busybody.' The reference was to the foreign policy of Palmerston, which had at this time disgusted even his colleagues so much that only party loyalty kept him in place. Carlyle's proposals, however, went beyond what any politician had the sense to see was needed. We might have avoided many wars if we had been guided by his advice. He said that Britain had no real interest in continental affairs but trade, and should abolish the whole of ' that industry of protocolling, diplomatising, remonstrating, admonishing, and " having the honour to be." ' The consular service would serve all ordinary purposes ; and if anything was needed that could not be conveniently done through consuls or the post, ' special message-carriers, to be still called Ambassadors, if the name gratified them, could be sent when occasion great enough demanded.'

' For all purposes of a resident ambassador, I hear persons extensively and well acquainted among our foreign embassies at this date declare, That a well-selected *Times* reporter or " own correspondent," ordered to reside in foreign capitals, and keep his eyes open, and (tho sparingly) his pen going, would in reality be much more effective ;—and surely we see well, he would come a good deal cheaper! Considerably cheaper in expense of money; and in expense of falsity and grimacing hypocrisy (of which no human arithmetic can count the ultimate *cost*) incalculably cheaper! If this is the fact, why not treat it as such? . . . There are men now current in political society, men of weight tho also of wit, who have been heard to say, "That there was but one reform for the Foreign Office,—to set a live coal under it." . . .

'What England wants, and will require to have, or sink in nameless anarchies, is not a Reformed Parliament but a Reformed Executive or Sovereign Body of Rulers and Administrators,—some improved method, innumerable improvements in our poor blind methods, of getting hold of these.' Contrary to his custom, Carlyle then took a side, declaring 'Sir Robert Peel the one likely or possible man' to effect a reform; and bluntly telling an open secret of public business being hidden from the people.—'The men that sit in Downing Street, governing us, are not abler men since the Reform Bill than were those before it. Precisely the same respectable men in office; respectably commonplace in faculty,—while the situation is becoming terribly original! Rendering their outlooks, and ours, more ominous every day.'

With the second-sight of genius he explained the character of our 'inefficient' public Offices. The questions sent to them are 'not decided truly and rapidly, but with delays and wrong at last,' and they were occupied with things they should never touch at all. 'Stupidity, Darkness of Mind' was the cause of all our trouble. The Colonial Office in particular was busy upon questions 'almost all of which should have been decided in the Colonies themselves,'—which may serve to remind us that Canada was then the only colony with Home Rule, which it owed to Lord Durham and Charles Buller mainly.

'For empires or for individuals there is but one class of men to be trembled at; the stupid class that cannot see A class of mortals under which as administrators, kings, priests, diplomatists, &c., the interests of mankind in every European country have sunk overloaded, as under universal nightmare.' In short, the men atop were too incompetent to be tolerable any longer. 'Our poor grandfathers, so busy conquering Indias, founding colonies, inventing spinning-jennies, kindling Lancashires, took no thought about the government of all that; left it all to be governed by Lord Fanny and the Hanover succession, or how the gods pleased. And now we the poor grandchildren find that it will not stick together on these terms any longer; that our task is to discover some government for this big world; that the red-tape offices in Downing Street are near the end of their rope.'

Carlyle believed there were good enough men in England and plenty of them, tho not perhaps among the moneyed classes. So he proposed that the reforming prime minister should be free to choose the best heads of departments wherever he could find them, and grant every man so appointed a seat in Parliament as long as he holds the office. In other words, the Government should have 'power to elect a few members to Parliament.'

'Lord Tommy and the Honourable John are not a whit better qualified for Parliamentary duties, to say nothing of Secretary duties, than plain Tom and Jack; they are merely better qualified, as matters stand, for getting admitted to try them. Which state of matters a reforming Premier, much in want of abler men to help him, now proposes *altering*.

'Consider how *many* Toms and Jacks there are to choose from. The aristocratic class from whom members of Parliament can be elected extends only to certain thousands; from these you are to choose your secretary, if a seat in Parliament is the primary condition. But the general population is of twenty-seven millions; from all sections of which you can choose, if the seat in Parliament is not to be primary. Make it a last investiture instead of a first indispensable condition, and the whole British Nation, learned, unlearned, professional, practical, speculative and miscellaneous, is at your disposal! In the lowest broad strata of the population, equally as in the highest and narrowest, are produced men of every kind of genius; *man for man, your chance of genius is as good among the millions as among the units; — and class for class, what must it be!*[1] From all classes, not from certain hundreds now but from several millions, whatsoever man the gods had gifted with intellect and nobleness and power to help his country, could be chosen: O Heavens, *could,*—if not by Ten-pound Constituencies and the force of beer, then by a Reforming Premier with eyes in his head, who I think might do it quite

[1] Italics added.

infinitely better! . . . For,' as he was never weary of urging, 'it is Wisdom alone that can recognise wisdom: Folly or Imbecility never can; and that is the fatalist ban it labours under, dooming it to perpetual failure in all things.'

To 'Democratic friends' he did not fail to point out that his proposal gave effect to the essential truth in 'Democracy,' namely, 'that the able man be chosen, in whatever rank he is found.' Upon the Tories he urged 'What is extremely important too, you could try this method with safety; extension of the suffrage you cannot so try.'

The most Carlylian part of the third Pamphlet was the praise of Robert Burns,—the greatest of our Scottish writers, the best of whose songs and satires surpass anything of the sort in any literature, and are well worthy of the pains required to learn the vernacular words he uses. He was a kind of miracle, like Shakespeare, and a neglected contemporary of 'the meagre Pitt, and his Dundasses and red-tape Phantasms—growing very ghastly now to think of—presided over by a singular Heroic intellect called George the Third,'—the men who were then mismanaging our public business, men without reverence for intellect, feeling no need of it, and with no use for Robert Burns except as a mere exciseman.

It has often been remarked that Carlyle's proposal, to appoint as ministers men not in Parliament, was practised and worked well in the last big war (the Willy-and-Nicky war of 1914–18). It should be continued and extended. No other formal change would do so much to improve the administration of justice among us as to do likewise in appointing judges,—a thing that should be kept out of the hands of politicians as much as possible. Why should we demoralize the legal profession and bribe barristers into politics? Especially by the greatest and most absurd Lottery in the world, that of the English Lord Chancellorship!

The conclusion of the third Pamphlet is that tolerating incompetent governors leads to 'Social Ruin' and Revolution.

XVI

THE NEW DOWNING STREET

(1850)

THE fourth Pamphlet was on The New Downing Street, our Government Offices as they should be. It began by roundly cursing the stupidity of 'Governments in all European countries,' in a way that went to the hearts of journalists, whatever their paymasters made them say.[1] He was a "bonnie curser,"—it was a treat to read him. It was in the manner of Euclid laying down the Postulates that he wrote :—'Intellect *has* to govern in this world ; and will do it, if not in alliance with so-called "Governments" of red tape and routine, then in divine hostility to such, and sometimes alas in diabolic hostility to such ; and in the end, as sure as Heaven is higher than Downing Street, and the Laws of Nature are tougher than red tape, with entire victory over them. If there is one thinking man among the Politicians of England'—*what an if*!—'I consider these things extremely well worth his attention just now.'

Then he explained how in the Middle Ages the old Catholic Church opened a career to 'the noble soul in the lowest stratum of social thraldom,' so that 'the poor neatherd's son, if he were a Noble of Nature, might rise to Priesthood, to High-priesthood, to the top of this world, to be the Papa of Christendom, and Commander of all Kings' ; whereby 'the old Christian society continued healthy, vital, and was strong and heroic.' The thing most needed to make Europe happy now was some method of doing likewise under modern conditions.

'Universal-suffrage Parliaments' were of no use. The men they lifted up to be Premiers and Statesmen were wretched, ugly "Greeks of the Lower Empire," meaning the worst rogues in Europe. 'Dame Dubarry's petticoat,' said he, naming a mistress of Louis XV, 'was a better seine-net for fishing out Premiers' than a universal-suffrage Parliament. 'In England alone of European Countries the

[1] Told D. A. W. by surviving veterans in the nineties.

State yet survives ; and might help itself by better methods. In England heroic wisdom is not yet dead, and quite replaced by attorneyism : the honest beaver faculty yet abounds with us. I said there were many *kings* in England : if these can yet be rallied into strenuous activity, and set to govern England in Downing Street and elsewhere,—then England can be saved from anarchies and universal suffrages . . .' and delivered from the accumulated rubbish of a thousand years.

He mentioned slightly the superstitions surviving in England,—'bishops' nightmares' he called them. He always was partial to the pious, willing to laugh at bishops but scrupulous not to hurt any simple soul that might believe in Christ. But he violently attacked the Whig delusion that 'Government can do nothing but "keep the peace."' He showed that to be absurd by referring to the enormous revenues collected, out of all proportion to such modest duties. 'Our domestic peace,' he wrote, 'as good as keeps itself.' As for foreign affairs he insisted that there was not in sight 'the smallest need' for war. It is tragic to remember that the hideous Crimean War began in the beginning of 1854, and to read in this Pamphlet,—'In spite of editorial prophecy, the Czar of Russia does not disturb our night's rest.'

Time has happily answered the question whether the editors were right and he wrong. It is now agreed that our politicians were befooled by Napoleon the Little, and in their own metaphor, "put their money on the wrong horse" in the Crimean War, protecting the Turks against the Russians.

Proceeding to denounce the existing 'Constituted Anarchy,' Carlyle remarked that the meaning of the popular clamour was, "Find us men skilled,"—'*make* a New Downing Street, fit for the New Era!'

New ministries were needed, he said, a 'Minister of Works, Minister of Justice, Minister of Education,' and so on. The 'idle Seventy-fours' should all be used to carry to the Colonies 'streams of British Industrials' now idle at home, while the scoundrels in the Model Prisons could be employed on a railway across Canada, which had just been proposed.

Perhaps the most remarkable and successful part of this Pamphlet was the argument that the Colonies were important and precious to Britain. Ever since the United

States had succeeded in winning independence, our politicians had been trying to believe that Colonies were a nuisance as well as an expense, and should be encouraged to separate. This seemed to the Tories the sort of thing that loyalty to George the Third required, and to the Whigs it seemed to harmonise with their gospel of Freedom, so that there was practical unanimity. Carlyle intimated that both were wrong. Better governors indeed were wanted, and he suggested to choose them 'not from this or that poor section of the Aristocracy, military, naval, or red-tapist,' but 'wherever there are born kings of men'; and however that might be, he declared that the Nation needed the Colonies and meant to keep them, and would take a terrible revenge on any politician who 'contrived to cut off any real right the big British Empire has in her Colonies.'

Far from denying the need for Home Rule in the Colonies, he quoted with approval the best advice going as to the kind of franchise that would work best; and then he went on to lay down a right principle of the highest value both in politics and in private life:—'In the Colonies, as everywhere else in this world, the vital point is not who decides, but what is decided on! That measures tending really to the best advantage temporal and spiritual of the Colony be adopted, and strenuously put in execution; there lies the grand interest of every good citizen.'

So completely has opinion turned round that it takes an effort, now, for the reader to realise that what is said about the Colonies appeared ridiculous and a novelty in 1850. It seems commonplace to-day, which is all to the good. But on the main point we are still as stupid as our fathers were, and barely beginning to open our eyes to the truth Carlyle told,—that in politics and religion and many other matters, everything in fact but the like of cotton-spinning, our working creeds are superannuated absurdities at the best, and generally fictions as false as nursery fables. He was explicit and merciless. The Pauperism that even politicians thought appalling he called 'our Social Sin grown manifest'; and whereas it was the fashion to talk as if all the sin were on the part of the pauper, Carlyle insisted that 'to make one Pauper there go many sins.' The overflowing pauperism of the period was the result of many evils.—'Not one idle sham lounging about Creation upon false pretences, upon means which he has not earned, upon theories which he does not practise, but yields his share of Pauperism somewhere or other. . . . I perceive this of Pauperism is the corner where we must *begin*. . . . In the course of centuries, I can see the State become what it is bound to be, the keystone of a most real " Organization of Labour,"—and on this Earth a world of some veracity, and some heroism, once more worth living in !'

Here is the ideal to which Carlyle was then looking forward,—it is a dream which may yet be realised as dreams are,—with differences in detail.—' Wise obedience and wise command, I foresee that the regimenting of Pauper Banditti into Soldiers of Industry is but the beginning of this blessed process, which will, in the course of generations, make us all once more a Governed Commonwealth, and *Civitas Dei*,' or Kingdom of God. ' Waste-land Industrials succeeding, other kinds of Industry, as cloth-making, shoemaking, plough-making, spade-making, house-building,—in the end, all kinds of Industry whatsoever, will be found capable of regimenting. Mill-operatives' and others ' will say: " Masters, you must regiment us a little; we will enlist with the State otherwise ! " ' Which meant that they would insist on provision for regular employment, support in sickness and pension at the end of a long term or at a fixed age. ' This will go on, on the one hand, while the State operation goes on, on the other: thus will all masters of workmen be forced to incessantly co-operate with the State and its public Captains; they regimenting in their way, the State in its way, till their fields meet, so to speak, and coalesce, and there be no unregimented worker, or such only as are fit to remain unregimented, any more. O my friends, I clearly perceive this horrible cloaca of Pauperism is the point where we must begin.'

Of course, he was aware of what ' the Clubs and coteries ' were saying about Peel not wanting office any more; but he shared the general hopes, which it is certain now were more reasonable than the clubs supposed. As Mr. Charles Villiers said by and by,—" If there had been a meeting of the people of England between 1846 and 1850, Peel would have been put in the chair."

Of the contemporary *Hansard's Debates* Carlyle said plainly :—' In the sense of God's *truth*, I have heard no true word uttered in Parliament at all.' He admitted that Sir Robert Peel ' stands for his share among others ' of the ' lamentable unveracities uttered in Parliament. But the largest veracity ever *done* in Parliament in our time was of this man's doing,' he declared,—so that the Repeal of the Corn Laws by Peel made him now the hope of England; 'and "the Traitor Peel" can very well afford to let innumerable Ducal Costermongers, Parliamentary Adventurers, and lineal representatives of the Impenitent Thief, say all their say about him, and do all their do.'

A number of dukes can each make a plausible claim to be the original 'sublime goddess-born Ducal Individual' derided as the 'Ducal Costermonger'; but nobody has ever doubted that Disraeli was the only representative of the Impenitent Thief. It may have been the wording of this cautious certificate to Peel's good character which suggested what Wellington had soon to surprise the "Lords" by telling [2] them about Peel to the same effect.

[2] Chapter XXV following.

XVII

STUMP-ORATOR

(1850)

ON Saturday, 27.4.50, Mrs. Carlyle was enjoying a panorama in the forenoon, and on coming home found her husband nearly done with all he had to do on the fifth Pamphlet, Stump-Orator, which was to come out on May-day, 1.5.50. She tactfully waited till he had finished his work and eaten 'a very wholesome dinner.' Then she mentioned an invitation from Neuberg to a party in celebration of the golden wedding of his father and mother. "Surely, surely," was the answer, before she finished speaking.[1]

"25 Church Street, Hampstead," was the scene; but we can only look at them, like figures on the screen, for there was no reporter. At table Neuberg was sitting between Mrs. Carlyle and a Mrs. S., who used to make Mrs. Carlyle uncomfortable by bringing her face too close; but with Neuberg between, "I can stand Mrs. S. quite well,"—we have Mrs. Carlyle's own word for it, to Neuberg.[1]

The Pamphlet appearing in a day or two was very different from what the "genteel public" expected. The "Stump-Orators" most sternly reprobated were not poor "agitators," but the superfine gentlemen who found a road to glory and high place by talking bunkum on platforms and in Parliament. Yet there was no vituperation in the style of Juvenal. Perhaps the writer was mindful how narrowly he had himself missed being one of the Orators by trade, and felt like the looker-on at an execution who said,—"But for the grace of God, there go I." At any rate he did not play the satirist and curse, but explained the species, scientifically.—

'It lies deep in our habits, confirmed by all manner of educational and other arrangements for several centuries back, to consider human talent as best of all evincing itself by the faculty of eloquent speech. . . . Our earliest schoolmasters teach us spelling and pronouncing; rhetorics, logics

[1] Unpublished letters from Mrs. Carlyle to J. Neuberg.

follow. And onward to the highest university, it is still intrinsically grammar, . . . and society at large confirms with all its literary gazettes, parliamentary eloquences, the grand lesson we had. The talent that can say nothing for itself, what is it ? Nothing ; or a thing that can do mere drudgeries, and at best make money.

'All this' Carlyle declared 'astonishing,' and contradicted, maintaining :—'*First*, that excellent speech never was the chief test of human faculty. *Secondly*, that really excellent speech—the Bible and some other books' for example—'is apt to get confounded with sham-excellent, the very worst of human things. *Third*, that in these times, and for several generations back, there has been no really excellent speech at all, but sham-excellent merely.' He bluntly alleged 'a general insincerity of mind for several generations,' and explained how in the old ages, when Universities and Schools were first instituted, this function of the schoolmaster, to teach mere grammar, was the natural one, inasmuch as the priests and the nobles as well as the working men were learning their business mainly by apprenticeship.

So it should be still, he declared. 'The human creature needs first of all to be educated not that he may speak, but that he may *have something to say*. Eloquent unperformed speech, in Parliament or elsewhere, is horrible ! The art of speech is noble' only when 'considered as the last finish of education.' What had misled our schoolmasters was that 'dextrous talk' was the way to rise, especially in Law and Politics and the Church. 'Such a method as this, by trial of talk, for filling chief offices in Church and State, was perhaps never heard of before,' and was simply ridiculous. 'In the learned professions as in the unlearned, and in human things throughout, in every place and in every time, the true function of intellect is *not* that of talking, but of understanding and discerning with a view to performing !'

Most of 'our gifted souls,' Carlyle surmised, took to the 'mute Industrialisms,' turning 'human intelligence into the beaver sort' and achieving 'accumulation of capital' in abundance ; but 'if the gifted soul be not of taciturn nature, and aspire to sensible utterance, . . . and is not rich enough for Parliament' and shies at the Law and the Church, the only outlet for him is that of 'Literature, trying to write Books. . . . A crowded portal this of Literature, accordingly !' In short, the one method of rising in modern

England was to 'talk well with pen or tongue.' It was as if Chaos had broken loose, and 'Society become wholly a bag of wind ballasted by guineas.'

The result was that our governing men were good for nothing or worse. 'Unwise talk is matchless in unwisdom. Unwise work, if it persist, is everywhere struggling towards correction, for it is still in contact with Nature: not so with unwise talk, which addresses itself to the universal suffrages; and can find harbour there till all the suffrages are bankrupt.' On this point Carlyle's friend Thomas Spedding seems to have joined issue. His letter to Carlyle has been lost, but in the reply which remains [2] it is written:—'Folly *done* is a small matter; and instantly finds its correction. Once *speak* your folly, it is like sticking a lighted torch into piles of bituminous combustibility which lay harmless otherwise.' In the Pamphlet he went on.—

Not even in Parliament, 'the Talking Apparatus, is the essential function, by any means, talk. Not to speak your opinion well, but to have a good and just opinion worth speaking,—for every Parliament, as for every man, this latter is the point. Have a false opinion, (and) the better you *tell* it, the worse it will be. Everywhere your one salvation is, That you can discern and follow what the law of the case before you is, what the appointment of the Maker in regard to it has been. Get this out of one man, you are saved; fail to get this, you are lost.'

Then he touched a vital point in saying,—'The Age that admires talk so much can have little discernment for inarticulate work, or for anything that is deep and genuine.' The result is that what the Chinese call the right sort of man, the well-doer, is little noticed. 'Nobody can recognise him till once he get some public stamp of authenticity.' So men of natural ability are conspicuous by their absence in public business; and another thing that Carlyle dwells on is that Parliament makes the men in it rather worse than better. —'For it is not the function of any to wag the tongue of him and make it appear that he has done work; but to wag some other organs and to do work. The human creature who has once given way to satisfying himself with "appearances," the moral life of such human creature is rapidly bleeding out of him. By and by you will have a dead

[2] *T. Carlyle and T. Spedding*, by A. Carlyle, *Cornhill Mag.*, June, 1921, pp. 753–4.

parliamentary bagpipe, and your living man fled away without return!

'Such parliamentary bagpipes I myself have heard play tunes, much to the satisfaction of the people. Every tune lies within their compass; and their mind is ready as a hurdy-gurdy on turning of the handle: "My Lords, this question now before the house——". . . . While the galleries were all applausive of heart and the Fourth Estate looked enlightened—I have sat with reflections too ghastly to be uttered. A poor human creature and learned friend, once possessed of many fine gifts, possessed of intellect, veracity, and manful conviction on a variety of objects, he has now lost all that;—converted all that into a glistering phosphorescence which can show itself on the outside; while within, all is dead, chaotic, dark; a painted sepulchre full of dead men's bones! Discernment, knowledge, intellect, in the human sense of the words, this man has now none. His opinion you do not ask on any matter; on the *matter* he has no opinion, judgment or insight; only on what may be said about the matter, how it may be argued of, what tune may be played upon it to enlighten the eyes of the Fourth Estate.'

It is a guess that Carlyle had in his mind's eye here the Law-dignitary mentioned in *Model Prisons;* but his Lordship never claimed the "immortality" he might have won, if he had boasted of having suggested to Carlyle the phrase 'parliamentary bagpipes.' It soon was current in Parliament itself. Ruskin applied it to Gladstone; and members applied it to each other much oftener than appears in *Hansard*. So many voluble politicians have been so described in the fifties and sixties and later that looking at the phrase is like looking at a kaleidoscope,—*parliamentary bagpipes*. "Parliamentary bagpipes,"—it sounds like a summary of much of our history.

Carlyle insisted that '*all* manner of things and relations of things, *spiritual equally with material*,[3] all manner of qualities, entities, existences whatsoever, in this strange visible and invisible Universe, are equally inflexible of nature; that they will, one and all, with precisely the same obstinacy, continue to obey their own law, not our law; even as sulphuric acid declines to become sweet milk, though you vote so to the end of the world. Will Nature change, or sulphuric acid become sweet milk, for the noise of vociferous blockheads? Surely not.'

[3] Italics added.

The gist of much of this Pamphlet is old Stoicism up to date, recalling a maxim he was always fond of,—" The Soul of the World is just." The conclusion gives well the effect of hundreds, perhaps thousands of letters, which in the course of his long life Carlyle wrote to young men in a moral mist, who applied to him for advice.—

'Truly it ought to become better known what ruin to all nobleness and fruitfulness and blessedness in the genius of a poor mortal you generally bring about by ordering him to speak, to do all things with a view to their being seen! Few good and fruitful things ever were done on those terms. . . .

'Be not a Public Orator, thou brave young British man, thou that art now growing to be something: not a Stump-Orator, if thou canst help it. Appeal not to the vulgar, with its long ears and its seats in the Cabinet; not by spoken words to the vulgar; *hate* the profane vulgar, and bid it begone. Appeal by silent work, by silent suffering if there be no work, to the gods, who have nobler than seats in the Cabinet for thee! Talent for Literature, thou hast such a talent? Believe it not, be slow to believe it! To speak, or to write, Nature did not peremptorily order thee; but to work, she did. . . . There where thou art, work, work; whatsoever thy hand findeth to do, do it,—with the hand of a man, not of a phantasm; be that thy unnoticed blessedness and exceeding great reward. Thy words, let them be few, and well-ordered. . . .

'Brave young friend, dear to me, and *known* too in a sense, tho never seen nor to be seen by me,—you are, what I am not, in the happy case to learn to *be* something and to *do* something, instead of eloquently talking about what has been and was done and may be! The old are what they are, and will not alter; our hope is in you. England's hope, and the World's, is that there may once more be millions such, instead of units as now. *Macte; i fausto pede.*' (Go, and good luck go with you!) 'And may future generations, acquainted again with the silences, and once more cognisant of what is noble and faithful and divine, look back on *us* with pity and incredulous astonishment!'

Which was all utterly modest and sincere. Even the Latin tag from Horace was like him,—there was a touch of Scott's Dominie Sampson in the live prophet at Cheyne Row. Besides, it may serve to remind us that he had to write for the educated classes in England as they were then, and to them such a quotation would be familiar,—they were only just desisting from using such tags in Parliament.

It may be added that Carlyle had had to discover slowly for himself how public speaking tends to be either commonplace or false. His early training had misled him. He had been brought up to revere the pulpit, and his teachers intended to fit him to preach in it. At college he had learned to listen patiently to lectures. His own success as a lecturer would incline him to think well of eloquence; but he had come to see, and did not shrink from telling, the truth that the plain Englishman's prejudice against oratory was right, and respect for it wrong. 'Loose tongues,' as he wrote in this Pamphlet, 'are akin to lying ones; are insincere at the best, and go rattling with little meaning.'

This is inevitable. The bigger the crowd of listeners, the less can be taken for granted by whoever has to speak to them. That is why oratory is trashy. Thus the Christian and the Chinese Gospels, and all the best books in the world, reveal the truth as it can be quietly written or spoken to a few; and even the Sermon on the Mount, a composition like Plato's Dialogues and not a report, does not even purport to be what we mean by a "sermon," but a record of what Christ said quietly when, to avoid the multitudes, "he went up into a mountain, and His disciples came unto Him." Where is there any great speech or sermon successfully spoken and worth reading now? In any language, time or country? Echo answers,—where? The day is coming when this shall be as much a commonplace in Europe as in Asia, and the admiration of mere eloquence appear a weakness of adolescence. Yet on Mayday, 1850, it was a novelty in our Literature.

XVIII

IN THE MERRY MONTH OF MAY

(1850)

'ON a bright May morning' after *Stump-Orator* appeared, Carlyle and his wife took the train to Richmond, and then the omnibus to the commons, and strolled about together 'among the trees and the gorse.' They had biscuits with them, and cigars. He was always hankering for a house in the country, and this sort of thing was her way of emphasizing,—" You can get as much of the country as you need without leaving Chelsea."

In the middle of the month he was dining at Peel's " to meet Prescott," whom he heeded little, but he was glad to meet again Sir Robert Peel himself. He was ushered into the big drawing-room and picture gallery at Whitehall Gardens, overlooking the Thames and Westminster Bridge and the new Houses of Parliament still unfinished. The architect Barry, who was building them, was one of the guests to-night, and seemed to Carlyle " not such a fool as his pepper-box architecture would have led one to guess." On arrival Carlyle found Peel in talk with old Cubitt, a builder and architect who had once been a working carpenter, a " hoary, modest, sensible-looking man." The talk went on about the new buildings, Sir Robert telling of architects' perplexities regarding acoustics. People walked round looking at the pictures, till they all sat down to a sumptuous but tiresome dinner. No ladies were there ; but a son of Peel was at each end of the table. Peel sat in the middle, opposite Carlyle, with Lord Mahon on his left and an ambassador on his right.

When it was over and most of the guests departed, Peel took the rest upstairs and showed them his treasures of autographs,—Mirabeau and Dr. Johnson, Byron and Scott, to say nothing of Kings and officials.

When at last he dismissed them, the Bishop of Oxford, " Soapy Sam," insisted on taking Carlyle home in his carriage, to the surprise of some. They were old acquaintances, having met first in 1839 at Guy's Hospital,[1] and might have been seen riding together in London. " Sam is a very clever fellow," said Carlyle once of the eloquent bishop. " I do not hate him near as much as I fear I ought to do." Carlyle is " an eminently religious man," said the bishop, as if excusing himself.

A few days after dining at Peel's, Carlyle was on his way to make the usual after-dinner call, and met Sir Robert in the Horseguards' building, and saluted him. Peel returned the salute, came forward smiling, and shook hands with a cordial—" How are you ? "

Soon afterwards they met again at the dinner-table of the Ashburtons, and became better acquainted. Carlyle thought Peel ' a real statesman. He was fresh and hearty, with delicate, gentle, yet frank manners ; a kindly man. His reserve as to all great or public matters sits him quite naturally and enhances your respect. A warm sense of fun, really of genuine broad drollery, looks through him ; the hopefullest feature I could clearly see. He talked to us readily, on slight hint from me, about Byron (Birron he called him) and their old schooldays ; kindly reminiscences, agreeable to hear at first hand, tho nothing new in them.' Carlyle began to hope there might still be ' some valuable reform work ' in Peel, in spite of his ' conservatism and even officiality of view. He seemed happy and humane and hopeful, still strong and fresh to look upon,' and assuredly he was the only politician then alive in England in whom Carlyle had the ' smallest hope.'

[1] *Life of Bishop Wilberforce*, by A. R. Ashwell, I, p. 142.

XIX

CURSING KING CHARLES

(1850)

ON 31.5.50 Carlyle wrote to his friend Thomas Spedding at Keswick,[1] replying to a recent letter which has not been kept; but from the reply it appears that Spedding had quoted the ancient saying which Oxenstiern, the Chancellor of Sweden, had used in 1648 in talking to his son,—"Don't you know, my son, with how little wisdom the world is governed?"

'Oxenstiern,' wrote Carlyle, 'himself a supremely wise man, had no doubt seen with continual sorrow and protest how far reality fell short of the ideal pattern, in his time; as unluckily it does in all times. The peculiarity of certain times is that they *lose the very Ideal,* and consider it moonshine or a dream of the speculative mind; and wise men, like T.S., express themselves content with a stuffed sack for chief governor, and declare that he and a street constable will do! These latter seem to me very peculiar and alarming times—different from any that Oxenstiern ever dreamt of; and, indeed, unexampled under the sun, except in England since the "Nell-Gwynn Defender of the Faith" made out his "glorious Restoration" to these parts; certainly one of the damnablest cargoes that ever arrived here. Said extraordinary "Defender" (O God, Almighty Maker, how can any of us *laugh* at such a thing!) has introduced *new* products and manifold elements not dreamt of in English or human history before. To refrain from bursting into profane swearing (which, perhaps, is *sacred* swearing), I hurry on and say only, *Hell's Fuel,* so far as I understand it, is, was, and always will be, precisely such *un*ideal practices and ages as those introduced by said extraordinary "Defender." As if an age should say to

[1] *T. Carlyle and T. Spedding,* by A. Carlyle, *Cornhill,* June, 1921, pp. 753–5.

itself, " Sin against God's Laws was always prevalent: let us give up the notion of anything else but sinning against them." '

To explain such " sacred swearing " it may be added that Charles Stuart II was really worse than our histories show, —he was an utter liar and evil-doer.

XX

PARLIAMENTS

(1850)

THE sixth Pamphlet, dated 1.6.50, is called *Parliaments*, and begins by insisting again that his main object was,—to show that our only method to avert the open Anarchy impending was in reforming Downing Street rather than Parliament. He declared such anarchy 'the blackest of terrestrial curses' and 'the Apotheosis of Attorneyism'; and by clear implication compared the Premier, Lord John Russell, to a foolish Captain trying to navigate his ship round Cape Horn 'by his old Whig and other charts of the British Channel.' Then followed 'a few considerations upon Parliaments generally,'—some pages esteemed among the best in our Literature on Parliaments, worth a hogshead of Hallam's and De Lolme's.

'Parliament was at first a most simple Assemblage. Red William, or whoever' else was King, in short, would 'assemble all his working sub-kings about him . . . for a fortnight's space, oftenest about Christmas time,' and 'in earnest conference all morning, in freer talk over Christmas cheer all evening, in some big royal Hall of Westminster, Winchester or wherever it might be, with log fires, huge rounds of roast and boiled, not lacking malmsey and other generous liquor, they took counsel concerning the arduous matters of the kingdom; debating everything, as Tacitus describes the Ancient Germans to have done, two times: once sober, and once what he calls "drunk,"—not dead-drunk, but jolly round their big table;—that so both sides of the matter might be seen; and, midway between rash hope and unreasonable apprehension, the true decision might be hit. To this hour, no public matter can be settled in England till it have been dined upon.'

There was no other way then of 'making a law, or of getting one executed when made, except by even such a General Consult in one form or another. Naturally there established themselves modes of proceeding: such methods, with trials of ever new methods accumulating, getting sifted, rejected, adopted, and committed to record,—the vast elaboration, now called Law of Parliament, grew to be what we see.

'So likewise in the time of the Edwards, when Parliament gradually split itself into Two Houses, . . . nothing could be more natural down to the Century of Charles First, when being constrained by unforeseen necessity to do so, it took suddenly, like water at the boiling-point, a quite immense development of function. This Long Parliament, the first of such Assemblages, declared that it was Sovereign in the Nation, and more royal than any King, (and so) has set a flaming pattern to all the world, which now after centuries all the world is fruitlessly bent to emulate. This Long Parliament is definable as the Acme of Parliaments: the Father, this, of all Parliaments that have since been.

'But what I had to remark of this Long Parliament and its English predecessors is their veracity of purpose. Supplies did, in some way, need to be granted; grievances, such as never fail, did in some way need to be stated and redressed. The silent Peoples had their *Parliamentum*; and spake by it to their Kings who governed them. In all human Government, wherever a man will attempt to govern men, this is a function necessary as the breath of life. The old Parliaments came upon indispensable work; and were in earnest. No conclave of railway directors could be more intent upon business.'

Modern Parliaments, however, are living in 'changed times.' The Free Press has superseded them now and for ever in their function of articulating grievances, so that 'not the discussion of questions, only the voting of them, can veritably go on in St. Stephen's now. The honourable gentleman is oftenest very wearisome . . . his and his Constituency's *Aye* or *No* is all we want.'

Seventy-six years have passed since this appeared, and members of Parliament have not all learned it yet. The other great change, to which Carlyle drew attention and which also has not yet been sufficiently heeded, is that the Parliament is no longer the adviser to the King, it is itself the King or Government,—'a National Palaver recognised as Sovereign, a solemn Convocation of all the Stump-Orators in the Nation to come and govern us.' The chronic failure of even the 'British Parliament' to work well as a

'Sovereign Ruler' points to a 'sad conclusion' from 'all experience,'—'that Parliaments, admirable as advising bodies, and likely to be in future universally useful in that capacity, are, as Ruling and Sovereign Bodies, not useful, but useless or worse.'

In explaining this Carlyle wrote :—'Consider, in fact, a body of Six-hundred and fifty-eight miscellaneous persons set to consult about "business," with Twenty-seven millions mostly fools assiduously listening to them, and checking and criticising them :—was there ever since the world began, will there ever be till the world end, any "business" accomplished under these circumstances? . . . We may take it as a fact, That no Sovereign Ruler with six-hundred and fifty-eight heads, set to rule twenty-seven millions, by continually talking in the hearing of them all, can for the life of it make a good figure in that vocation; but must by nature make a bad figure, and ever a worse and worse.'

Then he recurred to the facts of history. The Long Parliament at London, and the National Convention in Paris, had both done 'the work of sovereignty with some effect' in revolutionary times; but neither was typical of the peaceful days we should all prefer. Both had been in earnest. The Long Parliament tolerated no reporters, and the Convention used what might now be described as a Guillotine Closure, and in both cases the issues raised were referred to a decision by violence. Thus in England the Long Parliament ran down to a 'Rump,' and was mastered by Oliver Cromwell; and Carlyle reminded his readers of how in like manner the Convention had to bow to its 'Committee of *Salut Publique*, consisting of Twelve, of Nine, or even properly of Three; in whose hands lay all sovereign-business, and the whole terrible task of ascertaining what was to be done.'

He clearly implied but nowhere paused to say plainly,—rather took it for granted as self-evident,—that the only thing in the executive line which a Parliament could do well or should try was to select a Premier, and leave him a free hand to organise aright our administration, now palpably breaking down in all directions. What seemed most urgent was to insist on the absurdity of the delusion, then far more prevalent than it is to-day anywhere, except perhaps in America, that men could make whatever "laws" they liked.—

'Practically men have come to imagine that the Laws of

this Universe, like the laws of constitutional countries, are decided by voting. It is an idle fancy. The Laws of this Universe are *not* changeable by voting! Neither properly are the Laws of any land. Voting is a method we have agreed upon for settling temporary discrepancies of opinion: a good temporary method, which does settle the discrepancy for the moment. Nay, if the votings were sincere and loyal, we might have some chance withal of being *right* as to the question, and of settling it blessedly for ever;—tho again, if the votings are insincere, selfish, . . . we have the sad chance of being *wrong*, and so settling it under curses, to be fearfully unsettled again!

'A series of votings with three-times-three readings, and royal assents as many as you like, cannot make a law the thing which *is* no law.' (Which means, cannot make any law duly passed and binding in a law-court a real Law in harmony with Nature and binding upon consciences.) In short 'the pretended "law" will abrogate itself one day.

'Eternal Law is silently present, everywhere and everywhen. By Law the planets gyrate in their orbits;—by some approach to Law the Street-Cabs ply in their thoroughfares.'

In explaining the need there would always be for even the 'New Downing Street' to know what people wanted and felt, Carlyle articulated a democratic sentiment worth mention when he said, that the most foolish man alive knows *something* better than the wisest; but Bismarck himself could not have been more scornful of 'the fool's vote' in considering 'what it is wise to do,' and so completely had Carlyle made up his own mind that he plainly wrote,—'If there can be no reform of Downing Street, I care not much for the reform of Parliament.' Perhaps there is not even in *Sartor* so much self-revelation as in the concluding pages of this Pamphlet.—

'Slave or free is settled in Heaven for a man. . . . Slaves are in a tremendous majority everywhere; and the voting of them—not to be got rid of just yet—is a nuisance in proportion. . . .

'The free man is he who is *loyal* to the Laws of this Universe; who in his heart sees and knows, across all contradictions, that injustice *cannot* befall him here. The first symptom of such a man is not that he resists and rebels, but that he obeys. As poor Henry Marten wrote in Chepstow Castle long ago,

> " Reader, if thou an oft-told tale wilt trust,
> Thou'lt gladly do and suffer what thou must."

Gladly; he that will go gladly to his labour and his suffering, it is to him alone that the Upper Powers are favourable, and the Field of Time will yield fruit. " An oft-told tale," friend Harry; all the noble of this world have known it, and in various dialects have striven to let us know it! The essence of all " religion " that was and that will be, is to make men *free*. Who is he that, in this Life-pilgrimage, will consecrate himself at all hazards to obey God and God's servants, and to disobey the Devil and his? With pious valour this free man walks through the roaring tumults, invincibly the way whither he is bound. . . . A man well worth consulting. . . .

'I would recommend your Lordship to attack straightway, by the *Industrial Regiments* or better otherwise, that huge Irish and British Pauper Question, which is evidently the father of questions for us, the *lowest* level in our " universal stygian quagmire "; and to try whether—without ballot-box—there are no " Kings " discoverable in England who would rally round you. And to be swift about it; for the time presses,—and if your Lordship is not ready, I think the ballot-boxes and the six points are fast getting ready.'

XXI

HUDSON'S STATUE, &c.

(1850)

An interesting trifle was a letter dated 28.6.1850 from Carlyle to Lord Sandwich, the father of Mrs. Baring, Lady Ashburton. It was to tell him, apparently in reply to a question, that the first Earl of Sandwich, "Sea-General Montagu," had been one of the Ironside Captains, and was the same Montagu who is mentioned in the Squire Letters.[1]

The work of June was finishing the seventh Pamphlet, Hudson's Statue, for publication on 1.7.50. This was the same Hudson about whom Carlyle had been reading in May, 1849,—the "Railway King" of the forties. £25,000 subscribed for a statue in his honour was then being returned to the subscribers, because he had been detected in cooking accounts and paying dividends out of capital. His exposure brought what Carlyle called 'the universal Hudson *ragnarök*, or "twilight of the gods,"' when it had become 'too clear no statue or cast-metal image of that Incarnation of the English Vishnu will ever be molten now! Why was it not set up; that the whole world might see . . . the enduring Brass Portrait and Express Image of King Hudson, as he receives the grandees of this country at his levees or soirees or couchees? . . . Why was not the Hudson Memorial completed? As Moses lifted up the Brazen Serpent in the wilderness, why was not Hudson's Statue lifted up? It might have done us good.'

Carlyle dwelt on the unusual sincerity of his adorers—'Undoubtedly there were two motives mixed, but both of them sincere,—as often happens in worship. "Transcendent admiration" is the origin of sacrifice; but also the hope of profit joins itself. If by sacrificing a goat, or the like trifle, to Supreme Jove, you can get Jove's favour, will not that be a good investment?'

[1] See note to Squire Letter XII in Appendix to the *Ls. and Ss. of O. Cromwell.* The Carlyle letter quoted seems to be unpublished, and is in the Advocates' Library, Edinburgh (May, 1925).

Then he derided our fashion of letting idle busybodies set up any statues in any way they liked. A lady, who was taken round London by him in a carriage in his old age, was fond of telling[2] how he dwelt upon the absurdity of ignoring the fact of our climate being moist, and setting up statues in the open air, unsheltered. But the main point of what he wrote now was our moral obtuseness,—making 'Supreme Hero and Supreme Scoundrel nearly indistinguishable. . . . Ugly columns and images are a real evil. They preach ugliness and have a bad effect. They sanction and consecrate artistic botching, pretentious futility, and the horrible doctrine that this Universe is a Cockney Nightmare. . . .

'To me this populace of British Statues rises aloft over the Chaos of our affairs like the living symbol and consummate flower of said Chaos. Perhaps as strange a Pantheon of brass gods as was ever got together in this world. They stand there, poor wretches, gradually rusting in the sooty rain; black and dismal,—when one thinks of them in some haggard mood of the imagination,—like a set of grisly undertakers come to bury the dead spiritualisms of mankind.'

In every department as well as politics, we seemed to shut our eyes to 'Nature and Fact,' and agree to settle everything by 'the account of heads,' mistaking 'the inmost meaning' of this Universe. 'The real "religion"' of a man is 'his *practical Hero-worship*,' and '"Property" is our God at present.' Thus lawyers are 'our Pontiffs, the highest Priests we have,' with 'an immense power among us,' because their business is with "Property"; while the Christian clergy, 'poor devils, shamming and endeavouring not to sham,' are worshipping a God like Mumbo-jumbo, masquerading in fantastic headgear, with nothing inside their heads but a tissue of 'incoherent incredibilities.'—It is easy to guess where Tennyson learned to make hymns to "Property, Property, Property."

[2] To D. A. W.

XXII

A PRIVATE HARANGUE

(1850)

MANY histories of what Carlyle used to say to Globe-trotters confirm the guess, that a passage in the seventh Pamphlet is as good a report as could have been made in shorthand, of a typical harangue in his house at Cheyne Row.

'Jefferson Brick, the American Editor, twitted me with the multifarious patented anomalies of overgrown worthless Dukes, Bishops of Durham &c., which poor English Society at present labours under, and is made a solecism by. To which what answer could I make, except, that surely our patented anomalies were some of them extremely ugly, and yet alas, that they were not the ugliest!'

Then said Carlyle.—" Have not you also overgrown anomalous *Dukes* after a sort, appointed *not* by patent? Overgrown Monsters of Wealth, namely; who have made money by dealing in cotton, dealing in bacon, jobbing scrip, digging metal in California; who are become glittering man-mountains filled with gold and preciosities; revered by the surrounding flunkies; invested with the *real* powers of sovereignty; and placidly admitted by all men, as if Nature and Heaven had so appointed it, to be in a sense godlike, to be royal, and fit to shine in the firmament, tho their real worth is—what? Brick, do you know where human creatures reach the supreme of ugliness in Idols? It were hard to know! We can say only, All Idols have to tumble, and the hugest of them with the heaviest fall: that is our chief comfort, in America as here.

" The Idol of Somnauth, a mere mass of coarse crockery not worth five shillings of anybody's money, sat like a great staring god, with two diamonds for eyes; worshipped by the neighbouring black populations; a terror and divine mystery to all mortals, till its day came. Till at last, victorious in the name of Allah, the Commander of the Faithful, riding up with grim battle-axe and heart full of Moslem fire, took the liberty to smite once, with right force and rage, said ugly mass of idolatrous crockery; which thereupon shivered, with unmelodious crash and jingle, into a heap of ugly potsherds, yielding from its belly half a wagon-load of gold coins. You can read it in Gibbon,[1]—probably, too, in Lord Ellenborough. The gold coins, the diamond eyes, and other valuable extrinsic parts were carefully picked up by the Faithful; confused jingle of intrinsic potsherds was left lying;—and the Idol of Somnauth once showing what it was, had suddenly come to a conclusion! Thus end all Idols, and intrinsically worthless man-mountains never so illuminated with diamonds, and filled with precious metals, and tremulously worshipped by the neighbouring flunky populations black or white;—even thus, sooner or later, without fail; and are shot hastily, as a heap of potsherds, into the highway, to be crunched under wagon-wheels, and do Macadam a little service, being clearly abolished as gods, and hidden from man's recognition, in that or other capacities, forever and a day!

"You do not sufficiently bethink you, my republican friend. Our ugliest anomalies are done by universal suffrage, not by patent. The express nonsense of old Feudalism, even now, in its dotage, is as nothing to the involuntary nonsense of modern Anarchy called 'Freedom,' 'Republicanism,' and other fine names, which expresses itself by supply and demand! Consider it a little.

"The Bishop of our Diocese is to me an incredible man; and has, I will grant you, very much more money than you or I would now give him for his work. One does not even read those Charges of his; much preferring speech which is articulate. In fact, being intent on a quiet life, you gener ally keep on the other side of the hedge from him, and strictly leave him to his own fate. Not a credible man;—perhaps not quite a safe man to be concerned with? But what think you of the 'Bobus of Houndsditch' of our parts? He, Sausage-maker on the great scale, knows the art of cutting fat bacon, and exposing it seasoned with grey pepper to advantage. Better than any other man he knows

[1] *Gibbon's Decline and Fall of the Roman Empire*, Chap. LVII; M. Elphinstone's *History of India*, Bk. V, Chap. III, pp. 334–7; and W. W. Hunter's *Indian Empire*, p. 327.

this art ; and I take the liberty to say it is a poor one. Well, the Bishop has an income of five thousand pounds appointed him for his work ; and Bobus, to such a length has he now pushed the trade in sausages, gains from the universal suffrage of men's souls and stomachs ten thousand a year by it.

"A poor art, this of Bobus's, I say ; and worth no such recompense. For it is not even good sausages he makes, but only extremely vendible ones ; the cunning dog ! Judges pronounce his sausages bad, and at the cheap price even dear ; and finer palates, it is whispered, have detected alarming symptoms of horseflesh, or worse, under this cunningly devised grey-pepper spice of his ; so that for the world I would not eat one of his sausages, nor would you. You perceive he is not an excellent honest sausage-maker, but a dishonest, cunning and scandalous sausage-maker ; worth, if he could get his deserts, who shall say what ? Probably certain shillings a week, say forty ; possibly (one shudders to think) a long round in the treadmill, and stripes instead of shillings ! And yet what he gets, I tell you, from universal suffrage and the unshackled ne-plus-ultra republican justice of mankind, is twice the income of that anomalous Bishop you were talking of !

"The Bishop I, for my part, do much prefer to Bobus. The Bishop has human sense and breeding of various kinds ; considerable knowledge of Greek, if you should ever want the like of that ; knowledge of many things ; and speaks the English language in a grammatical manner. He is bred to courtesy, to dignified composure, as to a second nature ; a gentleman every fibre of him ; which of itself is something very considerable. The Bishop does really diffuse round him an influence of decorum, courteous patience, solid adherence to what is settled ; teaches practically the necessity of 'burning one's own smoke ;' and does practically in his own case burn said smoke, making lambent flame and mild illumination out of it, for the good of men in several particulars. While Bobus, for twice the annual money,—brings sausages, possibly of horseflesh, cheaper to market than another !—Brick, if you will reflect, it is not 'aristocratic England,' it is the united Posterity of Adam who are grown, in some essential respects, stupider than barbers' blocks. Barbers' blocks would at least say nothing, and not elevate, by their universal suffrages, an unfortunate Bobus to that bad height ! "

Thus did Carlyle in 1850 mock the prevailing gospel of grab and " Devil take the hindmost," and " Glory in the highest " to money-men. Thus did he deride the service of Shylock, so to speak.—' Street-barricades rise for that reason, and counterfeit kings have to shave-off their whiskers, and fly like coiners ; and it is a world gone mad in misery, by bestowing its approbation wrong ! '

XXIII

LEIGH HUNT'S AUTOBIOGRAPHY

(1850)

AFTER reading Leigh Hunt's *Autobiography*, Carlyle wrote to him on 17.6.50[1]:—

'DEAR HUNT,—

'I have just finished your *Autobiography*, which has been most pleasantly occupying all my leisure these three days; and you must permit me to thank you. . . . I call this an excellent good book, by far the best of the autobiographic kind I remember to have read in English; and except Boswell's Johnson, I do not know where we have such a picture drawn of a human life. A pious, ingenious, altogether *human* and worthy book; imaging, with graceful honesty and free felicity, many interesting objects and persons, and imaging throughout a gifted, gentle, patient and valiant human soul, as it buffets its way through the billows of the time, and will not drown, tho often in danger; *cannot* be drowned, but conquers and leaves a track of radiance behind it: that, I think, comes out more clearly to me than in any other of your books;—and that is the best of all results to realise in a book. In fact, this book has been like an exercise of *devotion* to me; I have not assisted at any sermon, liturgy or litany, this long while, that has had so *religious* an effect on me. Thanks in the name of all men. And believe along with me that this book will be welcome to other generations as well as to ours. And long may you live to write more books for us; and may the evening sun be softer on you (and on me) than the noon sometimes was!

'Adieu, dear Hunt. I have often thought of coming up to see you once more; and perhaps I shall one of these days (tho horribly sick and lonely, and beset with spectral lions, go whitherward I may): but whether I do or not, believe for ever in my regard. And so, God bless you, prays heartily,

'T. CARLYLE.'

Old Hunt came to see him soon, overflowing with gratitude, and talking to Mrs. Carlyle and him, broke into tears.

[1] *Life of Thomas Carlyle*, by R. H. Shepherd, II, pp. 90–4.

XXIV

LADY ASHBURTON'S GRAND BALL

(1850)

ABOUT the same time there was a conjugal debate between Carlyle and his wife. Lady Ashburton was giving a grand Ball on 24.6.50 and wanted to see them there. Carlyle had never gone to a " Ball " in his life, and his wife had never meant to go to this one. So she was surprised to discover, about a week before the appointed day, that her husband was " quite determined for once in his life " to see an aristocratic Ball and present himself as promised.

" I've nothing to wear," said she, as if that were conclusive ; but he was ready to go without her, and said,— " If you choose to be so peevish and ungracious as to stay away, there is no help for you." When told, " I haven't a dress," he answered,—" I will pay for any dress you choose to get." She spoke of her horror of stripping herself and " being bare " at her age,—" and if I don't I'll be like no one else," said she, and was answered :—" True propriety consists in conforming to other people's fashions. *Eve I suppose had as much sense of decency as you have, and she wore no clothes at all.*"[1]

So on 19.6.50 the actor Macready and his wife Catherine were agreeably surprised by a call from the two Carlyles.[2] They talked about Sunday restrictions, to which Carlyle objected, and about railways and things in general, and Ireland in particular, in the tone of the *Latter-Day Pamphlets*. Mrs. Carlyle gave them one of the Pamphlets with a corrected sheet showing where Carlyle had struck out some praise of Macready by name, " thinking you might not like it." Which made the actor moralize,—" He little knows what value I set upon a word of praise from him." But the immediate urgent business of the call was to get the help of Mrs. Macready about the dress for " the Ball." " A white silk dress " was the outcome of the female discussion, at first " made high and long-sleeved, and then on the very day of the Ball," as Mrs. Carlyle told her cousin, " cut

[1] *J. W. Carlyle : Letters to her Family*, by L. Huxley, pp. 342–4.
[2] *Macready's Reminiscences*, edited by Sir F. Pollock, II, p. 353.

down to the due pitch of indecency. I could have gone into *fits* of crying when I began to put it on," she added, "but I looked so astonishingly well in it *by candle light*, and when I got into the fine rooms amongst the universally *bare* people I felt so much in *keeping*, that I forgot my neck and arms almost immediately."

What added to her complacency was that her husband "with his white waistcoat and white gloves" was more than passable, inasmuch as the men attending the Ball, tho they were of England's best, "were mostly horribly ugly."[3]

So she admitted she was glad she went.—"It is an additional idea for life, to have seen such a party—all the Duchesses one ever heard tell of blazing in diamonds, all the young beauties of the season, all the distinguished statesmen &c. &c. were to be seen among the six or seven hundred people present—and the rooms all hung with artificial roses looked like an Arabian Nights' Entertainment. Lady Ashburton receiving all these people with her grand-Lady airs was also a sight worth seeing." What pleased her best was "the good look" she got "*into the eyes* of old Wellington—one has no notion, seeing him on the streets, what a dear kind face he has."

Carlyle, who made notes as usual, was of the same opinion.—'From five to seven hundred select aristocracy; the lights, decorations, houseroom and arrangements perfect (I suppose); the whole thing worth having seen for a couple of hours. *Of the many women, only a few were to be called beautiful.*[4] I remember the languid, careless, slow air with which the elderly peeresses came into the room and thereafter lounged about,'—a typical thing which may still be seen,—a kind of soft swagger, resembling cats that are quiet, after dinner.

'Old Londonderry looked sad, foolish, and surly. His Marchioness, once a beauty you could see, had the finest diamonds of the party, Jane tells me.' It is amusing to find Carlyle recording which of the girls was the prettiest,—a boyish touch,—and noting that while the American minister, called Lawrence, seemed 'a broad, burly, energetically sagacious-looking man of sixty,' he had a 'frightful' wife, tall and lean, 'sallow, parchment complexion, chin like a powder-horn.' Prescott and the other Yankees appeared negligible. The men Carlyle liked best were both

[3] *Letters from J. W. Carlyle*, by Leonard Huxley, *Cornhill Mag.*, Nov., 1926, p. 630.
[4] Italics added.

old, Anglesey and Wellington. It was thirty-five years this month since Wellington was telling Anglesey at Waterloo the line of retreat to take if he were killed and Anglesey were left in chief command, when suddenly a cannon-ball hit Anglesey. It cost him his leg only, not his life; but Wellington had to look for somebody else to receive post-obit instructions. It is curious to consider that if that ball had hit Wellington, Waterloo might have been a French victory.

In later years Anglesey and Wellington had been in politics together; but all that was becoming like a dream to Anglesey now, for like Wellington, his leader in arms and politics, he was over eighty, tottering to the grave, as Carlyle was watching them both in the crowd at the Ball.

'Anglesey, fine-looking old man, trailing his cork leg, shows better on horseback. By far the most interesting figure present was Wellington, who appeared between twelve and one, and slowly glided through the rooms. Truly a beautiful old man; I had never seen till now how beautiful, and what an expression of graceful simplicity, veracity, and nobleness there is about the old hero, when you see him close at hand. His very size had hitherto deceived me: he is a shortish, slightish figure, about five feet eight; of good breadth however, and *all* muscle or bone;—his legs I think must be the short part of him, for certainly on horseback, at least, I have always taken him to be tall. Eyes beautiful light blue, full of mild valour, with infinitely more faculty and geniality than I had fancied before. The face wholly gentle, wise, valiant, and venerable; the voice too, as I again heard, is *aquiline*, a clear, perfectly equable (*un*cracked, that is) and perhaps almost musical, but essentially *tenor* or almost treble voice. He glided slowly along, slightly saluting this and that other'—(' speaking only when spoken to,' we read elsewhere);—'clear, clean, fresh as this June evening itself; till the silver buckle of his stock vanished into the door of the next room, and I saw him no more. Except Dr. Chalmers, I have not for many years seen so beautiful an old man.'

Carlyle and Wellington had known each other by sight for many years, in a friendly way, but never conversed. 'To speak *to* him, with my notions of his ways of thinking, and of his *articulate* endowments, was not among my longings,' the younger man confessed to himself, content to admire from a distance.

XXV

THE DEATH OF PEEL

(1850)

IN the latter half of June there was much debating in Parliament on our Foreign Policy; and what Carlyle had called the "Hercules-Harlequin" and busybody tricks of Palmerston the Foreign Secretary were condemned by a majority in the Lords. The Government was in danger even in the Commons, in spite of party loyalty, which did, however, make a formal victory secure for the time. In the debate the speech of Palmerston lasted five hours, and may be called his masterpiece as a blatherskite talking bunkum. He flattered the national vanity and misled our 'superfine vulgar' by falsely pretending we were justified in meddling with other countries, and were like the Roman Citizens of old, privileged persons everywhere. Well were his colleagues aware that it was dangerous nonsense, but it was popular, and so they stood by him; and there were plenty of place-hunters to back him up and party men ready to vote against their convictions. Aware that Peel had other reasons for wishing the Government to remain in power, Cockburn flattered him and begged for his support in this matter. But Peel was a man of conscience, and rising to reprobate Palmerston, delivered what John Bright used to call "that most beautiful, that most solemn speech," setting forth the true method of righteousness in practice, even in the darkest depths of Diplomacy, which he called a 'costly engine for maintaining peace.' Diplomacy could be used to prevent war, if applied to appease passions and check resentments; but if it merely continued an angry correspondence and kept up conflicts for the sake of some imaginary 'English interest,' it would then be 'a cause of hostility and war.' The moral victory was so complete that the vote was little heeded, and it was generally expected that Peel would soon be forming a new Government.

The next day was Saturday, 29.6.50; and Peel attended a meeting of the Commissioners arranging next year's Great Exhibition. It is said he made them happy by promising to

MRS. CARLYLE
From a photo which belonged to John Forster, and which David Masson said was the best likeness.

[*face p.* 288

support in Parliament the site in Hyde Park. According to Milnes' Commonplace Book,[1] he was in low spirits,—perhaps the political excitement had left him tired. At any rate, it was at the urgent request of his wife, who wished to distract his mind, that he went out for a ride that fine June evening. After six, while Carlyle was walking in Piccadilly near Hyde Park corner, and remarking that old Anglesey with his cork leg was not quite safe as he was riding there on a brisk and skittish horse capering among the carriages, Peel was on Constitution Hill, and, according to a witness, his horse took *both* to rearing and to flinging up its heels, and he fell off. Unfortunately he held on to the bridle, and that pulled down the horse so that its knees came on him, breaking the collar-bone and a rib.

Carlyle did not hear of the accident till Sunday evening, when he and Thackeray had gone out together to dine at Addiscombe, where Mrs. Carlyle was spending the week-end with Lady Ashburton. It was the height of the season, and there were so many guests that every room was taken up, and Thackeray and he returned together, hoping that the alarm about Peel's injuries was exaggerated.

On Monday, Henry Chorley and Carlyle together went to a Club to see a bulletin, 'which pretended to be favourable.' They went to the neighbourhood of his house to gather tidings, and found a great 'crowd simmering about' on the same errand, and carriages swarming in 'all the back space' of Whitehall. On Tuesday, placard-bulletins were 'hoisted up from hour to hour,' as the police could not make themselves heard by 'the crowds of working people' wanting to know; and before midnight he died. Lady Ashburton brought the news to Carlyle's house on the Wednesday morning.

On Thursday (4.7.50), Mrs. Carlyle was writing to her cousin Helen[2] that Lady Ashburton had been 'deeply attached' to Peel.—'She is off into the country again to escape parties; came here on her way, all in tears, and asked Mr. C. to come by himself *this* week—as one asks the clergyman when one is in affliction!—Indeed this death has produced a greater dismay than any public event of my time. . . . Mr. C. is mourning over him as I never saw him mourn before—went to-day to look at the house where he lies dead.'

[1] *Life of R. M. Milnes, Lord Houghton*, by T. Wemyss Reid, I, pp. 443–4.
[2] *J. W. Carlyle : Letters to her Family*, by L. Huxley, p. 344.

'I still remember,' wrote Espinasse,[3] 'the tone of sadness, blended with resignation, in which at that time he said to me: "The world is a poor slave, and will always be governed in a low way."'

As soon as the death was known, the shops were shut in London, Liverpool and elsewhere, and the flags were half-mast high. In Parliament much was said. The old Duke of Wellington, 'in tears, with broken voice,'[4] described what he called "his most striking characteristic. . . . I had a lively confidence in his truth, in his justice and in his invariable desire to promote the public service. In the whole course of my communication with him, I never knew an instance in which he did not show the strictest preference for truth. I never had, in the whole course of my life, the slightest reason for suspecting that he stated anything that he did not firmly believe to be the fact."[5]

'E'en in our ashes live our wonted fires.' Brougham was seventy now and had been twenty years among the Lords; but he was so jealous of the general grief about Peel that he 'went about saying, "Let every statesman take care and ride like a sack, and he may die like a demigod."'[6]

[3] *Literary Recollections*, by F. Espinasse, p. 182.
[4] *Sir Robert Peel*, by C. S. Parker, III, p. 546.
[5] *Life and Times of Sir Robert Peel*, by Charles Mackay, IV, pp. 608 and 624–5; and the *Life of Wellington*, by Sir H. E. Maxwell, II, p. 372.
[6] Wherein Brougham was mistaken. He lived to discover that nothing could make people speak of Brougham as they spoke of Peel.

XXVI

JESUITISM, &c.

(1850)

WITHOUT delay Carlyle completed for publication on 1.8.50 the eighth and last of the Pamphlets, Jesuitism, which seemed to his wife and others "such an admirable summing up." He called our times the 'Age of Jesuitism,' and said that Jesuitism meant,—to persist in believing what was plainly doubtful or incredible, as if it were serving God to blind one's intellect and believe what is untrue! 'What we have to complain of is, that all men are become Jesuits! That no man speaks the truth to you or to himself, but that every man lies, and does not know that he is lying, in regard to almost all things. . . . For this is the sad condition of the insincere man: he is doomed all his days to deal with insincerities; to live, move, and have his being in traditions and conventionalities.'

Carlyle analysed the character of 'Unsaint Ignatius,' the Spanish soldier Loyola, who began the business of the Jesuits. The paragraphs on that poor wretch approach more nearly than anything else in literature the ideal Day of Judgment of the ancient Egyptians. There is no make-believe,—it reads like Euclid, unanswerable. A common book of science, or even Darwin's *Origin of Species*, is hypothetic and fanciful in comparison. Poetical conjectures, giving Ignatius the benefit of any possible doubt, make him alive again to the reader. Whoever retains any esteem for the fellow is merely to that extent unable to understand what he has read.

Of course, 'Unsaint Ignatius' began life like the rest of us, as a helpless, greedy, and selfish little brute. But he grew little up,—he grew mostly down. He was the ideal soldier or mercenary murderer, developing unrestricted by a conscience. General Wolfe of Quebec was only a boy under twenty at Culloden, when Cumberland, it is said, bade him kill a wounded Highlander and was answered,—"I am not an executioner." Which would be pardoned to a young officer and a favourite,—maybe Cumberland had merely been thinking of giving Wolfe pleasure! It may be guessed with what gusto 'Unsaint Ignatius' would have leaped to obey an order like that, perhaps enquiring,—"Painlessly, Your Royal Highness? Or would you like to see him *chopped* up?"

So when a cannon ball smashed the legs of 'Unsaint Ignatius' and there was no more use for him as a soldier, at the time when Luther was awakening the world, he naturally sought spiritual service with the Pope. He was not a man to be bothered with a scruple when he had an order,—he would stifle consciences as readily as he would cut throats. As a soldier he had been more vicious than was common, and as a poet has explained, that is a habit which 'hardens all within, and petrifies the feeling.' So his new regiment of spiritual soldiers succeeded in making a new record in human depravity, believing any lies they were bidden believe, playing any tricks the priests prescribed, and giving a new substantive to modern languages,—Jesuitism, 'an idea for which there was in nature no prototype before.'

Gustavus and Cromwell delivered Europe by defeating them and all their associates, 'the Wallensteins and Lammerleins, the Lauds and Charleses'; but at the 1660 Restoration in England, sheer insincerity set in and truth went out of fashion.—'"Be careful how you believe truth," cries the good man everywhere: "Composure and a whole skin are very valuable. There is little certain truth going. If it isn't orthodox truth, it will play the very devil with you." . . . And this, then, is the horrible conclusion . . . that the great body of orderly considerate men, the good and pious, have unconsciously abnegated the duty of acting or speaking the truth; and fancy that an amalgam of truth and falsity is the safe thing. In parliament and pulpit, in book and speech, we have to report that Human Speech is not true.'

Too long have flattering critics beguiled the British Public by saying that Carlyle was angry and exaggerated here, and that 'an Englishman's word' was honoured abroad. That is untrue. When it is said, it is usually in flattery or mockery. It may be news to some Englishmen, but it is as sure as death, that there is no tribe of savages so simple, no people in the world so ignorant, as to believe that Englishmen are more truthful than other people.

Chinamen, that is, non-official Chinamen, are sometimes so spoken of, but never Englishmen. Well might every race in Europe be admonished as Hamlet's mother was by her son.—

> 'Mother, for love of grace,
> Lay not that flattering unction to your soul,
> That not your trespass, but my madness speaks:
> It will but skin and film the ulcerous place,
> Whilst rank corruption, mining all within,
> Infects unseen. . . .
> Repent what's past; avoid what is to come.'

There is a vernacular proverb in a land where the English govern much but dwell little,—" There are three dangers,—the horns of an ox, and the heels of a horse, and the tongue of an Englishman."

In this Pamphlet Carlyle implied that the God of the Bible was incredible, and said that 'a man's "religion" consists not of the many things he is in doubt of and tries to believe, but of the few he is assured of, and has no need of effort for believing.' Accordingly the 'modern man's religion' was such as might have been expected of pigs, 'if the inestimable talent of Literature should, in these swift days of progress, be extended to the brute creation, so that swine, (I mean fourfooted swine), could communicate to us on paper what they thought of the Universe.' Whereupon he gave a humorous sketch of Pig Philosophy, such as Swift might have written but no other man of letters on record, full of fun, yet making one feel uncomfortably how much we modern men resemble swine. He went on to declare that Jesuitism had infected with its hypocrisy the Fine Arts also, and Literature in particular. 'Nowhere, not even in the Pope's Church of St. Peter, is there such an explosion of intolerable hypocrisy' as when men gather at some 'Royal Picture Gallery, Museum, or other divine Temple of the Fine Arts.' He instanced the New Houses of Parliament,—a 'wilderness of stone pepper-boxes with their tin flags atop,'—expensive and ugly, but insisted that such madness was the inevitable result of the Fine Arts 'divorcing themselves from *Truth*.'

In short, we should learn to work and to speak the truth, in the Fine Arts as in all other things. To every Nation 'its Believed History is its Bible,' and our Shakespeare might have made an epic of ours if he had been set to do it, and not wasted in the playhouse. 'The black deluge of

Consecrated Falsity' would be followed by better days. 'We shall all yet make our *Exodus* from Houndsditch, and bid the sordid continents, of once rich apparel now grown poisonous *Ou'-clo'*, a mild farewell!'

Indeed, the reports of the best of Carlyle's disciples then frequenting the house show that 'Jesuitism' was a substantial instalment of the *Exodus From Houndsditch*, so far as he ever intended to write anything of that sort. 'All that is *true* is your "religion,"' he tells the reader, comforting him against the despondent drivel of the divines of his day by saying:—'Not because Heaven existed, did men know Good from Evil; the "because" lay quite the other way. It was *because* men felt the difference between Good and Evil, that Heaven and Hell first came to exist. . . . The "open secret of this Universe"' he identifies with the "divine sense of Right and Wrong in man," which he calls 'the indisputable God's-message still legible in every heart.'

In a final word of adieu to his immediate readers, the dear-book-buying public, he bids them 'be thankful for your ennui,' and take it as 'a perpetual admonition' to get something noble to do, something better than yachting or deer-stalking.

XXVII

CRITICS OF THE PAMPHLETS

"CARLYLE'S Pamphlets will amuse you," wrote W. E. Forster when they appeared, in a letter to his brother-in-law in India, whom he called "Carlylish."[1] "They have had an immense reading, but probably less effect than almost any of his writings. They are so one-sided in their stern, almost lurid gloom, and preference of the past to the present; and besides, it is too late now to try to whip the world into good manners. It has grown past the flogging age. Still, the power of his sincerity is great, and he wields his whip sincerely enough, as I saw plainly this time last year, when travelling with him in Ireland."

This was the mark of Carlyle,—entire sincerity, a rare and beautiful thing. He would not have been nonplussed at any point by the rejoinder,—"Let us see you do it yourself." As La Fontaine has said:—

> 'Ne faut-il que délibérer,
> La cour en conseillers foisone;
> Est-il besoin d'exécuter,
> L'on ne rencontre plus personne.'
>
> When nothing is needed but talking aloud,
> Advisers and councillors come in a crowd;
> But when it is sure there must something be done,
> To do what is needful there's never a one.

It is difficult now to realise how original Carlyle was in Politics,—so many of his original ideas have been found right and become commonplace. Discussing his *Chartism*, *Past and Present*, and *Latter-Day Pamphlets*, his biographer in the *Times* of 7.2.1881 has well remarked:—'It is astonishing how, under uncouth, rhapsodical phraseology, lie many ideas which are now the common property of most educated men. *The novelties and paradoxes of* 1840 *are, to a large extent, nothing but the good sense of* 1881.[2] Who would not now echo Mr. Carlyle's protests against the supposed omnipotence of Parliament?' Or in short against the delusion

[1] *Life of W. E. Forster*, by T. Wemyss Reid, pp. 149–50. [2] Italics added.

that human nature can be shaped to order. And who now denies he was right about the West Indies? 'If all wise men are now haunted by a sense of the necessity of working out reformations really worth anything in the souls of the individuals, to whom do they owe this so much as to Mr. Carlyle? Who recognised the duty of spreading education earlier or more clearly than he? We say nothing of the keen eye for the detection of rogues and impostors, or of those ingenious epithets of his which, attached to some blustering, swelling piece of fraud, acted like a stone tied to the neck of a dog flung into deep water. It is enough to say that again and again he reminded, in his own way, his generation of stern truths which it was in danger of forgetting.'

Walt Whitman was one of the best of the later writers who discussed the politics of Carlyle, and he dismisses with derision the suggestion that America has anything to complain about, declaring[3]:—'I doubt if he ever thought or said half as bad words about us' (Americans of the United States) 'as we deserve.

'How he splashes like leviathan in the seas of modern literature and politics! One needs to realise the squalor, vice and doggedness ingrained in the bulk population of the British Islands, with the red tape, the fatuity, the flunkeyism everywhere, to understand his pages. Tho he was no Chartist or Radical, I consider Carlyle's by far the most indignant comment or protest anent the increasing poverty and degradation of the homeless, landless twenty millions, while a few thousands, or rather a few hundreds, possess the entire soil. . . .

'The array of British thought as existing to-day, *but with Carlyle left out*, would be like an army with no artillery.'

[3] *Specimen Days in America*, by Walt Whitman, 1864, and pp. 261–2 of the 1887 edition.

XXVIII

THE RETURN OF MAZZINI, &c.

(1850)

BY July, 1850, reaction was in full swing. It seems to have been in talk about Italian defeats that Carlyle remarked[1] :—" When I first met Mazzini, I thought him the most beautiful creature I had ever seen, but entirely unpractical." " He twaddled," said Mrs. Carlyle. But neither of them in the darkest hours of defeat dissembled their sentiments. Carlyle admitted that the Austrian victory at Novara " showed what Dutch bottom could do," and that " whatever material progress there has been in Italy " might be due to the Austrians ; but he concluded,— " I hope they will be driven out."

It seems to have been in July that the German patriot and poet, Moritz Hartmann, was in London. Sitting with the Carlyles in their drawing-room, he told them the history of the Frankfurt Parliament, of which he had been a member, and was comforted by their sympathy.[2] As Carlyle wrote to a publisher [3] to whom he was soon recommending Hartmann, he had seen at once that this stranger was ' an amiable intelligent man,' and after several talks and reading a ' very clever ' book of his, discovered him to be ' a scholar, poet, and man of sense and humanity,' and he ' has the beautifullest beard in Nature ! '

Hartmann had long contemplated a popular Life of John Huss, for which Carlyle believed him well qualified, inasmuch as his mother-tongue was Czech, and he was a Bohemian by race, and had ' rummaged the Prague archives, &c. &c.' and was ' actually a man of natural intelligence. He is nothing of the truculent revolutionist ; far from it ! He is one of the mildest (and) clearest of young German celebrities.'

[1] *Literary Recollections*, by F. Espinasse, p. 107.

[2] For Moritz Hartmann's reports, see his *Bilder und Busten*, 1860, and *The Birth of Modern Italy*, by J. W. Mario, pp. 219–20.

[3] *Life of Thomas Carlyle*, by R. H. Shepherd, II, pp. 96–7, but the date needs correction, as T. C. left London 31.7.50.

According to Hartmann's reports, Carlyle lamented the failure of the Frankfurt Parliament; but after finishing his lamentations over it, astounded his visitor by praising the Russian despotism! To listen to him, we are told, 'was like sitting by a rushing torrent and watching the waves roll one after the other. Carlyle was enthusiastic for the Emperor Nicholas and the Russian form of Government; and in France he was hoping for a great deal from General Cavaignac, a sort of Cromwell, who would put an end to the Parliamentary velleities of the French. His sharp unaffected soldierly language seemed Cromwellian.

'Suddenly Mrs. Carlyle started. A voice in the hall had reached her ears. Her eyes sparkled and opening the door she grasped the hands of the visitor in a transport of joy. It was Joseph Mazzini, and his friends had not seen him since 1848. Carlyle ceased talking, and with his stork-like legs in one long stride reached his guest, who was not less moved. I shared the sentiments so vividly depicted on the faces of all three (tho I did not know at once who it was). Carlyle remarked with a melancholy sigh,—"Your hair has grown somewhat greyer since I last saw you." Mrs. Carlyle caressing his beard with her hand exclaimed with tears in her eyes and a faltering voice,—"Aye, how white it has grown!"

'When Mazzini began to narrate events, the defender of the most absolute despotism followed him through all the phases of the Italian Revolution, as if he were the Cassius of this Brutus.'

Gladly would Mazzini have done at Rome as the men of Londonderry did in 1689, and said, "No Surrender!" That was what Carlyle had been anticipating last May that they might do; but tho Mazzini and his men were ready to "fight till Rome was ashes and ruin," and "yield only with life," the non-combatants would not take the risk, and the French bullies sent to restore the Pope were allowed to walk in.

Mazzini had waited in Rome awhile, but apparently by accident he was not made a martyr, and it was the hope of checkmating in some way the plans of Napoleon the Little that had brought him from Switzerland to Paris in 1850, and thence he came over to London. In describing how Carlyle received him, Hartmann added,—'I have seen Carlyle the same, with men of the most varied parties.' Which recalls the testimony of Leigh Hunt.[4]—

[4] *Autobiography of Leigh Hunt*, Chap. XXIV.

'I believe that what Mr. Carlyle loves better than his fault-finding, with all its eloquence, is the face of any human creature that looks suffering, and loving, and sincere; and I believe further, that if the fellow-creature were suffering only, and neither loving nor sincere, but had come to a pass of agony in this life, which put him at the mercies of some good man for some last help and consolation towards his grave, even at the risk of loss to repute, and a sure amount of pain and vexation, that man, if the groan reached him in its forlornness, would be Thomas Carlyle.'

A few weeks later Mrs. Carlyle was writing to her cousin Helen.[5]—'I was immensely glad the other day to receive—Mazzini! I did not think I *could* have felt so very glad. He looks much better than I expected and is in excellent spirits—he has a greyish *beard*—which is altogether a new feature—as before he wore only black mustachios—but this beard he begged me to believe was no *efflorescence of republicanism* but *necessitated* in the first instance and then persevered in because found so convenient—"for you must recollect, my Dear, that in the old times I needed always to have a barber to shave me—and in the camp with Garibaldi, and flying for my life, I could not of course take everywhere with me a barber! And so my beard had to grow and now and then be cut with a scissor."

'For the rest he looks much as he did and is the same affectionate, simple-hearted, high-souled creature—but immensely more agreeable—talks now as one who had the habit of being listened to—and has so much of interesting matter to tell. Imagine his going to live in a mad-house at Marseilles! While waiting for a false passport—he "thought they would not seek him amongst *mads*, decidedly." And another time at Geneva he lodged in the *same* house with the magistrate who was empowered to discover him—sure that the magistrate would look for him in every house before his *own*—and they lived under the same roof for fifty days.'

[5] *J. W. Carlyle: Letters to her Family*, by L. Huxley, pp. 344–5.

XXIX

MIGHT HAVE BEENS

(1850)

WHEN by and by Carlyle was asked, "Did you ever think of going into Parliament yourself?" he replied that he did think of it about the time of the *Latter-Day Pamphlets.*—"I felt that nothing could prevent me from getting up in the House and saying all that." But, according to Espinasse,[1] 'his wife immediately raised the formidable objection that he would have in that case to keep late hours, and he never recurred to the subject.' It seems strange that official employment should be possible after the appearance of the *Latter-Day Pamphlets*, and stranger still, tho true, that if Peel had lived, Carlyle might have been tried in the Ministry of Education.

W. Bingham Baring, now Lord Ashburton, was one of the richest and most respectable men in England. He had been an M.P. till he succeeded to the peerage, and a successful politician. He had been one of the ministers who stood steadily by Peel, and at the same time he was a devoted disciple of Carlyle, and shared his ideas on social reconstruction in general and education in particular.[1] England was then the worst-educated of all the Protestant countries in Europe. Between leaving Eton and going to Oxford, Ashburton had studied six months in the University of Geneva, which "opened his eyes," as he said himself,[1] and that explains what 'Dicky Milnes' has certified, that "he had an unquenchable thirst for information."[2]

In 1850 it seemed as likely as anything can be that when Peel returned to power as Prime Minister, which seemed impending when an accident killed him, Ashburton would have been one of his ministers, and probably the head of a new Education Department, with Carlyle as permanent official under him to organise the business. Carlyle was not only a leading man of letters, but had also

[1] *Literary Recollections*, by F. Espinasse, pp. 193, 92–101.
[2] *Monographs*, by R. M. Milnes, Lord Houghton, p. 235.

been for years an elementary teacher, and was familiar with the French, German, and Italian literatures as well as the Latin and Greek classics. He had all the qualities that go to ensure success in administration. So Espinasse is justified in his opinion[1] that, if Peel had lived, the friendship of the Ashburtons would have led Carlyle 'to serve his country as a "doer," and not merely as a "speaker."' To show how readily Carlyle would have turned away from writing, he tells how he once heard him say,—"Goethe was the most successful speaker of the century, but I would have been better pleased if he had done something."

Of course, Carlyle would have been equally ready to work at the organization of labour or of emigration; but the "forty thieves" of the day, as the money men controlling our politics are called in the lobbies, would never have allowed anything to be done that would tend directly to raise wages. Education was the immediately practical thing. The longest speech Ashburton seems ever to have made was an excellent address to the elementary teachers of the diocese of Winchester.[1] There can hardly be room for a doubt that if only Peel had been spared a few years longer, Ashburton would have reorganized our elementary education far better than was done about twenty years afterwards. But after the death of Peel, Ashburton kept out of politics, and Carlyle resigned himself to see public business in the hands of others, and returned to writing history. When a man has done as Byron did, and simplified his politics into a detestation of all existing governments, it is time to—think of something else. What next?

XXX

IRELAND AGAIN

(1850)

THE Pamphlets were better received in Ireland than in England, and the one on Downing Street had an amusing sequel. There was a passage that ran:—'The notion that any Government can be a No-government, without the deadliest peril to the Commonwealth, was never my notion, and I hope it will soon cease to be anybody's. But if it be the correct notion, as the world seems at present to flatter itself, I point out improvements and abbreviations. Dismiss your National Palaver; make the *Times* newspaper your national palaver, which needs no beer-barrels or hustings, and is *cheaper* in expense of money and of falsity a thousand and a million-fold. Have an economical red-tape drilling establishment, and fling out your orange-skin among the graduates, when you want a new premier.' Which means,—choose the premier by lot, among passably qualified men.

The suggestion made in derision was taken seriously by a gentleman who wrote from—

'COLERAINE,
'*July* 21*st*.[1]

'DEAR SIR,—

'You mention an admirable project in p. 17 of your "Downing Street." But why should not something be done as well as said? There is small chance for such a project if it be put before the said "Palavering Parliament." Why not do something yourself? Say you start a paper at the beginning of next session; you write a leading article now and then, to explain the *pros* and *cons* of certain questions before the House, to explain the nature of the difficulties which it is necessary to meet, and to give statistics when necessary, and let the rest of the paper be open to any M.P. in the way you propose. I would readily subscribe £10 a

[1] *Conversations with Carlyle*, by Sir Charles Gavan Duffy, pp. 153–7.

year until there are sufficient funds to carry it on, and surely I shouldn't be the only one who would give as much. . . . I shall not be remiss in subscribing, and in persuading those real M.P.'s with whom I am acquainted, to write instead of speaking, and in inducing the mere effigy M.P.'s to assist you with their subscriptions.

'Yours Sincerely.'

For the fun of the thing, Carlyle sent this with a covering letter to Gavan Duffy on 27.7.50, and went on to give his news.—

'These "Pamphlets" are now out of my hands, thank God. Such a universal howl of astonishment, indignation, and condemnation seldom rose around a poor man before. Voice of the "universal dog-kennel"—whap thap! Bow-wow! No *human* response hitherto, or hardly any, but that also will come so far as needful, I have no doubt. Thank your *Nation* critic, however; the news of such insight on his part was really welcome.

'My poor *liver* is gone almost to destruction with all this and with the summer heats, and other fell *et ceteras;* I seldom in my life felt more entirely worn down, and am now straight for the country.' He was about to go to Wales for some weeks, and thence to Scotland, and concluded with a paragraph on a line of agitation he had been advising Duffy about, and which reads in the light of later history as if it had been written with uncanny 'second-sight,' or prophetic vision.—

'Your "Tenant Agitation" looms out very big on me, and I must say it wears a more business-like aspect than any of the previous "agitations," and, I could fancy, may give work to all the "authorities" (on your side of the water and ours) for a generation or two to come! Yes, that is the heart of the matter, and a terrific universe of "work" lies *there* before we get to a solution of it! *Cosa fatta ha capo*—to end one must *begin*. That is true, too. *Suaviter in modo* then,' (gently in the manner), 'and God be with you.

'Yours ever truly,

'T. CARLYLE.'

XXXI

SEEING BATH, MERTHYR TYDVIL, &c.

(1850)

IT was Charles Redwood, the honest attorney practising at Cowbridge,[1] whom Carlyle was going to visit, and writing to tell Redwood that he would arrive at Cardiff by steamer on Thursday, 1.8.50, Carlyle remembered how in 1843 his friend had come to meet him, and he said,—"If engaged, don't mind; your man will perfectly serve the turn; tell him he is to look out for *an elderly thin man of your own stature; he will know him by his grim look, sober clothing, grizzled temples, and white hat*—the last mark perhaps the best."

It seems to have been merely an accidental coincidence that Carlyle was to be writing a Life of John Sterling next year, and that Sterling went to school at Cowbridge, and had spent many of his early years thereabouts. Carlyle was coming to rest in the country and not to work there. Since his last visit to Wales, in 1843, the good Quaker Redwood had become an intimate friend. He had been sending Christmas boxes to Mrs. Carlyle regularly, containing Welsh mutton, sheep's milk cheese, and so on, and whenever he came to London he was welcome at Cheyne Row, and spent many a happy evening there. He wrote in the *Examiner*, and in 1839 had published a book on *Folk Lore*. In short, as a credible reporter tells us,[2] it was 'a case of literary friendship from the first.'

On Wednesday, 31.7.50, Carlyle took train for Bath, where Savage Landor, an old man of seventy-five now, was expecting him. He found Landor at home, awaiting him, with no other company but 'a nice Bologna dog. Dinner not far from ready; his apartments all hung round with

[1] *Carlyle's Holidays in Wales*, by John Howells, *Red Dragon Magazine*, April, May, and June, 1884; and also *Carlyle Letters*.

[2] *Wales as Carlyle saw it Forty Years Ago*, by James Harris, in the *Red Dragon Magazine*, December, and perhaps 1881, but the year is uncertain.

queer old Italian pictures; the very doors had pictures on them. Dinner was elaborately simple. The brave Landor was really stirring company: a proud, irascible, trenchant, yet generous, veracious, and very dignified old man; quite a ducal or royal man in the temper of him; reminded me something of old Sterling, except that for Irish blarney you must substitute a fund of Welsh choler. He walked me through the Crescent, Park, &c., in the dusk ' till ten o'clock, and then went home to bed, and left his guest to go alone ' smoking along the streets ' and studying the town as much longer as he liked.

Carlyle found Bath ' decidedly the prettiest town in all England. Nay, Edinburgh itself, except for the sea and the Grampians, does not equal it. Regular, but by no means formal streets, all clean, all quiet, yet not dead, winding up in picturesque, lively varieties along the face of a large, broad sweep of woody green sandstone hill, with large outlook to the opposite side of the valley; and fine, decent, clean people sauntering about it, mostly small country gentry, I was told, " live here for £1200 a year," said Landor.'

Carlyle had always rather liked Landor; and after this visit the liking was mutual. In 1852 Landor told Forster [3]:—" I am a great advocate for hero-worship; and when you have looked closely into Carlyle, you may discover him to be quite as much of a hero as Cromwell."

Next morning Carlyle went to Bristol and took the steamer to Cardiff, where Redwood was awaiting him, and drove him in a gig to his new home at Boverton village, within a mile of a shore most suitable for bathing and in sight of the Somerset hills across the water. Redwood's mother was now dead, and daily after breakfast Redwood went to his office at Cowbridge and left Carlyle alone. Carlyle was happy. He called the house a " Hermitage," and assuredly it combined the pleasures of a well-served house with those of loneliness. Nearly every day for the three weeks he was there he was bathing in the sea, and riding far on the good swift pony ever ready in the stable, among the ' straggling, sleepy, sluttish-looking villages.'

Redwood himself seemed ' to have less intercourse with his neighbours than any other man now living '; but he ' liked and honoured ' his guest, and made him feel at home.

[3] *W. S. Landor, A Biography*, by John Forster, p. 454.

Tho fussy and fidgety, he was 'friendliness itself, poor fellow; disclosed a great quantity of passive intelligence amid his great profundity of dullness: nay, a kind of humour at times,' and perhaps Carlyle was chaffing his wife at a safe distance when he wrote to her from that house that Redwood also 'certainly excelled in *good temper* all the human beings I have been near lately. . . . More like an angel than a Welshman. Perfection of temper!'

On Thursday, 15.8.50,[4] Redwood did not go to office, but instead of doing so conveyed Carlyle away towards the mountains lying in the north, and about twenty miles from Cowbridge they beheld Merthyr Tydvil, the place of mines and ironworks. Carlyle told his wife.—

'In 1755 Merthyr Tydvil was a mountain hamlet of five or six houses, stagnant and silent as it had been ever since Tydvil, the king's or laird's daughter, was martyred here, say 1300 years before. About that time (1755) a certain Mr. Bacon, a cunning Yorkshireman, passing that way, discovered that there was iron in the ground—iron and coal. He took a 99 years' lease in consequence, and—in brief, there are now about 50,000 grimy mortals, black and clammy with soot and sweat, screwing out a livelihood for themselves in that spot of the Taff Valley. Such a set of unguided, hard-worked, fierce, and miserable-looking sons of Adam I never saw before. Ah me! It is like a vision of Hell, and will never leave me, that of these poor creatures broiling, all in sweat and dirt, amid their furnaces, pits, and rolling mills. For here is absolutely "no" aristocracy or guiding class; nothing but one or two huge iron-masters; and the rest are operatives, petty shopkeepers, Scotch hawkers, &c. &c. The town might be, and will be, one of the prettiest places in the world. It *is* one of the sootiest, squalidest, and ugliest: all cinders and dust-mounds and soot. Their very greens they bring from Bristol, tho the ground is excellent all round. Nobody thinks of gardening in such a locality—all devoted to metallic gambling.'

There is nothing here inconsistent with the gospel of work. Carlyle disliked the sight of the slaves of the metals and the slave-drivers, because they were dirty, ignorant, and living at random. The right sort of work, which a

[4] Date fixed by a letter of T. Carlyle, first printed in the *Times Literary Supplement*, 10.6.1920.

man should do or die, is not what comes to hand, nor yet what is paid the best. The hardest task of life is to discover what to do. To be wide-awake and look where one is going is the method of Carlyle. The organisation of labour he was calling for would have made Merthyr Tydvil a happy place.

XXXII

TO SCOTSBRIG

(1850)

MRS. CARLYLE in the meantime was raising her annual household earthquake, and enjoying long letters from her husband every day. Perhaps the last reply she sent him to Boverton was one dated 20.8.50, which ran:—

'Only a little note to-day, Dear,
"That you may know I am in being,
'Tis intended for a sign."

'And a sign, too, that I am grateful for your long Letters,—my only comfort thro' this *black* business,' (housecleaning) 'which has indeed "flurried me all to pieces." To-day's' (Letter) 'did not come by the morning post; not till twelve, when I had fallen so *low* for want of it that I might have had no news for a week! It is sad and wrong to be so dependent for the life of my life on any human being as I am on you; but I cannot by any force of logic cure myself of the habit at this date, when it has become a second nature. If I have to lead another life in any of the planets, I shall take precious good care not to hang myself round any man's neck, either as a locket or a millstone! . . .

'I am now going to lie on the sofa and have Geraldine read a novel to me all the rest of this day,—writing makes me "too fluttery for anything." . . . Give my kind regards to poor dear Redwood, whose feelings I can well understand.

'Ever your affectionate
'JANE CARLYLE.'

Saturday, 24.8.50, seems to have been the day of departure, and on that day, as he wrote from Scotsbrig five days afterwards to Redwood,[1] having four hours to wait at

[1] *Carlyle's Holidays in Wales*, by John Howells, *Red Dragon Magazine*, April, May and June, 1884.

Llantrissant, he accomplished it 'among the green fields. I got out a book and tobacco, and spreading my pea-jacket by way of carpet, lay down on the sunward side of a solitary bush.'

He reached Gloucester that night, and found its streets interesting on the Saturday night; but slept badly, and so went to Birmingham by train next day, and did better there. On Monday he went to Liverpool, and left by steamer that night for Annan, on the way to Scotsbrig.

The port of Annan was not deep enough for big steamers, and the steamer plying between it and Liverpool was now near its last voyage on that run. So Carlyle's disagreeable experience on it was described to his wife with a kind of double meaning only half-intended,—he was reconciling himself to the closing of his favourite route, by the sea.

The night was soft and beautiful as the steamer ran down the Mersey. Then as the night advanced, "This way the *gents' cabin*, sir," said the steward. 'In truth it was almost worth a little voyage to see such a cabin of gents. The little crib of a place, which I had glanced at two hours before and found six beds in, had now developed itself into the sleeping-place of at least sixteen of the gent species. There they all lay, my crib the only empty one; a pile of clothes up to the very ceiling, and all round it gent packed on gent, few inches between the nose of one gent and the nape of the other gent's neck; not a particle of air, all orifices closed. Five or six of said gents already raging and snoring. And a smell! *Ach Gott!* I suppose it must resemble that of the slave ships in the middle passage.' (Meaning the voyage across the Atlantic.) 'It was positively immoral to think of sleeping in such a receptacle of abominations.'

He spent the night on deck instead, and on landing 'appealed to Goody and posterity.' The latent reference was to one of Cavaignac's stories. "Vous êtes des injustes" (you are unfair to me), said a drunken man whom boys were annoying. "Je m'en appelle à la postérité" (I appeal to posterity). 'My poor dear!' his wife wrote back, Friday, 30.8.50. 'That was the worst journey, "but one," I ever read of.' This was another echo of French wit,—say "worst but one," for there's a *crush* towards badness. The letter went on.—'One good thing will come of it, I hope; and that is a certain sympathy with Quashee! You will be more disposed henceforth to grant to your black brother the compensation of unlimited pumpkins! Such is the only benefit that I ever get from being made miserable. Exceptional natures may be "made perfect through suffering." But where the moral digestion is weak, the more miserable one is, the more one grows—"What shall I say? —bad, upon my honour."' (The last quotation was from the talk of Mazzini.)

Resting at Scotsbrig and considering what next, Carlyle wrote to his wife on 4.9.50.—'I find it good that all one's ugly thoughts—ugly as sin and Satan several of them—should come uninterrupted before one and look and do their very worst. Many things tend towards settlement in that way, and silently beginnings of arrangement and determination show themselves. Why, oh! why, should a living man complain after all? We get, each one of us, the common fortune, with superficial variations. A man ought to know that he is *not* ill-used; that if he miss the thing one way he gets it in another. Your "beautiful blessings," I have them not. I cannot train myself by having them. Well, then, by doing without them I can train myself. It is there that I go ahead of you. There, too, lie prizes if you knew it.'

This is a fine instance of the method of the Stoic Epictetus in practice, blended with the human craving to get ahead of others. Two days later he wrote again.—'Nothing so like a Sabbath has been vouchsafed to me for many heavy months as these last ten days at poor Scotsbrig are. Let me be thankful for them. They were very necessary to me. They will open my heart to sad and affectionate thoughts, which the intolerable burden of my own mean sufferings has stifled for a long time. I do nothing here, and pretend to do nothing but sit silent. . . . One should be content to admit that one is Nothing: a poor, vainly struggling soul, yet seen with pity by the Eternal Powers, I do believe, and whose struggles at worst are bending towards their *close*. This puts one to peace when nothing else can; and the beggarly miseries of the mere body abating a little, as with me they sensibly do, it is strange what dark curtains drop off of their own accord, and how the promise of clearer skies again visits one. These last three days have been of surpassing beauty—clear, calm September days, the sky bright and blue, with fluctuating masses of bright clouds. The hills are all spotted with pure light and pure shade; everything of the liveliest yellow or the liveliest green in this lower region. On riding up from the Kirtlebridge side hitherward, I could not but admit that the bright scene, with Burnswark and the infinite azure behind it, was one of the loveliest that I had anywhere seen. Poor old Annandale, after all! . . . A note to Lady Ashburton, after I arrived here, brought this answer yesterday. Great *Gaudeamus*' (meaning Rejoicing,—the first word and so the title of an old students' song,—Great Rejoicing) 'at the Grange, it would seem. Between life *there* and life *here*, as I now have it, it must be admitted there is a contrast. We are about the two extremes of decent human lodging, and I know which answers the best for me. Remember me generally to all friends. Good souls! I like them all better than perhaps they would suspect from my *grim* ways. Sometimes it has struck me, Could not I *continue* this *Sabbatic* period in a room at Craigenputtock, perhaps? Alas! alas!'

His wife would not hear of such a thing,—she had had her way about where to live, and would never risk anything that might revive the matter. Carlyle remained 'near a month' at Scotsbrig on this occasion, to the delight of his mother, who went a walk with him every day, and was "wonderfully cheerful," he wrote to his brother in Canada; but it saddened him to see how very frail she was. "Like snaw-drifts in thaw," as the song says, she was fading away to "the land o' the leal." "Her hand shakes rather worse," Carlyle wrote to his brother, and she was weak and fragile, "but in general she shifts along wonderfully. Twice or thrice she had a *washing* while I was there, and did it all herself and well. She reads with all the old eagerness; is ever full of interest and affection for you and me and all that pertains to her; occasionally even *jokes*, in her own genial way." Dr. John, his medical brother, was living at Scotsbrig, and "an immense help" to her.

XXXIII

SEEN BY CHILDREN

(1850)

WHILE now at Scotsbrig, Carlyle was having new clothes made by his usual tailor in Ecclefechan. He can still be seen through the eyes of the tailor's son, a little boy running errands then, but in 1896 himself " Mr. Garthwaite, the tailor of Ecclefechan." The little boy of 1850 was in 1896 an elderly man, articulate and downright, with sharp decisive features, and a vivid recollection of the summer of 1850.—

" Thomas Carlyle was a good customer of my father for many years," he said.[1] " His orders came at long intervals, but when one came, it was worth having, six pairs of trousers and 3 or 4 vests and coats.

" I was always much in awe of him, myself. One day I went to Scotsbrig to get an order he was to write. ' Where is he ? ' I enquired of Mrs. James Carlyle, the farmer's wife. ' In the room upstairs,' said she. I would have much preferred to get the order without a sight of him ; but we heard him calling out, ' Little Garthwaite ! ' That was his name for me. ' You'll need to go up,' said Mrs. James Carlyle.

" I recollect his voice was like a bell, clear, distinct and strong. I went upstairs, but by the time I reached the open door of his room, he had turned again to the table and recommenced writing. I stood watching as his pen ran over the paper, sheet after sheet. He seemed to be lost to everything but what he was doing. Standing on the landing, I knocked at the open door. He took no notice. There was a washing board at the other end of the landing. I went and kicked it. He took no notice. I hummed and coughed a good deal, as loud as I could. He never moved, but went on writing, sheet after sheet, for an hour as it

[1] To D. A. W. at Ecclefechan, 1896.

seemed to me. Then all at once he gave a sort of shout, 'Aw!' I took that to mean 'Come in.' So in I went. 'There is your order,' said he, pointing to it, lying ready on the table, and handing me at the same time a letter to post and—a penny!

"His brother Dr. John would have given me a shilling or two on such an occasion,—he was a very genial man and always put me at my ease,—truly a perfect gentleman,—quite different from Thomas!"

This was the last summer at Scotsbrig during which Carlyle was under the observation of another juvenile, his niece Margaret Hanning, now twelve years of age. Mrs. Hanning, who lived in Dumfries on an allowance from her brothers Tom and Dr. John, used always to come to Scotsbrig, fetching her two girls with her, to help her mother when "Tom" was there. "It was not merely that mother worried about him," she explained in 1895,[2] "tho Tom was greatly bothered by his stomach and took his meals, at least his dinner, alone. Besides that, he was always greatly followed by visitors. He sometimes enjoyed their company, and always was courteous to any he met or who came into the same room with him; but often he would take great pains to avoid them."

Her daughter Margaret Hanning, now Mrs. Leslie, then remembered and told a story [2] of events she had both seen and often heard her mother tell, and Mrs. Hanning, listening, corroborated her.—'Two gentlemen once called to see Uncle Tom and mother went to seek him, searching everywhere, calling "Tom, Tom!" all over the farm buildings. She then went down the lane, as far as a field called the Fairy Brae, a favourite resort of his. At last she remembered she had not looked into his bedroom. So she went there, and found him sitting before the fire. She said, "Is it possible you have been here all the time I've been calling for you all over the farm?" "And I am very sorry you found me," he replied. "Come on in," said she. "There's Mr. Johnston, an old Ecclefechan man home from India, and another gentleman from India, here, both wanting to see you very much. Come, brush yourself up." He did not brush up, but he came down,—he often walked about near the house in his dressing-gown. He went in to the

[2] Talk to D. A. W. at Comely Bank Farm, Oakville, Ontario, Canada, 28.9.1895.

visitors just as he was, and had a pleasant talk with them, and soon was in a fit of hearty laughing, and rubbing his left arm, which was a trick of his when thus enjoying himself.'

Mrs. Hanning, who was over eighty in 1895, could not remember that 'trick.' What she did recall was that her brother often leaned on his left elbow, when reading. It seemed likely that the children had noticed what escaped the rest, how he sometimes rubbed his left elbow,—a natural thing to do after leaning on it. Mrs. Leslie went on.—

'The happiest time we youngsters ever had was when we saw Uncle Tom coming. Never in my life did I hear him scolding or speaking cross to anybody. He was never *working* at Scotsbrig. My mother told me so at the time. He was only resting and being beside his mother, my grandmother.

'The one thing I remember he was particular about was getting his mail every day. The boys, our cousins, sons of Uncle James, had to go for it to the post office. One day they were skylarking with the rest of us children instead, putting a lot of us on the donkey at once, for the fun of seeing us fall off. We arrived at the side of Middlebie Burn, in sight of Uncle Tom on the other side of it, and he said,—"If you stay much later I'll get no mail to-day. One of you must go to the post office now." So John ran off to fetch the letters, the same who is now old John Carlyle of Langholm.

'Uncle Tom did not need to *shout* across the burn. I do not recollect I ever heard him shout. But he had a musical voice you heard easily.' Then she reminded her mother of a thing worth telling, and they laughed again at the recollection. It was in 1850.—'My sister Mary and I and cousin Janet and some more were playing noisily outside the house after dinner. My mother came out to make us be quiet for uncle's sake,—he sometimes slept after dinner,—and was crying "Hush!" when suddenly Uncle Tom's voice came like music through the open window,—"Never mind them, Jenny. Let them laugh as loud as they can." My mother said no more and we children all danced and shouted for joy.

'One of the things Uncle Tom used to say, and I've heard my mother repeat it, was,—"I wouldn't desire to see a greater sign of a knave than to see a man chuckling and laughing to himself."

'I can just remember my aunt, Mrs. Tom, or "Tom's wife," as granny called her. My mother used to get from her Tom's old dressing-gowns and cut them up to make into clothes for my sister and me; and once I heard Mrs. Tom speaking to granny about that and how clever my mother was, saying:—"Jenny is very good at making silk purses out of sows' ears." And noticing me, she said also,—"What a gleg" (or wideawake) "little thing that is. She looks as if *she* had been in the cotton trade for the last 30 years."

'Uncle Tom came to see us whenever he was at Dumfries when we were there, and used to give my sister and me, each of us, a big silver coin, bigger than the palm of my hand,' a crown piece, of course.

What had been a mystery to Mrs. Leslie all her life was now explained to her by her mother. "I never heard Uncle Tom say anything unpleasant about my father," said Mrs. Leslie, "and after I came over to live in Canada, noticed that my father always spoke kindly of him,—never blamed him in any way, and never said a harsh word about him. Yet once at Scotsbrig, the last summer we were there, 1850, when mother and granny and Uncle Tom were talking together, I heard Uncle Tom allude to my father in Canada as 'that thing,' which always was a puzzle to me. I never understood it, tho I have not thought of it for many years."

Her mother, Mrs. Hanning, said she remembered it.—"It was in the course of arguing to help my mother, who was trying to prevent me agreeing to join your father in Hamilton, Ontario. Your father was there then, and begging me to come to him, and offering to send money for the purpose. When he first went to America in 1841, I was persuaded by my mother to stay behind. He had lost in business all his money and mine too, and my youngest child then, Mary, was a baby a few months old. So I stayed as my mother advised. But it was for the baby's sake. I kept writing to him as often as I could discover his address, but he sent no reply for four years. Then he wrote and we began corresponding as if nothing had happened. By 1850 he was a foreman in the Great Western Railway Works at Hamilton. Everybody was against my going, but I was determined, and strange to tell, before I went away, which was in 1851, Mrs. Tom, Uncle Tom's wife, wrote to me,—'Go in God's name, and God be with you, my dear little Jennie.'" Mrs. Hanning quite understood she had her brother's blessing, saying,—"His wife would never have written like that, if he had not approved."

"To the end of his life," said Mrs. Hanning, "Tom sent me a copy of everything he published, with an inscription in his own handwriting." The books were produced. There was no mistake about the handwriting. Mrs. Leslie added:—"In his will Uncle Tom gave mother an even share of all his property, which made her independent when he died."

XXXIV

KINGSLEY, MRS. TENNYSON, &c.

(1850)

ON Sunday night, 8.9.50, Mrs. Carlyle was writing to her husband:—'To-morrow I shall lay out two sixpences in forwarding (Kingsley's) *Alton Locke* (*The Devil among the Tailors* would have been the best name for it). It will surely be gratifying to you, the sight of your own name in almost every second page! But for that, I am ashamed to say I should have broken down in it a great way this side of the end! It seems to me, in spite of Geraldine's Hallelujahs, a mere—not very well boiled—broth of *Morning Chronicle*-ism, in which *you* play the part of the *tasting-bone of Poverty Row*. An oppressive, painful Book! . . . All the indignation against existing things strikes somehow so numbly! like your father whipping the bad children under the bedclothes![1] But the old Scotchman (Saunders Mackay) is capital,—only that there never was nor ever will be *such* an old Scotchman. I wonder what will come of Kingsley—go mad, perhaps.'

The book was being published by Chapman and Hall on Carlyle's recommendation, and he read it 'swiftly, under the bright sunshine, by the sound of rushing brooks and other rural' noises. When he went away from Scotsbrig, he left the book behind for others to read. Of course, he wrote to the author as kindly as possible, but also truly, telling him the work was crude and he could do better, but bidding him persevere.—'You will have to persist; like a cannon-ball that is shot, you will have to go to your mark, whatever that be. . . . Come and see me when you are at Chelsea,' he concluded, and 'never heed the reviewers.'[2] Theology he never would debate with professional Christians; but the 'huge folios of St. Augustine,' which John Sterling had given him, he gave to Charles Kingsley.[3]

It seems to have been in 1850 that a wideawake young

[1] See *Carlyle Till Marriage*, Chap. X, pp. 37–8.
[2] *Charles Kingsley*, by his wife, I, pp. 234 and 244–5.
[3] *Ibid.*, II, p. 284, footnote.

woman was at Ecclefechan station, and saw Thomas Carlyle waiting for the train. His brother James was beside him, having driven him from Scotsbrig, and she heard him saying to James,—" Go away home, back to your work. Don't waste your time here, waiting for the train." So James departed.[4]

That would be on 27.9.50, and Carlyle's destination was Keswick, to spend a few days with his friend Thomas Spedding. Thence he went on to Coniston and stayed with the Marshalls, the same old friends, from Leeds originally, who figure in the Reminiscences. While he was there, Alfred Tennyson and his newly married wife came to call. They were honeymooning at Tentlodge near by, a cottage lent them by the Marshalls.[5]

Carlyle and the bride had never met before, tho each had heard from Tennyson about the other; and doubtless what the lady remembered would be as we are told,—" He slowly scanned her from head to foot, then gave her a hearty shake of the hand." Nobody but herself would notice he was scanning her, and what he wrote to his wife reveals what was in his mind :—' Mrs. Tennyson lights up bright glittering blue eyes when you speak to her; has wit; has sense; and were it not that she seems so very delicate in health, I should augur really well of Tennyson's adventure.' Next day he called at their cottage, and she used gratefully to remember how ' on hearing her cough, while the others were talking, he, " with his invariable kindness," stole round and shut the window, which was open behind her.'[5]

Carlyle reached home on 2.10.50, by which time his wife had gone to stay with the Ashburtons at the Grange in Hampshire. Next morning she was writing to him at length :—' I have put a lucifer to my bedroom fire, dear, and sat down to write, but I feel more disposed to lay my head on the table and cry. By this time I suppose you are at home; returned after a two months' absence, arrived off a long journey—and I not there! . . . It is the first time in all the twenty years I have lived beside you that you ever arrived at home and I away.' Which seems accurate, too, requiring only the correction of twenty-four instead of twenty.

[4] Told by her, Mrs. Janet Graham, to D. A. W. in Ecclefechan about 1896.
[5] *Alfred, Lord Tennyson, a Memoir by his Son*, I, pp. 333–4.

She went on to tell how another lady then at the Grange 'was in London yesterday, and saw my maid on business of her own, and brought back word from her that you were coming last night; and the shouts of laughter, and cutting "wits," with which my startled look and exclamation, "Oh, Gracious!" were visited when the news was told me as we sat down to dinner, were enough to terrify one from "showing feeling" for twelve months to come.' Whereat Mrs. Carlyle, who made no pretence of meekness, showed the lady in fault 'so plainly that I was displeased with her impertinent jesting that she made me an apology in the course of the evening.

'And now what is to be done next? You say, stay where I am. . . . It is quite out of the question my remaining here till the 20th,' as in short Lady A. desires, 'unless you accept the invitation, which Lady A. is again writing to you, to come here after you are rested,' which, of course, he had to do, and, as he expressed it in writing to Redwood, 'join her for three weeks among gay people in Hampshire.'[1] He would have done so, even if she had not been able to add such inducements as that Thackeray was coming, and Kinglake and Brookfield.

It was on this occasion, October, 1850, that the Rev. Mr. Brookfield sent a good story to his wife,[6] telling her that as he, 'Carlyle and Kinglake, stood under the porch, Sir William Montague strolled up and said, "What a glorious day this is. Upon my word, as I walked up the lawn and looked at this splendid edifice and you gentlemen grouped under this magnificent portico, I felt that I could imagine a variety of things." Carlyle shouted, of course,' which means that he laughed uproariously like a boy, instead of smirking acquiescence. This is the sort of thing that lets us see what Lady Ashburton meant when she said,[7]—"Coming back to the society of Carlyle after the dons at Oxford is like returning from some conventional world to the human race."

Before the end of October, Mrs. Carlyle and her husband were at home in Cheyne Row; and apropos of the Grange, here is what Carlyle wrote to Charles Redwood:[8]—'This is the Lord Ashburton's big mansion, the ancient "Grange"

[6] *Mrs. Brookfield and her Circle*, by C. and F. Brookfield, II, pp. 324–5.
[7] *Monographs*, by Lord Houghton, p. 251.
[8] Letter of 26.12.51, printed in *Carlyle's Holidays in Wales*, by John Howells, *Red Dragon Magazine* of June, 1884.

of the Winchester Monks, now for the last three centuries a secular abode of dignitaries.'

Some days after coming home, Mrs. Carlyle was writing to her friend Mrs. Russell at Thornhill.—'Home is always pleasantest to me after a long sojourn in a grand House; and solitude never so welcome as after a spell of brilliant people. One brilliant person at a time and a little of him is a charming thing; but a whole houseful of brilliant people, shining all day and every day, makes one almost of George Sand's opinion, that good honest stupidity is the best thing to associate with.'

XXXV

A SAUCY LITTLE GIRL

(1850)

IN a book of Reminiscences[1] Mrs. Janet Ross exhibits herself as one of the happiest and sauciest little girls in London about 1850. She was Janet Gordon then, the eight-year-old granddaughter of Mrs. Austin. Her mother was Mrs. Austin's child, and the addressee of Thackeray's epistle :—

> 'A nice leg of mutton, my Lucie,
> I pray thee have ready for me ;
> Have it smoking and tender and juicy,
> For no better meat can there be.'

It was to a house in Queen Square he was inviting himself, near where Jeremy Bentham and James Mill had lived, on ground now covered by Queen Anne's Mansions.

When her parents 'went to Mr. Rogers's Sunday morning breakfasts in St. James's Place,' old Rogers insisted that his 'baby-love' should come for dessert, and he seated her next to himself, as she proudly informs posterity sixty years afterwards. "This is my little Janet," said her mother once to Mr. Grote, when Mrs. Austin took them both to see the historian. 'The stately, courteous old gentleman,' according to the grateful Janet's report, 'took my small hand in both his.'—He may have been wearing his beautiful waistcoat with brilliant red collar and lapel.[2]—What she remembered is that he bowed to her and said: "I am indeed delighted to make the acquaintance of Mrs. Austin's granddaughter and Lucy's daughter." '

The daughter of Lucy Austin, Mrs. Gordon, was likely to be spoiled by the friends of the family. Tennyson named Mrs. Gordon as the model of his *Princess*, and according to Tom Taylor and Kinglake, reported by Mrs. Ross, Tennyson once 'burst out at dinner :—" I never loved a dear

[1] *The Fourth Generation, Reminiscences*, by Mrs. Janet Ross, pp. 13–22 and 28.

[2] Credibly described to D. A. W. by an eye-witness.

gazelle, but some damned brute, that's you, Gordon, had married her first." '

There is always a spot in the sunshine. Janet found both her grandfather Austin and Thomas Carlyle less deferential to her than Mr. Grote. Mr. Austin sometimes took her out walking,—and taught her to reverence Burke and Bentham so that she 'connected them in some dim way with the Bible'; but when the old gentleman was 'launched in a discussion, it was almost impossible to stop him.' When once she found him talking to Dr. Whewell, 'for a time I listened, but at length my patience was exhausted.' "But, grandpapa, grandpapa, I can't get in a word. Do stop him!" she cried to Whewell. 'After that' she was 'forbidden to enter the study unless specially invited,' and even then she 'was not to interrupt.'

This might be pardoned in a grandfather, but in a caller it was intolerable to her. 'The one of our many visitors to Queen Square whom I cordially disliked was Mr. Carlyle. He was a great friend of Mrs. Austin's, and professed to admire Lucykin, as he called my Mother, very much. One afternoon he had a discussion with her on German literature, and her wonderful eloquence and fire prevailing, Carlyle lost his temper,' in the opinion of eight-year-old Janet, 'and burst forth in his Scotch tongue: "You're just a windbag, Lucy; you're just a windbag." I had been listening with all my ears as my grandmother always spoke with such enthusiasm about him; but furious at my Mother being, as I thought, "called names" by so uncouth,' unfashionably dressed, 'a man, I interrupted, and exclaimed: "My papa says men should be civil to women." For which pert remark I was reproved by my Mother. Mr. Carlyle, however, was not offended, and only observed:—"Lucykin, that child of yours has an eye for an inference." '[1]

XXXVI

TAKING IT EASY

(1850)

ALL the time Carlyle was in the country, he had been suffering from dyspepsia and depression, but soon after he settled down again at home, he was able to report to Redwood that he was feeling better,[1] and for the next three months he was reading at large. When busy he used to be content to learn what was in the daily newspapers from his wife's report; but now he read many periodicals, old and new, and books also, Sophocles for one item, and Wycherley's dirty plays for another, tho he stopped about the middle of Wycherley, 'with real abomination.' It was a relief to turn to Scaligerana or the good things of Joseph Scaliger, in French and English, which he much enjoyed. While reading he was thinking of what to work on next. Ireland? or Education? Or some bit of English history, perhaps William the Conqueror? 'But what,' he thought, '*can* be done with a British Museum under fat pedants, with a world so sunk as ours, and alas! with a soul so sunk and subdued to its elements as mine seems to be?'

In November an American Globetrotter in London posted to him "to be forwarded" a letter from Emerson to Mazzini, and intimated that he had a letter of introduction to Carlyle himself, but would not deliver it because Carlyle had called the Yankees "eighteen million bores!" He was writing from Morley's Hotel. Carlyle went to it at once; but found the Globetrotter had left for Liverpool that morning. So on 14.11.50 Carlyle was writing to Emerson to explain the matter:—

'"Eighteen million bores,"—good Heavens don't I also know how many of that species we also have; and how with us, as with you, the difference between *them* and the eighteen thousand noble-men and *non*-bores is immeasurable and inconceivable; and how, with us as with you, the

[1] *Carlyle's Holidays in Wales*, by John Howells, *Red Dragon Magazine*, April, May and June, 1884.

latter small company, sons of the Empyrean, will have to fling the former huge one, sons of Mammon and Mud, into some kind of chains again, reduce them to some kind of silence again,—unless the old Mud-Demons are to rise and devour us all. Truly it is so I construe it: and if the Eighteen millions are well justified in their anger at me, the Eighteen thousand owe me thanks and new love. That is my decided opinion, in spite of you all!'

Then he went on to confess that he had never even read an American pamphlet written to answer and confound him and sent over. As for Emerson's own criticism, Carlyle admitted 'there is good in all' things, 'and if you even see an Oliver Cromwell assassinated, it is certain you may get a cartload of turnips from his carcase. Let us well remember it; and yet remember, too, that it is *not* good to be "at ease in Zion"; good often to be in fierce rage in Zion; and that the vile Pythons of this Mud-World do verily require to have sun-arrows shot into them and red-hot pokers struck through them, according to occasion: woe to the man that carries either of these weapons, and does not use it in their presence!' (The next sentence makes one feel as if in Cheyne Row looking over his shoulder as he writes, and hearing the street noises.—) 'Here, at this moment, a miserable Italian organ-grinder has struck up the *Marseillaise* under my window, for example: was the *Marseillaise* fought out on a bed of down, or is it worth nothing when fought? . . . And so, Peace to the brave that are departed; and To-morrow to fresh fields and pastures new!'—

According to Espinasse,[2] Carlyle was in 'a mournful mood' this winter. 'One day at that time I was chatting with Mrs. Carlyle while he sat by himself, grumbling occasionally and looking very gloomy. Mrs. Carlyle suddenly turned round and said to him, "You ought to write a book."' To which he answered 'sorrowfully, "I can't write as I used to do."' And Espinasse moralises upon his 'under-estimating' himself, inasmuch as in a few months he was writing 'the delightful biography of Sterling.'

[2] *Literary Recollections*, by F. Espinasse, pp. 187–8.

BOOK XIX

JOHN STERLING
(1850)

I

HELPING A STRANGER TO GET WORK

(1850)

IN September last Carlyle at Scotsbrig had been corresponding with his old friend the Glasgow merchant, David Hope,—the friend of Edward Irving long ago,[1]—about a possible trip to Iona, which was abandoned. From London on 3.12.50 he wrote to him another letter,[1] worth reading now for the glimpse it gives of a side of Carlyle's continual activity which was intentionally kept out of sight. We are left guessing the sequel, which matters to nobody now.—

'My Dear Sir,—

'Is your brother William still in these parts, and at all engaged in the teaching department? If so, will you let me ask you for his address?

'A very worthy poor Scotchman has just called upon me, much wanting instructions as to his method of attempting to get employment in that line, for which he is intrinsically well qualified, tho quite new in the ways of this big Babel; and I, in my great ignorance of such matters, have bethought me of your brother's experienced sense and humanity as one of the likeliest courses for entering upon this affair.

'We are puddling away in the midst of foggy frost, reek rain,' meaning Smoke rain, or rain falling full of soot from the smoke in the air,—'and "No Popery,"—getting up our "Crystal Palace" very fast (if that could do anything for us), and little else that I see. My two months of roaming, in Wales and the Scottish border, do not seem to have done much for me: I am the same complaining creature you have always known me; and shall likely continue such, I think. After all, as the Psalmist has it, "Why should a living man complain?"—Because he is a fool, I do surmise, and for no other reason. Believe me always,

'Very truly yours,

'T. Carlyle.'

[1] *Unpublished Letters of Carlyle* (to Edward Irving and David Hope), *Scribner's Mag.*, apparently April, 1893, pp. 416–25. See *Carlyle Till Marriage*, pp. 234–6, etc.

II

NEWS OF THE DAY

(1850)

LEIGH HUNT was now sixty-six years of age, and was endeavouring to revive a periodical called *Leigh Hunt's Journal*. To oblige him[1] Carlyle consented to touch up some of his unused historical manuscripts, which John Chorley was sifting, and so on 7.12.50, etc., there appeared in three sections, under the general title of *Two Hundred and Fifty Years Ago*, picturesque descriptions of two duels and an aristocratic disturbance at *Croydon Races*. A movie-picture would be dull in comparison, and could not be made so intelligible. But *Leigh Hunt's Journal* had soon to stop for want of capital, and Carlyle did nothing more. The rest of the manuscripts copied by Chorley lay unprinted till published as *Historical Sketches* in 1898.

Richard Owen, the naturalist of the Hunterian Museum, etc., spent several evenings with Carlyle this winter, including 20.12.50, talking mainly about their common friend John Sterling, and doubtless saying ditto to his brother Captain Sterling, who was begging Carlyle to deliver the memory of John Sterling from the theologians. Another topic of their talk was Foucault's Pendulum. A clever young Frenchman, Foucault, had lately hung in the Pantheon a truly wonderful Pendulum, a ball of metal suspended over a table by a long wire. When it was made to swing free and in one plane, it appeared to make the circuit of the table in the twenty-four hours, going leftwards, the reverse of the direction of the hands of a clock; while in reality it was the table and the Pantheon that were moving. Thus was made palpable the greatest of astronomical discoveries, the daily movement of the Earth.

"Can you not advise Professor Airy," Carlyle enquired of Owen,[2] "or some real mathematician or geometer, to undertake that business of Foucault's Pendulum, and throwing Euler and his algebra overboard, illuminate it

[1] *Corr. of Leigh Hunt*, II, p. 120; and see *C. on Cromwell and Others*, pp. 248–9.
[2] *Life of Richard Owen*, by the Rev. R. Owen, I, pp. 261–3.

for the geometrical mind? It seems to me the prettiest experiment made in this century, tho perhaps good for nothing otherwise. I have had a great wrestling with it in my own poor head,—which used to know some mathematics twenty years ago,—and a deadly suspicion haunts me, the fact itself being certain as fate, that nobody has yet in the least explained what the real causes and conditions of it are."

The chief excitement this winter was a row about Papal Aggression, of which the immediate cause was the same well-meaning "Reforming Pope," Pius the Ninth, who encouraged the Sicilians to revolt, without intending it, and whom Napoleon the Little had replaced in power, when the French armies had finished the Roman Republic in 1849. As soon as the runaway Pope felt safe at home in the Vatican, he had started playing funny tricks. The English fanatic Dr. Newman was preaching in 1850 that a miracle was coming,—"the people of England, who had for so many years been separated from the Church of Rome, were about of their own will" to return to it.—"Like pigs to their wallowing in the mire," might well have been the only answer. What made the nonsense seem serious was that the Pope had taken to calling his priests such names as "Cardinal Archbishop of Westminster," "Bishop of Birmingham," and so on, as if the miracle were taking place, and so instead of laughter, there was popular fury. Writing to Redwood on 23.12.50,[3] Carlyle concluded:—

'I do not enter much into the Papal Aggression affair; tho I am Protestant enough to view it with equanimity, and even with a kind of goodwill. It seems to me the old Pope ought really to be warned that *he* is out of the game, for one; that after having beaten out his brains for three hundred years with Cromwellian and other hammers, we do expect he will now die! If the poor English people can do this, I shall not be sorry. If they fail to do it, I shall understand that windbag knocked against windbag will infallibly further the collapse of things inflated; and so in any case the Papal Aggression is grist to my mill. I write nothing in these months, nor have any prospect of writing; but do suppose that if I live there may come such a time again. God bless you always, dear Redwood.

'Yours ever truly,

'T. CARLYLE.'

[3] *Carlyle's Holidays in Wales*, by John Howells, *Red Dragon Magazine*, April, May and June, 1884.

III

NEUBERG AND LARKIN, &c.

(1850)

NEXT day, 24.12.50, Carlyle was writing to Varnhagen von Ense in Berlin[1] describing his friend Neuberg. He had given Neuberg a card of introduction to Von Ense, which was handsomely honoured in due course.

'Herr Neuberg,' the letter ran, 'is a man of unostentatious but truly superior character; a most pious, clear, resolute, modest and earnest man; with excellent insights and faculties; well acquainted both with our literature and yours, and indeed knows England and English affairs better probably than any stranger you have met. . . . He was twenty years a merchant in this country, and then, finding himself possessed of a competence and totally without enthusiasm for more, decided to give up business, and live henceforth among intellectual objects.'

On the same day Carlyle received a letter from Neuberg in Bonn, and answered it at once,[2] telling about this letter to Von Ense, and going on:—'You seem to have found in Bonn all that you could reasonably expect. Whatever is wanting might gradually be added. . . . Employment . . . wherever you go will be a restless necessity for you. A man, in all countries, has to "wait at the pool"; to look out assiduously for opportunities and capabilities; snatching them up as they arise, and diligently paving for himself a way thro' the abyss by them. For it is an ever-fluctuating, madly boiling abyss, except so far as we can control it and subdue it, to one and all of us. . . .

'Your perfect knowledge of England and things English seems to offer you some specific possibilities of function among Germans at present. . . . Old Arndt, in your picture, looks charming; an excellent piece of old-German stuff. I am delighted to hear of his vigorous delving and

[1] *Last Words of Thomas Carlyle*, 1892, pp. 257–61.
[2] Letters perhaps unpublished.

hoeing; but wish withal he would write us another Book: some autobiographic or other selection of his experiences in this world. . . .'

This "Father Arndt," as they called him in Germany, was an old professor at Bonn, and also the poet and historian who had inspirited his countrymen in the valley of the shadow of Napoleon, and made their famous song, *Was ist des Deutschen Vaterland*? (What's the Germans' Fatherland?) He was an old man of eighty now at Bonn, but had still ten years to live there. He left Reminiscences behind him, but whether Carlyle's suggestion was told to him, let German editors tell,—what he himself did not need to be told was that all Germany would be glad to hear him.

Another professor now at Bonn who had had a share in making history was Dahlmann. In 1848 he had gone into politics and become the leader of the constitutional Liberals. By this time he had returned to his professorial teaching and writing of history. Neuberg had described him and now Carlyle wrote:—'I once read a Book of Dahlmann's on the English Civil War, which corresponded very well to your account of him. Heavy and hard as pig-iron; a solid methodic history of that event,—with the religion, the soul of the whole business, "omitted by particular desire." I remember he ends by saying that the good issue in such countries is so plain that "a man may hit it, shooting blindfold"; a suffrage parliament, namely; that is (or was then) the good issue, according to Dahlmann.'

Then Carlyle told the news of his life in the country and his health, and ran on:—'The World, with its Papal Aggressions, Crystal Palaces, and such like, is and remains a great ass. Enchanted Ass, for there is always a man imprisoned there, poor devil!' The reference was to the Golden Ass of Apuleius. The letter ends with his wife's regards, and praise from both of them for Neuberg's letters in the *Leader*.

Before the year was out Carlyle received a letter from a young man, Henry Larkin, who became a neighbour and a friend and one of his most efficient helpers, a sort of volunteer secretary for press work with a genius for index-making. Larkin was particularly grateful to Carlyle for strengthening his faith in Christ, which was embarrassing, and he wrote to him to show that Oliver Cromwell had been more straightforward than Carlyle had represented on two occasions. He was surprised and delighted with a prompt reply, 29.12.1850, saying :[3]—

'It is a real satisfaction to me to be chidden from that side of the Cromwell controversy. . . . I do not find that essentially we differ at all in our notion about those matters either of the Protectorship or of the Kingship ; but if the business were raised into *speech* between us, one knows not how far it might still go ! A fact is a fact, and all men that do see it, must see it alike ; but what each man will then say upon it—how you, or I, or Oliver will then see best to *name* the fact—there we shall by no means be sure to be alike. Goethe says, "The instant we begin to speak, we are more or less wrong." With many thanks for your good-will to me, and much fellow-feeling with you in your reverence for Oliver, whom I only wish both of us, and all men, could a little resemble. . . .

'Yours very sincerely,

'T. CARLYLE.'

This ended Larkin's hope of altering the conclusion about Cromwell ; but he assures us :—'Altogether the letter was a great satisfaction to me ; and in times of depression, "You, or I, or Oliver" often recurred to me' with encouragement.

[3] *Henry Larkin on Carlyle and Mrs. Carlyle, Brit. Quarterly Review,* July, 1881, Vol. 74, pp. 29–31.

IV

WRITING "JOHN STERLING"

(1851)

IN the first week of the new year Carlyle and his wife were conducted through Pentonville Prison by Prison-Inspector Perry, who pleased him by warmly agreeing with his dislike of much he saw there, and called a "villainous putrefaction of benevolent Tartuffery." The Inspector and he would both have preferred to punish rather than pet the 'Devil's Regiments of the Line.'

By this time it was plain that Emerson never would write a Life of John Sterling; and in that event Carlyle felt bound to do it. In many talks with Richard Owen and others, and in reading old letters, he was quietly considering the materials available, but he did not begin to write till February. Writing to Neuberg in Germany,[1] he said he was 'silent' or even 'idle' in January, trying to 'gather a little strength,' contemplating the social chaos in which the people were weltering, 'amid the cheers of all for their Crystal Palace.' He rather liked the sight himself of the 'gigantic bird's cage,' as he watched it in his daily walks, and saw it gradually rising like an exhalation in Hyde Park; and he always praised Paxton, 'whose ingenuity is the soul of it, and *enables* him to employ tens of thousands upon it at once. Never in the world's annals, I believe, was there a *building* of such extent finished in ten times the *time* by hand of men.' The punctual completion of it and that it could be all rebuilt elsewhere without loss of material, —'that I call clever; the rest is like to be all fudge and boisterous ostentation.' He had thoughts of quitting London till the show was over.

One Wednesday evening, 15.1.51, a letter to Germany told that Neuberg's friend the homeopath Wilkinson came to tea at Cheyne Row,—"*a man of prodigious talent,*"— according to Emerson, writing to Carlyle this year. On the same evening Mr. Foxton called, 'and another Ci-devant

[1] Letters partly unpublished.

Reverend of still more ardent pretensions. Heterodoxy without limit was the consequence ; heterodoxy, with some touches of homeopathy and of better things. Foxton is not a genial man, but he is a healthy and practical ; reminds you of an English weaver who has found that his loom won't go. A wonderful good humour in him, considering his situation as Ci-devant. . . .'—Ci-devant means aforetime, and during the French Revolution 'des Ci-devants' or Aforetimers meant those who by title or position belonged to the old regime ; but on this occasion the expression Ci-devant was humorously extended to a class that Carlyle narrowly escaped belonging to himself, the professional Christians who had outgrown their creeds entirely and quitted the trade. Ci-devants of that sort might be forgiven for feeling a little ill-humour, were it only like that of the witness who was asked,—" Are you not a barrister yourself ? " and replied,—" I used to be, but I reformed, and now I mean all I say."

Theology was common talk then and " good copy " in the Press. It was as a Ci-devant martyr or sinner that John Sterling had been cursed of late in religious newspapers ; and now Carlyle was about to write his life and champion that meritorious class of men. Speaking of the man himself, Carlyle said,[2]—" Sterling was a beautiful figure in our literature, but he has never done anything," which Espinasse explains by saying that novels then 'counted for nothing' to him. Mrs. Carlyle 'said in her incisive way' that Sterling " wanted back-bone." When Espinasse asked,—" Was Sterling not ambitious ? " Carlyle replied :—" He had his ambition as we all have," and added, " Sterling liked to be in the van, like Forster of Rawdon," meaning the William Edward Forster of the Education Act.

About the middle of January Robert Chambers of Edinburgh sent the first of the four volumes of his *Life and Works of Robert Burns* ; and Carlyle did much more than merely acknowledge the gift and return thanks. He read it with pleasure and wrote to give what help he could. He indicated material that might be new to Chambers, and suggested to divide the history more firmly into masses, into epochs, distinct books, and chapters, declaring [3] :—

[2] *Literary Recollections*, by F. Espinasse, pp. 218–9 and 215.

[3] From copies of original letters of T. C., made by C. E. S. Chambers of Edinburgh. He owned the MSS. and was grandson of Robert Chambers, the addressee.

'It is a bold and genial notion, that of intercalating Burns's Poems into the prose narrative of his life, and treating them as little bursts of musical utterance in the grand unrhymed practical tragedy which he enacted under this Sun! Beyond doubt such is their real character; and into that category they must ultimately come with all readers: but to handle them so, in the present stage of the business, and for readers in this epoch, is attended with peculiar difficulties. I remember Allan Cunningham used sometimes to say that he thought of such a plan, but durst not venture. We are well pleased to see you grapple with these abstruse natural obstacles; and doubt not that you will give a good account of them yet.'

On 20.1.51 Carlyle was writing in his journal: 'It is man's part to deal with Destiny, who is *known* to be inexorable. It is the woman's more to deal with the man, whom, even in impossible cases, she always thinks capable of being moved by human means; in this respect a harder, at least a less dignified, lot for her.' One of the absurdities of Froude was to suppose this reflection arose out of 'the domestic atmosphere' of Cheyne Row! In truth it seems likely to have been suggested by a recent 'most melancholy interview' with Lady Bulwer Lytton, the wife of poor Bulwer Lytton from 1827 to 1836, and then for forty-two years his tormentor. 'Can do nothing with the poor lady's novel, I fear,' wrote Carlyle about her in his journal, 30.12.50, referring, no doubt, to a novel of hers, in which she made her husband the villain. Of course Mrs. Carlyle sympathised with her, and called Lytton "a lantern-jawed quack"![2] Carlyle could not see how to do any good in the matter, and merely moralised in his journal about the unhappy pair (30.12.50),—'How the Furies do still walk this earth, and shake their "dusky glowing torches" over men and women!'

About the end of January he went to the Grange, and perhaps because his mind was full of the Ci-devant John Sterling, he did what he usually avoided, talked theology with clergymen; but, of course, they were "broad" enough to know that the dogmas of the creeds are not worth debating now, and to agree with the good apostle James, the brother of Jesus, rather than with Paul, inasmuch as the only Christianity that matters is righteousness and mercy, peace on earth and goodwill. It is a curious fact that most of the clergy of Scotland thought so through the eighteenth century, preaching "plain moral sermons" and being decorously silent about other "doctrine." Such had been the Faith of all sensible people in Scotland down from the days of George Buchanan at the Reformation. To debate about dogmas was deemed pugnacity and want of sense. But after the French Revolution it became the fashion to affect a little more patience with piety, and, like Wellington, go to church to set a good example to the "common people." The fact is that the superstitious part of Christianity, especially the piffle in the creeds, had been completely discredited among people of sense in Scotland for many generations. This is the key to the reticence of Carlyle that puzzled Froude. What puzzled people in Scotland was that a man of so much sense and one who was superior to hypocrisy should have so much patience with "religion."

On this occasion Bishop Thirlwall was one of the guests at the Grange, and also Trench, then Dean of Westminster, and the Stanleys, Sir John Simeon, and "Dicky" Milnes and others addicted to divinity and delighted to find Carlyle willing to be drawn out for once. To quote Carlyle's own confession in a letter, he made 'a dreadful onslaught' one evening 'on—what shall I say? properly the *Church*—in presence of Trench and the Bishop. Trench affected to be very busy reading, and managed extremely well. The Bishop was also grand and rationally manful, intrinsically agreeing with almost everything I said. Poor Simeon, a gentleman in search of a religion, sate stupent in the whirlwind of heterodox hail, and seemed to feel if his head were on his shoulders.'

Carlyle returned home and began writing the *Life of John Sterling* early in February. Before the end of March, there was little remaining but to make the manuscript plain for the printers, fit in the letters quoted, and see it through the Press. The nearest approach to affectation in Carlyle was his too-modest—conscientiously modest—uncertainty whether the work was worth publication. His wife and John Forster took him seriously and 'warmly voted for immediate printing.' A man should always consult his wife, especially when she is sure to advise what he knows is right.

JOHN STERLING.

[face p. 336

V

THE ASHBURTONS, HERR TAUCHNITZ, &c.

(1851)

NEUBERG was in London in the first week of March,[1] perhaps to save Carlyle, when he was busy at *John Sterling*, from any bother over a pretty thing that Lord Ashburton and his wife were doing. As soon as they saw that Carlyle intended to go deeper into European history, they started procuring, as if for their own amusement, quantities of ' biographical prints, portraits of distinguished men of the eighteenth and earlier centuries.' Of course, ' the affair was wholly entrusted to Carlyle to bring into order,' and the engraver Doyle was joined with him, to save him trouble. On the German side Neuberg and by and by Professor Magnus co-operated, while ' Thiers was employed to collect for her ladyship in France.'[1] The mere collecting took over a year. Besides getting engravings, Ashburton had some copies of pictures made, particularly one of a fine portrait at Charlottenburg of Frederick and his sister Wilhelmina as children. This copy being given to Carlyle became the best ornament of the drawing-room at Cheyne Row.

The rules Carlyle followed in this matter were :—1.— ' The best possible likeness ' was preferred. 2.—Indispensable that the artist ' have actually seen the individual,' so that even an Erasmus by a Vandyke was not wanted. 3.—' No grudge of fair cost.'

Writing to Neuberg after he went home to Bonn, Carlyle had an interesting item of news. ' Herr Tauchnitz, a huge eupeptic man in showy apparel, with the cross of some Legion of Honour or Dishonour at his buttonhole,' called and promised to pay £25 for printing the *French Revolution*. There was no legal obligation to pay anything for copies to be sold abroad, and that was why he gave himself airs. He ' affected to have a soul above ducats,' but rashly boasted of having paid Thackeray £100,—which made Carlyle think £25 too little, but he said nothing.

[1] Neuberg letters, partly unpublished.

VI

JOHN CHORLEY AND OTHERS

(1851)

CARLYLE was 'the most attentive of listeners' to anyone who knew what he was talking about, according to Espinasse,[1] who gives instances. At a soiree at John Chapman the publisher's house in the Strand, Carlyle was seen 'listening during the best part of an hour' to Dr Elliotson, explaining Animal Magnetism.

It was in March, 1851, that John Chorley quite completed the sifting and copying of the unused manuscripts of Carlyle's work on English history. He was a favourite at Cheyne Row all his life. He had great knowledge of Spanish Literature, and one of the things Carlyle advised him to write was a book on the Spanish Drama. 'Another specialty' of his was the English navy, and Espinasse reports :—'This was a topic on which Carlyle delighted to hear him dilate. I remember passing a pleasant hour listening to Chorley while he described to Carlyle the hardships and privations endured in the Polar regions by the officers and men of a Government Arctic Expedition, and the devices by which the officers endeavoured to keep up the spirits of their men.'

John Chorley was rich, poor fellow, or what is called independent. He had been able to get out of business early; and his 'chief recreation was solitary performance on the bassoon.' He had no need to work, and published nothing worth mention but an occasional review in the *Athenæum,* when his brother Henry was on its staff. He sauntered through life serenely as Shakespeare might have done, if satisfied with his surroundings at Stratford,—enjoying his books and his bassoon, and earning the gratitude of posterity by preserving from the fire the Historical Sketches. He and Erasmus Darwin, brother of the better-known Charles, were typical of 'Carlyle's most intimate friends,'

[1] *Literary Recollections,* by F. Espinasse, pp. 146, 230–3.

says Espinasse,[1]—' not at all what the world calls distinguished, but prized for quiet intelligence, refinement of manners, and purity of life.'

This Darwin and Carlyle one day in conversation made a curious computation,—they counted 'that there were in town on any day during the London season, three thousand families at whose dinner-table a man of any note would be welcome.'[1] Such 'lion-hunting,' as the ladies called it, was then the fashion.

One of the literary events of this Spring was the appearance of the ecstatic John Ruskin's *Stones of Venice*, about which Carlyle wrote to Ruskin on 9.3.51,[2] describing the book as 'a strange, unexpected, and, I believe, most true and excellent *Sermon* in Stones, from which I hope to learn in a great many ways. The spirit and purport of these Critical Studies of yours are a singular sign of the times to me, and a very gratifying one. Right good speed to you! It is a quite new "Renaissance," I believe, we are getting into just now: either towards new, *wider* manhood, high again as the eternal stars; or else into final death, and the mask of Gehenna for evermore! A dreadful process, but a needful and inevitable one; nor do I doubt at all which way the issue will be.' This explains what is told us[3] by an old aunt of Mr. Wedgwood and of Charles Darwin's wife.—

One Sunday, 30.3.51, was turned into 'an impromptu public day' by unexpected callers, including both the Darwins, Erasmus and Charles, and 'Mr. Carlyle who was very pleasant,' and who 'amused me,' she said, when Ruskin's *Stones of Venice* was being highly praised, 'by his summing up the moral of the book,—that you must be a "good and true man" to build a common dwelling-house.'

Before the printers had started on *John Sterling* in May, Carlyle had resumed the study of Danish, which he had dipped into some time before, intent on seeing anything to be seen in Scandinavian history. Whatever the reason, that was a common direction then of curiosity in Scotland. Perhaps it may have been because so many families in Scotland had come from there. The Ambassador Bunsen was willing to help, but could do little. One of his Secretaries, Dr. Pauli, came to Cheyne Row several evenings to make himself useful, and was declared by Carlyle to be 'an

[2] *Life, &c., of John Ruskin*, by W. G. Collingwood, I, pp. 151–2.
[3] *Emma Darwin, A Century of Family Letters*, II, pp. 130–1.

intelligent, laborious young man, but not deeper in Norse than myself.' He was able to give a lesson or two in Anglo-Saxon, that was all. Carlyle considered whether to go to Denmark, to study there awhile; but ended by looking around for some other subject for the present, and leaving Scandinavian history aside for more than twenty years.

Carlyle and his wife together this summer attended Thackeray's lectures on the English Humourists,[4] the same that were afterwards often read again in America, for like Emerson and many others, Thackeray did not speak his lectures, he merely read them. But he read them very well, and was a popular performer. It may have been soon after the first delivery of them in London that Mr. Venables heard something memorable. Carlyle 'liked Thackeray himself,' he tells us,[5] 'and never spoke of him with the contempt which, before he became intimate with Dickens, he expressed for "the infinitesimally small Schnüspel, the distinguished novelist."' But Carlyle 'never insisted on the faultless excellence which involves some negative qualifications. He had naturally but little sympathy with Thackeray's instinctive dislike of greatness, as it is exemplified in his antipathy to Marlborough and Swift. I think it was after a conversation between them on the character of Swift that I heard Carlyle say,—"I wish I could persuade Thackeray that the test of greatness in a man is not whether he would like to meet the man at a tea-party."'

[4] *Life of W. M. Thackeray*, by L. Melville, I, p. 282, etc.
[5] *Carlyle's Life in London*, by G. S. Venables, *Fortnightly Review*, Nov., 1884, p. 605.

VII

THOMAS WOOLNER & CO.

(1851)

A YOUNG man then frequenting the house was Thomas Woolner.[1] Coventry Patmore had lately persuaded Carlyle to spare four sittings of a couple of hours each for a medallion by this promising young sculptor, who was about to go to the gold-diggings in Australia, as he could not get at home the work he wanted to do. He hoped the medallion would bring him work, and so it did by and by. Meanwhile, when seeing *John Sterling* through the press, Carlyle was paying Woolner for a facsimile of the medallion, which he sent to his sister in Dumfries, telling her: 'It really seems to me, and to some surer judges, a rather clever thing,—as certainly to the little sculptor himself: a very good young fellow, who we hope will come into notice yet.'

One evening this summer Woolner brought to the house a big bumptious fellow, William Bell Scott, the forty-year-old son of a respectable Edinburgh engraver known to Carlyle, and himself now a drawing-master at Newcastle by trade, and artist and poet by choice. Ten years ago this Scott had written an impudent letter to Carlyle, rebuking him for omitting to glorify the business of artists in his lectures on Heroes. There was no answer. When Carlyle's *Cromwell* appeared, he published *More Letters of Oliver Cromwell*, in mockery of the history, but to the end of his life was left guessing whether Carlyle knew of the existence of his satire. What makes him worth mention is what Carlyle did when Mr. Scott's brother David died,—a far better man and artist,—and a book canvasser in London was falsely saying that a set of illustrations to the *Pilgrim's Progress* was sold "for the private benefit of the artist's mother."

'Carlyle subscribed,' Scott tells us,[2] 'but having some misgiving, wrote me at once, saying if this was the truth, "then undoubtedly some effort should be made by such as recognise your brother's genius." Altho, as I explained at

[1] *Thomas Woolner*, by Amy Woolner, pp. 11, 12, 65.
[2] *Autobiographical Notes of the Life of William Bell Scott*, Vol. I pp. 268–9, etc.

once, the assertion was a base device of the canvasser, this generous, prompt, and friendly act bound me to Carlyle for ever.'

So when Mr. Scott came to London a few weeks afterwards, he tells us, Woolner 'and I went out to Cheyne Row to spend an evening by invitation. . . . So peculiar a Scotchman (as Carlyle) in voice and manner I was not prepared to meet. Natives of the same province recognise at once the clay from which each other must have originally sprung; no amount of schooling can change him or hide the peasant origin from being seen by another of the same locality, although the acutest Londoner does not seem to detect it. But here, face, dress, manners, and accent were all alike those of a man rather proud of his humble and provincial antecedents, one not at all ambitious of being a citizen of the world. His conversation was exactly like his *Latter-Day Pamphlets*, only more damnatory, and his descriptions of people and things—he did not care so much for talking of books—were admirably terse, vivid and vigorous, but . . . anatomical; his voice, emphatic enough, was like the rattling of pebbles and boulders driven against each other in a spate.

'"Ah!" said he, "you're an artist," pronouncing the first syllable of the word like *air*, which I had not heard even in Edinburgh for a long time back. "But you're something more" (teacher of drawing, in fact). "Ah, well, I can make nothing of artists, nor of their work either." Let the reader remember he had just been sitting to Woolner for his medallion. "Empty as other folks' kettles are, artists' kettles are emptier, and good for nothing but tying to the tails of mad dogs. So little do I care to venture on these speculations, I have never been at an exhibition all the many years I have lived in London." This was disappointing, this boasting combined with ignorance. But he was intolerant only because truth and justice, or the want of these, were ever present to his mind. His speech obeyed the strictest veracity and kindness. The furnishing (of the sitting-room) was not exhilarating. . . . Nothing but common ugly portraits were on the walls, particularly the smug face of Francis Jeffrey. . . .

'Woolner had imbibed quite a devotion to Carlyle, and a sort of worship of Mrs. Carlyle. She was actually that evening in a rather low dress, a fashion much decried, gone out indeed, and to anyone with thin arms and no "bust" to speak of, a monstrous mistake and self-deception.' It was the fashion, however, and what seemed low in Cheyne Row was called "high in the neck" in Society, where Bishop Blomfield was saying he had *never* seen anything like what now met his eyes at the dinner-table, "at least, not since I was weaned."[3]

'The talk chancing to be on drawing and its benefits,' wrote Woolner in an article for students,[4] 'Carlyle told us that he never in the course of his life so ardently desired anything as in his youthful days he desired to learn the art of drawing: but that in the circumstances of his life there was no possibility, and it had been to him a lifelong regret.[5] He said he believed that no man ever took more pleasure in reading than he had done all his life, and that most of what he knew had been obtained from books; but were he asked which alone would be of most advantage to a man during his career, for sharpening his faculties, giving him a clearer perception of facts, and a love of truth,—the power to read or the power to draw—he should say that on the whole drawing was the more valuable.'

This is very like him, and probably correct in substance tho not literally accurate. He plainly wished to say what he truthfully could that would be polite to his hearers; and it should be noted that it was for sharpening the perceptive faculties and giving a love of truth that drawing was preferred. For communicating with others or obtaining general knowledge there was no suggestion of comparing the power to draw with the power to read.

On the way back to town, Woolner told Scott that the arts were going to the dogs, and sculpture in particular He had only had one small commission in many years. He had been writing poetry, "But poetry is not my proper work in this world," said he. "I must sculpture it, not write it. If a man undertakes to plough a field, but shies off with a gun in his hand and brings back any amount of game, would his master thank him? That's my case, and, unless I take care, my master conscience will have something to say that I shan't like. I have noticed his eye glaring at me already." Which goes to show that Scott was right in deeming Woolner a disciple of Carlyle.

[3] *Leaves from the Note-books of Lady Dorothy Neville*, Chap. XIV, p. 245.

[4] *Where to Draw the Line: a Word to Students*, by T. Woolner, R.A., in *The Magazine of Art*, 1892, pp. 7–11.

[5] Miss M. Carlyle Aitken, Carlyle's niece, has told D. A. W. she also had heard her uncle say so.

VIII

EXHIBITION AND PEACE CONGRESS

(1851)

WHAT had brought Mr. Scott to London was doubtless the Exhibition in Hyde Park, which was opened on the first of May, and was filling the town this season, so that, as Carlyle complained to the publisher Chapman,—"You can't get along Piccadilly."[1] Of course, he had to take his wife to see the show, but their curiosity was soon satisfied. He declared that the Crystal Palace 'surpassed in beauty of effect and arrangement all the edifices I have ever seen or read of, except in the Arabian Tales, but there the merits of the business ended,' and the Exhibition itself was only a well-got-up 'piece of nonsense.'[2]

He was certainly right in thinking it was not a place for study, and when it was suggested that Exhibitions might tend to improve manufactures, he thought of Richard Arkwright and replied:—"The grandest specific set of improvements ever made in manufactures was effected, not in a big Glass Soap-bubble, presided over by Prince Albert and the General Assembly of Prurient Windbags out of all countries, but under the torn Hat once of a Lancashire Pedlar and Barber, who chanced to have a head that he could employ in *thinking* under said Hat!"

While thus deriding the decorative department of Politics and 'the *Win-dust-ry* of all Nations,'[3] Carlyle was delighted to bless a small side-show,—which was really no part of the affair itself, but was fitted into the Exhibition for the sake of its crowds,—the fourth meeting of the Peace Congress, 22, 23 and 24.7.1851. The previous meetings had been at Paris, Brussels, and Frankfurt in recent years; but the revival of the ancient ideal of peace on earth was not a novelty. Old Samuel Rogers, now eighty-eight, but making many calls in his carriage this summer, and receiving many

[1] *Life of George Eliot*, by J. W. Cross, p. 138.
[2] *Letters to Neuberg*.
[3] Letter of 29.10.51, in *Last Words of T. Carlyle*, p. 262.

visitors, the Nestor of the Exhibition year, had heard Tom Paine toasting long, long ago,—" The Republic of the World ! " A much younger man, Sir David Brewster, only three score years and ten as yet and prominent in Exhibition work, was the appropriate Chairman of the Peace Congress.

Politicians were conspicuous by their absence there, 'sensible of each other's infirmities,' perhaps, and shrugging their shoulders at peace talk ; but the good Chairman had the pleasure of intimating on the opening day, 22.7.51, letters of adhesion from Archbishop Whately and the Archbishop of Paris, and from Barthélemy Saint-Hilaire, Hippolyte Carnot, Victor Hugo and some others, including his old acquaintance, Thomas Carlyle, whose letter was one of the few that were read to begin the proceedings.[4]

'CHELSEA,
'*18th July*, 1851

'To the Chairman of the Committee of Arrangements (Peace Congress)

'SIR,—

'I fear I shall not be able to attend any of your meetings ; but certainly I can at once avow, if, indeed, such an avowal on the part of any sound-minded man be not a superfluous one, that I altogether approve your object, heartily wish it entire success, and even hold myself bound to do, by all opportunities that are open to me, whatever I can towards forwarding the same. How otherwise ? " If it be possible, as much as in you lies, study to live at peace with all men " ; this, sure enough, is the perpetual law for every man, both in his individual and his social capacity ; nor in any capacity or character whatsoever is he permitted to neglect this law, but must follow it, and do what he can to see it followed. Clearly, beyond question, whatsoever be our theories about human nature, and its capabilities and outcomes, the *less* war and cutting of throats we have among us, it will be the better for us all ! One rejoices much to see that immeasurable tendencies of this time are already pointing towards the result you aim at ; that, to all appearance, as men no longer wear swords in the streets, so neither, by and by will nations ; that, among nations too, the sanguinary *ultima ratio*' (or

[4] *Elihu Burritt*, by Chas. Northend, pp. 121–3 ; and *Home Life of Sir David Brewster*, by Mrs. Gordon, pp. 215–222.

last resource, meaning war), 'will, as it has done among individuals, become rarer and rarer; and the tragedy of fighting, if it can never altogether disappear, will reduce itself more and more strictly to a *minimum* in our affairs. Towards this result, as I said, all men are at all times bound to co-operate; and, indeed, consciously or unconsciously, every well-behaved person in this world may be said to be daily and hourly co-operating towards it—especially in these times of banking, railwaying, printing, and penny-posting; when every man's traffickings and labourings, and whatever industry he honestly and not dishonestly follows, do all very directly tend, whether he knows it or not, towards this good object among others.

'I will say further, what appears very evident to me, that if any body of citizens, from one, or especially from various countries, see good to meet together, and articulate or reiterate these or the like considerations, and strive to make them known and familiar,—the world in general, so soon as it can sum up the account, may rather hold itself indebted to them for so doing. They are in the happy case of giving some little furtherance to their cause by such meetings, and, what is somewhat peculiar, of not retarding it thereby on any side at all. If they be accused of doing little good, they can answer confidently that the little good they do is quite unalloyed, that they do no evil whatever. The *evil* of their enterprise, if evil there be, is to themselves only; the good of it goes wholly to the world's account without any admixture of evil: for which unalloyed benefit, however small it be, the world surely ought, as I now do, to thank them rather than otherwise.

'One big battle saved to Europe will cover the expense of many meetings. How many meetings would one expedition to Russia cover the expense of? Truly I wish you all the speed possible; well convinced that you will not too much extinguish the wrath that dwells, as a natural element, in all Adam's posterity; and I beg to subscribe myself, &c.

'T. Carlyle.'

IX

WILLIAM HARCOURT AS DEVIL'S ADVOCATE

(1851)

AMONG the new arrivals in London this season was William Harcourt, the same who is now so well remembered by rich men in England for recasting the Death Duties in 1894. In 1851 he was a big bumptious fellow of twenty-four, who had just pleased his father by taking a good place in the degree list at Cambridge, and having got on the staff of the *Morning Chronicle* as a political journalist, he was planning to read law and make his subsistence secure in the law-courts first of all, and then take to politics.[1] He fancied himself an authority on history,—a favourite pen-name of his by and by was "Historicus,"—and from the first he was distinguished for wit and impudence. Indeed he was remarkably like a young man who once electrified the elders, when invited to pray at a prayer-meeting, by profusely thanking God for His infinite goodness to mankind, in having made the present generation such an immense improvement upon any that had gone before. A gentleman in Homer had already said so, but he did not know that,—it is an old, old story.

Harcourt's biographer places 'his experience of Carlyle' soon after he came to town; and soon after the letter to the Peace Congress appeared in the newspapers is the likeliest date. What tempted young Harcourt would be the hope of maybe scoring over Carlyle, and the confident expectation of being seen and heard debating with him on equal terms. It may have been at some dinner-table that they met, for he was acquainted with several of Carlyle's friends. Wherever it was, 'Carlyle was extolling Cromwell,' when Harcourt intervened and said:—

"It is a remarkable fact that all Cromwell's institutions

[1] *Life of Sir William Harcourt*, by A. G. Gardiner, and see page 61 for the quotations following. Where these are amplified, it is on the authority of the Right Hon. Augustine Birrell, who was the source of Mr. Gardiner's information, having heard the story from Sir William Harcourt.

crumbled with his death. Would it not be true to say that Ignatius Loyola has produced more permanent effect on mankind? After all, Oliver Cromwell cut off the head of Charles the First, whose son was *restored* to the throne. He abolished both Houses of Parliament,—they are sitting at this moment. Now Ignatius Loyola won back a great part of the Continent from the Reformers to the Church of Rome; and the Institution he founded is as influential as ever to-day." And so on to that effect, Carlyle sitting grimly silent till he finished.

Then Harcourt received the reprobation he deserved for defending plain rascality, and the debate ended suddenly. The more is the pity that we have no report but his own of what was said to him. A generation afterwards, when he had reached about the age of Carlyle in 1851, and was talking to one young enough to be his son, he told what he remembered or had decided to tell, but all he would say that Carlyle had said to him was,—" Young man, ye may be very clever; I daresay ye are, as ye're just from the University; but allow me to tell ye, ye are going straight to the bottomless pit."

Accepting this as correct so far as it goes, there is a humorous sneer in it at Harcourt's crudity in supposing anyone in London heeded the University. The reference to " the bottomless pit " was positively polite. As Harcourt had no superstition, there was no danger of hurting his feelings; and as his father and grandfather were clergymen, and he was aiming at a public career himself, it was courteous, almost excessively courteous, to presume he was a Christian. At any rate, when he told the story he was " chuckling and gurgling " with delight, tho he would need all his impudence to " save his face " in 1851, and never encountered Carlyle again.

X

JOHN STUART MILL AGAIN

(1851)

IN 1851 the Irish Tenant League authorised Lucas and Gavan Duffy to offer John Stuart Mill a seat in Parliament[1]; and Gavan Duffy coming to London to see him about it applied to Carlyle for an introduction, and at once was introduced.[1] But Mill was a civil servant, unable to go into Parliament without resigning his post, and as he explained in his *Autobiography*, that 'precluded even consideration of the proposal.' Which was a calamity to the nation, considering how much we have suffered since then from the ignorance of politicians about what the Irish wanted Mill to teach the Commons, the elements of Political Economy and the absurdity of the Irish land-laws.

It is worth the consideration of politicians whether they should not minimise the risk of any such calamity recurring by making it settled law that civil servants of every sort, local and national, and maybe teachers too and railway servants and others, including miners, whenever work in the mines is properly organised, should have a lien on their posts if elected to Parliament, and so be all of them available as candidates if ever required. But what concerns us now is Carlyle's talk with Duffy on this occasion. He said that tho able to introduce anyone to Mill, he and Mill had ceased to see much of each other.—

"Mill has one faculty in great perfection, the power of setting forth his opinions with a lucidity which no one in England can match. What he aims to make you see, you see as plainly as a conspicuous object set in the sunshine. He has the habit of approaching everything by the way of logical analysis, and when he brings that method to bear upon a question, he gets out of it nearly all it can yield him. There are probably quite other qualities in it, not at

[1] *Life in Two Hemispheres*, by Sir Charles Gavan Duffy, II, p. 39; *Conversations with Carlyle*, by the same, pp. 166–71; and the *Autobiography of J. S. Mill*, p. 279.

all to be detected by logical analysis, and altogether unsuspected by him. Of the true relations of things in the universe, Mill has small insight or none. He is inclined to scream and shriek about matters of no real importance, and to believe in unrealities of various sorts." In short, "Old Sterling the thunderer,"—of the *Times*,—"used to say there was a good deal of sawdust" in Mill's essays.

After pausing a little for anything Duffy might have to say, Carlyle went on to describe Mill in the Reform Bill era,—"an innocent young creature, with rich auburn hair, and gentle pathetic expression,"—and he told the story of his ancient intimacy with Mill, and Mill's infatuation with the Mrs. Taylor, whom he had married this April. There was humour not intended in Carlyle's wondering at Mill believing Mrs. Taylor "the paragon of womankind, which she is not." Mrs. Carlyle struck in: — "She is a peculiarly affected and empty body. She is not easy unless she startles you with unexpected sayings. If she is going to utter something kind and affectionate, she speaks in a hard stern voice. If she wants to be alarming or uncivil, she employs the most honeyed and affectionate tones. 'Come down and see us,' she said one day (mimicking her tone). 'You will be charmed with our house, it is so full of rats.' 'Rats!' cried Carlyle. 'Do you regard them as an attraction?' 'Yes' (in a soft voice). 'They are such dear innocent creatures.'"

When Carlyle confessed he could not account for Mill's ceasing to visit him, Gavan Duffy said,—"If he heard your estimate of Mrs. Taylor, there need be no difficulty in accounting for the change." Which was not far wrong, and the best guess possible before the *Reminiscences* of Carlyle revealed how Mrs. Taylor, a 'vivid' and 'very Will-o'wispish "Iridescence" of a creature, meaning nothing bad either,' had been introduced at Cheyne Row and tried to 'tutor and twirl' Mrs. Carlyle, 'but got taught better before long, to her lasting memory.' It is an old familiar story,—the sages were separated by their women. "It is the pillow that sunders families," say the Muslims.

The next time Carlyle encountered Mill after introducing Gavan Duffy, Mill deliberately averted his head and avoided Carlyle, almost as if cutting him. "Mistake was impossible," said David Masson,[2] reporting this as

[2] To D. A. W.

Carlyle had told it to him at the time. "Mill was absent-minded, but Carlyle extremely wideawake, and he had very good sight, and he told me he saw that Mill had seen him."

He was not alone in this misfortune. Mrs. 'Platonica Taylor,' as he called her, now Mrs. Mill, monopolised the unfortunate man, and estranged Mill from most of his friends, including even his mother and sister.[3]

[3] See *Life of J. S. Mill*, by W. L. Courtney, Chap. VI; and *Carlyle on Cromwell and Others*, pp. 171–4 and 276.

XI

MALVERN, &c.

(1851)

IT was not want of company for himself that made Carlyle regret Mill's withdrawal from society, which followed when Mrs. Taylor, becoming Mrs. Mill, took possession of him. As Carlyle said to Mr. Chapman, in complaining of the Exhibition,[1] he was 'worn to death with bores all summer, who present themselves by twos and threes in my study, saying, "Here we are, &c., &c."' While correcting the proofs of *Sterling*, he was also looking round for new work. On 12.7.51 Mrs. Carlyle was writing to her friend at Thornhill, Mrs. Russell:—"The longer one lives in London, one gets of course to know more people, and to be more invited about; and Mr. C. having no longer such a dislike to great parties as he once had, I fall naturally into the current of London life—and a very *fast* one it is."

He had often heard about the new-fashioned "water-cure" from John Forster, Bulwer Lytton and others, and the time had now come when, as he said, he was to "pay his tax to contemporary stupor" and try it. His first thought had been of trying it at Darmstadt, and that was what made him prophesy to his friend Thomas Spedding of Keswick,[2] that when he came to town to see the Exhibition, 'You will not find me here. I seriously meditate flying beyond seas till the vile banquet of the children of the wind, with all its tumults and eloquent eructations, be fairly over. One dead dog is bad; but fifty of them stranded at Blackfriars Bridge on a hot day, what can you do with these? The nostril and the soul alike turn away with abhorrence from *such* an Ecumenic Council.'

The printing of *John Sterling*, however, was not nearly finished by the end of July, and he had to remain in England to do the proofs. In sending this news to Neuberg,[3] he

[1] *Life of George Eliot*, by J. W. Cross, p. 138, etc.
[2] Letter printed in *Thomas Carlyle and Thomas Spedding*, by A. Carlyle, *Cornhill Magazine*, June, 1921, p. 758.
[3] Letter probably unpublished.

described a new book on Physiology, by their common friend Wilkinson the homeopath, as 'a most surprising Book,—shadows and analogies being apparently all the same to it as facts and measurements and substances,—a very cloudland indeed, with abundance of broken rainbows scattered about.' Bating only the rainbows which are uncommon, this fits so many volumes that it deserves to become a commonplace.

The whole of August, Carlyle was at Malvern with his wife as guests of Dr. Gully, the leading practitioner of the new cure, who had pressingly invited them again and again, writing to Carlyle,—" Only come and I will cure you." Mrs. Carlyle went " as bodyguard, not as patient "; but grew tired of looking on and became a patient too, " for fun." The doctor did his best to repeat on Carlyle the miracle he had worked on Bulwer Lytton; and Carlyle did all he could to help him. Mrs. Carlyle was writing to William Allingham soon after the " cure " began:[4]—'A lady told me the other day that it was " quite delightful to hear from the *bathman* how *sweetly* Mr. Carlyle took his baths! His *only regret*, the bathman said, being that he was not kept *longer in the pack!* " So you see the cold water must be acting favourably on his faculty of patience and resignation, if on nothing else.'

It was too late. The Edinburgh doctors of long ago with their too plentiful mercury and castor-oil had done organic mischief beyond repair; and Carlyle's dyspeptic sufferings which had lasted thirty years had to last for thirty more. He was grateful to Dr. Gully all the same, and so was his wife, who told him,—" The more I think of these people,"—Dr. Gully and his daughter and the rest,—" the more I admire their politeness and kindness to us. I don't remember ever in my life before to have stayed a whole month in anybody's house without ever once wishing to be away." They had enjoyed the pure air and quiet, and continued to use the water, " compressors, sitting baths, packings " and so on, for a while longer; but in a month or two the tired dyspeptic was to let go the little hope he had, and say the water-cure had " done me no ill, and not traceably very much good."[5] Looking back at it many

[4] *Letters to William Allingham*, pp. 140–1.

[5] Letter of 29.10.51 in *Last Words of Thomas Carlyle*, Longmans, p. 263. It is corroborated by letters to Emerson, 25.8.51, to Mrs. Aitken, his sister, 11.10.51, etc., etc.

years afterwards, when old and ill, he called 'water as a medicine the most destructive drug I ever tried'; but no such feeling appears in the letters of 1851, and there is no evidence that he ever tried water as a drug after then.

Sydney Dobell and his wife were at Malvern this month,[6] and saw much of the Carlyles. In a few weeks Dobell sent Carlyle his articles on Christianity, Currer Bell, etc. In thanking him, Carlyle said he found his "notions all very beautiful in the given time and circumstances," and soon was bidding him "send me anything you may write. Whether I dissent from it or not, I shall be very glad to read it."

At the end of August, the Carlyles 'rolled off for Worcester' together and then parted, she for Manchester to stay with Geraldine Jewsbury, and he for Scotsbrig, 'full of gloom and heaviness, and totally out of health, bodily and spiritual. Prussian Friedrich, and the Pelion laid on Ossa of Prussian Dryasdust, lay crushing me with the continual question, "Dare I try it? Dare I not?"'

The gloom was partly due to an unpleasant parting from his wife, which was rather a novelty in his experience. She had been in a bad temper, and supposed he was coming close to her for a farewell kiss with a lighted cigar in his mouth, when in truth he was only trying to whisper that he had given half a crown to a maid who had to be tipped. The offended wife abused him there and then without reply—why brabble before strangers? She was aware it would worry him all the way to Scotland, as he admitted it did, in explaining. She condescended to write a long letter and mention she had 'quite forgiven' him, before she received his explanation, that he had not been thinking of kissing.—'What you, in your kind assiduity, were aiming at,' he wrote, 'I had not noticed or surmised. You unkind woman, unfortunate with the best intentions, to send me off in that humour with such a *viaticum* through the manufacturing districts! I thought of it all day; yet *with sorrow*, not with anger, if you will believe me.'

He stayed at Scotsbrig several weeks, resting and pondering whether to tackle Frederick, or to drop him, as he had already dropped William the Conqueror and "the Cid," the hero of Spain. After reading the books available, he found, —'I can make less of the Cid than I expected, and cannot

[6] *Life and Letters of Sydney Dobell*, I, pp. 235–7.

get any clear face view of him at all.' What inclined him towards the modern hero Frederick alias Friedrich was the greater prospect of having reliable facts to handle. But he said nothing of all that at Scotsbrig, where he read aloud the Life of Dr. Chalmers, which his mother could enjoy, when talk ran dry. 'He tired of gossip very quickly,' remarked [7] young John Carlyle, a nephew diligently observing him, the son of his youngest brother James, the farmer at Scotsbrig. 'When there was nothing more to be said,—"Let us be learning something," he would say, and start some one reading, or read aloud himself.' Such was Carlyle's notion of culture, the same as that of the Chinese sages or Benjamin Franklin,—mere quiet reading.

In a letter he wrote from Scotsbrig, 10.10.51, there is a reflection natural at a time when he was turning his attention aside from current politics to history:—'I am sick of the stupidity of mankind—a *servum pecus*.' This is a phrase of Horace, meaning a servile herd, and Horace like Carlyle was provoked to apply it to his fellow-beings by human readiness to imitate others and run after them. 'I had no idea till late times what a bottomless fund of darkness there is in the human animal, especially when congregated in masses, and set to build Crystal Palaces, &c., under King Cole, Prince Albert and Company. The profoundest Orcus,' place of death, 'or belly of Chaos itself, this *is* the emblem of them.'

An invitation to address a crowd at the opening of a 'Working-Men's Reading Room' at Carlisle reached Scotsbrig too late. He was in London by 19th September. It was sent after him, and in explaining his absence, he wrote [8]:—

'After all, it is not by speaking visitors and transient strangers, however wise and well-disposed, that any benefit can be done you,—only by wisdom daily present and busy.

'I hope that by degrees your leading men (furnished with good and wise books, not with bad and foolish ones, which are worse than none) may become the rallying point of all the sincere and serious-minded workers in Carlisle, that they may try what can be achieved towards self-culture (the true aim of every human soul) by earnest co-operation in this kind.'

[7] Verbally to D. A. W. in 1896.

[8] Letter to Robert Lattimer, Secty., reprinted in the *British Weekly* (10.10.1918), from the *Carlisle Journal*.

Then came something perhaps suggested by the talk of Neuberg who had much experience at Nottingham of this sort of thing.—

'Mechanics' Institutes and the like modern establishments seem to me to be dying because of their fatal belief in the efficacy of platform operations and the saving nature of public speaking. Better march with a minimum of drumming!'

'I wish you cordially well, with thanks for the honour done me.'

XII

TO PARIS

(1851)

BEFORE the Ashburtons left London this year for Homburg and Switzerland, Carlyle had promised to spend a few days with them in Paris when they were returning. So on Thursday, 25.9.51, he set out and took the train for Newhaven, along with Browning and Browning's wife and child and maid. He had gladly delayed his departure for a day for the sake of their company.[1]

As he was sitting on the steamer's deck at Newhaven he beheld a man distributing religious tracts in German, French and English, and being repulsed by many with anger and contempt. The tract-distributor seems to have been refreshed by the courteous silence of Carlyle. At any rate he did not enquire his language, but bestowed upon him abundantly German tracts, and French and English, which were all gravely accepted, and 'served me well as waste-paper,' recorded the pilgrim.

The paddles began to turn about half-past one, and the next seven or eight hours were spent in watching fellow-passengers and the various shades of sea-sickness. They spent the night at Dieppe, for the sake of Browning Junior, still under three. The sight of Dieppe harbour reminded Carlyle that John Knox had passed through there, three centuries before. Mrs. Browning was agreeably surprised to find how much she was liking her fellow-passenger, and has proudly reported[2] that he said to her child,—"Why, sir, you have as many aspirations as Napoleon!" That he might have said the same to almost any healthy juvenile, she did not suspect.

Carlyle explored Dieppe in the evening and the morning, remarking among other details the abundant beards, and the absence of rags among the poorest,—'old clothes all

[1] *Excursion to Paris,* in *Last Words of Thomas Carlyle,* pub. Longmans, etc., pp. 149–91.

[2] *Life and Letters of Robert Browning,* by Mrs. S. Orr, pp. 172–3–4.

accurately patched, a thrifty people.' The name of the 'rue d'Ecosse' (street of Scotland) he also noticed, and the old churches, the fine natural harbour, 'mouth of a river, broad gap in the chalk cliffs,' and the clean streets with 'water flowing in the gutters,' the barracks and the big cannon. Among the morning dandies loafing about he saw one of the London pattern 'of ten years ago, with hands in coat-pockets, and a small stick rising out from one of them!'—The bakers were 'naked from the waist, all but a flannel waistcoat and cotton nightcap,' and soldiers 'in red trousers walked everywhere.'

It was after breakfast when Browning and Carlyle 'strolled out along the quay' their hotel was on,[1] and near the end of the quay 'an immense flaring crucifix stood aloft'; and this is likely to have been the time and place when Carlyle 'glancing towards the figure of Christ said,—"Ah, poor fellow, *your* part is played out."[2] Which delighted Browning, were it only as a mark of confidence, for in public, if not altogether in private, Carlyle was silent about superstition, as had long been the custom among men of sense in Scotland.

They took train for Paris, and in two hours were at Rouen, 'Joan of Arc's last resting-place and the scene of many singular things.' He admired its trees and gardens, pleasant meadows, and clear air, 'a lovely place, compared with Manchester.' Thence their train ran up the valley of the Seine and crossed and recrossed the river, which seemed 'swift but not bigger-*looking* than the Thames at Chelsea.' Some of the station names recalled the figures that haunt the memory, Charlotte Corday for one. The land they looked out upon was pleasant to the eye, with its copses and vineyards, but seemed as if slit into ribbons, and not well enough cultivated, the ploughing 'shallow and ill-done.' By four o'clock they were punctually approaching Paris, and he recognised after twenty-seven years the blunt height and castle of St. Cloud.

XIII

THIERS AND OTHERS

(1851)

AT the station the fellow-travellers separated, Carlyle being bound for the Hotel Meurice, where the Ashburtons were awaiting him, and the Brownings going to another; but Mrs. Browning had the pleasure of reporting,—' He spent several evenings with us, we three together. He is one of the most interesting men I could imagine, and you come to understand perfectly when you know him, that his bitterness is only melancholy, and his scorn, sensibility. Highly picturesque, too, he is in conversation; the talk of writing men is very seldom so good.'

He called on nobody else but General Cavaignac, who was out of town. This was the brother of his friend the Republican writer, Godefroi Cavaignac, who by this time had gone farther than to the country. He had died in 1845, and only his bronze statue was now to be seen in Paris,—at Montmartre.

On the night of arrival, Friday, 26.9.51, the Ashburtons took Carlyle to the theatre after dinner, and he noticed in the stalls ' a clever energetic set of faces visible there, far superior to such as go to Drury Lane; among them, pointed out by Lady Ashburton, who had met him, (General) Changarnier. Strange to see such a man sitting sad and solitary there to pass his evening. A man of placid baggy face, towards sixty,' fifty-eight past; ' in black wig, and black clothes; high brow, low crown, head *longish;* small hook nose, long upper lip (all shaved), corners of which, and mouth generally, and indeed face generally, express obstinacy, sulkiness, and silent long-continued labour and chagrin. I could have likened him to a retired shopkeeper of thoughtful habits, much of whose savings had unexpectedly gone in railways,' meaning speculation in shares. ' Thomas Wilson of Eccleston Street resembles him in nose and mouth; but there was more intellect in Changarnier, tho in a smoke-bleared condition.'

Changarnier had risen in the army by long good service,

assisted in keeping order in 1848, and for two years commanded the National Guard of Paris and the troops there; but in January, 1851, he had been removed from that post as too honest a man by the President, Louis Napoleon, *alias* Napoleon the Little, who was then preparing to make himself Emperor by violence. At the impending *coup d'état* of 2.12.51 Changarnier was to be arrested and banished. He lived to return in 1870 to serve his country in war, and when the war was over, he was one of those most useful to Thiers in reorganising the French army,—assuredly a man worth seeing.

Next afternoon, Saturday, 27.9.51, Carlyle saw Thiers himself ushered into Lady Ashburton's drawing-room. Ashburton and he were afoot, about to go out, their horses ready at the door of the hotel; but they subsided into chairs on sight of such a caller, and the talk lasted more than two hours,—Ashburton and wife, Carlyle and Thiers, and no others. Thiers was a thick-set, 'little, brisk man' from the south, fifty-four years of age, 'with a round, white head, close-cropt, and of solid business form and size; round fat body tapering like a ninepin into small fat feet, and ditto hands; the eyes hazel and of quick, comfortable kindly aspect, small Roman nose; placidly sharp fat face, puckered eyeward (as if all gravitating towards the eyes); voice of thin treble, peculiarly musical;—gives you the notion of a frank social kind of creature, whose cunning must lie deeper than words, and who with whatever *polissonnerie*,' or naughtiness, 'may be in him has absolutely no malignity towards anyone, and is not the least troubled with self-seekings. He speaks in a good-humoured treble *croak* which hustles itself on in continuous copiousness, such a copiousness as even Macaulay cannot rival,' and Carlyle had never heard before. His 'remarkably fine voice' makes his talk distinct tho quick, flowing on 'in a monotonous low gurgling key, with occasional sharp yelping warbles, very musical all, and inviting to cordiality and *laisser-aller*' (letting yourself go). "Oh bah! eh b'en lui disais-j—" (Oh bah! and as I was saying to him). Essentially a "bon enfant," a good fellow, was Carlyle's impression of his real character, 'with the addition of *coquin*' or knave, which in this private note here quoted may not mean what men commonly mean by coquin or knave, but only that he fell short of the high standard which Carlyle thought becoming in a man of such intellect.

His arms and legs were at rest, his tongue alone did the entertaining, 'the hazel eyes with face puckered round them looking placidly animated. Not the least officiality is in his manner.' He lets you choose the topic, and 'can give you clear and dainty response about anything.'

Thus Lady Ashburton had just been purchasing a fine Sèvres vase. Thiers 'flowed like a tide into pottery in general' for 'half an hour,' with details of his own doings as a minister encouraging Sèvres,—not monologue but conversation, many questions answered.

Aware of what interested Carlyle, Lord Ashburton had been looking the day before at some of the "Associated Workmen." Thiers struck into that next and had much to say worth hearing, anecdotes and facts and 'political and moral criticisms, good of their kind. One master of "Associés"' (or foreman or manager of co-operative workmen, so to speak) this one 'perhaps a hatter, "ruled like a Cromwell,"—tho by votes only; and had banished and purged out the opposition party, not to say all drunkards and other unfit hands: "tel régime de fer"' (such iron discipline) 'was the *indispensable* requisite,' and so in short the method of 'Association could never become general among workmen. Besides, it forbade *excellence*: no rising from the ranks *there*, to be a great captain of workers,—as many, six or seven of whom he named, had done by the common method,'—as if "grab and get on" were the true gospel of life, and command of cash a proof of excellence!

Thiers went on to say,—the Association method is 'applicable only to hatters, chair-makers, and tradesmen whose market is *constant*. Try it in iron-working, cotton-spinning, or the like, there arrive periods when no market can be found, and without immense capital you must *stop*. (It is a) good thing, however, for keeping men from chômage,' (idleness), 'for "educating" them in several respects. (It is a) thing to be left to try itself,—is not, and never can be, the true way of men's working together.'

Carlyle had a letter for Michelet, then a professor in the Collège de France, from which he was soon to be removed for refusing to take the oath of allegiance to Napoleon the Little. At present he seems to have been out of town, and when Carlyle enquired about him, he found that Thiers had small esteem for Michelet. It may be recalled,—what Thiers was sure to be painfully aware of,—that in his essay on the *Parliamentary History of the French Revolution*[1] Carlyle had plainly intimated that the *History of the French Revolution* by Thiers was 'as far as possible from meriting' its 'high reputation.' It presented an impossible conception of the event, lacked footnotes, and was so full of errors that it was possible 'to find four errors per hour' in reading it! But the critic added,—'he is a brisk man of his sort; and does tell you much, if you knew nothing.'

So the talk of Thiers would now mean,—'you should think less of Michelet than of me.' Carlyle's note informs us that he expressed 'good-humoured contempt for Michelet and his airy syllabubs of hypothetic *songerie*' (or dreams) 'instead of narrative of facts. "Can stand le poète in his *place;* but not in the domain of truths"—a sentence commented on and expanded, which indicated to me no great *æsthetic* sovereignty on the part of M. Thiers,—leave him alone then! Our conclusion was, M. Michelet was, perhaps, a bit of a *sot*' (or simpleton); 'M. Lamartine, who had meanwhile come in course, too, being definable rather as a *fat*' (or twaddler)—'a hard saying of mine, which Thiers with a grin of laughter adopted: and so we left Parnassus à la Française; and M. Thiers, who could not stay dinner, took himself away.'

In fairness to both the critics we should remember that at this time Michelet was still working on his French Revolution, and only the earliest part of his great history had been completed,—down to Louis XI, what he calls the Middle Ages.[2] When his history was more advanced, only modesty would have hindered Carlyle in praising a history of the Revolution that so cordially followed his own lead, and maybe even Thiers would have had a better feeling for one who, like himself, had been victimised by Napoleon the Little. Michelet was a man of high heroic temper, who devoted his life to history, and found wisdom its own reward, whereas Thiers was the ambitious journalist-politician, who had not leisure to make his books *much* more accurate than the newspapers, and who remained himself, in spite of all his gifts, a little, but only a little, better than a man of the world. Thus it is possible Lady Ashburton did not know how Carlyle had written about him, and was merely

[1] See Miscellanies, and *Carlyle to "The French Revolution,"* pp. 397–8.

[2] In the latest edition, this first part is in the first eight volumes. Volumes IX to XIX begin with the Renaissance and end when the Revolution was beginning. Then follow the nine volumes of his *Revolution Française*.

led by what she saw with her quick woman's eye to tell Carlyle,—" He thinks you do not respect him sufficiently." Which made Carlyle punctilious in politeness to him now and always.

His opinion of Thiers compared with Guizot is in his notes, and may have been told to the Ashburtons on this occasion, before they separated to dress for seven o'clock dinner.—'Of Frenchmen known' (to me), 'Guizot included, I consider Thiers much the best man. A healthy Human Animal, with due *beaverism* (high and low), due vulpinism, or *more* than due; in fine a *healthy* creature, and without any "conscience," good or bad. Whereas, Guizot—I find him a solemn *intriguant.*' "Un intrigant austère" had been Talleyrand's description of Guizot. Carlyle goes on:— 'An Inquisitor-Tartuffe, gaunt, hollow, resting on the everlasting No, with a haggard consciousness that it ought to be the everlasting Yea: to me an extremely detestable kind of man. So I figure him,—from his books and aspect, and avoided to speak with him while he was last' in London. 'Heaven forgive me if I do the poor man wrong; practically I have only to avoid him.'

On the Sunday Carlyle and Ashburton rode out together sight-seeing. First they went to the Champ de Mars. There they joined in a crowd of thousands, paying each his franc or half-franc for admission, and saw the show, of which the chief item was inflating a balloon. Then they rode to Passy and other places, ending with the Bois de Boulogne and the Place de la Concorde.

One of the differences between 1851 and 1824 was that the streets had pavements now. The Palace where lately Louis Philippe reigned was now an 'Exhibition place for Arts et Métiers.'

The 'two inevitables' at the Ashburton dinner-table in Paris were Prosper Mérimée, 'le gentleman auteur' and incarnate 'Comme-il-faut,' and Laborde, a traveller. They were of the sort that run in couples, like Rosencrantz and Guildenstern. It was Mérimée who told at table that somebody said,—" Thiers est un polisson; mais, Guizot, c'est un drôle." Thiers is a rascal, but Guizot is a joker. This would likely be to corroborate himself in running down Thiers, when Carlyle was upholding him. Mérimée was in the political background, but one of Louis Napoleon's men.

Carlyle was going about a great deal alone and also with Ashburton, intent on seeing all that could be seen quickly of the modern Elysium. Those were the days when "good Americans when they die go to Paris," and money-men in many lands felt towards it as the Indian Emperor towards his palace,—"If there is a Heaven on Earth, it is there!" Lady Ashburton's mother, Lady Sandwich, who had left Paris reluctantly in 1848, was now living there again. On Monday, 29.9.51, she had them all to dinner, the Ashburtons, Carlyle, and the 'two Inevitables,' and in addition two titled folk with nothing to say and some others, including Thiers and his wife,—'a brunette of forty, pretty enough.' Carlyle was glad to see for once a 'dinner wholly in the French fashion,' but his own share of it was small,—'a slice of undone beef,' gathered out of some 'kickshaws,' with a little bread, of course, and 'a drop of good sherry and tumbler of *vin ordinaire*.'

Over coffee after dinner he tried to have another good talk with Thiers, but Mérimée was now present, with abundance to utter but nothing to say, and 'nothing notable' is the report. Carlyle was glad to go, receiving from 'the good old lady' hostess twenty drops of her "Jeremy," a laudanum preparation to make him *sleep*. She had doubtless heard from her daughter how much he was suffering from want of sleep. Unfortunately it was too early for bed, when they reached Meurice's. The 'two Inevitables' returned with them, and in the Ashburtons' drawing-room Mérimée began to repeat the Paris patter about German Literature:—"Jean Paul is a hollow fool of the first magnitude. Goethe is the *best*, but (he also is) insignificant, unintelligible, a paltry kind of scribe *manqué*, as it seemed," a scribbler who had failed!

Carlyle could stand no more of it. He lighted a cigar and adjourned to the street. "You impertinent blasphemous blockhead!" was 'sticking in his throat,' as he confessed in his notes, and he felt it better to retire in silence. 'Such was the sin of *the Jews*,' he wrote, as well as of 'so much that goes on still.' He did not return till after Mérimée had gone away, and there was nothing to face except the good-humoured banter of the Ashburtons. But after such an internal earthquake, even ten drops of the "Jeremy,"—all he ventured to take, the rest he poured out of the window,—could not make him sleep. He decided to go home on Wednesday, or Thursday at the latest.

Most of the Rue de Rivoli had been built since his visit to Paris in 1824,—much had happened since then. What struck him as he watched the well-dressed men on the streets was the disappearance of the species "gentleman." The two revolutions since 1824 had not been without effect. Or was it the season? Were they all like Cavaignac in the country? he asked himself. On sight of Louis XIV in the Place des Victoires one morning, "Comment?" said he to 'two little dumpy men in white wide-awakes: "Est-ce qu'on a laissé *cela,* pendant la république?"—Have they left that standing during the republic?—They grinned a good-humoured affirmation.'

One thing he now did for the Ashburtons may have been privately intended by them for his pleasure mainly,—'surveying two large batches of Booksellers' Prints, marking the defects, &c.' He saw alone or in company with Ashburton many places associated with interesting events, including the 'old pale-dingy' Temple, where a policeman on duty had 'never heard of Louis XVI, or his imprisonment here.' When Ashburton was in shops, searching for bronzes and clocks, etc., Carlyle preferred to sit in the carriage at the door, drinking *vin ordinaire* and charming the coachman by providing it for him, too; but he was seeing below the surface of the passing show, discerning many things, and in the tradesmen detecting signs of efficiency and strong character and some '*sincerity* of greed and eagerness. A reflection rose gradually that *here,* in the industrial class, is the real backbone of French society: the truly ingenious and strong men of France are *here,* making money,—while the politician, &c. &c., class is mere play-actorism, and will *go to the Devil* by and by! "Assuredly," as Mahomet says.'

He bought a dog's collar and string for Nero, as a gift to his wife; and came home alone by Calais on Thursday, 2.10.51. Between Dover and London he slept in a railway carriage for the first time in his life, and told Browning[2] that for the next eight days he did little *else* but sleep. During the working hours of four of these days, however, 4 to 7.10.51, he made a detailed record of all he remembered of this visit; and he carefully erred on the side of politeness by sending his compliments to Thiers.

It was only afterwards when it was too late that he heard from Browning how Béranger could yet be seen at times 'in his white hat, wandering along the asphalte.'[2] He had not thought of him in time, and concluded a long letter to Browning,[2] "How I should like to see the flap-hat of the old Chansonnier!"

"Kossuth (*Koshoot*) is coming!" cried little Lewes to Carlyle, when they met in the street on 10.10.51,—" Kossuth is coming!" "Yes," was the answer, "but Kossuth will *go* again; that is perhaps the beautiful part of the news! All nonsense *goes*, if it cannot be prevented from coming." When mentioning this to his sister, Carlyle explained that Kossuth, who was then on an American frigate, on the way to England, was going to receive a great reception when he landed. 'To me he is hitherto nothing but a bag of mutinous playactor *wind*, very doubtful whether he *is* anything more to anybody; and I mean to keep well clear of him for the present.'

XIV

THE LIFE OF JOHN STERLING

(1851)

ON 11.10.51 Carlyle was writing to a sister and telling as the day's news,—'my poor little book is coming out to-day or soon,' which fixes the date of the publication of the *Life of John Sterling* and raises a problem much discussed. Was this "humbug" or "cant," this constant depreciation by Carlyle of all his own works? Plainly neither, but merely a way of talking, the idea inspiring which was that modesty or self-depreciation is the duty of all men. It is a general fashion in China, appearing there an elementary rule of politeness, and surely it is a way of doing that helps to keep the peace. In Carlyle it was doubtless suggested by our own religion, and confirmed by his love of truth. As anyone can see in others, men are continually liable to mistake about themselves or anything that is their own. Self-praise or praise of anything belonging to oneself would seem as wrong to any sincere Christian as to any Confucian sage. "If I bear witness of myself, my witness is not true," said Jesus himself. "The works that I do bear witness of Me." The first duty of every teacher should be by precept and example to teach us to shun self-praise and suspect those who practise it.—Which would, at least, diminish advertising.

The book on Sterling was swiftly successful and is one of the most popular biographies in our language; but even Carlyle had not been able to make a good story out of the events of a life so humdrum as his. The only thing interesting about him was his moral evolution. Handicapped by having money enough to be idle when he liked, Sterling avoided common frivolity and grew into harmonious activity, which is the best human happiness, by dint of doing daily the duties at hand and finding guidance in the voice within. By a happy marriage he emancipated himself from sexual sentimentalities, as a disciple of Carlyle should; but he suffered all the other current ailments of intellectual adolescence, including political measles and religious mumps, and recovered perfectly from them all,—decidedly an interesting "case."

When Mrs. Carlyle was asked,—"What did John Sterling do to deserve a 'Life'?" she did not explain how he had been vituperated by the clergy for shedding their creed, and how Carlyle, who was a literary executor jointly with the Archdeacon, had been appealed to by Sterling's relatives to clear his memory. "*Induced* Carlyle *somehow* to write it," was Mrs. Carlyle's reply. This was wifely indeed, recalling Stella, the spouse of Dean Swift, who, when told that the Dean had written well about another woman, said he could write well about anything, and mentioned his sermon on a broomstick.

The preponderating figure in the book, resembling Falstaff in Shakespeare's plays, is Coleridge, whose 'transcendental moonshine' had misled Sterling, and made him a curate for eight months. The Chapter upon Coleridge (VIII of Part I) is the most readable chapter in the history of religion in England. It is a real treat to see and hear a celebrated saint and philosopher at home, as if in his shirt sleeves, exhibited as Goethe says the characters in Shakespeare are, like a clock with a crystal dial, which shows the internal works as well as the time of day. There is no caricature, no distortion. The story is as delightful as anything in *Don Quixote* and full of Nature's own humour, the contrast between reality and appearances.

For a long time Coleridge had been the most conspicuous of English philosophers. "He is very great in monologue," admitted Madame de Staël, when she could not get him to listen to her, "but he has no idea of a dialogue." His contemporaries heeded him devoutly. He was teaching the clergy a new set of shibboleths, a new way to distil their water of life, with general approval. Society was in a funk of infidelity, and eager to stampede in any direction away from it, to show an example to the people. So the living portrait of Coleridge in this book was resented at the time as too good a likeness; but fashion follows fashion, in shibboleths as in clothes, and all that Coleridge wrote, and the books about him, will soon serve only for a few notes to future editions of the *Life of John Sterling*.

This book was, moreover, the kind of *Exodus from Houndsditch* which it came natural to Carlyle to write. It handsomely met the challenge in the common reviewers' question,

—" Can you tell us your private opinion as to the place where wicked people go ? "[1] No room was left for doubt that to Sterling and his biographer, Hell was a superstitious nightmare and Theology as dead as Astrology. Whereupon professional Christians and reviewers in conventional newspapers began bow-wow-ing at ' the melancholy Polyphemus of Chelsea,'[2] and comparing him to Voltaire for his ' levity and mockery ' and lack of respect for ' the Christian ministry.' ' The genuine Geordie,' or Rev. George Gilfillan of Dundee, demanded,—" Christianity is either false or true. Which ? Do you call the clergy liars ? &c."

It is cruel, but permissible to a biographer of Carlyle, to point out the proof in Gilfillan's own biography that what was really resented was Carlyle's candour. On 1.9.51, six weeks before *John Sterling* was published, Gilfillan was writing to a friend likely to review it and mentioning almost casually, that the creed of Carlyle was merely " Naturalism," or the " cold granite of Natural Religion." So it was not needful for him to read the book to know that. If only Carlyle had suppressed what Gilfillan called the " few rabid sentences of infidelity," that is to say, if he had left simple persons to suppose he thought the clergy true prophets and John Sterling in fault for thinking differently, he would have received nothing but praise from the like of Gilfillan, instead of being " scourged everywhere."

Ridiculous as it seems to-day, the " scourging," as Gilfillan called the vituperation of the book, was merely what might have been expected at the time. In telling the true story of the life of his friend Sterling, Carlyle had let out the secret that men of sense no longer took Heaven or Hell seriously and literally. The outcry against " John Sterling " showed that many professional Christians were still depending on Hell, like the Church of Rome in Béranger's delightful ditty, " The Death of the Devil."—

St. Ignatius was surprised at table by Satan, and agreed to drink with him. So they clinked their glasses. Ignatius dropped poison into the other's glass, and the Devil died. But instead of the blessings Ignatius expected, he received the curses of his colleagues. All the clergy were crying,—

[1] *Second Gallery of Literary Portraits*, by George Gilfillan, p. 125; corroborated.

[2] *Third Gallery of Literary Portraits*, by George Gilfillan, pp. 313–7. Also *George Gilfillan*, by R. A. and E. S. Watson, pp. 78, 155 and 195.

" Good-bye for us to Power and Money now. God will be greater than the Pope. We've lost our Father! The Devil is dead! The Devil is dead!" So Ignatius himself had to take the place of the deceased, and by dint of thefts and massacres, wars and plagues, he outdid him so much that the angels in Heaven, looking down, were pitying men more than ever, and lamenting the death of the Devil.

It would have served the clergy right, and none should have blamed Carlyle, if he had answered scoff with scoff. He had struck oil. A rich reward of fame and money was within easy reach. But he did not feel called to risk distressing genuine Christians, and could appreciate the misgivings of his friend, the Dumfries editor, Aird, who told Gilfillan that the *Life of John Sterling* was "very able and interesting," but admitted "it might have been as well to let the poor forlorn sheet lightning die away in its cloud."[3] Carlyle thought differently and had not shrunk from telling the truth when he saw it right to do so; but assuredly, after doing that, he wished for nothing but to live at peace with all men, and so he acted on the good old rule,—" Let them say whatever they like."

It remains to be added that doubtless one of the reasons for the success of the book was its unconscious revelation of himself. John Sterling had been more than a friend, he had been a disciple.

[3] *Poetical Works of Thomas Aird, with a Memoir*, by the Rev. Jardine Wallace, p. liii.

XV

ON CHRIST AND IMMORTALITY

JOHN STERLING was only one of many disciples. Espinasse assures us[1] that Carlyle was always patient and beautifully courteous to religious enquirers; but that religion was not a topic 'to which he cared often to advert or dwell on long.' When once Espinasse was proving these statements to an inquisitive friend[2] by many instances, his sister interposed a correction, saying,—" I heard Carlyle swearing with my own ears." Her brother and she then recalled the whole of the talk she was thinking of.

Leigh Hunt had said, " The Glasgow people are so stingy that they would not subscribe to put down Hell." Defending Glasgow and answering Hunt, Carlyle quoted Burns's words,—" The fear of Hell's the hangman's whip, to hold the wretch in order," and said it was " scarcely desirable to abolish the terror of Hell all at once." This involved the usual contrast between Hunt's " unlimited faith " in human goodness and Carlyle's matter-of-fact adherence to older opinions, which he defended on this occasion by saying,—" Every man must feel that he is a damned scoundrel," which horrified Miss Espinasse, but meant no more than what Shakespeare put in Hamlet's words,—" Use every man after his desert, and who should 'scape whipping ? " Seeing the horror on her face, her brother, who afterwards explained[2] that she was hard of hearing and had missed the point, fraternally turned to her and popped the question,—" Fanny, do *you* think we could get on without Hell ? " " Hell, Hell ! ! ! " she ejaculated with a shudder, and was silent ; Carlyle coming to her rescue with, " Ah, she hasn't turned that over in her mind yet ! "

" Carlyle is not one but many men," said Mrs. Carlyle to Espinasse, who added that he once heard Carlyle disapprove

[1] *Literary Recollections*, by F. Espinasse, pp. 195–200.

[2] Espinasse to D. A. W., who was present when Mr. Espinasse's sister thus corrected him, and pp. 195–200 of his *Literary Recollections* here quoted were supplemented by what Mr. Espinasse said verbally to D. A. W. Italics added.

of introspection, and say,—" I never troubled myself about my faults, it was only not struggling enough." Yet he quoted with awe one of Cromwell's exclamations on his deathbed, the text,—" It is a fearful thing to fall into the hands of the living God."

Even 'for the Church of England, *apart from its theology*, he had a certain toleration,' but when Lord John Russell created a new See of Manchester, 'he used strong words of reprobation.' With equal plainness he denounced the "rubbishing Puritanism" of latter-day dissenters and the "hollow compromise" of Unitarianism, 'tho he admitted that many clever and worthy people were Unitarians.' "There are two young men," he said once to Espinasse, naming William Maccall and another, "who took up with it and are now completely stranded." With the Broad Church movement, tho F. D. Maurice and Charles Kingsley were 'personal friends' of his, 'he had only moderate sympathy,' predicting 'in a half-contemptuous tone,—"they will get up something" as a substitute for the Thirty-Nine Articles and the rest.' He called Jesus "a beautiful moral phenomenon," and the Bible "a grand symbol, if one could take up with it," and speaking once to Espinasse of the hold Christianity had on human nature, he said,—" It will be a long time before they give it up."

Admonishing Emerson about the plain speech on Christ and immortality in Emerson's Essays, Carlyle had written,—'I dare say you are a little bored occasionally with "Jesus," &c., as I confess I myself am, when I discern what a beggarly Twaddle they have made of all that, what a greasy Cataplasm to lay to their own poltrooneries;—and an impatient person may exclaim with Voltaire, in serious moments:—"Au nom de Dieu, ne me parlez plus de cet homme-là!"' (In the name of God, never mention that fellow to me again!)

When no pious souls whose feelings should be spared were listening, Carlyle was plain-spoken about both Christ and immortality. Professor Blackie had called upon him in 1848,[3] and came occasionally afterwards, and once was shocked to hear him declaring how much "sham" there was in both 'Scottish and English Universities, British Houses of Parliament' and 'orthodox theologies.' Espinasse was 'the sole listener' to that dialogue. When

[3] *John Stuart Blackie*, by A. M. Stoddart, I, pp. 241–2, and *J. S. Blackie's Letters to his Wife*, p. 125.

Blackie said that he discovered in Goethe "a lack of sympathy with earnest men, Luther for instance," Carlyle replied,—"It could not well have been otherwise, since Luther was a Savage, and Goethe anything but that."

The evening was fine, and they all three adjourned to the back garden for a smoke; and there it was that Blackie started praising John Wesley, and between the puffs Carlyle burst forth with,—"*Damn Wesley for bringing in a Jew-nosed God!*"[2] Then seeing the poor Professor's consternation, he 'graciously added, "Well, I withdraw the damn!"'

According to Espinasse, who was 'too much accustomed to Carlyle's strong sayings to be surprised at anything,' he used to say that he never felt spiritually at ease until he left the Churches behind him, and went out into the bare desert where was a temple not made with hands. He was fond of repeating the reply of Confucius to some anxious Chinese enquirer,—"You ask me what death is, I know not what life is; you ask me what Heaven is, I know not what Earth is"; and 'speaking of the darkness in which the destiny of man is shrouded,' Carlyle told Espinasse, "It would never do for us to know the plan of the campaign."

"What are we?" he asked at another time, and went on to answer the question,—"A thought shot down from yon blue sky." Perhaps in answer to Espinasse quoting what he had written that "walking is a series of falls," he said as if 'jubilantly trustful,'—"Defeat is victory," and once, but only once, he launched forth hopefully, saying that in the end the beautiful would be supreme. To illustrate his meaning he mentioned what he had doubtless noticed in the *Acta Sanctorum* (Deeds of the Saints), 'that in describing their celestial visions, the saints dwelt chiefly on the beauty and splendour of the Heaven revealed to them. In time, he prophesied, beauty would be all in all. "For the few?" asked Espinasse. "No!" he replied, "for the many."'

'I was foolish enough,' says Espinasse, with true Boswellian candour, 'to inflict on him a vague notion of mine that a man's fate in the other world might depend on the state in which he was when he arrived in it from this world. Carlyle gave me and my theory no encouragement, silencing me at once with the concise and emphatic rejoinder, "We know nothing about it!"'

XVI

SPIRITUAL OPTICS

(1851)

AFTER the death of Peel, Carlyle had given up the hope of being allowed to do anything in current politics. The organizing of national education had to be left to other hands in later generations, and the organizing of labour is hardly yet begun,—to our immeasurable loss. To name one item only,—we can hardly count even the cost of the stoppage of the coal-mines in 1926. But our country's loss has been the world's gain. "Heaven makes no mistakes." The time of Carlyle, which might have been consumed in wrestle with the sons of darkness in our provincial idol-caverns, was given to the *Life of John Sterling* and the history called by the name of Frederick.

When giving the *John Sterling* its finishing touches in April he wrote in his journal :—'In the spiritual world, as in the astronomical, it is *the earth* that turns and produces the phenomena of the Heavens. In all manner of senses this is true ; we are in the thick of the confusion attendant on learning *this ;* and thus all is at present so chaotic with us. Let this stand as an *aphoristic saying* ? or work it out with some lucidity of detail ? Most true it is, and it forms the secret of the spiritual epoch we are in.'

What may have suggested it is thus stated by a biographer of Kant.[1]—'Two centuries and a half before his time, Copernicus (whose cell at Frauenburg on the Frisches Haff makes him a neighbour of Kant) had restored to the sun that central rank in our system from which traditional astronomy had long ousted it. *Kant looked upon himself as a Copernicus of mind.*' In short, he supposed his formulas told the truth in a final way.

Which was not so absurd as it seems. The makers of such formulas all feel like that. Carlyle ignored Metaphysics as merely morbid ; but he saw sense in some of the

[1] *Kant*, by William Wallace, p. 155, Blackwood, 1882. Italics added.

sayings of Kant, and esteemed him the best of his sort. It is really touching to see how even the best of philosophers was only human after all, and began to be absurd when he was thinking of himself. As Burns has put it :—

> ' But, och ! mankind are unco weak,
> An' little to be trusted ;
> If *self* the wavering balance shake,
> It's rarely richt adjusted ! '

Perhaps the funniest of Froude's misunderstandings of Carlyle was apropos this entry in the journal. Imagining Carlyle an exaggerated Froude preoccupied about " creeds," he guessed that, by the "Exodus from Houndsditch," Carlyle meant " sketching the outlines of a creed which might hereafter be sincerely believed." It was because Carlyle had never done such a thing that Froude imagined he left undone the " Exodus from Houndsditch ! " In truth Carlyle would have found nothing but material for laughter in such a notion. If he had lived to the age of Methuselah, he would never have taken to tinkering creeds.

Not long after the *John Sterling* came out, Carlyle " worked out with some lucidity of detail " the idea which had occurred to him in finishing it, on a MS. printed after his death. Apparently he had not thought it worth printing, but it is worth reproducing here, with thanks to Froude, poor fellow, for drawing attention to it.—" Heaven has a use for even our blunders," as pious folks used to say. Spiritual Optics meant optical illusions of the mind's eye, so to speak. The sensible reader of Carlyle will find nothing needing explanation.—

' SPIRITUAL OPTICS

' Why do men shriek so over one another's creeds ? A certain greatness of heart for all manner of conceptions and misconceptions of the Inconceivable is now if ever in season. . . . Be not so much alarmed at the opulences of this world. Whether they be of the hand or the mind, whether consisting of St. Catherine's docks, blooming corn-fields, and filled treasuries, or of sacred philosophies, theologies, bodies of science, recorded heroisms, and accumulated conquests of wisdom and harmonious human utterances—they have all been amassed by little and little. Poor insignificant transitory bipeds little better than thyself have ant-wise accumulated them all. How inconsiderable was the contribution of each; yet working with hand or with head in the strenuous ardour of their heart, they did what was in them; and here, so magnificent, overwhelming, almost divine and immeasurable, is the summed-up result. Be modest towards it; loyally reverent towards it; that is well thy part. But begin at last to understand withal what thy own real relation to it is; and that if it, in its greatness, is divine, so then in thy littleness art thou! *Lass Dich nicht verblüffen,* "Don't let thyself be put upon." "Stand up for thyself withal."' (Or—Do not be bluffed.) 'That, say the Germans, is the eleventh commandment; and there is not, perhaps, in the whole Decalogue a more important one.

'Except thy own eye have got to see it, except thy own soul have victoriously struggled to clear vision and belief of it, what is the thing seen and the thing believed by another or by never so many others? Alas, it is not thine, though thou look on it, brag about it, and bully and fight about it till thou die, striving to persuade thyself and all men how much it is thine. Not *it* is thine, but only a windy echo and tradition of it bedded in hypocrisy, ending sure enough in tragical futility is thine. . . . If men were only ignorant and knew that they were so, only void of belief *and sorry for it,* instead of filled with sham belief and proud of it—ah me!!

'The primary conception by rude nations in regard to all great attainments and achievements by men is that each was a miracle and the gift of the gods. Language was taught man by a heavenly power. Minerva gave him the olive, Neptune the horse, Triptolemus taught him agriculture, &c. The effects of *optics* in this strange camera obscura of our existence, are most of all singular! The grand centre of the modern revolution of ideas is even this—we begin to have a notion that all this *is* the effect of optics, and that the intrinsic fact is very different from our old conception of it. Not less "miraculous," not less divine, but with an altogether totally new (or hitherto unconceived) *species* of divineness; a divineness lying much nearer home than formerly; a divineness that does not come from Judæa, from Olympus, Asgard, Mount Meru, but is in man himself; in the heart of everyone born of man—a grand revolution, indeed, which is altering our ideas of Heaven and Earth to an amazing extent in every particular whatsoever. From top to bottom our spiritual world, and all that depends on the same, which means nearly everything in the furniture of our life, outward as well as inward, is, as this idea advances, undergoing change of the most essential sort, is slowly getting "overturned," as they angrily say, which in the sense of being gradually turned over and having its vertex set where its base used to be, is indisputably true, and means a "revolution" such as never was before, or at least since letters and recorded history existed among us never was. The great Galileo, or numerous small Galileos, have appeared in our spiritual world too, and are making known to us that the sun stands still; that as for the sun and stars and eternal immensities, they do not move at all, and indeed have something else to do than dance round the like of us and our paltry little dog-hutch of a dwelling-place; that it is we and our dog-hutch that are moving all this while, giving rise to such phenomena; and that if we would ever be wise about our situation we must now attend to that fact.

'I would fain sometimes write a book about all that, and try to make it plain to everybody. But alas! I find again there is next to nothing to be said about it in words at present—and indeed till lately I had vaguely supposed that everybody understood it, or at least understood me to mean it, which it would appear that they don't at all.

'A *word* to express that extensive or universal operation of referring the motion from yourself to the object you look at, or *vice versa*? Is there none?' (Optical Illusion.)

'A notable tendency of the human being in case of mutual motions on the part of himself and another object, is to misinterpret the said motion and impute it to the wrong party. Riding in this whirled vehicle, how the hedges seem to be in full gallop on each side of him. . . .

'It is very notable of the outward eye, and would be insupportable, did not the experience of each man incessantly correct it for him, in the common businesses and locomotions of this world. In the uncommon locomotion it is not so capable of correction. During how many ages and æons, for example, did not the Sun and the Moon and the Stars go all swashing in their tremendously rapid revolution every twenty-four hours round this little indolent Earth of ours, and were evidently *seen* to do it by all creatures, till at length the Galileo appeared, and the Newtons in the rear of him? The experience necessary to correct that erroneous impression of the eyesight was not so easy of attainment. No. It lay far apart from the common businesses, and was of a kind that quite escaped the duller eye. It was attained nevertheless; gradually got together in the requisite quantity; promulgated, too, in spite of impediments, holy offices, and such like; and is now the general property of the world, and only the horses and oxen cannot profit by it. These are notable facts of the outward eyesight and the history of its progress in surveying this material world.

'But now, will the favourable reader permit me to suggest to him a fact which, though it has long been present to the consciousness of here and there a meditative individual, has not, perhaps, struck the favourable reader hitherto —that with the inward eyesight and the spiritual universe there is always, and has always been, the same game going on. Precisely a similar game, to infer motion of your own when it is the object seen that moves; and rest of your own with menadic storming of all the gods and demons; while it is yourself with the devilish and divine impulses that you have, that are going at express-train speed! I say the Galileo of this, many small Galileos of this, have appeared some time ago—having at length likewise collected (with what infinitely greater labour, sorrow, and endurance than your material Galileo needed) the experience necessary for correcting such illusions of the *inner* eyesight in its turn— a crowning discovery, as I sometimes call it, the essence and summary of all the sad struggles and wrestlings of these last three centuries. No man that reflects need be admonished what a pregnant discovery this is; how it is the discovery of discoveries, and as men become more and more sensible of it will remodel the whole world for us in a most blessed and surprising manner. Such continents of sordid delirium (for it is really growing now very sordid) will vanish like a foul Walpurgis night at the first streaks of dawn.

'Do but consider it. The delirious dancing of the Universe is stilled, but the Universe itself (what scepticism did not suspect) is still all there. God, Heaven, Hell, are none of them annihilated for us, any more than the material woods and houses. Nothing that was divine, sublime, demonic, beautiful, or terrible is in the least abolished for us as the poor pre-Galileo fancied it might be; only their mad dancing has ceased, and they are all reduced to dignified composure; any madness that was in it being recognised as our own henceforth. . . .'

On another loose sheet he wrote.—

'Singular what difficulty I have in getting my poor message delivered to the world in this epoch: things I imperatively need still to say.

'1. That all history is a Bible—a thing stated in words by me more than once, and adopted in a sentimental way; but nobody can I bring fairly into it, nobody persuade to take it up practically as a *fact*.

'2. Part of the "grand Unintelligible," that we are now learning spiritually too—that *the Earth turns*, not the Sun and heavenly spheres. One day the spiritual astronomers will find that *this* is the infinitely greater miracle. The Universe is not an orrery, theological or other, but a Universe; and instead of paltry theologic brass spindles for axis, &c., has laws of gravitation, laws of attraction and repulsion; is not a Ptolemaic but a Newtonian Universe. As Humboldt's "Cosmos" to a fable of children, so will the new world be in comparison with what the old one was, &c.

'3. And flowing out of this, that the work of genius is not *fiction* but fact. How dead are all people to that truth, recognising it in word merely, not in deed at all! Histories of Europe! Our own history! Eheu! If we had any vivacity of soul and could get the old Hebrew spectacles off our nose, should we run to Judæa or Houndsditch to look at the doings of the Supreme? Who conquered anarchy and chained it everywhere under their feet? Not the Jews with their morbid imaginations and foolish sheepskin Targums. The Norse with their steel swords guided by fresh valiant hearts and clear veracious understanding, it was *they* and not the Jews. The supreme splendour will be seen *there*, I should imagine, not in Palestine or Houndsditch any more. Man of genius to interpret history! After interpreting the Greeks and Romans for a thousand years, let us now try our own a little. (How clear this has been to myself for a long while!) Not one soul, I believe, has yet taken it into him. Universities founded by monk ages are not fit at all for this age. "Learn to read Greek, to read Latin!" You cannot be *saved* (religiously speaking too) with those languages. What of reason there *was* in that! Beautiful loyalty to the ancients. . . . Beautiful truly so far as it goes! But the superfœtation'—or the rot—'is now grown perilous, deadly, horrible, if you could see it!

'Old piety was wont to say that God's judgments tracked the footsteps of the criminal; that all violation of the eternal Laws, done in the deepest recesses or on the conspicuous high places of the world, was absolutely certain of its punishment. You could do no evil, you could do no good, but a god would repay it to you. It was as certain as that when you shot an arrow from the Earth, gravitation would bring it back to the earth. The all-embracing law of Right and Wrong was as inflexible, as sure and exact, as that of Gravitation. Furies with their serpent hair and infernal maddening torches followed Orestes who had murdered his mother. In the still deeper soul of modern Christendom there hung the tremendous image of a Doomsday when the All-just, without mercy now, with only terrific accuracy now, would judge the quick and the dead, and to each soul measure out the reward of his deeds done in the body—eternal Heaven to the good, to the bad eternal Hell. The Moslem, too, and generally the Oriental peoples, who are of a more religious nature, have conceived it so, and taken it, not as a conceit, but as a terrible fact, and have studiously founded, or studiously tried to found, their practical existence upon the same.

'My friend, it well behoves us to reflect how true essentially all this still is: that it continues, and will continue, fundamentally a fact in all essential particulars—its certainty, I say its infallible certainty, its absolute justness, and all the other particulars, the Eternity itself included. He that has with his eyes and soul looked into Nature from any point—and not merely into distracted theological, metaphysical, modern philosophical, or other cobweb representations of Nature at second hand—will find this true, that only the vesture of it is changed for us; that the essence of it cannot change at all. Banish all miracles from it. Do not name the name of God; it is still true.

'Once more it is in religion with us, as in astronomy—we know now that the Earth moves. But it has not annihilated the stars for us; it has infinitely exalted and expanded the stars and Universe. Once it seemed evident the Sun did daily rise in the east; the big Sun—a Sun-god—did travel for us, driving his chariot over the crystal floor all days: at any rate the Sun *went*. Now we find it is only the Earth that goes. So, too, all mythologies, religious conceptions, &c., we begin to discover, are the necessary products of man's god-made mind.'—

Apparent motion or optical illusion or whatever else we call the traditional mistakes in Spiritual Optics, there is an old German song which puts that human weakness so well as to teach us patience with it. The author is the greatest of all poets,—" Anon." The song is worthy of Horace at his best, indeed, there is nothing of Horace so good. Béranger might have written it, but no other Frenchman in history. Surely humour is better than either pity or terror for teaching us the truth. The absent-minded folk who cling to creeds outworn resemble the fuddled hero of this song.—

Straight from the tavern I am come here.
Old road, how odd to me now you appear!
Right and left changing sides, rising and sunk,—
O, I can plainly see,—Road, you are drunk!

O what a twisted face *you* wear, my Moon,—
One eye shut, t'other one round as a spoon!
Who would have thought of it? Shame on you, shame!
You have been fuddling, you jolly old dame!

Look at the drunken lamps, see how they wheel,
Nodding and flickering round as they reel!
Not one among them all stands in his row,—
Look at the drunken lamps,—see how they go!

All in an uproar are things great and small,—
I am the only one steady at all.
Here is no safety for sober good men,
So I'll go back to the tavern again.

BOOK XX

BEGINNING 'FREDERICK'

(1851–53)

I

HERBERT SPENCER AND CARLYLE

(1851)

IN October, 1851, George Eliot's Mr. Lewes brought Herbert Spencer, then aged thirty-one, to see Carlyle. Seven years had passed since Spencer had sent him his first Pamphlet and felt grateful for a sympathetic note about it. When Spencer was an old man himself, he reflected on the contrast between his own behaviour and Carlyle's, inasmuch as he himself sent only a circular acknowledgment of the presentation copy of a book, and 'commonly no acknowledgment at all' for a Pamphlet. 'A note such as that which I received from Carlyle' was never to be expected from him,—which is interesting, as maybe the nearest approximation to humility discoverable in Herbert Spencer.[1]

A letter to a friend at the time shows Spencer's impression in 1851.[2] 'I spent an evening at Carlyle's some fortnight since. His talk is little else than a continued tirade against the "horrible, abominable state of things." He was very bitter against the Exhibition amongst other things, and was very wroth at the exposure to the public of such disgusting brutes as the monkeys at the Zoological Gardens. He talks much as he writes. You would hardly recognize him by the likeness you have. He has much colour in his cheeks while your portrait suggests pallor. He is evidently fond of a laugh and laughs heartily. But *it is so useless to reason with him*[3] that I do not want to see much of him. I shall probably call to look at him two or three times a year. His wife is intelligent but *quite warped by him.*'[3]

After two or three more calls, 'always in company with Lewes,' the newest of our philosophers 'ceased to go' to Cheyne Row, because he feared the 'fierce argument' he foresaw; and his disciples shuddered by and by to hear that when Carlyle was questioned about Spencer he called him, "an immeasurable ass."

[1] *An Autobiography*, by Herbert Spencer, I, pp. 230–1 and 379–84.
[2] *Life and Letters of Herbert Spencer*, by D. Duncan, p. 378.
[3] Italics added.

II

ON TEMPERANCE, CATHERINE II, &c.

(1851)

JOHN STERLING was selling well,—so much the worse for its author's popularity with most professional Christians. The same was true of the *Latter-Day Pamphlets* and most politicians. When Carlyle came home from Paris in the first week of October, 1851, he settled down to steady reading about the history of Europe before the French Revolution. The only trifle of other business worth mention is that he got from Mazzini a letter of introduction for the Brownings to George Sand, whom Mrs. Browning worshipped—till she met her. In sending it on 28.10.51, Carlyle replied to Browning's suggestion to return to Paris in the Spring.—' If I were to go to France, I think my next object would be Normandy rather; to see the Bayeux tapestry, the Grave of W. Conqueror, and the footsteps (chiefly Cathedrals I believe) of those huge old Kings of ours. I read a Ducarel (French Englishman of 1750) the other week, who roused all my old aspirations for a while. But after all it is better to sit still.' This agrees with what appears in other letters, such as those to Neuberg and to Varnhagen von Ense. He had settled down to reading history, but he was not yet sure that it would be best to write about Frederick. He was now sating his curiosity in order to see and determine that, and had by no means lost hope of some day writing about William the Conqueror and Company, either instead of Frederick, or after he had finished with him.

About the same time, the assistant-editor of the *Westminster Review*, the Miss Evans known as "George Eliot," was trying to coax articles out of him, regretting that her *Review* had not got the article on the Opera which had appeared in Procter's (Barry Cornwall's) *Keepsake* and been much quoted in the Press.[1] ' Carlyle called the other day,'

[1] *Life of George Eliot*, by J. W. Cross, pp. 136–40.

she was writing in November, 'strongly recommending Browning the poet, as a writer for the *Review*, and saying "We shall see," about himself.'

She was only one of many editors then doing likewise.[2] It was at a later date, apparently, that an enterprising editor offered him a thousand guineas 'for a description of the Derby Day, to which his name should be appended.' But it seems to have been about this time that Robert Rae, the 'Secretary of the Scottish Temperance League, called at Chelsea with a view to prevail upon him to write something for the *Scottish Review*—a shilling quarterly the League was then publishing. Mr. Carlyle was profoundly interested in the temperance question. He entered heartily into conversation with Mr. Rae on the subject, perceiving at a glance, we doubt not, the sincerity of his visitor. He was greedy of information about the progress of the work the League had in hand, and felt so much sympathy with it, that he would have written an article for the *Scottish Review* but for the fact that he had already refused similar applications from old friends, magazine and review editors, in London. Besides, were he to contribute an article, he added, there would be no end to the applications that would flow in upon him from other quarters; (and) so, reluctantly, he had to say no.'

On 15.10.51 Mrs. Carlyle was writing to her cousin Jeannie at Liverpool:[3]—'Mr. C. has been sleeping like a top and eating vigorously since his return from Paris—the Ashburtons . . . are now in town. She brought me a woollen scarf of *her own knitting* during their stay in Switzerland and a cornelian bracelet, and a similar scarf only smaller for Mr. C.—in fact I believe the dear woman would never have done all that knitting for *me*, unless as a handsome preparation for doing the comforter for Mr. C.' Which was a good guess. 'She is really "what shall I say?—*strange* upon my honour."' This was a humorous quotation from Mazzini's way of telling of attentions he received from female adorers. The letter runs on.—'On her first arrival in London she staid only two hours and drove down here with these things. I was gone out. So she left them—with Mr. C. whom she saw—and then wrote me a note of invitation to the Grange,' which in short was first refused and then renewed some weeks later and accepted, both ladies being "what shall I

[2] *Thomas Carlyle*, by W. Howie Wylie, pp. 246–7.
[3] *J. W. Carlyle: Letters to her Family*, by L. Huxley, pp. 351–3.

say ? *strange* upon my honour," whimsical at least, as petted wives are prone to be after forty or fifty, when they have long been spoiled, and have not had children, to draw their thoughts out of themselves.

On 29.10.51 Carlyle was writing to Varnhagen von Ense:[4]—'If I were a brave Prussian, I believe I should forthwith attempt some picture of Friedrich the Great, the *last* real *king* that we have had in Europe,—a long time till the *next*, I fear—and nothing but sordid anarchy *till* the next. But I am English, admonished towards England;—and Friedrich, too, is sure enough to *be* known in time without aid of mine.—And so I remain in suspense.' In short, why don't you or some genial Prussian do it ? Advice as to maps is asked, and as to books about Catherine II, the only other royalty remarkable for superior sense among Frederick's contemporaries. Carlyle confessed his curiosity about her, assuring Von Ense,—'Catherine is a most remarkable woman;—and we are to remember that, if she had been a *man* (as Francis I, Henry IV, &c.) how much of the scandal attached to her name would at once fall away.'

This letter was given to Neuberg to take to Berlin and deliver along with a packet of autographs, precious to Von Ense. On the Sunday after it was written, Neuberg came to Cheyne Row at 5 p.m. to dine with the Carlyles, no others present,—which gave 'time to talk' without restriction. Carlyle was in the full flood of reading about the age before the French Revolution. It was no new thought. The Archenholtz he was now handling, "precise, exact, copious, dullest of men," had been the first book he ever read in German, thirty years before, and was now re-read "with satisfaction and instruction."[5]

Not Frederick and Catherine alone, but also Voltaire and Pitt,—the Great Commoner, one of his earliest heroes,—swarms of departed potentates and priests arising from the abysms of the Middle Ages, culminating in Czar Peter and Martin Luther, soldiers of fortune of heroic quality in their shabby trade, and generals of every sort and hosts of other spirits, male and female, in common clothes, or in armour or buckram or eighteenth-century regimentals, or wigs and decorations as extinct to-day as the plesiosaurus, they were reluctantly rising before the mind's eyes of the historical

[4] *Last Words of Thomas Carlyle*, pp. 261–4, Longmans, etc., 1892.
[5] Quoted from a letter to Neuberg.

magician, as if to a day of judgment, and he was asking himself,—can they be shown again?

Voltaire's volumes were familiar,—like a tale that has been told; but he had now to read the thousands of letters of Voltaire, and also the writings of Frederick himself, which were as flat as stale beer. Preuss, Lloyd, and Jomini, Retzow and Ranke, Archenholtz and Zimmermann, Denina and Nicolai, etc., etc.,—to say nothing of contemporary Italian, French, and English books,—no witch of Endor ever had cruder materials for working miracles in recalling the dead. Neuberg was ready to send cargoes more of all that could be got in Germany, but little of it was worth more than rotten coffins: mere wood, and wet, the best of it, and as fuel good for little but raising smoke. No wonder Varnhagen von Ense was filled with misgivings, declaring that Carlyle would not be satisfied with a store of materials already immense, but "wanted to increase it to the colossal."

Dead wood and wet: but here was a magician who could raise a flame at last, and show to living eyes once more the departed dead, hovering like shadows awhile above the eternal darkness.

III

ADVICE ABOUT READING

(1851)

WRITING to his sister Jean, Mrs. Aitken at Dumfries, on 12.11.51, about a book he had sent her the day before, Carlyle bestowed upon her some advice about reading still worth looking at.—

'I think it is a pity that you did not get some weightier kind of Books, out of which real knowledge might come to you; for example, Books of History, which you could read carefully, having a Map at hand, and attending to the *chronology*, that is, keeping both places and dates steadily before you:—for example, have you ever read any good History of England (Hume's, Henry's); Robertson's *Scotland;* Robertson's *America*, a most entertaining book; his *Charles the Fifth*, etc., etc.? There is a good stock of such Books; and that is the way to read with advantage.

'I recommend also Homer's *Iliad*, and Translations of all the old Greek and Roman Books, called *Classics;* of which Jack, I believe, has some store; at any rate plenty of them are to be had now comparatively speaking, and very cheap. It would be worth your while to have some solid good Book always at your hand when you have a little leisure. Take some thought of this; and, after consulting Jack, *and still more your own real notion,*[1] ask me to help in any way I can.'

The conclusion is the best of this advice, recalling the old advice which may be prehistoric:—

> "Fall to it," meaning to reading, "as you find your stomach
> serves you:
> No profit grows, where is no pleasure ta'en:
> In brief, sir, study what you most affect," or like the best.

[1] Italics added.

IV

IN A CHELSEA BACKYARD, &c.

(1851)

ON 1.12.51 Mrs. Carlyle went to the Grange, leaving her husband to follow. On Saturday, 6.12.51, he was still at home, and instead of going out for his usual early walk, he said to the maid that he would clean the flagstones in the backyard, as she was too ill to do it. It took him three-quarters of an hour and ten or twelve pails of water and plenty of hard scrubbing. He thought of Cobbett's words,—"Dirt shall not be around me, so long as I can handle a broom"; and when he had cleaned the 'greasy clammy flags,' he washed himself and sat down to breakfast. Reporting to his wife, he said it was his 'chief act of virtue' since she went. The steady reading which filled his working hours was not counted.

The weather was 'absolutely perfect' the next day, Sunday, and he took much exercise out of doors, riding and walking. He went to dine at Anthony Sterling's, South Place, expecting 'a mutton-chop with Ford,' instead of which it was a 'grand dinner, Mrs. Ford and the girls all dressed like tulips,' Anthony himself 'in white waistcoat, all very grand indeed,' which made Carlyle thankful to Fate that he had not come in a pilot jacket, as he nearly did. He usually dressed like other people when he went to a dinner-party, but on this occasion was taken by surprise.

The guest of the evening was the Richard Ford who revealed Velasquez to picture-admirers in England, and wrote a handbook for Spain so good that it became a model for handbooks. Carlyle confided to his wife that Ford was a man 'without *humour* or any gracefulness or loveability of character,' but 'not the worst of men to dine with at all; has abundance of authentic information—not duller than Macaulay's, and much more certain, and more social too—and talks away about Spanish wines, anecdotes and things of Spain.'

V

AT THE GRANGE, MACAULAY, &c

(1851–52)

MEANWHILE Mrs. Carlyle at the Grange had unusual news to send to a cousin.[1] She and Lady Ashburton were dressing dolls for a Christmas tree, and there was a tacit strike of the servants.—'The very footmen won't *carry the dolls*. . . . When told to bring one or desire the maid to bring one they simply disappear and no doll comes!—I remarked on this with some impatience yesterday, and Lady A. answered,—" Perfectly true, Mrs. Carlyle —they won't *bring the doll!*—I know it as well as you do—but what would you have me do?—turn all the servants, men and women, out of the house on account of these dolls? for it *would* come to *that*—if I made a point of their *doing anything in the doll line!* Perhaps it would be the right thing to do—but then what should we do next week without servants when all the company come?" Such is the slavery the grandest people live under *to what they call* their "*inferiors*."'

It seems to have been on the Thursday following, 11.12.51, that Mrs. Carlyle wrote a bright letter to Kate Sterling, a daughter of John and a granddaughter of old Sterling, the "thunderer" of the *Times*, whose phrase is quoted. The "President" mentioned is Napoleon the Little, and the "row" was his "coup d'état" at Paris, on 2.12.51.—

'THE GRANGE,
'*Thursday*.

'DEAREST K.,—

'I don't know what I was "born with in my mouth" but it could not have been "a silver spoon" anyhow,—and if anyone ever presented me with a *charm* I must have left it, I think, beside my teacup. For certainly there is not "in all England" (your grandfather's phrase) a poor woman more liable than myself to having "the pigs" run thro'

[1] *J. W. Carlyle: Letters to her Family*, by L. Huxley, pp. 354–7.

things! Here I have been living these ten days in the midst of "a terrestrial paradise," "woods and wilds whose melancholy gloom, &c.," terraces and fountains and artificial lakes, "regardless of expense,"—and for any good I have been able to take of it all, I might as well have remained sitting before my own dead wall in Cheyne Row! Not once have I crossed the threshold, my dear! and am thankful to have had only one day in bed.—The cold I caught so suddenly that night became much worse on my arrival here, and has kept me so thoroughly wretched that I really think I should have gone home ere now, to my own red bed, but for the fact that both Lady Ashburton and Lady Sandwich'—the mother of Lady Ashburton,—'have fallen ill also,—and *even as I am* I am *up to* more than either of *them*, and can do them some good by staying.—I don't *go* much *on doing good*, in a general way. All that Unitarian twaddle about "thinking only of others," "studying the welfare of others," &c. &c., I leave to Miss R. and the like of her. But Lady Ashburton has been extremely kind to me for many years, and our relative positions afford so few opportunities for my showing her any *practical* gratitude that when one does offer itself I am naturally very glad to seize it.—Lord A. has been from home for a week, and if I were not here to sit with her in her bedroom, her situation amidst all her grandeur would be rather desolate.—And as for Lady Sandwich with her French manners, it requires all the good sense I can bring to bear on her to keep her *quiet*. There being about a quarter a mile of corridors and staircases between the bedrooms of the two, I get plenty of *indoors* exercise at least, in travelling from the one to the other! But in this way I have hardly any time to myself—to write my own letters or think my own thoughts—besides that when I do get to my own room for a little, I need to lie on my sofa with my eyes shut to rest my wearied spirit. I look forward to Saturday with perfect terror. The House is to be filled with people on that day, and if Lady A. cannot appear, I shall have to *do* them all myself,—with this cold!

'While Lady A. was coughing and blowing her nose this morning, *I* was taken with a violent fit of *sneezing!* "Gracious!" she exclaimed, when she could speak, "*what* do you suppose, Mrs. Carlyle, is the meaning of all this?" "I could do without knowing the meaning of it," I said, "if I could only predict the end of it—*what* is going to become of us on Saturday?" "Oh, the end," said she, "of the end there can be *no* doubt. Mr. Salmon will have to come and read the funeral service over us all—and I shall send him a note to-day to prepare him!"

'Poor Saffi'—the Italian "triumvir," a friend and colleague of Mazzini,—'has written me 2 charming letters, one in English, one in Italian, and has received no answer to either. The English letter I will send you, but don't lose it, keep it for me. I was very frightened at first that they would all rush into that row—strange that nobody should have as yet shot the President—but there is a good time coming, please God!—Did you see the account of General Cavaignac's arrest? That man *does* everything and *suffers* everything like a man out of *Plutarch's Lives!*—If the young lady to whom he is affianced don't have the spirit and wit to effect his escape, someone else must. Why not I?

'Ledru,' meaning Ledru-Rollin, "the tribune of the Revolution" of 1848, as he has been called,—'seems to have miscalculated strangely. Lady Sandwich who is a violent Aristocrat was scolding me the other night about my faith in Ledru,—adopted from Mazzini entirely. At last she exclaimed:—"Mrs. Carlyle, Ledru must either be or have been *your Lover!* Only that, only a passion, could have so blinded and perverted your judgment." Lady A. looked up from her work (a doll's shift) and asked gravely: "Was he ever your Lover, Mrs. Carlyle?" "Never," I said laughing, "the very reverse of that!" "The very reverse of that!" repeated Lady A. "What does that mean, I wonder? Oh, I have it! You mean to say that he had prevented somebody else from being your Lover!!!" . . .

'Your Affectionate,

'J. W. Carlyle.'[2]

It is likely the last remark emanated from the lively old Lady Sandwich with her "French manners," and that in writing A. was a slip of the pen for S.

Edward Fitzgerald was now in town and calling on his friends.[3] He found Carlyle alone and was told about 'the Water System' at Malvern. "It has done me a very little good," said Carlyle to him, adding,—"I would be quite well if I threw my books away and walked about the mountains; but that would be 'Propter vitam, &c.,'"—

[2] Apparently an unpublished letter,—thanks for it are due to Prof. W. H. Woodward. [3] *Letters of Edward Fitzgerald*, I, p. 272.

for the sake of keeping alive, giving up what makes life worth living. In short, as Fitzgerald said in reporting the talk in a letter this month to Tennyson's brother, 'Nature made him a Writer: so he must wear himself out writing Lives of Sterling, &c., for the Benefit of the World. Thackeray,' for his part, 'says he is getting tired of being witty, and of the great world: he is now gone to deliver his Lectures at Edinburgh, having already given them at Oxford and Cambridge.'

After which he was to fetch his two daughters with him to the Grange, where Carlyle in the meantime had joined his wife on 13.12.51. Carlyle could read there almost as well as at Chelsea, and enjoyed the sight of the notabilities that crowded the house, including the Chancellor of the Exchequer, Sir Charles Wood, Lords Grey and Lansdowne, Twisleton and Clough, and women and many others nameless now,—nearly all, excepting the Carlyles, complacent first-class passengers in the quickly-moving, never-ending train of life. One who much interested Carlyle was Macaulay, and he described him in letters from the Grange to his brother John and a sister.—

'He and I did very well together; and I felt his departure a real loss to the party. . . .

'He was a real acquisition while he lasted. A man of truly wonderful historical *memory*, which he has tried in extensive reading, and has always lying ready, with this or the other fact, date, or anecdote on demand: in other respects, constantly definable as the sublime of commonplace; not one of whose ideas has the least tincture of greatness or originality or any kind of superior merit except neatness of expression. He speaks with a kind of gowstering' (blustering) 'emphasis; laughs occasionally (*not* at things really ludicrous, but where a laugh is demanded by the exigencies of the case) with a loud wooden but frank and good-natured tone:—he is on the whole a man of really peaceable kindly temper, and superior sincerity in his Whig way. . . . Grandson of a Highland Minister, and really very much (intrinsically) like a Highland Minister himself, tho "preaching" in a very different element, and with a stipend immensely enlarged!'

"I used to think my husband the most copious talker, when he liked, that was anywhere to be fallen in with," wrote Mrs. Carlyle now to her friend Mrs. Russell, "but Macaulay beats him hollow! in quantity."

For lack of reporters, all that Carlyle said, or Macaulay or any other, is like water spilt upon the ground; but there is a glimpse of a pleasant evening in Mrs. Carlyle's letters to a cousin.[1] On Christmas Eve the Christmas tree stood decorated in the servants' hall, and forty-eight children with their schoolmistress and mothers and most of the servants were ranged around, while Lady Ashburton, attended by her husband, Carlyle and his wife, and the clergyman and his wife and two daughters, 'distributed the presents, calling up each child by name and saying something graceful and witty along with the doll, top, or whatever it might be. Mr. C. had begged to have a map of the world in pieces given to *him*, which was done very cleverly. "Thomas Carlyle—the Scholar," shouted her Ladyship, and the *Scholar* himself advanced. "*There* is a map of the world for *you*—see that you put it all together and make the pieces fit." *The Scholar* made his bow, and looked as enchanted as any little boy or girl among them.'

Next night was Christmas, when the servants had a ball of their own, which lasted till six in the morning; and for eight days more Carlyle continued reading history, alongside Thackeray, who was writing his *Esmond*,[4] while Lady Ashburton was a genial hostess to Mrs. Carlyle and Thackeray's two daughters and many more. The Carlyles came home together on 2.1.52, with Thackeray and his two girls in the train along with them; and also, as Carlyle wrote to his brother next day, 3.1.52,—'In the Train we came upon Milnes and his Wife, just returning from *Palmerston's*, the theme now of all tittle-tattle that has nothing else to play upon. Milnes, himself looking fat and elderly, reported Palmerston to be "happy"' . . .

Milnes was one of the few who were standing by Palmerston now, when Lord John Russell dismissed him from his ministry for being too prompt in welcoming a month ago the December Coup d'État at Paris; and the happiness Milnes remarked was a sign of the times, for in a few weeks Palmerston had what he called "his tit-for-tat with John Russell," by defeating the Government, which made Lord Derby the Prime Minister, and Disraeli the Chancellor of the Exchequer and the leader in the Commons.

[4] *Mrs. Brookfield and her Circle*, by C. and F. Brookfield, II, pp. 368–9.

VI

A WITTY OLD WOMAN

(1852)

LADY SANDWICH was meditating an early return to Paris, which Mrs. Carlyle was regretting, for she was always fond of the lively old lady, now seventy-two. Indeed it had been for the pleasure of her company as much as for any other reason that Mrs. Carlyle had gone to the Grange for December; and one of the best of all the good stories she tells in her letters may be dated about then. She wrote to her cousin after coming home:[1]—

'The old Countess (Lady Sandwich) is decidedly one of the most entertaining and agreeable people I know. I was talking to her of A.B., saying I wondered she did not get married, with sixty thousand pounds.

'"Married?" said Lady Sandwich—"what *are* you thinking of?—Who would marry anything so ugly?"

'"But really," I said, "she is not after all so very ugly. She is Ladylike—has a very nice figure, a good skin, and hair,—is not too old—is accomplished, amiable; men don't need all that usually to help them to marry sixty thousand pounds."

'The old Countess sat staring at me till I had done and then exclaimed almost indignantly:—"Great God, Mrs. Carlyle, what nonsense you *are* talking! Just imagine that nose on a pillow!" But unless you had seen the nose, you cannot enjoy the fun of this speech. That is the style of the thing.'

The witty old woman did not continue in Paris, but returned to England and was in her eighties when she died, which is itself a certificate of good character. Mrs. Carlyle was of course in the right in their debate; but it is likely they were merely chaffing, for if not it is hard to understand why Mrs. Carlyle did not answer as she might have done,—"All cats are alike in the dark."

[1] *J. W. Carlyle: Letters to her Family*, by L. Huxley, p. 360.

VII

COMFORTING BISHOP THIRLWALL

(1852)

ANY Government that is unjust seemed "organised rascality" to St. Augustine; and such indeed was the empire now being prosperously set up in Paris by the deluded people and soldiers. In taking the like of Napoleon the Little for their leader, they were almost as preposterous as the Egyptians adoring cats, or perhaps any of their contemporary European neighbours, and in one way they were worse. The "empire" meant war, for its hosts of idle fighting men wanted better loot than they could get in Algiers. The "coup d'état," the political crime of violence perpetrated in Paris in December, 1851, was followed by a general panic in England, which was more reasonable than we can now realise. London had long been a temptation to fighting men as "a glorious city to sack."

On 28.1.52 the wisest of the Bishops, Thirlwall, had a long walk and talk with Carlyle in the Parks, and reasoned with him earnestly about the evil designs of the French, 'astounded' at his indifference, and himself 'full of almost frantic apprehensions.'

"Hardly a shadow of a probability" of French invasion would Carlyle allow. "A temporary insult to our coasts" was the utmost possible for a long time to come, and he added :—"If we had to bestir ourselves, out of the abominable Hudsonism" (or commercial gambling) "and rotten canting confusion now everywhere prevalent, and fight for ourselves like men or be slaughtered as fat swine, it would probably be a great advantage to us at the end of the account!" Whereby the Bishop was comforted, if not entirely convinced.

Carlyle wrote to Neuberg[1] that the terror-stricken in England as yet were mainly 'the writers in the *Times*. As for me I rather welcome the "Brummagem French Cromwell" (such as he may turn out), and thank him for stopping the "900 talking attorneys" at any rate: one clearly useful thing (after 40 years' trial) if he never do another!'

[1] Letter apparently unpublished.

VIII

HENRY LARKIN IS TURNED FROM LITERATURE

(1852)

MORE than a year after receiving the letter from Carlyle of 29.12.50,[1] Henry Larkin wrote again and incidentally revealed without intending it that he meant to take to writing. "Again by return of post," he tells us,[2] "I received as kind a letter as one man ever wrote to another. And that letter finally decided for me that literature was not a possibility to which I could ever look, without some far more urgent call than any I had yet been conscious of."

The letter was typical, and is still worth reading.—

'CHELSEA,

29th March, 1852.

'DEAR SIR,—

'Your letter is very kind and good; and I know very well, by old experience of my own, what it means. In a world so full of contradiction and confusion I may honestly accept your loyal feeling towards me with thanks and satisfaction; and to yourself also it signifies much that you have such feelings, and have found some course for them, in days like ours. Persist in that disposition, whatever hindrances occur, so long as you can.

'If I have ever taught you any truth, let me offer or reiterate this one advice about it, That you be earnest, without delay, to *do* it; and not at all earnest to *say* it, but rather careful *not* to say it, till the irresistible necessity arrive. If such necessity never arrive, then understand that *you* are all the richer; you have the thing still circulating in your blood and life, and have not thrown it out of you, it or any part of it, by speech. This is truer than perhaps you think at present; you will see it better by and by. Of all the devouring Molochs to which souls "pass through fire," and are burnt, too truly, into phantasmal

[1] Book XIX, Chap. III.

[2] *Carlyle and Mrs. Carlyle, A Ten Years' Reminiscence*, by Henry Larkin, *Brit. Quart. Review*, July, 1881, pp. 28–84, and for the letter, pp. 31–2.

inanity and *death*-in-life, there is none comparable, in horrible efficiency and all-destructiveness, to the eloquence Moloch (called " Literature," " Stump Oratory," &c., &c.) who stands crowned as a god among these poor bankrupt generations! " Do with all thy might what thy hand findeth to do " : speak of the same only to the infinitesimal few; nay, oftenest to nobody, not even to thyself! . . .

'Yours sincerely,

'T. CARLYLE.'

This letter shaped aright the life of Henry Larkin, and gives a clue to the book he wrote in 1886[3] to " explain " Carlyle :—' His heart was sick of perpetually exhorting and admonishing. He longed to be *doing* something, instead of writing and talking about it: to be a leader, not a mere prophet. He felt he had been commissioned to *do* something effectual; and he could find no practical outlet for his powers and energy. This was the pent-up secret of Carlyle's life.'

For the simple persons who need theories, Larkin's is as good as any other, tho far enough from the truth. In the absence of other details about him, it may be as well to note what an Irish antiquarian has reported,[4]—' this Larkin seems to have been of the Welsh or English Larkins, who are akin to the Irish, the modern representatives of the Irish clan O'Lorcain, County Wexford.' Like other English Larkins, this one seems to have been bred a Protestant, and assuredly he had by this time become a devout evangelical Christian. We will see more of him in years to come.

[3] *Carlyle and The Open Secret of His Life*, by Henry Larkin, pp. 73–4, etc. (Kegan Paul, Trench, Trubner & Co., 1886.)

[4] Samuel Scott, now in Ayr, but from Derry, where he is better known: an undoubted expert in such matters.

IX

PUBLIC AND PRIVATE OUTLOOK

(1852)

CARLYLE did not need to learn from Thiers and other exiles whom he met at the Ashburtons' that Napoleon the Little was a common scamp. He had seen the fellow in London. 'Not long after the coup d'état,' Espinasse was speaking to Carlyle about it[1] 'as a feat likely to commend itself to Cromwell's biographer,' but was grimly answered that Louis Napoleon had "done some very ugly things." Carlyle went on to 'talk much of Louis Napoleon's aggressive designs,' says Espinasse, 'and being myself of French extraction, I was rather indignant when he declared that France, if she did not take care, would be partitioned one of these days.'

He never dissembled his contempt[1] for 'the wretched kind of men we had for governors,' saying England was governed by "a miserable bureaucracy." Once at Cheyne Row Espinasse heard Professor Craik enquire of him,—"Who are the men you would put in their place?" "I am one," Carlyle replied, "You are one, and he is one," pointing to Espinasse, and 'adding something in a tone of unforgettable bitterness about being "crushed down here."'

Yet there was no animosity whatever in the curses he bestowed on our politicians. He agreed with Gavan Duffy and others in disesteem for Lord John Russell, declaring he "thought of nothing but his quarter's salary," while speaking of that political unfortunate, after seeing him, as "having something of the old English gentleman about him." The nearest approach to an exception to this was about Russell's rival, Disraeli, the new Messiah of the Tories, whom Carlyle called "Ou' Clo'." He told Espinasse[1] that 'the last chapters of *Tancred* (1847) convinced him that its author was a thorough quack.' As for Palmerston he called him[1]

[1] *Literary Recollections*, by F. Espinasse, pp. 193–5, and in one detail, conversation of Espinasse.

"the ugliest man I have ever seen," and "the chief anarch of England."[2] When Duffy described Palmerston's pleasant appearance and popularity in the House,[3] but said he thought him merely "a playactor cast in the part of a patriot statesman," Carlyle concurred, and called him "a fitting leader for an age without sincerity or veracity." But even here his main objection was to Palmerston's pandering to popular folly, by meddling in continental affairs which were really no concern of ours, in a way that was sure to land us as it did in needless wars.

To Neuberg in Germany he wrote on 1.3.52[4]:—'All men *laugh* hitherto at the new ministry, with Disraeli for Chancellor King of the Moneybags; but to me it gives no laughter, only gloomy thoughts (when I attend to it at all), as a Belshazzar Handwriting on the wall![5] When once the Stump-Orator is actually Sovereign of England, there will be strange sights here as elsewhere! But we cannot help it, and must not too much mind it.'

Meanwhile he was soliloquizing in his journal:—'Took to reading about Frederick the Great soon after my return from Paris, at which, with little definite prospect, I continue. Was at the Grange three weeks, a huge company coming and going. Lonely I, solitary almost as the dead. Infinitely glad to get home. . . . Keep reading Frederick.' (Names the books.) 'I make slow progress, and am very sensible how *lame* I now am in such things. *Hope* is what I now want. Hope is as if dead within me for most part; which makes me affect solitude and wish much that I had even one serious intelligent man to take counsel with. But this is weak, so no more of this; know what the inevitable years have brought thee, and reconcile thyself to it. An unspeakable grandeur withal sometimes shines out of all this, like eternal Light across the scandalous London fogs of time. Patience! Courage! Steady, steady!' He ended by once more asking himself, 'Can Frederick be my next subject—or what?' It was a question that often recurred to him, as he went on reading steadily, without hasting, without resting,—like the Sun.

Neuberg was supplying him from Germany with all the books available 'about "Vater Fritz"' (Father Fritz), but

[2] *Life of R. M. Milnes, Lord Houghton*, by Wemyss Reid, II, p. 477.
[3] *My Life in Two Hemispheres*, by Sir C. Gavan Duffy, II, p. 52.
[4] Letter apparently unpublished.
[5] See Daniel v.

had to let Carlyle pay for them, being admonished,[4]—'Otherwise I really cannot apply again.' Carlyle confessed to him[4] he was 'gaining little new love for the man. . . . In my present indeterminate humour, nothing strongly solicits me elsewhither; and tho there seems no greater likelihood of my ever making a Book upon Friedrich, I may at least go on as long as it amuses me.

'I very greatly want some *human* details about the inward structure and condition of Fr.'s army . . . I honour Fritz greatly for being a man of unsubduable healthy elasticity and shiftiness ("burning his own smoke" to a really great extent).'

On All-Fool's-Day, 1.4.1852, Carlyle was writing in his journal again:—'You talk fondly of "immortal memory," &c. But it is not so. Our memory itself can only hold a certain quantity. Thus for every new thing that we remember, there must some old thing go out of the mind; so that here, too, it is but death and birth in the old fashion, though on a wider scale and with singular difference in the *longevities*. Longevities run from 3000 years or more to nine days or less; but otherwise death at last is the common doom.'

X

ADVICE TO A TEACHER

(1852)

IN April Carlyle received a letter from Canada. His elder half-brother John, the 'Wee Jack' he played with in childhood, had long been a farmer there, and now the son of John, a new James Carlyle, was a teacher by trade, and applying to his Uncle Tom for advice in his studies. He received an immediate and long reply.[1]—

'CHELSEA, LONDON,
19th April, 1852.

'DEAR NEPHEW,—

'I am glad to hear, by your letter, that you are intent upon self-improvement; to increase one's knowledge of profitable things, and in all ways cultivate one's immortal soul, is surely the duty of every creature according to his opportunities. . . .'

As for advice: 'Since you are at the trade of Teaching, your first care ought to be to perfect yourself more and more in all the branches you are required to teach. Nothing is more frightful than a Schoolmaster who is himself ignorant, or ill-informed, upon the things he is trying to impart to his scholars. Beyond and before all other pursuits, you must make yourself master of whatever you are teaching, or likely to be called at any time to teach. To begin with the beginning: Your handwriting, for example, though promising and tolerable, is by no means good *enough;* the way to improve it, and there is no other way, is to *practise daily;* write every day, *trying* to do better' . . . and in short get 'a good hand,—swift, distinct, simple, and without waste of room. Then there are Arithmetic, Geography, English Grammar. . . . Many schoolmasters I have seen who were *not* intelligent of Arithmetic and its principles; they taught it, as they worked it, by rote, and had no knowledge of principles. Do you not imitate these; if you are

[1] Shown to D. A. W. in Toronto, 1.10.1895, by James Carlyle himself, who allowed it to be transcribed.

still in that situation, get yourself a good book of Arithmetic.' . . . He names a book and tells how to use it,—' labouring incessantly with your whole strength (which is the real secret of success in all attempts in whatever direction). . . .

'In the rear of Arithmetic, and essential for a Schoolmaster who will rise above the lowest sphere of his business, are Mensuration, Geometry, Algebra, and the whole field of Mathematics; a very noble subject, useful in all manner of ways; — and a subject withal in which a man of real sense can make his own way, to any length, without help of a teacher. Indeed there are few or no subjects on which a man of real sense,—real industry, honesty, and steadfast perseverance,—cannot make his own way; and if you do make it, it is better in many respects, and far more productive for you, than if a teacher had helped.

'For English Grammar,' he praised '*Cobbett's* little book' as 'one of the clearest and best,' and said: 'Cobbett is otherwise a great example to you: he began life here in London as a wandering lad, barely able to read, who was obliged to *enlist;* as a private soldier he took to study, while others were idling and drinking; and he ended as a man of solid cultivation, and of high mark in the world.'—He named two books on Geography and remarked.—' Almost any Book you can pick up on that subject, will open a wide field of enquiry and improvement for you: I recommend that, and all the astronomy you can acquire, as very useful.—Beyond and in advance of all these subjects, lie Foreign Languages, especially French and Latin. . . . Cobbett learned French with hardly any master (except perhaps a chance hint about the pronunciation). . . .

'With regard to reading for general improvement . . . read whatever good Books you can find. . . . Read no *fool's* Book if you can help it; fly from a fool as you would from poison, in your reading and in all other pursuits of yours! . . . It is less important to a man that he read many Books, than that he read a few *well* and with his whole mind awake to them. This is indisputably certain. A very small lot of Books will serve to nourish a man's mind, if he handle them well—and I have known innumerable people whose minds had gone all to ruin, by reading carelessly too many Books. It is like omnivorous *feeding*. . . . The wisest men I have known in this world were by no means great *readers; good* readers I should rather say, of a *few* Books that were wise,—and having an *abhorrence* of all

Books they found to be *foolish*. A man gathers wisdom only from his own sincere exertions and reflexions ; and in this it is not really very much that other men can do for him ; but whatever help there is, he will find with the *wise* alone. . . . Read *well* whatever books you can get that you *understand* to be good ones ; try them well with your own judgment, earnestly, but yet humbly and loyally ; you will get *more* light at every step, and see better what country, what path is *ahead* of you if you do this as you ought.

' As to subjects for reading,' he praised history, and named books and added as usual,—' Chronology and Geography are the *lamps* of History. . . .

' Give my kind wishes, remembrances and regards to your Father and Mother : we have drifted far asunder since that night I stayed in their hospitable house at Cockermouth ; may all good be with them always, and with you.

' Yours truly,

' T. CARLYLE.'

In his old age James Carlyle told warmly how much he had treasured this letter all his life, and profited by it. He almost had it by heart. He became a much-respected teacher and ultimately teacher of teachers in Toronto. After many years he came to England to see his uncle, and in short we are to see him again in 1879.

XI

THE LONDON LIBRARY IN DANGER

(1852)

THE letter to his nephew of 19.4.52 would be written in the afternoon or evening hours, and not allowed to interfere with his regular work of reading history. The same may have been true of even such a matter as the London Library row, which occupied most of his spare time in the first half of this summer.

The London Library was now 'regarded as a social institution of great utility which political leaders and writers felt it a duty to support.'[1] Its Secretary and factotum, J. C. Cochrane, appointed in 1840 in the way we have seen,[2] had died this spring at the age of seventy-three;[1] and his right-hand man and assistant, John Edward Jones, was hoping to succeed him,—a very reasonable hope, considering the modest salary and all the circumstances. Unfortunately for Jones, Mr. Gladstone had marked the post as a proper plum for a Neapolitan protégé of his, James Lacaita. Besides its salary, the post gave openings to a social climber which made it attractive to many, and any one could see that Lacaita with such a champion made Jones impossible. Carlyle was sorry for Jones, but also concerned for the Library, which he had taken such pains to start. He could not discover anyone in London, Italian or other, who had ever heard of Lacaita before. Gladstone called to satisfy him without success. 'From Gladstone's own account to me,' he wrote, 'I figured him as some ingenious bookish young advocate, who probably had helped Gladstone in his Pamphlets underhand,—a useful service, but not done to the London Library particularly.'

The Pamphlets referred to were the "Two Letters to Lord Aberdeen," which had caused a sensation in 1851 and had a large circulation.[3] The biographer of Gladstone, John

[1] *Carlyle and the London Library*, by Frederick Harrison, pp. 93–4.
[2] *Carlyle on Cromwell and Others*, pp. 102–4.
[3] *Life of W. E. Gladstone*, by John Morley, I, pp. 390–7.

Morley, has told what confirms the shrewd guess of Carlyle.[3] It was Lacaita who in 1850 was the first to open Gladstone's eyes to the abominations of Naples,—"the negation of God erected into a system of Government." Lacaita was the legal adviser to the British Embassy, when Gladstone came there, and 'they talked politics and literature day and night' together.[3] The success of the Pamphlets made Gladstone naturally grateful, but considering that Lacaita was a new arrival in England and not even "naturalised" as a British subject till 1855,[4] it cannot be denied that John Morley was most discreet in saying nothing about the attempt to thrust him on the London Library in 1852.

Assuredly Lacaita could not have had a better champion. Gladstone "has no convictions," said Carlyle to Espinasse,[5] "but he is a long-headed fellow." The difference between them about this matter was their irreconcilable points of view. Carlyle was utterly downright, and after hearing Gladstone out, said to him plainly,—"The proposal is quite inadmissible. The post ought to be given to an Englishman."

In excuse of Gladstone, one may recall what Sir James Graham was writing in his journal a few months later,[6]—'It is melancholy to see how little fitness for office is regarded on all sides, and how much the public employments are treated as booty to be divided among successful combatants.' Which was a sentiment creditable to Sir James, and all the more so that it seems to have been sincere. It was a private note, made soon after Disraeli and his Tories had been beaten, and when Graham could have been Chancellor of the Exchequer, if he had not insisted on standing aside in favour of Gladstone.

On this occasion when Gladstone failed to persuade Carlyle to back his pet, he determined to disregard him and push the job through the committee. Carlyle's way of preventing him is a good model solution of the ever-recurring problem,—how to succeed in public affairs tho honest.

Confined by influenza, and so unable to attend the committee, Carlyle sent his wife in the second week of May 'to communicate my notions to Forster: namely, that Jones should be made interim manager; that first of all a thorough

[4] *Dictionary of National Biography*, Supplement III.
[5] *Literary Recollections*, by F. Espinasse, p. 195.
[6] *Life of W. E. Gladstone*, by John Morley, I, p. 446.

examination and illumination of the Library's *condition*, from the very heart to the surface of it, should be had,—whereby we might know what *kind* of Librarian might now be the best for us ;—and that not till after that should any Election, or movement towards an Election, be made by any one of us.' In this way Carlyle obtained the time he required to checkmate Gladstone. To Jones Mrs. Carlyle was to ' signify . . . in some kind way that he must not pretend at all to be head Librarian, in case there were one, tho his deserts were known and would be attended to.'

Forster agreed entirely, but plainly told Mrs. Carlyle that nothing would be done but appoint Lacaita. Gladstone was " stirring Heaven and Earth," and the committee " perfectly certain " to oblige him, as most of the members, " Milman, Lyttleton, Milnes, Hallam, etc." were " malleable material, some of it as soft as butter, under the hammer " of a possible minister. Mrs. Carlyle was " quite of Forster's way of thinking " ; and so was her husband for a day or two. Yet he felt it was " contrary to common honesty "[7] to let the Library be utilised for the convenience of a " miniature Panizzi."[8] So if he could not prevent it, he told Helps[7] that he felt bound to " go before the thing, and in some softest but perfectly audible way *protest* against such a proceeding, and refusing absolutely I, for one, to have any hand in it more or less, openly dismiss myself from the Committee before they proceed to so untenable an operation."

On 10.5.52 Carlyle remarked in a letter to his brother John,—' Gladstone, I think with Forster, will probably succeed : but he shall not do it without one man at least insisting on having Reason and common Honesty as well as Gladstone and Charity at other men's expense, satisfied in the matter ; and protesting to a plainly audible extent against the *latter* amiable couple walking over the belly of the former.'

On 12.5.52 he was writing more hopefully to Forster, who had promised to help him.[8]—' Dear Forster, This project of Gladstone's must be resisted à l'outrance : I find also that there are " possibilities " (in spite of your evil prognostics), and if there were not, that such must be *made*, and prosecuted with energy and without delay. The Committee (of

[7] *Correspondence of Sir Arthur Helps* (1917), pp. 108–10.
[8] John Forster papers at South Kensington, T. C. Letters, 12. and 28.5.1852.

which every one of *us* is a constituent atom) has no more right to do this thing than your Henry would have, if you sent him for a cut of salmon, to buy it, with your money, of some meritorious Fishmonger (Neapolitan or other) who had a cut *extremely in need of being sold.* With what face would Henry present malodorous salmon to you, and brag of his "charity," done at your expense! This seems to me the exact position we occupy, whether we recognise it or not; and we, each of us, shall intrinsically deserve horsewhipping if we play false to it,—and don't bring home simply the *best salmon* we can find. . . . We are called each honest Henry of us to resist to the death. . . .'

On the same day Carlyle summoned Arthur Helps from the country:—[7]

'Dear Helps, The London Library is in danger! I myself am incapable of stirring out,' having influenza. Then, after a full account of the position, 'Come up to town, and lodge yourself within reach of me, the earlier the better, but at least a week before next Committee meeting. Unless actually held, as I myself am, you are actually bound to this, somewhat as your groom would be if he saw one of your horses about to be stolen by a cadger, and could prevent it by a little running. . . . I have no candidate of my own; on the whole, no wish in the matter except that what is honest be done by the Committee. . . . Sure enough, Gladstone might saddle Kossuth or King Bomba on the L. Library, or put the L. Library altogether in his pipe and smoke it to white ashes, without entirely ruining one's prospects in this immense Universe! These things I . . . will keep in mind; and yet . . . come,—at once if you can.'

As additional inducement he promised, "My remaining capabilities of speech shall all be devoted to you; and before the day comes I hope to be myself on my feet again." Accordingly he 'spent many headaches writing about that Gladstone foray'; and without any apparent intention that way, maintaining a gravity like Dean Swift's, he set Society buzzing and grinning, for Gladstone was already the prig of politics, the advertised *incorruptible*, and for a motion peculiarly his to be publicly opposed as "contrary to common honesty" delighted everybody within wind of it. This multiplied the applicants. Not counting foreigners, there were 250 Englishmen alone before the end of May,—

which was fatal to the hopes of poor Jones, but not less so to Gladstone and Lacaita.

The last scene was at the committee meeting on Saturday, 12.6.52. The hundreds of applicants had then been reduced to a short leet of eleven, among whom W. B. Donne, a Norfolk man, was easily first favourite, a scholar of distinction and personally known to Spedding, Milnes and others. 'Speeches were spoken, manœuvring went on' with plenty of 'real politeness, candour, and delicate management.' Carlyle's answer to Gladstone was merely,—"we should go to a vote as we are not convincing one another"; whereupon the President (Lord Devon) collected the written votes and counted them 'amid considerable stillness,'—eighteen for Donne, and for Lacaita four,—Gladstone and Bunsen, Lyttleton and Lansdowne. Unanimously they voted esteem for Jones "and recognition of our obligation to do something for him in the way of permanent promotion." As for Lacaita, he became a professor of Italian in a London College,[4] etc.

Thus was the London Library saved from a job. It continued to prosper without any more history, growing like a tree.

XII

FREDERICK AND VOLTAIRE AS THE HEAVENLY TWINS

(1852)

MEANWHILE through all the influenzas and Library bothers, Carlyle was steadily reading and becoming more and more familiar with the men and women of the eighteenth century, but his hero Frederick was not altogether like the woman who inspired the poet Burns,—'But to see her was to love her, Love but her, and love for ever.'

There are ominous words in a letter to Neuberg of 2.2.52,[1]—'I continue reading Books about Vater Fritz, gaining *little new love for the man'*;[2] but there was a redeeming quality turning the balance in Frederick's favour,—'a man of perfect *veracity*, in spite of his fox-like cunning, and French-polished completely *royal* ways, I clearly perceive him to have been.' Such a quality in a man absorbed all his life in the work of Government made him an ideal specimen for Carlyle's purpose, which was to convince us benighted Europeans of the truth which Confucius taught the Chinese five centuries before Christ, that public business was real and difficult work, and that the prosperity of a people depended upon its being done well. In Europe hitherto any fool who could get the job was presumed to be able to do it.

On the last day of May Carlyle was telling Neuberg,[1]—"He does increase in beauty to me, the intrinsic bright-sheet-lightning soul of Vater Fritz does, and so I continue to read about him . . . the world offering to me nothing elsewhere so inviting. I have even tried what I could to go through the 5000 letters of Voltaire for his sake, the Pirithous of that Theseus,"—Pirithous and Theseus being the Greek David and Jonathan, or, so to speak, the Heavenly Twins. "Voltaire also has his *lightning* element and holds

[1] Letter apparently unpublished.
[2] Italics added.

of the Gods, after all," added Carlyle, as if reluctantly convinced, in spite of his pious prejudices. So it was not by accident that Voltaire became the spiritual hero of the great history. Frederick was an outright disciple of Voltaire, and not to be understood apart from him. It was Voltaire that made him a freethinker of the right sort, a real *free*-thinker, like a disciple of Confucius, tolerant of all religions as of Æsop's fables.

XIII

CHEAP BOOKS, &c.

(1852)

ONE of the literary excitements this summer was a row among the booksellers. According to Carlyle's private letters,[1] the 'little' booksellers were willing to do business for a profit of 15 per cent or 10 per cent of the price, while the 'big booksellers insist on taking from 45 to 60 per cent of the sale price for the mere act of selling any new book.'

Carlyle sympathised with the 'little' booksellers, and did not conceal his opinion, and when the debate was ending he was thus writing to one of them, Robert Chambers, who became a 'big' one in the end, but was always more an author than a publisher, and wrote many good books, besides being the author "anon" of the book which in 1844 anticipated Darwin, 'The Vestiges of Creation.' He had been calling on Carlyle lately, and the letter was to enquire where to see a certain old ballad, but went on:—'The Paternoster Row Grandees have received their quietus much more speedily than could have been expected; and must feel rather absurd, one would think, under this new aspect of affairs! There is likely to be a great cheapening of books by and by, and an immense increase of reading in consequence,—which, if it were certain that we should get truth and sense to read, or if it were all one (as it is to a dreadful degree all *two*) whether we read sense and truth or falsity and nonsense, would be an indisputable benefit for mankind! Anyhow, we must try it; and *then* see what next.'

Carlyle did not like the *Vestiges*, the authorship of which he would know before now. Like many another teacher by trade, he was too keenly conscious how prone men are to

[1] Unpublished. The letter to Robert Chambers here quoted was dated 27.5.52, and is taken from a copy transcribed from the original MS. by C. E. S. Chambers, a grandson of the addressee, Dr. Chambers.

feel and act on the moral level of our arboreal ancestors, and so he was averse to anything that might make it more difficult for them to straighten themselves and look up. But the *Vestiges of Creation* never diminished his goodwill towards Robert Chambers, nor did the *Origin of Species* by and by prevent him from liking Charles Darwin.

XIV

CARLYLE AND LEWES ON COMTE, &c.

(1852)

T. S. BAINES was living by professorial lecturing and learned editorial work and journalism; but what makes him interesting to-day is his faithful report of an interview with Carlyle this July. He talked about it for thirty years afterwards, and printed it when Carlyle was dead.[1]

In 1852 he was a man of twenty-nine, and assistant to Prof. Sir William Hamilton in Edinburgh, and came to London early in July. One hot Monday afternoon he called on Lewes, who was now so much esteemed for his writing in his new weekly, the *Leader*, that Espinasse says Carlyle was calling him "the Prince of Journalists."[2] Baines tells us he found him :—

'Busy at his desk, writing notices for the *Leader* in his shirt sleeves. Having denounced the weather in gay and lively terms, he pressed me to remain to dinner, suggesting that if I did we might walk over to Chelsea in the cool of the evening, and pay a visit to Carlyle. I accordingly remained, and about seven or eight o'clock we started on our evening walk. Crossing the High Street, Kensington, we struck into Young Street, where Lewes pointed out to me a house with bow windows in which Thackeray then lived. This led to his giving me various recent illustrations of Thackeray's skill, humour, and dexterity as a draughtsman, pencil sketches of Lewes himself (and others) hit off amidst the music and talk of social evening parties.

'Arrived at Cheyne Row we found Mr. Carlyle at home, while Mrs. Carlyle was not in, (but) was expected soon. We were shown into a comfortable room on the ground floor and presently heard Mr. Carlyle descending. He gave

[1] *Athenæum*, No. 3101, dated 2.4.1887, pp. 449–50. This report by Mr. Baines himself supersedes all other reports of this interview.

[2] *Literary Recollections*, by F. Espinasse, p. 282.

us a cordial welcome, and sat down at a little distance on a rather straight-backed chair. He was dressed in darkish clothes, wore a deep black stock,' the kind of neck-tie then usual, ' and a dark-green tail coat with a velvet collar.

' On such a day it was impossible to avoid the weather, and that was first discussed. Carlyle explained, with a good deal of humorous detail and emphasis, how he had sought shelter in various back-rooms, striving to secure some nook of shadow in comparative coolness.

' He then went on to speak generally of the peculiar heat of London and the suburbs in the later summer months. He said that when he first came to town he thought the habit of going away in August, so common with the Londoners, was a mere superstition which he, as a man of independent judgment and character, ought to resist. Accordingly one August he determined to remain in London, while his friends decamped to the country, the Continent, and the seaside. At first the days tho warm were tolerable enough, the nights being fairly cool and refreshing. But as the month went on the sultry air seemed to thicken and consolidate itself. A dense mass of breathless, heated, arid mist covered the face of the heavens. There were no cool grey clouds in the morning, no breath of refreshing air or dew at night, but the same exhausted, oven-like, stifling atmosphere night and day. " It was more like Tophet," said the sage, " than anything I had ever felt or imagined."

' " Ah ! " replied Lewes, lightly waving his hand towards his friend, " Ah, my dear fellow, you'll know more about that by-and-by."

' The contrast between the two men was striking. Lewes with his light badinage was lounging back in an easy chair, his frock coat thrown open, and revealing the greater amplitude of shirt front from (having) no waistcoat ; Carlyle sitting straight up on his chair, with his deep stock and high waistcoat, absorbed in the vivid realization of the past, and with the set, almost rigid air of reflective intensity and self-centred strength.

' The talk then passed to the *Leader*, and Carlyle bitterly denounced the local newsman as illustrating the Age in doing, in a shambling and inefficient way, the special duty he undertook. He never folded the paper properly so that it could be comfortably read. " Every Saturday," groaned the sage, " I have the trouble of refolding the paper, with all the discomfort and irritation of delay from being compelled to do for myself what this wretched impostor ought to have done to my hand." He then turned on Lewes, and said rather abruptly,—"Are those papers on Comte nearly come to an end?"

'Lewes replied that the series was not yet completed.

'"Ah!" said Carlyle, "in the meantime they are so much lost space to me. I generally look through most of the *Leader*, but I never read a line of those papers. Do you think anybody reads them?"

'On this Lewes bridled up a little, and replied in decisive tones,—"Oh, yes, they are exciting great interest in the English Universities, and especially at Oxford. I have letters from Oxford that show (that)."

'"Ah!" retorted Carlyle, "I looked into Comte some years ago, and soon found he was one of those creatures that bind the universe up into bundles, and set them all in a row like stooks in a field—one of those fellows who go up in a balloon with a lantern to examine the stars. I was soon done with him."

'Carlyle (had) recently been taken by his friends to see *Faust* acted by a German company. Lewes was anxious to know the result, and questioned (him). Carlyle spoke well of the Mephistopheles,—"represented with dramatic skill and finish," and was fairly satisfied, but he did not care for the play as a whole, intimating that it was unfit for acting, and could never be successfully rendered on the stage.

'Carlyle then referred to Dickens as an actor, having recently seen him perform. He gave it as his opinion that Dickens's genius was essentially histrionic and mimetic; that with his faculty of keen and minute observation, his general alertness of mind and body, his mobile power of gesture and expression, he had all the requisites of a successful actor; and that had he lived at a great period of the drama, in the Elizabethan Age for instance, his genius would have found its appropriate outlet on the stage. He would have become a popular comic actor, writing a humorous piece now and then perhaps, as was the custom. But while living under different conditions and working with his pen, his books still retained and revealed the native genius of their author. They had the sustained, if rather jerky liveliness, the pleasant tricks and mannerisms of humorous portraiture on the stage. He was in short a born actor.

'Mr. Lewes spoke highly of Helps' *Conquerors of the New World and their Bondsmen.* Carlyle agreed in the main, but with exceptions and limitations. Helps had not evinced sufficient mastery over his materials. He was too concerned to show the extent and variety of his researches, and had thus introduced into the text a good deal that ought to have been shovelled over into the universal dustbin.

'Mrs. Carlyle came in then and welcomed us in a bright and cheery way. She provided us at once with cooling drinks, lemonade, soda-water, and stronger elements for those who cared for them. I sat for a short time on the sofa with Mrs. Carlyle, and found her chatty and pleasant, tho rather incisive in speech and manner. Presently, through a spontaneous change, Mr. Lewes engaged Mrs. Carlyle in conversation, while Mr. Carlyle joined me.

'He enquired in the kindest manner after Sir William Hamilton, whose assistant I then was. He gave me some interesting recollections of his intercourse with Sir William during the time he lived in Edinburgh, recalling the finished courtesy and dignity of his manner, his wide reading and solid erudition. He mentioned that in those days Sir William lived in rooms in a back street near the Register House, and added that, whenever he passed his windows at night, however late, his light was always burning, and that he believed he regularly spent the greater part of every night amongst his books.

'Carlyle's conversation was very like his books, and much of it as good as almost anything I had ever read in them. The new impression was of his real kindness of heart, the deep latent sympathy of his nature. There was a peculiar gentleness in his tone, an accent of deep and sincere feeling in his voice, in speaking of Sir W. Hamilton, and especially in referring to his crippled condition from paralysis.

'On taking leave Mr. Carlyle proposed to go with us part of the way. As I was a stranger, he and Mr. Lewes kindly walked with me to Sloane Street, and saw me into an omnibus there. On the way some reference was made to politics. The first Derby Ministry had recently been formed, and Disraeli become a member of the Government for the first time.' (Chancellor of the Exchequer, it may be added, and Leader of the Commons.) 'In reference to this I remember that Carlyle, waving his arm towards Westminster, said that we had now a weltering chaos of parties, a reeking cauldron of anarchical political strife, in which all the lowest elements, including a mouthing verbalist and juggling adventurer like Disraeli, had come to the top.'

After seeing Baines into his bus, Carlyle and Lewes walked on together, and it may have been this night that a bit of talk took place, which Lewes recorded without date in his *Goethe*.[3]—'I remember once, as we were walking along Piccadilly, talking about the infamous *Buchlein von Goethe*, Carlyle stopped suddenly, and with his peculiar look and emphasis said,—"Yes, it is the wild cry of amazement on the part of all spooneys, that the Titan was not a spooney too! Here is a Godlike intellect, and yet you see he is not an idiot!—Not in the least a spooney!"'

[3] *Story of Goethe's Life*, by G. H. Lewes, footnote, p. 206 of the 1884 edition; Book IV, Chap. VI.

XV

OFF TO GERMANY ALONE

(1852)

DURING the Willy-and-Nicky war of 1914–18, it was said by some who should have known better that the great history of Frederick, which Carlyle was now about to begin to write, had been instigated and even partly written by men employed by the Prussian Government. The Kaiser had brought out a special edition of the German translation of it while the war was in progress, and at the beginning of the bloodshed tried to pose as another Frederick, which only showed what a fool he was. The historical fact is that Prussian officialdom did what it could to discourage Carlyle, for a plain and obvious reason. Like all the other reactionary Governments of Europe, the Prussian one was anxiously orthodox. Officials seeking favour and promotion were present and punctilious at religious parades, and could only shudder at the suggestion of showing afresh how much Frederick the Great was a disciple of Voltaire, and a mere "philosophe" or free-thinker, such as would not in 1852 be tolerated in Government service. Varnhagen von Ense, who was old enough to please himself, tells a good story in his Memoirs.[1] At one of Metternich's famous breakfasts at Paris in 1810, Varnhagen found Dr. Gall 'engaged in a vehement discussion on religion with Count Sternberg.' There was 'great violence and harshness on both sides,' tho both agreed that religion was 'necessary. "For," said Sternberg, "what would the world come to if the common people were not in some degree kept within bounds by religion?" "And," said (Dr.) Gall, "what would become of us if our princes and rulers were not somewhat held in check by religion?"' Even Varnhagen von Ense now shared the official uneasiness, and was unwilling to encourage Carlyle's enterprise.[2]

[1] *Memoirs of V. von E.*, translation called *Sketches of German Life, &c.*, by Sir A. Duff Gordon, p. 163.

[2] Letter from V. von E. to Neuberg, 14.6.1852, apparently unpublished.

Carlyle had written to him in June[3] with great frankness, but remarking :—'I have no definite *literary* object of my own in view, to animate me in this enquiry ; nothing but a natural human curiosity, and love of the Heroic, in the absence of other livelier interests from my sphere of work at present. . . . That I should ever write anything on Frederick seems more and more unlikely ; but perhaps it would be good that my *reading* upon him, which has been a kind of intermitting purpose with me all my life, should now finish and complete itself at last. Accordingly friend Neuberg, I believe, has now another small cargo of Books on the road for me ; nay other wider schemes of enquiry are opening : one way or other, I suppose, I ought to play the game out.'

This and more to the same effect may have seemed in the Germany of the fifties Voltairian dissimulation ; but it was merely Carlyle's way of not committing himself. Such was the method of Jesus in behaviour, according to the best of our recent commentators on the Gospels.[4] Assuredly such was the way of Carlyle all his life. It was like the great Napoleon's method of strategy, for he said, "I never had any plan of campaign," but in short remained always ready to do what seemed best at the time of action. So in Germany this year and for another year to come, Carlyle could truly say that he had not yet undertaken a history of Frederick, but was only thinking of it.

Thus after writing to Varnhagen, he was writing to Emerson (25.6.52) and remarked,—'I am not *writing* on Frederick the Great ; nor at all practically contemplating to do so. But, being in a reading mood after those furious *Pamphlets* . . . and not being capable of reading except in a train and *about* some object of interest to me,—I took to reading, near a year ago, about Frederick, as I had twice in my life done before ; and have, in a loose way, tumbled up an immense quantity of shot rubbish on that field, and still continue. Not with much decisive approach to Frederick's *self*, I am still afraid ! The man looks brilliant and noble to me ; but how *love* him, or the sad wreck he lived and worked in ? I do not even yet *see* him clearly ; and to try making others see him—?—Yet Voltaire and he *are* the celestial element of the poor Eighteenth Century ; poor souls.

[3] *Last Words of Thomas Carlyle.* Pub. Longmans, etc., pp. 265–72.

[4] Leo Tolstoy. See, e.g. Aylmer Maude's *Life of Tolstoy, Later Years*, pp. 35–6.

'I confess also to a real love for Frederick's dumb followers: the Prussian *Soldiery*.—I often say to myself, "Were not *here* the real priests and virtuous martyrs of that loud-babbling rotten generation!" And so it goes on; when to end, or in what to end, God knows.'

Which seems to show that Neuberg had succeeded in finding for Carlyle the books about Frederick's army which he wrote for some months ago. To return to the letter to Varnhagen von Ense.[3]

'A project has risen here of a little tour to Germany of which the chief justification to me,—tho the *female* mind withal has other views in it,—would be to assist myself in the enquiries after Frederick. To look with my own eyes upon Potsdam, Ruppin, Rheinsberg, Küstrin, and the haunts of Frederick; to see the Riesengebirge country and the actual fields of Frederick's ten or twelve grand battles: this would be a real and great gain to me. Hohenfriedberg, Soor, Leuthen, I could walk these scenes as truly notable ones on this earth's surface; footsteps of a most brilliant, valiant, and invincible human soul which had gone before me. . . . Then at Berlin, one could see at least immensities of *portraits* . . . engravings, &c., &c., which are quite wanting in this country; as well as all manner of books to be read or to be collected and carried home for reading;—not to mention oral enquiries and communications, or the very sight of friends who might otherwise remain always invisible to me!

'In short, I think it not unlikely that we may actually come, my Wife and I, this very summer; and try the business a little; for there are Homburg or other watering-places in the game too, and we really both of us need a little change of scene, after so many years of this Babel. The drawbacks are sad incapacity, especially on my part, for sleeping, for digesting, for supporting the conditions of travel,—which are sport to most people, and alas are death to poor us! However, if the motive energy *were* sufficiently great? We can both of us' in short speak German, and 'I have a certain readiness in bad French as well. Miss Wynne eagerly urges the attempt, on hygienic grounds; others urge, and in fact, there is a kind of stir in the matter, which may perhaps come to something.'

Then he went on to enquire about the possibility of getting 'open-aired and above all quiet' lodgings for himself and wife in Berlin, which was to be their headquarters, and concludes:—'Miss Wynne, home from Paris this good while, seems as well as ever, and quite beautiful again. We all salute Varnhagen.

'Yours always,
'T. CARLYLE.'

Varnhagen at once replied that Berlin was deserted in summer, especially by the professors; so that he should go there only at the end of September. Whereupon Carlyle remarked to Neuberg,—'Æsthetic teas in German are not likely to be much lovelier to me than the like phenomena in England—ach Gott! Cultivated men of the "silent" (practical) sort, whom I might hope to meet with there, would be far more instructive and far more welcome to me.'

'It is not as a joy but as a necessity that I can much contemplate a visit thither,' he wrote to Neuberg, and said his offer to be a companion was 'a real temptation—very seductive,' and would be welcome if still convenient to Neuberg when the time came.

Mrs. Carlyle declared Neuberg 'as suitable a guide and companion as humanity could well afford.' She had been following the foreign correspondence very closely, and bidding Neuberg write to her, and it explains better than anything yet published what happened at Cheyne Row.

Neuberg told Carlyle of estates that had been offered to him, and Carlyle advised him to think of buying one to 'trim up a home for yourself. Depend upon it, that is a considerable point for a man; to be anchored even by the possession of a House, a Library, a Dairy, Garden, and good conveniences for *living* whatever life one may have,—this is greatly preferable to no anchorage at all. As to England, if you have quite done with trade, there really is very little that cannot be overtaken by visits. *I have serious thoughts myself, many a time, of fairly lifting anchor out of this empty noise, and steering towards some discoverable habitation that were at least silent, and furnished with* NOT-*dirty air to breathe.*[5] Age is and should be earnest, sad even, tho not ignobly but nobly sad; and empty grinning apery of commonplace creatures and their loud inanities ought to be more and more shut out from us as the Eternities draw nigh. You, in your own thoughts, may find occupation for yourself wherever you are; and whether the world takes

[5] Carlyle underlined only *not* before dirty.

any notice of it or takes no notice, is really not the question with a man. . . . Never mind my counsels, given without knowledge of the really deciding elements.'

Whatever the 'really deciding elements' in the long-pending domestic question, to stay or not to stay at Cheyne Row, Mrs. Carlyle had made up her mind she would never leave London, and soon was writing to Neuberg,—"We have taken a lease of this house for thirty-one years—that should serve our time, I think!" To clench the matter, she proceeded to spend over £300 in structural alterations, chiefly by enlarging the big front room on the first floor which was the "library." So through the hot days of July the masons and carpenters were in possession, and Carlyle was 'banished to his dressing-room closet upstairs' and 'continued,' as his wife told Neuberg,—'hanging on by the eyelids (as sailors say) to his usual life of study with dignity.'

She enjoyed directing the workmen, had no wish to go to Germany, and bade him go 'off to Scotland to be out of the way.' Towards the end of July he yielded and went by steamer to Dundee, and stayed some weeks with Thomas Erskine of Linlathen there, within reach of sea-bathing, and enabled by his friend's kindness to work six hours a day as regularly as if at home,—better indeed than was possible at home when the bricklayers and carpenters and painters were in possession. Most of his leisure there was given to the translation of *A Day with Frederick*, which was printed sixteen years later as an Appendix to the History. 'Very flat, but I daresay very *true*,' was what he called it in conclusion,—'a Daguerrotype of one of his days.'—To-day one might rather compare it to a very good film, showing the old King inspecting his property with his bailiff, as if one were looking at him and overhearing all he was saying. The Bailiff, Herr Fromme (or Mr. Good), had a 'wonderful talent of exact memory,' and 'wrote down everything, directly on getting home.'

From Dundee Carlyle went to Scotsbrig, where he hoped his wife would join him for the visit to Germany; but she was begging him to go without her, telling him the house would not be ready for two months, and that she much enjoyed superintending the work, and as for Germany saying plainly at last, 6.8.52,—'It would be anything but a *pleasure* for me to be there.' Describing work in the house, she said,—'The two carpenters are very conscientious and assiduous. . . . When it comes to putting everything in order again, it will be a much greater pleasure than going to Germany, I can tell you.'

Her sincerity in this appears beyond a doubt from what she was writing to her cousin Helen about this time.[6]—'The German scheme is lying quiet, only now and then such phrases as "It will do till we go to Germany"—"When we go to Germany we will, &c." strike a sudden terror into my mind. . . . For a whole year. . . . Mercy, that *will* be awful!'

As late as 17.8.52 he was writing doubtfully to Neuberg admitting that it seemed a duty to go,—he would never have a better chance,—'at least to Berlin. Tho my acquaintance with Frederick somewhat ripens, I do not at all feel such a love as will go through fire and water.'

A few days later he was writing to his wife half-humorously,—'My own private perception is that I shall *have* to go to-morrow week in a Leith steamer for Rotterdam. I wait, however, for your next letter. The ass does swim, I sometimes say, if you fling him fairly into the river, tho he brays lamentably at being flung. Oh, my Goody! Is there no help at all, then?'

So it was settled to her satisfaction,—Friday evening, 27.8.52, the day of departure.

The parting with his mother was tenderer than usual; but it was over, and he was entering the booking office of Ecclefechan railway station, when friends who had come to see him off remarked that he seemed to be surprised by a bulky packet in the pocket of his coat. He took it out and opened it,—a bundle of the best of home-made bannocks, the same as his mother used to stuff his pockets with when he was a boy and going to school or college. In shaking hands a few minutes later, it was easy to see his eyes were wet.[7] He was never to see his mother again till he came to see her die, and tho he could not know that, he guessed and feared.

[6] Undated letter, *J. W. Carlyle*: *Letters to her Family*, by L. Huxley, p. 364. Dr. Huxley dates conjecturally, July, 1852.
[7] *Thomas Carlyle*, by W. H. Wylie, pp. 21–2.

XVI

THE VOYAGE ACROSS

(1852)

"YOUR voyage is likely to take thirty-six hours," said Dr. John in taking leave at Leith on Friday evening, 27.8.52; but the steamer did not start till midnight and met bad weather.[1] 'Laden to the lip with iron, the uneasiest of little kicking wretches' took over eighty hours, reaching Rotterdam about noon on Tuesday, 31.8.52.

Besides an elderly couple from Kirkcaldy, there were two more fellow-passengers, young law students on their way to a German University, Shand[2] and Honeyman; and Honeyman said[3] of Carlyle:—"I cannot say that he spoke either much or little. He was just agreeable: often silent, always answering pleasantly when addressed, occasionally remarking something or joining pleasantly in ordinary conversation. He helped Shand and me with practical advice which we found useful afterwards as to how to find our way about. As a preliminary to the University, we had to learn German; and he advised us to take Wilhelm Meister as a text book."

Arriving at Rotterdam about noon, "I recollect he walked about Rotterdam with us that afternoon. I never saw him again."

The fact was that during the night he could not sleep at all, and therefore abandoning the hope of seeing Amsterdam or the Hague, he escaped from the hotel to the Rhine steamer between five and six next morning, and soon was sleeping there on the cabin sofa, 'four hours, and again four hours, deep, deep,'—the best sleep he had had for a week past, or was to have, for many weeks to come.

Talking German he soon made 'agreeable acquaintances'

[1] Writing on Tuesday, 31.8.52, Carlyle mistook the date for 1st September.

[2] Afterwards the Judge, Lord Shand. In December, 1902, D. A. W. heard of his talk and got an introduction; but Shand was then ill, and never recovered.

[3] Afterwards a Glasgow writer, P. S. Honeyman, who told this to D. A. W. on 13.12.1902.

among fellow-passengers, and looking round upon the country below the level of the river, ‘ kept from drowning by windmill pumps,’ he felt ‘ astonishment and admiration at the invincible industry of man.’ The weather was fine, the landscape more and more agreeable, and before the day was done, he could see far-off the ‘ beautiful mountain group ’ of ‘ the Seven Hills.’

XVII

THE RHINE, COLOGNE, EMS, &c.

(1852)

NEXT day he landed at Cologne, and was almost sorry he did. As he afterwards told the pious Thomas Erskine, who was naturally curious about the Cathedral,—'Cologne, &c., I got no good of, but rather mischief; the sight of those impious charlatans doing their so-called "worship" there—a true devil-worship, if ever there was one,—and the fatal brood, architectural and others—*Puseyites* and enchanted human apes that inhabit such places—far transcended any little pleasure I could have got from the supreme of earthly masonry, and converted my feeling into a sad and angry one.'

It is an old story, but a true one,[1] that the German Ambassador Bunsen once showed Carlyle the plans for the completion of Cologne Cathedral, and getting no remarks of the sort he was seeking, did not take the hint but put some question which was answered,—"It is a very fine Pagoda, if ye could get any sort of a God to put in it." Bunsen burst out laughing,—he and Carlyle were alone together, and it was only in public that officials had to be orthodox.

The picturesque scenery as he went up the river was more pleasant to Carlyle than cathedrals, 'but surely,' he wrote to his wife, 'the most picturesque of all objects was Neuberg, standing on the beach' at Bonn to welcome him. 'My journey has had nothing that was not pleasant and lucky hitherto,' was the gist of a long detailed narrative he sent her, in return for a letter she sent to him when he was in Neuberg's house, which, he told her, 'seemed to me the kindest I had got from you this long while, almost like the old ones I used to get.'

Neuberg's sister who kept house for him had ready for "the Master," as Neuberg always called this visitor, the

[1] Froude expressly says Carlyle confirmed this to him.

'best chamber in the Coblentzer Strasse.' On seeing a German bed for the first time, Carlyle enquired,—"Do the Germans mean one to sit in one's bed?" He *would* have his window open, and was kept awake by cocks outside, altho the house was quiet.

The Saturday's work was examining the University library, and noting names of books. About twenty were borrowed, to be read at some paradise in the Seven Hills fit for a Rip Van Winkle. They were to stay a week there. Meanwhile at Bonn he tried a back room, the farthest from the fowls, and fortified himself by a tub of cold water as a help to sleep. It was on this visit to Germany that he told Neuberg to tell his sister not to neglect cold water,—"there is a certain morality in it," he said, recalling[2] his wife's praise of it, and maybe Malvern and Dr. Gully. They heard him splashing in the middle of the night, 'and there was a strong smell of tobacco smoke.'

Neuberg lost no time. They inspected Roland's Eck. It was crowded and noisy. Then they tried Hunef, 'a small sequestered village' on the other side of the river. It seemed sleepy by day; but at night its bells were like Cathedral bells, and the watchman's horn was loud. Back to Bonn in the morning, "Will you take me up again?" he asked Miss Neuberg, in a tone of comical despair; and next day when she enquired,—"Have you slept better?" he answered by telling an old story. A man tried how little food his horse could live on, and gave it daily less till one morning he found it dead!

So Neuberg and he decided to take away the books borrowed in Bonn, and finish notes from them elsewhere, and for the rest to abandon hopes of study beyond these, and concentrate on what could be done by a man on short allowance of sleep,—gather books or information about them, and see places and portraits.

Excepting Arndt, 'a sturdy old fellow of eighty-three, with open face, loud voice, and the liveliest hazel eyes,' the savants at Bonn were not sirens.—'Miserable creatures lost in statistics' they seemed to a visitor with nerves on edge. He did not need to make an effort to tear himself away.

Going on Friday (10.9.52) by steamer to Coblentz, Carlyle beheld 'the grandest thing' that Germany could show him,

[2] This and any other detail not in any letter is taken from the article *Carlyle and Neuberg* in *Macmillan's Magazine*, Aug., 1884: by Dr. Sadler, who learned it from Neuberg's sister.

the Rhine; no longer sauntering as in Holland, wriggling as if reluctant to reach the sea, like a rich and healthy old man dodging death as long as possible; but rushing in its prime past hills and towns and castles, between trim banks, 'much broader than the Thames at full tide, and rolling along many feet in depth, at a rate of four or five miles an hour, *without voice,* but full of boiling eddies, rolling strong and calm for three or four hundred miles, the most magnificent image of silent power I have seen, a world-river.'

The fellow-passengers were now a mixed crowd, scenery-seekers and rich wandering Jews. Neuberg was with him, and at 2 p.m. they landed at Coblentz and took bus up a side valley to Ems, past fields bespangled with the kind of lilies Germans call Zeit-lose (Time-loose), because they bloom both late and early in the year.

They slept three nights at Ems, and made progress with the books; and in idle hours surveyed the earthly paradise of a fashionable watering-place, inhabited by 'devil's-servants' mainly and their flunkies, 'a place as from the opera direct.' There was gambling every night, the Russians conspicuous there; 'a street like half a mile of the brightest part of Rue de Rivoli'; fantastic promenades and music by the river-side. They watched the sinners dancing once, a show not easy to forget. One old woman 'careering about in a sprightly manner,' says Neuberg, 'he nicknamed "Zeit-lose"—Time-loose.' He must have felt like Tam o' Shanter watching the witches.

On Sunday as they listened to the band he said,—"I wish they'd play the Hundredth Psalm in honour of the Lord's day." On this their last evening there, they took a donkey cart to Burg Nassau, illustrious as the birthplace of William the Silent and other heroes, and there Carlyle plucked a flower which he sent to his wife.

Next day they went by river from Coblentz to Maintz, reputed the most picturesque run on the Rhine, and among the crowds on the steamer remarked a sprinkling of Irish, who were 'lilting' about 'the vine-clad hills.' Carlyle and Neuberg saw 'old Maintz' as well as they could by 'cat's light,' and talked about printer Faust and others, and then took train to Frankfurt.

XVIII

FRANKFURT AND HOMBURG

(1852)

WHEN Carlyle was shaving at Frankfurt next morning, Tuesday, 14.9.52, looking through the window to the lively square, he caught sight of a face 'among the trees' which he recognised, the face of Goethe. 'Ach Gott! Merely in stone,' he wrote to his wife,—'I had so longed to see that face alive; and here it was given to me at last, as if with huge world irony, in stone, an emblem of so much that happens.'

The Grand Duke of Weimar was in Italy, but his Secretary was a Scot abroad, a Mr. Marshall, and he was now awaiting the travellers here, having arrived the night before to do the honours of Frankfurt. Neuberg and he conducted Carlyle to Goethe's father's house. "Salve!" (Hail!) said Carlyle, taking off his hat as he stood before it. They entered and were shown the inside, and wrote their names in silence. They next inspected the Hall where the 'old Kaisers were all elected,' looked at the fair going on, perhaps also at the Inn, which Goethe's grandfather had kept, and certainly the grim-looking Ghetto, where hung the Red shield, *Roth Schild*, a sign which supplied a surname to the money-broker whose descendant lately offered Carlyle a blank cheque in vain. At last the three sightseers went to the top of the highest steeple, and sat there sipping beer and smoking, surveying from above.

By 5 p.m. Neuberg and Carlyle had taken leave of Marshall and Frankfurt, and were in the bus which brought them about seven o'clock to quiet quarters known to Neuberg on the fringe of Homburg. The town was within five minutes' walk, and Neuberg and Carlyle surveyed it together that evening. 'The *Kursall*,' Carlyle told his wife, was 'a public set of rooms, finer than some palaces, all supported by gambling,' and on going through it he beheld 'such a set of damnable faces—French, Italian, and Russian, with dull English in quantities—as were never seen out of Hell before! Augh! It is enough to make one turn cannibal. An old Russian countess sat playing Gowpan-fuls ' or two-hand-scoops ' of gold pieces every stake, a figure I shall never forget in this world.' In the music-room, however, he recognised ' a mournful tall lean princely man,' whom he had met at the Ashburtons' in June, a Duke of Holstein-Augustenburg whose father had pensioned Schiller. He was here with his family.—Homburg had been originally a health resort, and was not altogether a Monte Carlo.

In the next two days Carlyle tasted its waters, and making a ' duty-call ' had an unexpectedly pleasant hour or more with the genial Augustenburgs, the mother ' a fine broad motherly woman,' and two sons and two daughters, a happy family. The latest London news at Homburg was the death of Wellington. In the Schloss he saw many portraits and plenty of books about Frederick; but it was not his cue to stay. He could only note the names of books that were new to him, and finish his ' book-excerpting ' and return the books he had borrowed at Bonn.

He decided to do no more in the way of reading, and wrote to his wife from Homburg:—' Reading of books I find to be impossible. The thing that I can do is to see certain places and to see if I can gather certain books. Wise people also to talk with, or enquire of, I as good as despair of seeing. *All* Germans, one becomes convinced, are not wise! On the whole, however, one cannot but like this honest-hearted hardy population, very coarse of feature for most part, yet seldom radically *hässlich* (disagreeable); a *sonsie* look rather ' (*sonsie* meaning pleasant to look upon in every sense, mind, body, and character): ' and very frugal, good-humouredly poor in their way of life.'

XIX

IN THE FOOTSTEPS OF LUTHER

(1852)

ON Friday, 17.9.52, Carlyle and Neuberg went to Cassel, pausing some hours on the way to look at Marburg, ' a strange most ancient town,' and to see there a chamber now used for keeping hay, but in 1529 the scene of the famous conference of the Reformers, when Luther, Melanchthon and Co. held grave debates on doctrine with the Swiss Zwingli and others, and ' found no end, in wandering mazes lost.' Tho Cassel was noisy with watchmen's horns and pipes, town-clocks and rattling carts, their landlord tried to persuade them to linger, saying,—" If you stay over Sunday, you'll see the artificial waterworks playing. You should stay." " I would not stay," Carlyle replied, " even to see Hassenpflug hanged, which would be a much grander sight." The respectable Tory minister of that name Carlyle described as " a tyrannous, traitorous court minion," and the people were calling him Hesse's " Hass und Fluch," Hate and Curse. It was a real pleasure to Carlyle, as he wrote to his wife, to see the fellow's windows broken, as they drove past on the Saturday morning.

Arriving at Eisenach, they went at once to the castle on the Wartburg where Luther was sheltered in 1521, and climbed the ' short stair of old worn stone ' which led to Luther's room, where he was concealed and laboured at his translation of the Bible,—' a very poor low room, with an old leaded lattice window,—to me,' Carlyle wrote to his mother, ' the most venerable of all rooms I ever entered. Luther's old oak table is there, about three feet square, and a huge fossil bone—vertebra of a mammoth—which served him for footstool. Nothing else now in the room did certainly belong to him ; but these did.'

Neuberg was touched to see how reverently Carlyle laid his hands upon the fossil and upon the table also, which he kissed ; and he said to Neuberg,—" There is no more sacred spot in the whole earth for me to stand upon than this." They were shown the mark on the wall which was made by Luther's inkstand, when he flung it at the Devil; and saw the 'outer staircase close by the door where he speaks of often hearing the Devil make noises.' Then getting the window opened, the visitors could look as Luther did 'down the sheer castle wall into deep chasms (and) over the great ranges of silent woody mountains.' There were portraits by Cranach of Luther's father and mother, copies of which were by and by made for Carlyle by Tait, and are now hanging in the house at Chelsea; and a portrait by Cranach of Luther himself, far better than any Carlyle had seen yet:—'a bold effectual-looking rustic man, with brown eyes and skin; with a dash of peaceable self-confidence and healthy defiance in the look of him. . . . Poor and noble Luther! I shall never forget this Wartburg, and am right glad I saw it.'

They spent Saturday night at Gotha, where they lodged in sumptuous rooms in an old quiet inn, and Carlyle slept in the very room where Napoleon breakfasted, after being beaten at Leipzig. By noon on Sunday they were in Erfurt, with its crooked narrow streets and old-fashioned over-hanging walls, and there they beheld 'the very room where Martin Luther lived when a monk,' with its lead-glazed window looking to the west over cloistered courts and roof-tops. 'A poor old oaken boxie with ink-bottle and sand-case' was shown as Luther's, and another portrait of him by his friend Cranach, far better than an engraved copy of it which Carlyle's mother had, inasmuch as the original showed 'a noble face,' he wrote to her, 'the eyes not turned up in hypocritical devotion, but looking out in profound sorrow and determination, the lips too gathered in stern but affectionate firmness.'

They reached Weimar on the Sunday night, where the obliging secretary Marshall was expecting them, and "would take me into Heaven if it depended on *him*," said the grateful Carlyle. Not only were a librarian and an editor ready to dine with them at Marshall's, and the Goethe and Schiller houses 'opened by favour' for their inspection, but also 'the quietest rooms in Germany' had been engaged at the inn; and sure enough he was to have a good night's sleep there, but first he sat up late to send his mother a full report. He explained to Neuberg that he had promised her to trace the footsteps of Luther.

XX

AT WEIMAR

(1852)

ON Monday, 20.9.52, Carlyle saw all that Weimar had to show him of Goethe and Schiller, reporting to his wife in a letter that day that 'Neuberg is better than six couriers, and is a friend over and above.' They were two hours in Goethe's house, and on the book-shelves there he found the last book he had ever sent Goethe, Taylor's *Survey of German Poetry*, and sticking in it a crumb of paper torn from some essay of Carlyle's own, 'still sticking in' where Goethe left it, 'after twenty years.' In Schiller's house they spent an hour, and saw 'the room where he wrote, his old table (and) the bed where he died.'

When they were standing by the graves of Goethe and Schiller, 'it was an affecting moment' to Neuberg. When last he had stood there, it was alongside the Marian who became his wife and was now lost for ever. He wrote to his sister that he felt she was standing beside him now, and he added,—'How pleased she would have been to hear of these doings. . . . By degrees one learns that remembrance is a holier and richer possession than flattering hope.' Thus was Neuberg thinking as he stood silent beside the others. "The heart knoweth its own bitterness, and a stranger doth not intermeddle with its joy."

Next morning when Carlyle and Neuberg were at breakfast together and about to depart, in came the Secretary Marshall 'looking highly animated.' His Grand Duchess, the mother of the Grand Duke who had called at Cheyne Row and was now in Italy, and herself a sister of Czar Nicholas, had seen the name *Carlyle* among the visitors, and hearing from Marshall who it was, had despatched him with an immediate invitation to dinner at three o'clock. Tho this delayed them for a day, Carlyle confessed to his wife,—'It must be owned the honour done me was to be recognised; and I was very glad to oblige Neuberg by a touch of Court life, which he would not otherwise have seen.'

Now in those days a tall hat was required to be on the

head of every man approaching such a place as the Grand Ducal Palace of Weimar, and Carlyle had only a common wideawake. So when he went to his bedroom to dress for dinner, he found an anonymous present from some German friend upon his toilet table,—a fine new hat, conventionally perfect. Invisible to him, the faithful Neuberg was eagerly watching, and saw him take the hat out of the box, put it on his head, and look at himself in the glass attentively. Then he flung the hat upon the floor and kicked it into a corner.[1]

Society had to suffer the sight of Carlyle going to Court in a wideawake. The dinner lasted two hours, three to five, Carlyle sitting next the Grand Duchess. Her husband at the other end of the table was a Grand Duke, the son of Goethe's patron, but now, alas, 'a kind of imbecile,' which did not prevent him 'looking' like a gentleman, and having 'an air of solemn serene vacuity, which is itself almost royal.'

To Neuberg the Grand Duchess appeared 'a fine and stately old lady.' Carlyle was sitting beside her, and told his wife that she had 'once been extremely pretty, tho hard always as nails or diamonds.' He had to 'maintain with energy a singularly empty intellectual colloquy, in French chiefly, (but partly) in English and in German. The lady being half-deaf withal, you may think how charming it was. She had a thin croaky voice; brow and chin recede; eyes are blue, small, and of the brightness and hardness of precious stones.' "We noticed," said Neuberg, "that tho she was full of politeness and attention, she never smiled." They were glad to get away, soon after five, and what Carlyle remarked of her was only,—"Poor soul, the heart is frozen out of her."

'In driving back,' wrote Neuberg, 'he laughed a good deal at the thought of having been at the Grand Duke's in a wideawake.' But on reflection he admitted to his wife and brother that it was a 'rather troublesome dramatic affair. . . . Schiller's house and Goethe's,' which had surprised him by their smallness, 'and the thought that their lives had lain in such a scene made the matter worse and worse. Weimar is quite a little spiritual puzzle to me.'

[1] Carlyle's letters are supplemented by Neuberg's, but neither tells this story, tho there is an allusion by Neuberg. See also *Macmillan's Magazine*, August, 1884, p. 288. The full details as here told were given by Neuberg to his sister, and by her to a lady who told D. A. W.,—the late Mrs. Allingham, the artist.

XXI

IN THE FOOTSTEPS OF FREDERICK

(1852)

LEAVING Weimar on Wednesday, 22.9.52, Carlyle concentrated attention for the rest of this pilgrimage on the footsteps of Frederick. The next stage was Leipzig, where he saw the fair and bought some books, and drank a glass of wine in Auerbach's Cellar. They reached Dresden that night,—a change from Leipzig 'as from the tumult of Cheapside into the solitude of Bath.' There was much to see near Dresden, where Frederick had done much business both as a king and as a general, and Dresden itself was 'a very interesting old capital.' 'Miss Bölte and other sages' were expecting him eagerly, and gladly would Carlyle have stayed a week with them, 'if sleep had been attainable. But, alas! it was *not*.' The Dresden hotels were like a pair in contemporary Ireland, of which it was said,—" Whichever you go to, you lie awake most of the night, wishing you had gone to the other."

So on Saturday they went up the Elbe by steamer, and after climbing 'a high peak called the *Bastei*' found sleeping quarters at Nieder Rathen, 'in a little country inn literally washed' by the river, 'which is lying in the moonshine as clear as a mirror and as silent.' Their next stage was also up the Elbe, and on Monday morning before breakfast they walked over all the riverside battlefield of Lobositz, under the guidance of a native. To make the night's sleep secure and let him see the interior, Neuberg took him that day into beautiful quarters,—Teplitz, a watering-place 'in the so-called Saxon Switzerland, amid the Bohemian mountains,' north-west of Lobositz. Their road was the famous " Pascopol," familiar to the readers of the Frederick history.[1]

On Tuesday, 28.9.52, they went by road to Zittau, east of the Elbe, the town that made Prince Karl infamous

[1] *History of Frederick the Great,* Book XVII, Chap. V, etc.

'till all memory of him cease,' says the historian, for wantonly burning it in 1757,—'there are devilish things sometimes done in war.'[2] It may have been on this day that Carlyle read on the Townhouse of Zittau an inscription he admired,—it is equal in wisdom to the best of proverbs:—'Bene facere et male audire regium est,'—To do good, and have evil said of you, is a kingly thing.[2] At Herrnhut, not far from there, Carlyle and Neuberg saw 'four hours of the stillest life you ever saw or dreamed of.' The 'tourist's note' on Herrnhut is worth reading. It is in the *History of Frederick*.[3]

Thence the railway took them to 'moory Frankfurt' (-on-Oder), where he inspected the battlefield of Kunersdorf,[4] and on Thursday, 30.9.52, he and Neuberg arrived in Berlin.

[2] *Ibid.*, Book XVIII, Chap. V.
[3] *Ibid.*, Book XV, Chap. XIII.
[4] *Ibid.*, Book XIX, Chap. IV.

XXII

AT BERLIN

(1852)

HE was only nine days at Berlin,—the whole tour did not last seven weeks. Yet he learned so much in so little time that one is reminded of the miracle of the loaves and fishes; and in this instance the method of genius was simple common sense intensified. He concentrated on what he was doing. Thus he went to a Museum where Frederick's clothes were kept. The Keeper was more than polite. He insisted on showing the visitor everything in the place. Carlyle declined to look, explaining what he wanted. 'It was as if one should go into an inn to take a chop, and they insisted he must eat everything in their store.' The Keeper contended this and that; but at last the visitor was allowed to look at the 'military old clothes' he had come to see. He looked at nothing else, and departed feeling he had really no business even with these.[1]

From Berlin he sent David Masson a testimonial Masson wanted, as to his fitness for teaching English Literature in University College, London, an employment Masson duly got this year.

Meanwhile the Berliners were ready to lionize Carlyle as much as he would let them, which delighted Neuberg, who wrote to his sister:—'We have been invited to a great many dinner-parties, &c., whereby I have become acquainted with all sorts of local authorities. Everywhere, for earnestness and power, Carlyle forms a striking contrast to most of the people whom we meet.' By Sunday, 3.10.52, he had already seen 'Potsdam, Sans Souci, &c.' He remarked to Neuberg,—"We lead a pretty *fast* life here."—It was doubtless for Neuberg's sake that Carlyle endured the festivities, for on 5.10.52 Neuberg confided to his sister that if he then came home, Carlyle would not remain a day longer.[2]

[1] *Thomas Carlyle*, by Moncure D. Conway, pp. 63–4.

[2] Many of Neuberg's letters are in *Macmillan's Magazine*, August, 1884. Other authorities for what follows are: Varnhagen von Ense's report,

One of these dinner-parties has become famous. It was on Tuesday, 5.10.52, at the house of Edward Magnus, the banker. The painter Cornelius and another artist were among the guests, but pietists preponderated in the august persons of Herr von Olvers, the Director of the Museum, Privy-Councillor Wiese of the Clerical Department, and Privy-Councillor Abeken of the Foreign Ministry. Pietism was then a road to promotion in Berlin officialdom.

They talked of Goethe. After much had been said in his honour, Wiese 'could not refrain from lamentation,'—like one of the friends of Job. He turned up his eyes and made other pious gestures.—'What a pity it was that so great a genius as Goethe, so gifted a man, had lacked the blessing of saving faith, and did not use his powers to the service of the Lord! Should not have more purely devoted himself to the service of Christian Truth! And should have had so little' . . . and so on. 'A number agreed with this in a lively manner,' said one who was there,—canting in chorus to the same tune, till they noticed with alarm that Carlyle was 'ominously silent . . . his hands impatiently twisting his napkin, restless and making cross faces. At last he laid his arms straight on the table, and bending forward said in his lumbering slow way in halting German in a loud voice.—

'"Meine—Herren! Weiss—denn—keiner von Ihnen—die alte—Geschichte—dass Jemand die Sonne gelästert hat—weil er—seine Cigarre—nicht—an ihr hat anzünden—können?"'

"Gentlemen—does then—not one of you—know—the old story—that somebody once cursed the sun—because—he could not light—his cigar on it?"

The saints were silenced, feeling, as Wiese said afterwards, 'ashamed of having misunderstood this Englishman.' The others were happy. "I could have kissed him," said one. According to Magnus, Cornelius had begun by echoing Wiese, but after this he seems to have taken his cue from the stranger and let himself go; and when Carlyle 'made all sorts of side-thrusts at the painters for their pictures of Christs and Madonnas,' Cornelius jovially called him several times,—"a Godless man."

printed in German in *Last Words of Thomas Carlyle* (Longmans), pp. 287–9. See also his Correspondence, reviewed in *Bentley's Miscellany*, XLVIII (1860), pp. 471–8. Also the *Life of George Eliot*, by J. W. Cross, pp. 179 and 182, giving what Magnus told in 1854.

Varnhagen von Ense had lost no time in visiting Carlyle, who returned his visit, but wrote to his brother about Varnhagen :—' In him is no help at all : a lively-talking pleasant, *official* kind of man ; I understand every word of his German, and feel with regret how little it can do for me. Poor fellow, he is ten years older than myself, and has had many slaps too . . . a very vigorous old fellow, with cunning grey eyes, turn-up nose, plenty of white hair, and a dash of dandy, soldier-citizen and Sage . . . and he goes to Miss Something's soiree every night,—whither I would never follow him, and " don't intend to." '

Which illuminates their talk. Carlyle was enquiring about books on Friedrich. Varnhagen von Ense said :— " I can only reply in the same words as Dr. Vehse,—' Not one, but a hundred.' "

Neuberg must have looked very puzzled at this, for Carlyle explained to him,—" I ask him for fish, and he answers there are plenty in the sea."

'The worst is,' wrote Varnhagen to Miss Bölte in telling this, ' what you say and know of him, that he can lay aside his whimsical manner and be polite and attentive according to time and circumstances.'

Tho he lacked the leisure to ' be polite and attentive ' in Miss Somebody's soirees, he made acquaintance with Preuss and Rauch and everybody he wanted to know. On Thursday (7.10.52) he waited on Tieck, who was now in his eightieth year, and seemed to him ' a beautiful old man, so serene, so calm, so sad.'

Tieck, however, had dandy tastes, and did not like the visitor. He explained it all to Varnhagen by and by. The clothes of Carlyle were more than unfashionable, they were positively " negligent " ; and tho it was plain he was far from well—" he looks lamentable in spite of his red cheeks " —his complaints about noisy bedrooms and curtainless beds were nonsense, and his manners positively " boorish."

Tieck's lack of humour made him see no fun in a saying of Carlyle,—" I should think no one could die at Berlin, for in beds *without curtains* what Christian could give up the ghost ? " Tieck perhaps took this for metaphysics, and hardly dissembled his disapproval.

Their conversation was in German. When Tieck began talking about Coleridge, Carlyle ' broke into uncontrollable laughter.' Tieck said he asked him ' with chilling seriousness,'—" Why do you laugh ? "

Carlyle stopped suddenly, and 'in a serious tone and with a serious expression,' replied :—

"Oh, no! I know quite well that about Coleridge much is to be said seriously," and so on.

"Then why did you laugh?" demanded Tieck, but 'no answer was given to this.' *The only answer possible would have hurt the old man's feelings.*

"Foolish vanity," thought Tieck, who has not a laugh in all his forty volumes; and whatever he said to him, told Varnhagen that Carlyle's views of the greatness of Frederick were "mad," and that "it would be better if he did not write about him."

This was the general opinion of the Berlin savants. They were entirely helpful; but officialdom felt no wish to see the great king revealed to modern Germany as he really was, the disciple of Voltaire. It might be dangerous, and they comforted each other with the assurance it was impossible. The historian Heinrich Leo in particular was loud to this effect. He is "a husky, wooden kind of man," said Carlyle to Neuberg, and added with reference to the learned Leo's books,—"suspicion of a Quack withal." Berlin had no such feelings. Leo proved to Varnhagen that in the very nature of things Carlyle was sure to fail, because Frederick was a Prussian King or nothing, and, said he,—"For Prussia and Prussian greatness Englishmen, even Germanized Englishmen, have simply not got the sense, just as anglicized Germans like Bunsen lose it entirely."

Which was not so absurd as it sounds. For one thing the miracle Carlyle was about to perform in *Frederick* was unique in literature, and it is likely to continue so. The best heads in Berlin could not be blamed for not anticipating it. He was far from anticipating it himself. He was recoiling from the subject. As he wrote to his sister,—'The sight of actual Germany, with its flat-soled puddlings in the slough of nonsense (quite a different kind from ours, but not a whit less genuine) has hurt poor Fritz very much in my mind; poor fellow, he too lies deep-buried in the *middens-tank* (or dung-hill), even as Cromwell was; and then he is not half or tenth-part such a man as Cromwell, that one should swim and dive for him in that manner! In fact tho I have not yet quitted the neighbourhood of Fritz and his old cocked-hat, his fate is very uncertain with me; and every new German *Book* I read about him, my feeling is, All up with Fritz. In Germany I could not even get a good portrait of him,—tho they spend the year round in singing dull insincere praises to him in every key; and have built a huge bronze and granite monument to him in Berlin, at the cost of perhaps half a million, worth next to nothing. They have the mask of his dead face, however; a fiercely shrivelled plaster cast. . . . The face of a lean lion, or else partly, alas! of a ditto *cat!* The lips are thin, and closed like pincers; a face that never yielded;—not the beautifullest kind of face. In fine why should I torment my domestic soul writing his foreign history? He “ may go to France for me! ” ’

XXIII

HOME AGAIN

(1852)

ON Saturday, 9.10.52, Carlyle and Neuberg went by train from Berlin to Cologne, and parted next morning, while friends of the faithful Neuberg 'escorted' Carlyle to Malines, where he slept on Monday. Next day he went on by train and, embarking at Ostend on Tuesday night, 'was safely floated to the Customhouse Stairs,' and thence by boat and river steamer came to Chelsea Pier and Cheyne Row on Wednesday afternoon, 13.10.52.

As he rushed upstairs his wife's voice met him,—"Take care of the paint." The painters were still busy. Next day he went into town and sent the hospitable Magnus a Spanish book he had promised, and on Friday his wife and he went together to the Grange. Mrs. Carlyle needed a rest, and the painting and cleaning that remained to be done could go on without her. From the Grange he reported to Neuberg:—

'We lead the usual strenuously-idle life, and hear of things only at a pleasant distance, and feel bound to treat them (in the English fashion) with contempt. Alas, I grudge the bright days of time one loses; for there is absolutely no saving of them here. We have agreeable enough people, Thackeray among them.'

Returning home on Tuesday, 2.11.52, he wrote to Neuberg three days later describing his sensations in the much-altered house. The enlargement of his "library," on the first floor, was an improvement for which he strove to be grateful; but all his old arrangements were upset, 'from the position of my bath and towels to that of my books and papers. I never in my life felt so utterly *demoralised* (in the Napoleon sense)'—old habits needing to be changed—'as in these two days since I actually got home again, and sat down face to face with the chaotic heap of *facts* which are around me and within me, and which must be conquered or they will abolish me. The changed house is but a top-stone to other disorder. Pray for me; I really require the good wishes of friendly souls.'

Acknowledging the arrival of a box of books, which Neuberg had sent from Germany, he said:—'What can be the meaning of one man's "helping" another, if you do not loyally try to help me, it would be difficult to say! For the rest, I have not at present the least notion of ever writing upon *Friedrich;* so far as the eye of imagination can reach I do not even see the possibility of such a thing. But here are the materials; a long wish, at any rate, is gratified; and if at any time such a purpose do take me, I can set about it with what strength is left. Something I must do! But something far more out of the inmost heart would be the desirable thing to do. Here also I have need of your prayers; nay here chiefly, or here alone. Let us hope, let us hope; above all things, let us be *silent!*

'Returning from the Grange, I found, among other masses of rubbish, four numbers of a Methodist Magazine, containing at distant intervals through six months, a criticism of me; which I glanced over, and found very strange. I stand before that poor Methodist, it clearly appears, as one of the most portentous black immeasurable monsters, threatening (unless I be a humbug and fool, of which he has a wavering timid hope) to eat up the Solar system and submerge mankind! The "misunderstandings" of men by one another sometimes rise to the enormous. All this has given me many thoughts for these two days.'

XXIV

WHAT NEXT?

(1852)

IN his working hours, Carlyle was reading heaps of books, and on 9.11.52 soliloquized in his journal.—

'My survey of the last eight or nine years of my life yields little "comfort" in the present state of my feelings. Silent weak rage, remorse even, which is not common with me; and, on the whole, a solitude of soul coupled with a helplessness, which are frightful to look upon, difficult to deal with in my present situation. For my *health* is miserable too; diseased *liver* I privately perceive has much to do with the phenomenon; and I cannot yet learn to sleep again. During all my travels I have wanted from a third to half of my usual sleep. For the rest I guess it is a *change of epoch* with me, going on for good perhaps; I am growing to perceive that I have become an old man; that the flowery umbrages of summer—such as they were for me—and also the crops and fruits of autumn are nearly over for me, and stern winter only is to be looked for—a grim message—such, however, as is sent to every man. Oh ye Supreme Powers! thou great Soul of the world that *art* just, may I manage this but *well*, all sorrow then and smothered rage and despair itself shall have been cheap and welcome. No more of it to-day. I am not yet at the bottom of it; am not here writing wisely of it, even *sincerely* of it, tho with an effort that way. The votes of men, the respectabilities, the &c., &c., have been too sacred to me. It must be owned, too, the man has had such a set of conditions as were not always easy to govern, and could not by the old law-books be treated well.'

Growing 'old,'— of course. In writing as in talk, a great deal is taken for granted. When a man is approaching sixty, Nature gives him many hints. In a letter to Neuberg

true man of official men in England, or that I know of in Europe.' Watching the 'sumptuous procession' from the second-floor windows of Bath House, he saw nothing in it 'of the least dignity' except the four thousand soldiers. 'The car or hearse, a monstrous bronze mass,' was an ugly object, and with its 'incoherent huddle of expensive palls, flags, sheets, and poles,' it was 'more like one of the street carts that hawk door-mats than a bier for a hero. Disgust was general at this vile' thing, but as it passed all people remembered what was inside it, and 'stood in deep silence and reverently took off their hats. In one of the Queen's carriages sat a man conspicuously reading the morning newspaper. Tennyson's verses are naught. Silence alone is respectable on such an occasion.'

He wrote to his mother that he would soon 'recover his feet,' which means his health and sleep. 'All clouds have their bright sides too; and, on the whole, I hope to get to a little *work* again, and that is the consolation which surpasses all for me.'

He completed in December his translation of *A Day With Frederick*, which had occupied him at Erskine's house last summer; but what next was still a question. Thus on 5.12.52 he was soliloquizing in his journal.—'The elements of our work lie scattered, disorganised, as if in a thick, viscous, chaotic ocean, ocean illimitable in all its three dimensions; and we must swim and sprawl towards them, must snatch them, and victoriously piece them together as we can. *Eheu*! Shall I try Frederick, or not try him?'

XXV

DIZZY AND JEWS IN GENERAL

(1852)

COMING to London as a Member of Parliament late in 1852, Gavan Duffy resorted regularly to Cheyne Row.[1] On Sunday afternoons he and Carlyle used to walk in the parks together, and often they might have been seen on the grass at the back of the house with two or three others sitting or standing about, discussing politics and things in general. There was now a real Irish party in the Commons, and the first thing they wanted was tenant-right. Disraeli was willing to deal with them, but not so his leader, Landlord Derby, nor Dublin Castle. So when Disraeli brought in a bad Budget in December, Duffy and Company turned the scale against his crowd, and the Government went out.

In telling Carlyle about this, Duffy said :—" Tho I voted against them, I could not help having a certain sympathy for Disraeli for the indomitable pluck with which he faced his enemies, at the head of a party which distrusted him only a little less " than those opposite. " The Peelites seemed to hate him with a preternatural animosity, but I had never heard that he had done anything cruel or cowardly against them or anyone else. He was a political gladiator, no doubt, as Bolingbroke and Canning had been before him," (which refers to Dizzy's jibes in the final debate, when he called a Mr. Goulburn a " weird Sibyl," and told Sir James Graham that he regarded him but did not respect him, and so on.) " It is idle," said Duffy, " to complain that he struck deft blows at his opponents ; that is his vocation."

" A base vocation ! " Carlyle exclaimed. " The case is not a perplexing one at all, it seems to me. A cunning Jew gets a parcel of people to believe in him, tho no man of the smallest penetration can have any doubt that he is an

[1] *Conversations with Carlyle*, by Sir C. Gavan Duffy, pp. 179–80 ; and *My Life in Two Hemispheres*, by Sir C. G. D., II, pp. 46, &c.

impostor, with no sort of purpose in all he is doing but to serve his own interests. He is a man from whom no good need be expected, a typical Jew, ostentatious, intrinsically servile, but stiffnecked in his designs."

"*Jus diabolo detur,*" (do justice to the Devil), Duffy interposed. "Let it be remembered that he exhibits a generous courage on behalf of his race, in face of the fierce hostility of the party which he leads. He is true, at any rate, to the interest and honour of his own people, which counterbalances a multitude of sins; and I have a personal satisfaction in seeing a race, who are persecuted for a crime committed centuries and centuries before they were born, reassert themselves."

Carlyle replied: "They are paying for sins of their own, as well as of their ancestors. They are an impotent race, who have never distinguished themselves in their entire history by any estimable quality. Some of them clamber to what they call prosperity, but, arrayed in the showiest garniture, there is always an odour of old clo' about them. They make great quantities of money up and down, and glorify the speculator who makes most as the most venerable of mortals. When of old any man appeared among them who had something to tell worth their attention, one knows how such a one was received by the Israelites, and their vices of character are intractable."

Duffy did not deny that it was mainly in denouncing Disraeli that Carlyle was serious in this debate. What was said about Jews in general was partly chaff, the key to which was that in 1852 the Jews had only recently received the full rights of Englishmen, and many vain fellows among them were trying to go to the other extreme and glorify themselves as the chosen race. Queen Victoria was believed to be secretly proud of her Jewish blood; and even in our own day her grandson the Kaiser, "Runaway Will," was said to be fond of boasting of descent through her from King David!

Neuberg was a Jew, and Carlyle did not need to be told that the Jews were like other men. It would be strange indeed if they were different, as they vary in stock from blacks to Scandinavians, and are not like a clan, which is all akin, but like some of the Indian castes,—of multiple stocks and really united by their religious faith. Thus even in the time of Jesus, the Pharisees were 'compassing sea and land' to make proselytes.

XXVI

A MERRY CHRISTMAS

(1852)

ON 23.12.52 Carlyle was writing a long letter to his good Quaker friend in Wales,[1] Charles Redwood, and after thanking him for the usual 'well-replenished Christmas box,' containing a turkey and mutton and cheese, he gave details of his recent domestic history, including the alterations and repairs of the house and his travels in Germany. 'I had not one night's sleep all the time, if you know what that means. It is not yet many weeks since we got the last of the unclean creatures (painters and varnishers) out of the house, and they have to come back next summer and "finish everything." . . . My poor wife has suffered a good deal, but is not nearly so low as I, and appears to be mending faster. Let me not forget to add that I too am mending; that the house is improved for the rest of one's life, that my nerves are perhaps better than before, and thus, on the whole, that all shall be "well that ends well."

'I am not quite idle, tho I cannot, even in the language of flattery, be described as working in a visible manner. Frederick the Great has cost me huge reading, and it was after him alone or mainly that I kept enquiring in Germany lately; nevertheless it seems to me I never can embark on writing a book about him, so little lovely is the man to me, so dim, vague, faint, and contemptible is the account I get of his life-element, is (too often) his life-element itself to me! He will walk the plank, I think, or has walked it, and I must try something else. Adieu, dear Redwood. I send you many grateful thoughts and am silent.

'Yours ever truly,

'T. CARLYLE.'

On Christmas Day an English friend who was passing called to wish the Carlyles a Merry Christmas and "made a note" of what followed. William H. Brookfield was his

[1] *Carlyle's Holidays in Wales*, by John Howells, in the *Red Dragon Magazine*, Cardiff, April, May and June, 1884.

name,—an Inspector of Schools. He was the son of a Sheffield solicitor, and a Cambridge graduate who had entered the Church, and had the honour of refusing a bishopric,[2] but only because it was in the Barbadoes and he had hopes of one at home, and meanwhile had his inspectorship. He was a handsome man and a popular preacher, and his wife was a niece of Hallam the historian,—" Dryasdust."

What is said to have spoiled his chance of a bishopric in England was a sermon he had preached one Sunday at Berkeley Chapel on the " Temptation in the Wilderness."[3] When he 'mentioned that it was not absolutely necessary to salvation to believe that Christ was tempted by the conventional physical Devil, Lord Shaftesbury who was present rose, hat in hand, and left the Church. He subsequently went to Lord Palmerston and said to him,—" We can't make Brookfield a Bishop. It's impossible, the man's *a Free-thinker !* " ' It should be explained that Palmerston was trying to make the ministry popular by letting his relative Shaftesbury select the bishops. According to Goldwin Smith, the prizes of the Church of England were regularly political spoils, so that Shaftesbury's scruples were rather a credit to him under the circumstances,[4] and his superstition about the Devil was not so silly as it may seem to-day. Incredible as it may sound, as recently as 6.7.1850, John Ruskin calling with his young wife at tea-time at Cheyne Row, had set himself to badger Carlyle about religious opinions in presence not only of Mrs. Carlyle and Mrs. Ruskin, but also of five others, including Mrs. Wedgwood, Erasmus Darwin, and De Vere, the poet and Puseyite. The ecstatic John persevered till he had made sure of the joyful discovery that " the Devil " had no personal existence at all ! The only Devil he need fear was that within each of us ; and—what may have upset poor De Vere—that no power can " clip the wings " of that Devil but one's own.[5]

Some weakness in the lungs had made Brookfield spend the winter of 1851–52 at Madeira, and how he spent the Christmas of 1852 was recorded by him on 29.12.52 in his diary.[6] 'Let me try to describe dining with Carlyle on

[2] *Mrs. Brookfield and Her Circle*, by C. and F. Brookfield, I, p. 116.
[3] *Ibid.*, II, p. 441.
[4] *Reminiscences by Goldwin Smith*, pp. 284–5.
[5] *Letters from J. W. Carlyle*, by Leonard Huxley, *Cornhill Magazine*, Nov., 1926, pp. 629–30.
[6] *Mrs. Brookfield and Her Circle*, &c., II, pp. 378–81, initials replaced by names.

Christmas Day. I was en garçon (alone), Mrs. Brookfield being at Clifton, nursing her father. I staid in till about three, writing a letter or two; when I sallied out with the intention of calling on the Henry Taylors at Mortlake. *En route* by an omnibus to Battersea Bridge I resolved to call and bid Merry Christmas to the Carlyles, who are but three minutes from it; Mrs. Carlyle was at home; and while we sate chatting the Moralist himself and a friend went out at the front door. The servant was dispatched by Mrs. Carlyle to call him back to shake hands with me. He instantly returned, introduced his friend, chatted a bit, advised me how to proceed to Henry Taylor's, about which small everyday practical matters he always shows lots of practical common sense. "I don't think any boats are running to Mortlake now at all; or if there be you shouldn't be on the water so late with your ailments of chest or what not; just go down by a steamer to Vauxhall for twopence, and then take train for Henry Taylor."

'I begged him to go out for his walk, and I would stay a little with Mrs. Carlyle, and away he went. Soon after he had gone she asked where I was to dine. "Oh, I was going to dine at home." Well, but wouldn't I stay and eat with them at five o'clock—they had no dinner but mutton, and no company but that cousin who went up in a balloon for science.'—There were two cousins of Mrs. Carlyle called John Welsh, one rather foolish and talkative, and this one who was more sensible, "the silent cousin," a mathematician and astronomer esteemed by Carlyle and employed at Kew Observatory, where he became Superintendent this year, and had previously been assistant.[7] Brookfield's report goes on.—'I said it was a temptation I felt neither any call nor power to resist—and I would give up Mortlake, take half an hour's walk, and be there again at five.

'I did so, and returned before five, and Carlyle came in a few minutes afterwards; and so coming into the room where I sate and hearing that I was to stay, he put out his hand, and with genial hospitable face, said, "Well, you're a glorious fellow,—that's right—&c." I interrupted with some playful palaver about being the envy of 1,999,999 people that day, so we settled down to dinner. Note (as Matthew Henry keeps saying) how his language falls into commonplace when he has his heart engaged by a

[7] *Letters from J. W. Carlyle,* by Leonard Huxley, *Cornhill Magazine,* Oct., 1926, pp. 493, &c., and Nov., 1926, pp. 622, &c.

common feeling. "Well—you're a glorious fellow"—simply what a schoolboy would have said who was really pleased, like a thump on the back. The repast was soup, followed by a haunch of wonderfully Lilliputian but good mutton with potatoes.

'Carlyle either felt or affected humorous despair at having to carve this joint, and consulted me, finally turning it over to me. I said the proper way of cutting a haunch was so-and-so; but that had been defeated by the peculiar way in which Ap Morgan had cut up his sheep, more like a heathen priest than a Christian butcher.' The mutton was a present from Mr. Redwood in Wales;[8] but it had been cut up by a local butcher, and Brookfield continues:—'Mrs. C. said, "it's not the butcher's fault; it was to have been only a leg, but when you agreed to stay the loin was added."

'Carlyle now and then put a bit of what he thought one ought to like—of leg, of loin, or of fat, on one's plate with a sort of genial, homely hospitality which was touching. There was wonderful nut-brown from the neighbouring "Cricketers," Port and Sherry, to which Madam presently added a bottle of excellent Madeira. Meanwhile, the talk was incessant, but remarkable for nothing but cheeriness. Then came woodcocks, and, finally, a Christmas plum pudding with brandy sauce—which brought on my story of the Saddleworth elector at York in Montague Wilson's contest about twenty-five years ago. At one of the open Taverns he called to the waiter: "Waiter, ha' ye nowt better nor woin?" "No, sir, nothing better than champagne, port, sherry, whisky, gin, brandy, &c." "Way then! bring us a quart of that stuff we hed we't pudding." Carlyle laughed like a volcano at this—and twisted it many ways in the course of the evening.

'After dinner and wine (he) and I adjourned upstairs for a pipe of York River Tobacco—over which he talked characteristically, chiefly about Education. Then downstairs to cheerful tea—and so made an end at ten o'clock, and I went home in an omnibus with the silent cousin who had dined with us, bearing with me half a dozen old pipes of Carlyle's and the one he had used that evening, for a memorial of a day that I felt very grateful for and not a little elated by.'

[8] Unpublished letter.

XXVII

MORE ABOUT CHRISTMAS

(1852)

THE next day was Sunday, 26.12.52, and when Neuberg came to tea that day, the maid was out, and he had the pleasure of helping Mrs. Carlyle to make the toast at the parlour fire and carry the tea-things up and down stairs. "Quite Arcadian!" he wrote to his sister.[1]

Carlyle gave him a copy of the new and fourth edition of "Hero-Worship," remarking,—"Nothing astonishes me so much as that the people continue to buy my books. It is as marvellous as the feeding of Elijah by the ravens."

Neuberg may have spoken as he wrote to his sister:—"There is a greater amount of prosperity visible in England at present than I have ever before noticed. The number of turkeys, oyster-barrels, fish-baskets and game displayed in the shop-windows is almost incredible."

Carlyle said:—"English people at Christmas eat themselves as full as they can hold from a feeling of religious duty, and lay it all to Christ."

Writing to his brother John a day or two later, Carlyle said that the English seemed to him to use Christ as a painted cobweb to hide Eternity, saying,—"Drink away, my jolly ones,—no fear of being damned after all,—Christ is there!"

What he said now would give Neuberg an opening for the latest conclusion of German research, such as he had been learning at Bonn and was soon to be setting forth in the *Westminster Review*. The purport of it was that our Christmas is merely a continuation of the pagan feast 'at the turn of the year.' The Prince of Peace was represented by a child asleep on a sheaf of corn, and the pagan belief was that this was also the God of Marriage, the same who was worshipped at Upsala along with Odin and Thor, the good God Frier. He rode on a boar with golden bristles,

[1] Letter from Joseph Neuberg to his sister, 27.12.52, in *Macmillan's Magazine*, August, 1884, p. 289.

according to Neuberg, who declared that he 'is still commemorated at Christmas-time at Oxford,' when 'the procession of the Boar's head,' Frier's symbol, 'is solemnised,' by dons without misgivings, not knowing what they do.

When Neuberg rose to go at half-past ten o'clock, Carlyle and his wife together escorted him most of the way to the Strand, where he was living.

Lady Ashburton was ill, confined to bed on Christmas Day, but on New Year's Day (1.1.53) she was writing to Mrs. Brookfield :[2]—'You cannot think how very pleasant your letter was yesterday morning, coming as it did to a still sick bed as a gleam of sun from out of doors. . . . I have had long letters from my friends.' She was explicit about the weather and some match-making, but said not another word about her own illness, which seems characteristic, and all the more so because Mrs. Brookfield was an intimate to whom she wrote freely. There is unconscious self-revelation, however, in these sentences :—

'It is very nice to see such complete absorption in our clan friendship, only one would like to have a little share oneself where one feels such great regard. . . . On the whole, I constantly say to myself, you cannot help it, you are made to have acquaintances, not friends, your lot is cast in an age where no one wants friends, where all that people want from associating with each other is given by acquaintanceship ; and if the term friend is still used it is a mere homage to an extinct form. Having said that and turned very uncomfortably over to the other side of one's mind, to see if anything not so dreary could come, I there always find my dear old Prophet Carlyle, and has one any right to more than one such friend in a lifetime ?'

[2] *Mrs. Brookfield and Her Circle*, by C. and F. Brookfield, II, pp. 381–2.

XXVIII

DEMOCRACY AND THE IRISH

(1853)

As this winter went on, 1852–53, 'I saw Carlyle under a new aspect,' reports Gavan Duffy.[1] 'Among friends he was still simple and genial; but he was much run after by inquisitive Americans, and as they wanted to interview him, he got into the habit of uttering, almost as soon as his visitors had settled down, the sort of harangue they expected. . . . His conversational manner disappeared (then), and his language came forth in a strong unbroken stream, while, like the Ancient Mariner, he fixed the spectator with his glittering eye.' Here is a sample, 'addressed to some Irish-Americans.' He told them :—

"Irishmen may be assured there is no one in England wishes ill to Ireland, as they have come to imagine. Quite the contrary, good men on all sides would applaud and assist any practical method for her relief. If I were given the task of lifting Ireland out of her misery, I would take counsel on all sides with men of practical knowledge on the best means of setting the people to work. I would ask such assistance from Parliament as might be necessary, and then carry out my scheme with unabating stringency. Whoever would not work must starve. I would begin with the work-houses, where men have delivered themselves up as bond slaves to society, by the confession that they cannot exist by their own labour; and at the outset I would organise *them*. By and by I would transfer my workers to the Bog of Allen, or elsewhere, and bring them into contact with work to be done. *Organisation is the essential basis of success, and I believe every trade must finally get itself organised as much as it can,*[2] even the trade of authorship, so that each man would be put to the work he was fittest to do, and

[1] *Conversations with Carlyle,* by Sir Charles Gavan Duffy, pp. 181–6.
[2] Italics added.

not left wasting his strength and spirit in a totally useless direction.

"If a wise scheme like this were opposed—as, indeed, it is sure to be—*one might rely on the sense of the community for maintaining it.*[2] If the Ministry of the day set themselves against it, men of sense should say[3] to them, Get out of that, you ugly and foolish windbags: do you think the Eternal God of Nature will suffer *you* to stand in the way of His work? If you cannot open your eyes and see that this is a thing that must be done, you had better betake yourselves elsewhere—to the lowest Gehenna were fittest—there is no place for you in a world which is ruled, in the long run, by fact and not by chimera. This is the course which ought to be taken. Men of sense might get the thing done, but men of no sense, not at all.

"In democracy there is no help. Universal suffrage might be worth taking, and then men of sense would discover the limited use of it. For my part, if I could consult my horses, I would certainly ask them whether they preferred oats or vetches, quite sure they are the best judges on *that* point; but if they presumed to question the propriety of the road I was travelling, I would say,—'No, my worthy quadrupeds, it is not to London I am going, but in quite another direction. I am going to Greenwich, for reasons too tedious to mention, and so let us set out without more delay.' The notion of settling any question by counting blockheads, or referring it to the decision of a multitude of fools, is altogether futile. The wise man must ponder on the right path in the silence of his own heart, and when found take it, tho the whole multitude brayed at him with its many heads, which most probably they would—for a time."

As soon as Carlyle paused, John Forster assured Duffy,—"There is no dislike of Irishmen in England, and no assumption of superiority."

Carlyle said,—"If there is dislike, it arises from the way Irishmen conduct themselves in England. They often incur[4] disfavour by their private performances. Irishmen who know better must teach these persons to live quite differently, and they ought not to feel the slightest necessity for championing blackguards, because they happen

[3] Original text, *would*.

[4] In the original, "entitle themselves to." This is the chief of the small corrections made with the permission of Sir C. G. D.

to be Irishmen. The curse and destruction of Ireland is her putting up silently—even contentedly, it would seem—with lies and falsities, and making heroes of manifest liars. Till this practice ends, her case is hopeless."

'After a harangue,' Gavan Duffy explains, 'there was generally a conversation on the subject of it. Carlyle listened patiently to dissent, and justified or illustrated his opinions calmly.' Thus it was that apparently in the course of the talk that followed this harangue, he said,—"The Scottish peasantry are gifted with silent intrepidity and valour. Their constant submission to the Divine Will, and their strict veracity, are qualities which it would behove Irish peasants to imitate, for, to say the truth, I have not found these qualities plentiful among them, nor the plain speaking which comes of honest thinking."

"You have never seen an Irish peasant in his natural condition," said Gavan Duffy, in reply to this, "only a population resembling a famished crew just escaped from shipwreck; the Irish peasantry are intrinsically pious, generous, and veracious. The shiftiness and evasion, which they sometimes exhibit in the witness-box, are the devices of a people harassed by cruel laws and harsh masters. They evade, but they will not violate, the sanctity of an oath." He went on to tell at full length an anecdote to prove this, and received a patient hearing, and was not told, as he might have been, that nobody ever doubted that Irish peasants were superstitious. What Carlyle remarked when he finished was,—"The stories current of them by writers of their own country give the impression of an idle, reckless race, with a levity which is not agreeable, but painful, to contemplate."

This only started Duffy afresh, with a new anecdote to show how wise they really were, and how different from what Maxwell and Lever had represented.—'In a dear summer, as the famine periods are called, a small farmer was induced by his wife to send out his father to beg, equipped with a bag, a staff, and half a double blanket. After he was gone,' she looked for the other half of it 'to make sure he had not carried it off. When the house had been ransacked in vain, the farmer thought of asking his little son if he had seen it. "Yis, father," the boy replied. "I have put it by till the time comes when I'll want it.' "What will you want with it," enquired the farmer. "Why, father," replied the boy, "you see, when I grow up to be a big man, and I'll be sending you out to beg, I'll want to put it on your back." '

Carlyle said,—" It is a homely apologue, intended no doubt to illustrate the force of example. We may safely assume that the old man was recalled from his begging and put in the most comfortable corner of the cabin after that."

" Yes," rejoined Duffy, " and you must remember it is the apologue of an Irish peasant."

XXIX

BROOKFIELD AND OTHERS

(1853)

AT noon on Friday, 14.1.53, old Henry Hallam the historian, past seventy-five now, called to tell his niece, Mrs. Brookfield, that he would dine with them next day, and she and her husband hastened to collect a party he would like to meet. Mr. Brookfield has recorded in his diary:[1]—'I to Carlyle's. Found him alone eating his dinner. He was excessively pleasant and human. He laughed greatly at my wishing Mrs. Carlyle and himself to "use their influence with each other to come."'

Both of them went, and so did Tom Taylor and James Spedding, Captain Sterling and others, and as Sydney Smith used to say, "There was Hallam, with his mouth full of cabbage and contradiction."

On Monday, 24.1.53, Mr. Brookfield wrote in his diary.—'Went out at 2.30 to St. James's to arrange for adult Baptism to-morrow. Overtook Carlyle, on his way to Diorama,'—a kind of panorama, like the best of the movies, pictures of reality. Brookfield went on.—'He spoke of Alfred Tennyson and his domestic life. I said marriage was dipping into a pitcher of snakes for the chance of an eel, and that Alfred Tennyson had found an eel. He went off on this, railing a good deal, and said eels had a faculty by very natural transformation for becoming snakes.

'I said what a tragi-comedy life is. A walking funeral was just before us. "Aye, there goes a bit of it," said he, "a small hole, and an insignificant look down into it by these people, and then an end of it. Another leaf from the great big forest has rustled down."

'We passed Tattersall's. He said he had once gone there when he first came to London, and saw iron-faced taciturn men *in earnest*. An ecumenical council could not have been more serious. I said they would have talked a great deal more.'

[1] *Mrs. Brookfield and Her Circle*, by C. and J. Brookfield, II, pp. 383–90.

After discussing an odd-looking cabman familiar to them both, Carlyle 'said he had sometimes thought that, if a man had met William the Conqueror and blown a pistol through his brains and manured a field with him, he would even in that case have produced good turnips, but a very expensive cartload it would have been.' And then they separated, Brookfield going to arrange a Baptism, and Carlyle to look at a Diorama, as an agreeable change from his morning's work of reading German histories and biographies.

Neuberg had now come to live in England; and in writing to invite him for Tuesday evening, 25.1.53, to meet the big and beautiful Charlotte Williams Wynne and 'good little Montégut' of the Revue des Deux Mondes, Carlyle was frank about the German authors, saying:—'Nox and Chaos! No dumber people have been found, not even the English, than these respectable Teutonic cousins: what great actions they have done, what great platitudes (mere *silence audible*, a dreadful kind of silence) they have uttered about them! I think it is "the nature of the beast."'

This was like a bubble rising to the surface of the mud through which he was diving, a bubble which showed that the diver was yet alive, and not a lonely bubble,—there were many more. Thus a few days later he was writing to Neuberg again:—'On this Earth, I believe there is nowhere so intense a blockhead, so fatal to himself and mankind, as your learned College one who never dreams but he is a prophet and shining light! . . . So academical, learned, and yet so totally *in*human, pedantic. . . . In fact I am very ill off, as every man, indeed, in this world is, who is following a work of *his own* in it,—and leaping ditches and hedges with his loaded cart, instead of following the beaten Dilettante highways, the goal of *which* is unhappily not so delightful as the smooth travelling on them!'

Gavan Duffy had been saying he needed shelves for books in his Pimlico lodgings. He happened to be out of town when suddenly Carlyle remembered that there were shelves in his garret which might serve. So he wrote to Duffy on 6.2.53, describing the shelves awaiting delivery to him, and mentioning a man he might know.[2]—'One "Thomas Muloch, Dublin," sends me an acrid little pamphlet the other morning, solemnly denouncing and damning to the Pit, really in a rather sincere and devout manner, "*both* the Irish Churches," (Protestant and Catholic), in the name of

[2] *Conversations with Carlyle*, by Sir C. Gavan Duffy, pp. 187–90.

Jesus, and of *any* instalment of salvation to Ireland, of which country he is a passionate lover. I have thought a thousand times, since seeing Ireland, to much the same effect, in the name of still higher entities and considerations —tho virtuously holding my peace on the subject. The "Churches," alas, alas! Of all preachers and prophets and divine men wanted in Ireland,' and in short elsewhere, the most wanted 'is the Divine Drill-Sergeant who, with steel whips or by whatever method, would teach poor canting slaves to *do* a little of the things they eloquently say (and even *know*) everywhere and leave *un*done. Poor Muloch! Really *is* there any such *totally* accursed *sin* as that . . . in this illustrious thrice-hopeful epoch of Free Press, Emancipation, Toleration, Uncle Tom's Cabin, and the rest of it?'

While common respectable sinners may smile at such a fuss being made over 'leaving undone the things we ought to have done,' and count it a mere oddity of Carlyle to be so much in earnest about that, nobody can deny that the steel whips have been sore on us since 1853.

From February, 1853, Carlyle and Neuberg were looking round for some deserving German out of work in London, who might be employed 'on weekly wages, and to save him from worse' to hunt for Books and Prints in the Museum on Prussian affairs, and do similar mechanical work, such as copying German. In the absence of more important tasks,—for Chorley had finished sifting and sorting all the unpublished MSS.,—the faithful Neuberg was willing; but Carlyle told him,—"*You*—not by any means! And if I even find nobody,—who knows?—'One's coat *can* be cut *according* to the cloth.' I leave it peaceably to the Powers." We will see by-and-by the kind of copyist they got for wages, —Frederick Martin,—the would-be Judas of this history.

Writing to his mother on 13.2.53, Carlyle mentioned anxiety about Mazzini, who was then busy with an insurrection in Milan. He said they had news of his safety, tho 'if the Austrians could catch him, they would shoot him down like a mad dog: but they cannot quite; and that too is a kind of comfort.' Mazzini escaped as usual, and soon was safe in London again.

Mrs. Carlyle was able to go out this winter, and credited to cold baths in the morning the improvement in her health; and this February was the time of the most enjoyable snowstorm she had seen in London. 'On the first night of the snow,' she wrote to Mrs. Russell, 'I *walked* home through it from the theatre, with my bonnet hanging on my back part of the way, one minute taking myself a "slide," and the next lifting a handful of snow to eat it! In fact, that almost forgotten Scotch-looking snow had made me perfectly *drunk*, or I should never have "tempted Providence" in such a distracted manner! I escaped safe and sound' without a cold from it.

On Monday, 21.2.53, she was at another merry dinner at the Brookfields' in honour of old uncle Hallam, with Mrs. Procter, Monckton Milnes, Captain Sterling, and others. Next day, 22.2.53, Mr. Brookfield dined at home, but after dinner went 'to Carlyle's,' as he recorded.[1] 'Very pleasant indeed. He was in high good humour. Said that as a Scotchman he used to have the strongest aversion to Prelacy—but had come to think the Church of England upon the whole about the best thing of the kind going. He spoke in the strongest language about "our best righteousness being filthy rags." He walked home with me.'

There was humour in this way of talking as well as earnestness, and Mr. Brookfield could appreciate both. He had quite outgrown professional cant, and was so frankly free from superstition that before long Lady Ashburton had to bid his wife, when she was at the Grange without him, write to him:—"She hopes you won't risk your inspectorship in the vain attempt to drive common sense into fashionable heads."

On the last day of February Mr. Brookfield was at a "rout" at the house of Milnes, and noted in his diary:[1]— 'Coming away with the Carlyles I told the schoolboy's fable,—"There was once on a time a fox that fell into a well. A rabbit came and looked at him over the well side. Moral. This should teach us to beware of foxes." Carlyle laughed as much as ever I saw him do at anything, and said it was the profoundest piece of moral instruction he had ever heard.'

Profound indeed it was, recalling the parable of the Good Samaritan. "Beware of bothering yourself about others in affliction" was the sentiment both of the priest and of the Levite who 'passed by on the other side,' and of Brookfield's schoolboy, and more pardonable in the schoolboy than in his seniors. It is a sentiment springing from deep animal instincts of selfishness, inherited from our arboreal ancestors, and from animal and fishy progenitors even more remote.

XXX

DOING ALMS

(1853)

PERHAPS the nearest approach to fiction in the private letters of Carlyle is an occasional reference to money of his own which he was giving as money for which he was a trustee; but that was merely his poetical way of expressing his true feeling. He did think one should feel like a trustee in respect of one's possessions. That used to be a common sentiment in Europe, before the Christian religion evaporated. Another old-fashioned but beautiful feature of his character was his lifelong habit of doing even as Jesus commanded,—" When thou doest alms, let not thy left hand know what thy right hand doeth, that thine alms may be in secret."

This is an unusual difficulty to inquisitive biographers. A credible witness once told one of them [1] how he had seen Carlyle giving what seemed something insignificant, like small packets of tobacco, to several old women in a Dumfriesshire village, gruffly saying nothing to anyone but,—" Here, take that." Enquiry revealed that Carlyle had been making considerable presents of money to old acquaintances. The way of giving was intended to conceal what it was from idle observers, and even after many years they would not give details, so completely was the reciprocal duty of secrecy understood and taken for granted.

Sometimes, however, secrecy was not possible; and Carlyle was frank in writing to his old mother, and so it happened that in February of this year he told her of 'a long walk' he had taken 'into the country, to look after a poor Scotchman called Maccall, who is in very bad case just now. A man of much faculty; bred originally for preaching, and who *has* had congregations, twice, in England, but could not get on with them: Wherefore some seven or

[1] D. A. W.

eight years ago he gave up preaching altogether, and has been in London, with Wife and one child, trying to "live by his pen." At last he is broken down in health. Jane *begs*, from some of her rich friends, for poor Maccall. He is a good man, too, and high, tho too *lean*,—and harsh-edged, as a rusty *lipped*[2] razor!'

We are left guessing; but this may explain the following letter of 4.3.53 from Charles Dickens, which many years afterwards Carlyle handed to Neuberg.[3]

'1 JUNCTION PARADE, BRIGHTON,
Friday Evening, March fourth, 1853.

'MY DEAR CARLYLE,—

'Your letter has been forwarded to me here. I am at work on the seashore for a fortnight by way of change—this evening. To my great vexation, for there are very few men I can so ill afford to miss on any occasion as you.

'The Secretary of the Literary Fund is Mr. Octavian Blewitt, and the office is in Great Duncle Street, Bloomsbury, at the corner of Bloomsbury Square. In support of the applicant's appeal, a letter from himself will be necessary setting forth his case, and one of recommendation from you. If he be in such health that he can go out of doors, he will receive from Mr. Blewitt every possible attention and guidance. If he be not forthcoming, a word from you to the same gentleman would be all powerful. If you feel the least difficulty in moving in the matter or the least desire to avoid it, send the case to me, and I will do so, gladly. Lastly, if three guineas will be of any use to our unfortunate brother, I will place them at your disposal for him on your telling me that you will receive them.

'In his application, he must mention his literary claims; that is, he must state what books he has written, or what other literary work he has done. It is also expedient—if his claims be strong—that he should mention the nature of his present difficulties, and that such a sum would give him hope of conquering them. I particularly recommend him to see Mr. Blewitt if possible. He may make any use of my name. I am not now one of the relieving board, but I belong to an amazing body called the Council—whose functions I have never been able to discover—and I believe

[2] Scotch for *broken-edged*.
[3] Whose nephew lent the MS. to D. A. W.

my name would quicken a dull ear if his claim were addressed to any such.

'I shall be here until next Tuesday week, when I return straight home. Believe me heartily sincere in saying that I am wholly at your service in such a case, and that the word "trouble" is not in my vocabulary.

'I send this off in a hurry to save the post.

'Very faithfully Yours,

'CHARLES DICKENS.'

'Thomas Carlyle, Esquire'

XXXI

THE ATHENÆUM CLUB, &c.

(1853)

THERE was something of antique simplicity in the long friendship of the Carlyles and the Ashburtons, for Lord Ashburton was one of the richest men in England, and tho Carlyle was great as an author, he was sometimes derided even in literary circles for being "content with the wages of an artisan." While it was well known that Ashburton would have been delighted to find some way of enriching his friend, the only instance of anyone taking advantage of that was almost accidental.

Thomas Ballantyne, a journalist and a friend, was calling one day on Carlyle, and lamented that his paper, *The Statesman*, was in financial difficulties. He begged a loan for it of £50. Carlyle gave him £100, and a card of introduction to Lord Ashburton, who at once gave him £500, and afterwards helped him in various ways. It seems likely enough that Ballantyne's repayment to Carlyle of his £100 was in fulfilment of a promise to Ashburton.[1]

By March, 1853, Lady Ashburton was afoot again, and one evening quizzed Carlyle on his unwillingness to say "Yes" to her husband's entreaty to let him propose him "for immediate election" to the Athenæum Club. Ashburton was on the Committee of the Club, and said all he could. Carlyle thought he had made his "No" as plain as politeness allowed. But in March he found himself a member, with the entrance money and the subscription paid in a lump.

On his first night there, Ashburton and he were dining together, and in the reading-room he saw old Crabbe Robinson, who asked for his brother Dr. John, and the

[1] *Literary Recollections*, by F. Espinasse, pp. 240–5, but corrected by the statements to D. A. W. of David Masson and Dr. Hutchison Stirling. Both these gentlemen had heard from T. C. and Ballantyne detailed accounts of the matter.

friendly faces of Owen, Darwin, and others made him feel at home. ' Plenty of loungers here, if one wanted lounging,' he thought to himself. The Athenæum Club had a welcome new member, but it never saw very much of him. He was too busy, and too fond of home.

XXXII

TRYING TO START WRITING

(1853)

BEFORE March was out it was sure Carlyle was going to write on Frederick, for he was trying to start. He would not dine out at two, not even with Neuberg, to whom he wrote on 23.3.53 :[1]—' I cannot show myself before five—under penalty of *losing a day ;* which of course I am loathe to do.' He went on to tell he had just received ' a catalogue of the *Nicolai* Library at Berlin, from which the generous proprietor permits me to choose at will. This is magnificent ! There will be nothing for it now but actually to *begin*,—God knows how in the world, or whether ever, to *end*. At least I must cease abusing the poor Prussian Libraries. Here finally to a most fair extent, is *what they have ;* can *nothing* be made of it, then ? '

He spent Easter at the Grange, March–April, bound by a promise he lamented,—" nine days idle ! " Yet Bielfeld's books were awaiting him there, and his reading hours were never interrupted. This is as likely a date as any for Milnes' breakfast story.[2]—

Lady Ashburton to Carlyle at breakfast :—" How are you to-day ? " Carlyle :—" Battling with Chaos." Lady Ashburton :—" In this house you might have said Cosmos." When presently Carlyle said of someone,—" Send him to Chaos ! " Lady Ashburton said,—" You can't." " Why ? " " It's full."

Mrs. Carlyle, who had preferred to stay at home, wrote to her husband she was reading *Jeanne de Vaudreuil*, ' which, if Lady Ashburton felt down to reading a pretty religious book, you may safely recommend to her ; it is worth a dozen " preciosas." '

Lady Ashburton was enjoying, she said, " a lovely Easter,"[3] and perhaps what pleased her most and set

[1] Letter apparently unpublished.
[2] *Monographs*, by R. M. Milnes, Lord Houghton, p. 252.
[3] *Mrs. Brookfield and Her Circle*, by C. and F. Brookfield, II, p. 392.

London Society buzzing, was the fate of one of the guests, Massimo d'Azeglio, representative of the King of Sardinia, and lying abroad as usual, who spoke as one having authority to instruct a listening world what to think now of the Romans and of Mazzini in particular. Carlyle heard him out, and when he had finished deliberately replied:—"Monsieur, vous ne le connaissez pas du tout, du tout!"—"You do not know him at all, sir, not at all!"—and turned his back to him and sat down to a newspaper.

While this was still being talked about, the grateful Mazzini described Azeglio to his English friends[4] as "a true emanation of the Eighteenth Century" and a clever fellow, novelist and artist as well as diplomatist. It may be explained that nobody but Froude, who was not there, seems to have said Carlyle was rude. On this occasion Carlyle was like a judge who tells a man under trial he is guilty and passes sentence. He had helped "Young Italy" by discrediting Azeglio, but done it fairly, with all the simplicity of common sense and genius. Azeglio, in his eagerness to do his function and lie at large, had forgotten Mazzini was so well known in England that it was himself and not Mazzini who would be judged by what he was saying. Talking falsely of a man his hearers knew, he was teaching them to disbelieve what he said about strangers.

In the middle of dinner one evening, a note was handed to Ashburton,—"A fire visible somewhere in the neighbourhood,"—and he at once left the table and rode to the homestead on fire, six miles away. It was on his estate, and in spite of heavy rain he stayed to see the thing out and was not home again till about eleven. He looked "almost glad" when he came back, Carlyle observed, "tho to him also it will be a considerable loss, no doubt." The "gladness" would be that satisfied expression one may remark on the faces of men who have done well some unusual and difficult duty. It was such a trifle that the only reason for mentioning it is that Carlyle was fond of telling it,—a sure sign of his partiality for one who was among the most devoted of his disciples.

Returning home, Carlyle was still unable to please himself by anything he could write. He told Neuberg that he felt "so broken and confused by the restless, shadowy mode of life" at the Grange, "and the incurably unsuitable *dietetic* hours" that "I had to lie pretty much on my oars

[4] *Mazzini's Letters to an English Family*, by E. F. Richards, pp. 266–7.

for a week after," meaning that he did not try to write, but continued reading. No wonder common country-house visitors, whatever their possessions or decorations, were insignificant, like passers-by on the streets or figures on the films. Crowds of departed spirits were rising before his mind's eye, in the smoke of the fire he was kindling by such armfuls of decaying books. He was beholding awake the world as it had been in the eighteenth century, seeing it all against the background of Eternity, and considering how to show it again.

In describing to Neuberg on 13.4.53 what he was doing, Carlyle was making a kind of draft of the liveliest bit of the third of the opening chapters of the history he was now trying to begin,—the "Königsmark tragedy." What made him tell it now was that he wanted a portrait of a so-called "Duchess of Ahlden," and naturally explained to Neuberg who she was,—the cousin and divorced wife of the Hanover Duke who became the English George I. Thus she was the mother of George II, and through her daughter, grandmother of Frederick the Great; but in 1694 her handsome paramour Königsmark had been killed by her husband's servants, and herself shut up "in the old Castle of Ahlden, in the moory solitudes of Lüneberg Heath: to stay there till she die," more than thirty years afterwards. It was like Carlyle to want to see the face of such a grandmother of his hero Frederick.

It was not less like him to praise the "decorum of these Hanover Princes and official gentlemen," and leave us to guess for ourselves their obvious vulgar motives for hushing up anything that might make the English uneasy about the royal breed. "There are traces of a kind of Fate running through their history," wrote Carlyle to Neuberg now, discussing "these poor Hanover people," and declaring their fate "like that of a stupefied Atrides genealogy," the Greek kings in the Iliad. As Thackeray remarked, "The Fates are supposed to interest themselves about royal personages."

Meanwhile Carlyle, considering how to write on Frederick, was soliloquizing in his journal on 13.4.53.—'Still struggling and haggling about Frederick. Ditto, ditto, alas! about many things! No words can express the forlorn, heart-broken, silent, utterly *enchanted* kind of humour I am kept in; the worthless, empty, and painfully contemptible way in which, with no company but my own, with my *eyes* open, but as with my hands bound, I pass these days and months, and even years. Good Heavens! Shall I never more rally in this world then, but lie buried under mud and imbecility till the *end* itself (which cannot be distant and is coming on as with seven-leagued boots) overtake me? Several are to blame; for tho no one hates me, I think nearly *everybody* of late takes me on the wrong side, and proves unconsciously unjust to me, more or less destructive to me. Several are to blame, or to pity. But above all there is one. Thou thyself. Awake—arise! *Oh Heaven and Earth, shall I never again get awake, and feel myself working and alive? In the earth there is no other pleasure for me, no other possession for me, but that same; and I neglect it, indolently lie praying for it, do not rise and victoriously snatch it, while the fast-fleeting days yet are.*[5]

'Here are now ten years, and what account can I give of them? The work done in them is very small even, in comparison. Remorse is worthless. The remnant of the future, this yet remains to us. Endless German history books; dull, bad, mostly wearisome; most uninstructive, every one of them; Frederick, an unfortunate subject. In the heart of huge solar systems,—anti-solar rather, of chaff and whirling confusions,—I sometimes think I notice lineaments of a Fritz, concerning whom I *shall* have a word to say. Say it? Oh Heaven, that I could say it!

'The review and newspaper world, all dead against me at present, which is instructive too if I take the right point of survey for it, and look into it without jaundice of any kind. The *canaille* of talkers in type are not my friends then. They know not well what to say about me,' except in short to call him scoundrel. 'Well, out of that too I got new views. I myself was in fault, and the depths and immensities of human stupidity were not practically known to me before. A strange insight, real, but hardly fit for uttering even here, lies in that. "Who can change the opinion of these people?" That is their view of the world, irrefragable, unalterable to them. Take note of that, remember that.

'"The Gadarene Swine!"[6] Often, in my rage, has that incident occurred to me. Shrill snort of astonishment, of alert attention. "Hrumph!" "That is it, then!" "So sits the wind!" And with tails up and one accord at full speed away they go, down steep places to their watery

[5] Italics added. [6] Mark v. 1–20.

grave, the *Devil* being in them.'—One would think this was written in August, 1914! The note goes on.—

'Withal it is rather curious to remark also, as I do on various occasions, how, while all the talk and print goes against me, my real estimation in the world—alas, certainly without new merit of mine, for I never was so idle and worthless—seems steadily increasing—steadily in various quarters, and surely fast enough, if not too fast.' He was thinking of the increasing sale of his books, and concluded.—'Be true to thyself. Oh Heaven! Be not a sluggard. And so give up this and take to something like work.' So said, so done: Carlyle would take no holiday this year, in the country or elsewhere. Even Sunday had its daily task.

By this time the Ashburtons too were back in London. On 16.4.53 Mrs. Brookfield's latest baby was four weeks old, and Lady Ashburton, who was to be its godmother, was at tea with the Brookfields,[3] and Brookfield noted:—'Very pleasing to hear how affectionately she talked of Carlyle,' saying,—"There is nobody like him" And Brookfield told her,—"You are the only person in the world who dares put a ring through the nose of Carlyle."

She did not need to rejoin,—"Except his wife." That was a matter of course. Brookfield was himself an entirely happy hen-pecked husband, and could recognise others of the same sort at a glance,—Lord Ashburton for one, and Thomas Carlyle for another.

XXXIII

GLADSTONE, PANIZZI, &c

(1853)

THE Journal of Carlyle was intended for no eye but his own. The "agony inside" he was enduring while struggling to make a start but unable to do it was seen by nobody else at the time except his wife, who used to chaff him about it. It may easily be exaggerated by a reader of his journal who forgets that the journal was not a narrative, but a hurried jotting which merely reveals the mood of the moment. The key to his introspection is his almost Quixotic ideal of duty; and still more his superb ideal of history, which often made the best he could write seem trash. There can be no doubt he suffered from the strain of composition, especially when beginning a big work, and when wearied out and ending it. There can be equally little doubt that he generally enjoyed his work when he was doing it. We may believe he was suffering when he said he was, without supposing he continued to suffer when he was not saying so. Indeed he would have been called a happy man, but for his journal; and tho he was prone to look into himself when about to write in it, he hardly ever did so at any other time.

On 18.4.53 Mr. Gladstone introduced his first Budget as Chancellor of the Exchequer, extending the succession duty to landed property, and abolishing the taxes on soap and more than a hundred articles of food, including apples. This led Carlyle to make a small suggestion through Monckton Milnes, a supporter of the Government.[1] —

'If you could persuade Gladstone to take off that extremely scrubby little tax on foreign books—or, rather, on old foreign books, for the modern are oftenest worth less than nothing, and may be burnt at St. Catherine's (Dock) for aught I care—he may do a perceptible benefit to the one or two serious students still extant in this

[1] *History of Modern England*, by H. Paul, I, p. 293; and *R. M. Milnes, Lord Houghton*, by T. Wemyss Reid, I, pp. 480–1.

country. A perceptible benefit, not a great one – ah no; and on the whole if he won't, and can't, the Muses (with Panizzi's breech seated on the throat of them, and little conscious of crime in the posture, he, poor devil!) must still try to live if they can.'

Milnes exerted himself accordingly. The suggestion was too late for the current Budget; but Gladstone agreed to it, and made a note of it, and in due time abolished the 'scrubby little tax,' a magnanimous thing for Gladstone to do, considering what happened last year at the London Library.

On Friday, 22.4.53, Brookfield went in the evening after dinner to call on the Ashburtons at Bath House, and found there a large party that had been dining, both the Carlyles, Lushington and Venables, "Bear" Ellice, James Spedding and Milnes. The talk turning on a recent appointment of the Rev. Mr. Jackson to be Bishop of Lincoln, 'Milnes asked across the tea-table, "Brookfield, are you to be Jackson's successor at St. James's?" Carlyle peremptorily answered, "No! He's going to be nothing of the sort," as if repudiating any such arrangement,' wrote Brookfield proudly.[2]

The reference to Panizzi sitting on the throat of the Muses, without knowing he was doing anything amiss, needs explanation. In the British Museum Library there was a fine collection of books presented by George III, and called the King's Library. The rooms where these were kept were quieter than the general reading-room, where Carlyle could not read without a headache, and there were many of these books that related to eighteenth-century history. So about April Carlyle wrote what Espinasse[3] describes as a "calm, conciliatory letter" to Panizzi, applying for leave to read in these quiet rooms. According to Panizzi's own advocate and biographer,[4] Panizzi "answered in terms too severe, so much so that we purposely avoid making public anything which was simply the fruit of former quarrels,"—a prudent thing for a biographer to do, if Espinasse is right in saying Panizzi was "insolent"; and the biographer is mistaken in talking of former quarrels. Panizzi had been accidentally offended as already explained,[5] and doubtless

[2] *Mrs. Brookfield and Her Circle*, by C. and F. Brookfield, II, p. 393.
[3] *Literary Recollections*, by F. Espinasse, pp. 190–2.
[4] *Life of Sir Anthony Panizzi*, by L. Fagan, I, pp. 335–7.
[5] *Carlyle to "the French Revolution,"* pp. 362–3.

resented the recent Parliamentary Commission;[6] but tho he had long itched for a personal quarrel with Carlyle, to advertise the importance of Panizzi, he had never been able to get it. So now he saw his chance, and tho Lady Ashburton who knew him spoke to him, and Lord Clarendon at her instigation wrote to him, he would not let Carlyle read in the King's Library rooms, preferring rather to lie,—which came easy to Panizzi.

Carlyle had an interview with Hallam, "good old soul," who was ready to do all he could to oblige him, but the preposterous "fat pedant" Panizzi had "gained the ears of the working members of the Trustees,"[3] and so was able to maintain his No, and keep Carlyle out of the quiet rooms of the King's Library. He reckoned on a nice little row, to make the name of Panizzi famous in the land; but Carlyle knew better than to waste time on him. Panizzi could not shut the general reading-room, and Neuberg and Larkin could endure its stuffy air and make all needful notes and extracts. Carlyle wrote to his brother Dr. John in April that if Hallam could do nothing, he would 'quietly let the matter drop. After all, Books are not what will make me rise; it is astonishing what little *profit*, in any form whatever, one too often gets out of Books! With Prussian Books on Friedrich, for example, one might load a wagon; and the knowledge even Prussians have of Friedrich I find to be frightfully like *zero*, in spite of Books. Not one *genial* Book yet exists on the subject.'

He told Neuberg, "If the British Museum and Panizzi had never existed, I might then have got at the King's Library *without* headache." In the privacy of his journal he soliloquized about this:—'Never mind! No matter at all. Perhaps it is even better so. Intrinsically he hinders me but little. Intrinsically the blame is not in him, but in the prurient darkness and confused pedantry and ostentatious inanity of the world which put him there, and which I must own he very fairly represents and symbolises there. Lords Lansdowne and Brougham put Panizzi in; and the world with its Hansards and ballot-boxes and sublime apparatus put in Lords Lansdowne and Brougham.'

By this summer Carlyle was fairly started on a task too important to be interrupted by any personal squabble. The spiteful Panizzi was too silly to see what he was doing, and

[6] *Carlyle on Cromwell and Others*, p. 372, and Book XVI, Chap. XXII of this volume.

no more worth a quarrel than the cocks and the dogs in adjoining houses. What preoccupied Carlyle was the sight of the immense extent of the job he had undertaken, when he was feeling old and "well capable of being beaten by this time." He "wished he had never heard of Fritz," but grudged that so much labour should be lost. Besides, he felt it a duty to be doing something, and there was no more attractive work in sight. Neuberg was "taking the waters" at Kissingen this summer, and had decided to settle in London beside him. Miss Neuberg, his sister, who had kept house for him, was now married and living there.

Explaining to his brother Dr. John his difficulties in starting, Carlyle dwelt upon two, his 'want of sufficient Love for lean Frederick and his heroisms,' and first and foremost, 'the vague *shoreless* nature of the subject, which has been treated hitherto by hardly any man of superior understanding, and lies "like water spilt upon the ground."'

"One never goes so far as when one knows not where one is going." It was not merely a history of the lean Frederick he was now beginning to write; but a history of eighteenth-century Europeans. His visions of their doings possessed him. From this summer till February, 1865, his life was in that book. Details of daily life around were all but insignificant to him.

loud voice, "I thank you most kindly for all your attentions." "Oh, if I could but do you any good," I said. "Ye have done me good, mony a time," she answered. I went to bed to lie awake all night, listening for noises. John slept in the midroom. But the light of a new day found your mother better rather than worse. It was more the recollection of the state in which she had been (on Monday) than her actual state that kept us in agitation all yesterday. One thing that leads me to believe her life will be prolonged is, that she recovered out of that crisis by the natural strength that was still in her . . . entirely of herself. . . .

'I have just been to see if your mother had awoke; she has slept two hours. I asked her if she had any message for you, and she said, "None, I am afraid, that he will like to hear, for he'll be sorry that I'm so frail. . . ."'

'Was not that a beautiful old Mother's message?' remarked Carlyle in his reply, 23.7.53; and the conclusion of his long letter ran:—'I have done my task to-day again . . . a most dreary one. I am too old for blazing up round this Fritz and his affairs; and I see it will be a dreadful job to *riddle* his history into purity and consistency out of the endless rubbish of so many dullards as have treated of it. But I will try, too. I cannot yet afford to be *beaten*; and truly there is no other thing attainable to me in life except even my own poor scantling of work such as it may be. If I can *work* no more, what is the good of *me* further? We shall all have a right deep sleep by-and-by, my own little Jeannie. Thou wilt lie quiet beside me there in the *divine* bosom of Eternity, if neve[r] in the diabolic whirl of time any more. But this is too sad a saying, tho to me it is blessed and indubitable as well...

'I called on Lady Ashburton; les... urda... g than us[ual] is to have a last Addiscombe party ... y week, then go for the North. ... for ever my p...

'Adieu! Jeannie mine. God ... mother and thee! 'T. C.'

Mrs. Thomas Carlyle

By the time she received this ... heerful, and then she had written again, giving news ... was home on the first went to her uncle's in Liverp... he first time on arrival of August.[2] It is likely she s...

[1] *Carlyle's Holidays in Wales,* ...ne, 1884.

[2] Letter of T. C. to Charles R... by John Howells, *Red Dragon Ma*...

the significant present her husband had awaiting her this year. On her birthday, 14.7.53, it would only have bothered her, as she was away from home. The key to its meaning is that by the long lease and the expensive repairs to the house, she had now fairly anchored him as she had long wanted to do in their house at Chelsea. So his annual birthday present to her this year was a coloured lithograph of a wife shaving her husband. She holds his nose by her left hand; and while grasping the razor in her right, she is leisurely chatting with a caller. There is glass on the back as well as on the front of the picture, so that the endorsement can be read:—

'To my dear Jeannie, (14th July, 1853)
'from her ever-affectionate T. Carlyle (dealer in emblems).'

XXXV

HOLMAN HUNT AND CHRIST

(1853)

AT this time Holman Hunt and others were being vituperated by art-dilettantes and critics for their 'return to nature' in painting. "Pre-Raphaelitism" was the name of the new style, and Ruskin was their champion in the Press. In 1853 Hunt was living in Chelsea, and tells us:[1]—'Once when I was riding on the omnibus to Chelsea, the driver was talking about characters peculiar to the neighbourhood,' and speaking 'with amusement of Carlyle, of his staid aspect, his broad-brimmed hat, and his slow gait,' the driver added 'he had been told "as how he got his living by teaching people to write."'

What Holman Hunt could not understand, he wrote afterwards,[1] was how 'the revulsion of feeling that has grown up against Carlyle since his death can be maintained while his books are within reach. What a difference from the days when young authors such as James Hannay left my bachelor gatherings for a quarter of an hour, only to look up at the dark house of the great sage, and to distinguish the room he was sitting in by the light in his window! I had read all his books that I had been able to buy or borrow, and with all the reverence of my nature I had seen the living prophet rambling along the streets of the neighbourhood. . . . Curious as his aspect was in his slow perambulations, it was noticeable that never did the rudest boor or the most impudent gutter-boy fail to be chilled into dumb propriety when he passed; they were silenced in their noisy idleness by'—the sight of him, so to speak. 'It was noticeable to me that none of the thousand entertaining incidents of childish caprice and character, nor the endless surprises of whim in the grown-up children of men, ever made him pause or turn his head. . . .

[1] *Pre-Raphaelitism and the Pre-Raphaelite Brotherhood*, by W. Holman Hunt, I, pp. 346, 352–60.

'One day walking on a narrow pavement, passing a lady girded with preposterous hoops, he was well-nigh thrown to the ground; disentangling his foot, he recovered his balance and, unruffled, turned ceremoniously to the lady, raised his hat and made his bow, revealing neither annoyance nor sarcasm.

'A visitor, in leaving the Carlyles to come to me, had told Mrs. Carlyle of his intention, and the lady asked with interest about me and my work, a curiosity in which her husband somewhat participated. This induced me, when I had some pictures finished, to ask my friend to ascertain from her whether the prophet would honour me with a visit. Accordingly Mr. and Mrs. Carlyle came. On the first visit I need only say that he looked taller and younger than when muffled up outside, and that his face, despite a shade of joylessness, was one of the noblest I had ever seen. His large-orbited blue eyes, deep sunk, had upper lids drooping over the iris, the lower lid occasionally leaving bare the white below. The brow was prominent, the cranium domed and large, the hair shaggy. His nose and the lower part of his face had the stamp of grandeur, and his figure when unbent had a dignity of its own. Weakness revealed itself in the meagreness of his neck.' . . . His 'voice reached the treble when he wished to discourage interruption. He would have no dialogue, but the tenderness of the man bespoke itself in unaffectedness of gesture and the directness of his first word.

'Like all great men I have ever seen, he indulged in no pomposity. He assumed, not unnaturally however, that people—young people particularly—wanted to hear him talk, and did not expect him to listen. His enthusiastic comments upon my *Hireling Shepherd* and *Strayed Sheep* were far beyond my hopes,' and Hunt proudly quoted a letter from Mrs. Carlyle (13.4.53).—

'Dear Mr. Hunt,

'Will you oblige me by letting Mr. Watson see the Picture? Having raised his curiosity about it to a pitch, I feel myself responsible for the gratification thereof!

'Mr. Carlyle says "it is a really grand Picture! The greatest Picture that he has seen painted by any modern man!" And Mr. Carlyle being notorious for never praising except in negations ("not a bad Picture"—"A picture not wholly without a certain merit," etc., etc.), the present

outburst of positive praise evinces an appreciation of your Picture not to be exceeded by "any modern man!"
'Please recollect that you settled with him to come here some evening soon.

'Yours very sincerely,

'JANE W. CARLYLE.'

This naturally encouraged Hunt, when he had finished what he thought a masterpiece, to invite the Carlyles again to a private view; and perhaps his best bit of writing is his report of it. (1853).—

'Mrs. Carlyle had often in chatting to my friends let them know that she had been a noted beauty in her youth and an heiress, and that her friends were much averse to her marriage with Carlyle, but that she would not give him up. She said the same to me in turn. It seemed absurd that the lady who had by her marriage become one of the most renowned wives of her time—instead of being the wife of a respectable mediocrity—could be thinking of what she had given up for him. I observed that, in real fact, she was proud of her husband to the point of vanity. While he talked she placed herself behind him, and whenever something he said deserved special attention, she good-naturedly smiled across to me, nodded, and when at first I thought I must reply to some of his remarks, she held up her finger and shook her head. I saw her often afterwards, and think she was one of the proudest wives in the country.

'It was Carlyle's second visit to my studio that best revealed the inner nature of the man, when *The Awakened Conscience* and *The Light of the World* were just completed. He spoke approvingly of the first, but turning to the other, he spoke in terms of disdain.—

'"You call that thing, I ween, a picture of Jesus Christ. Now you cannot gain any profit to yourself, except in mere pecuniary sense, or profit any one else on earth, in putting into shape a mere papistical fantasy like that, for it can only be an inanity, or a delusion to every one that may look on it. It is a poor misshaped presentation of the noblest, the brotherliest, and the most heroic-minded Being that ever walked God's earth. Do you ever suppose that Jesus walked about bedizened in priestly robes and a crown, and with yon jewels on His breast, and a gilt aureole round His head? Ne'er crown nor pontifical robe did the world e’er give to such as Him. Well—and if you mean to represent Him as the spiritual Christ, you have chosen the form in which He has been travestied from the beginning by worldlings, who have recorded their own ambitions as His, repeating Judas’ betrayal to the high priests.

‘ “ You should think frankly of His antique heroic soul. If you realised His character at all, you wouldn’t try to make people go back and worship the image that the priests have invented of Him, to keep men’s silly souls in meshes of slavery and darkness. Don’t you see that you’re helping to make people believe what you know to be false, what y’ don’t believe yourself ? The picture I was looking at just now of the shallow, idle fool and his wretched victim had to do with reality ; this is only empty make-believe, mere pretended fancy, to do the like of which is the worst of occupations for a man to take to.” I tried here to declare that I did firmly believe in the idea that I had painted, more than anything I saw with my natural eyes, and that I could prove from his writings that he also did ; but he raised his voice well-nigh to a scream, and Mrs. Carlyle, standing behind, put up her emphatic finger and shook her head, signing to me.

‘ He vouchsafed but passing notice of my defence. “ It’s a’ wilful blindness. Ye persuade yourself that ye do believe, but it’s high time that ye gave up the habit of deluding yourself.” I tried again to say that he had himself written of the spirit of truth coming to men, and of the need of listening, and that no Spirit of Truth was so candid as that which Christ represents ; but he would not stop, and his good wife more vehemently beckoned silence.

‘ “ I’ll tell ye what my interest in the matter is. I have a screen at home, and on it I have put portraits, the best I can anyhow get—often enough I have to be content with very poor ones—of all the men that ever were on earth who have helped to make us something better than wild beasts of rapine and havoc ; of all the brave-hearted creatures whose deeds and words have made life a term of years to bear with patience and faith, and I see what manner of men most of these were—Socrates and Plato, Alexander, Pompey, Cæsar, aye, and Brutus, and many another man of the old time who won or lost in the struggle to do what they deemed the justest and wisest thing. By the help of these effigies I can conjure each up to my eyes as tho he were an old acquaintance, and I can call up more or less vividly many a man of the time that has come since; but that grandest of all beings, that Jesus of heavenly omens, I have no means whatever of raising up to my sight with any accredited form."

'Taking a long breath here, he proceeded as if to a new chapter: "I am only a poor man, but I can say in serious truth that I'd thankfully give one third of all the little store of money saved for my wife and old age, for a veritable contemporary representation of Jesus Christ, showing Him as He walked about while He was trying with His ever invincible soul to break down the obtuse stupidity of the cormorant-minded, bloated gang who were doing, in desperate contention, their utmost to make the world go devilward with themselves. Search has been made honestly, and imposture has striven to satisfy the desire to procure some portraits of Him, but not the faintest shadow exists that can be accepted, nor any legendic attempt to represent Him can be credited, notwithstanding your fables of King Abgarus of Edessa or of St. Luke or of St. Veronica's napkin.

'"Yet there were artists enough and to spare, and the sculptors' work has come down to us, filling all the museums of Europe. They adored their stone images of obsolete gods, and looked to the augurs of these as ruling their destinies, while the living mouth-piece of God, the giver of true wisdom, was amongst them. It was a shadow-land in which they searched for their gods, and so made images of Jupiter, of Apollo, of Hercules, of all the deities and deesses who put no bridle upon the will of their votaries, but left them to play into the hands of all the devils in Hell, from whose reign indeed they were not separated, unless forsooth they were only the creatures of purposeless fancy. Male and female, they were the rulers of a Heaven that all the intelligent among men had long ceased to believe in, spite of the statues by sculptors who made believe to believe. And these carvers of marble, had they only instead chiselled a faithful statue of the 'Son of Man,' as He called Himself, and shown us what manner of man He was, what His height, what His build, and what the features of His sorrow-marked face were, and what His dress, I for one would have thanked the sculptor who did it with all the gratitude of my heart for that portrait, as the most precious heirloom of the Ages.

'"Now I tell you, young man, you are doing exactly what the sculptors of Roman time did, and ye'll ne'er make your talent a benefit to your fellow-men of to-day and to them that come afterwards, if you go on working at worn-out fables. I have seen the pictures, all of them, by the great painters who have set themselves to portray Jesus, and what could be more wide o’ the mark? There’s the picture of ‘Christ disputing with the Doctors’ in our National Gallery by Leonardo da Vinci, and it makes Him a puir, weak, girl-faced nonentity, bedecked in a fine silken sort of gown, with gems and precious stones bordering the whole, just as tho He had been the darling of a Court, with hands and fingers that have never done any work, and could do none whatever, a creature altogether incapable of convincing any novice advanced enough to solve the simplest problem in logic. There are other notable presentations of conceptions of Christ in paint and marble familiar to us in prints, and they are all alike.” Here, raising his voice very high, he continued, “And when I look, I say, ‘Thank you, Mr. Da Vinci,’ ‘Thank you, Mr. Michael Angelo,’ ‘Thank you, Mr. Raphael, that may be your idea of Jesus Christ, but I’ve another of my own which I very much prefer.’

‘“I see the Man toiling along in the hot sun, at times in the cold wind, going long stages, tired, hungry often and footsore, drinking at the spring, eating by the way, His rough and patched clothes bedraggled and covered with dust, imparting blessings to others which no human power, be it king’s or emperor’s or priest’s, was strong enough to give to Him, a missioner of Heaven sent with brave tongue to utter doom on the babbling world and its godless nonsense, and to fashion out another teaching to supplant it,—doing battle with that valiant voice of His only against the proud and the perverse, encharming the simple by His love and loveableness, and ever disenchanting such as would suppose that the kingdom of Heaven that He preached would bring to Him or to His adherents earthly glory or riches; offering them rather ignominy and death. Surrounded by His little band of almost unteachable poor friends, I see Him dispirited, dejected, and at times broken down in hope by the immovability and spleen of fools, who being rich with armed slaves, determined to make the Heavens bend to them. I see Him unflinching in faith and spirit crying out, ‘He that hath ears to hear let him hear.’ This was a man worth seeing the likeness of, if such could be found.

‘“One painter indeed there was who had some gleam of penetration in him, and faculty of representation, and his works I look for wherever I can hope to find them. Albert

Dürer is that man, who illustrated the painful story of the Christ, the Man of Sorrows, in His babyhood nursed amid ruins, with Joseph ever toiling, and the Mother oppressed and haggard with thought, and the child without the carelessness and joy of infancy, being lean and prematurely sad, and then step after step of the same heavy burdened soul appears, until, with face worn and distorted, He ends His life of misery upon the Cross; but even Albert Dürer had canons of tradition which hindered him from giving the full truth, and I don't see what hope there could be in attempting to do now what he failed to do then. Take my word for it, and use your cunning hand and eyes for something that ye see about ye, like the fields and trees I saw here a year ago, and, above all, do not confuse your understanding with mysteries."

'And then as he turned to go he said, pointing to a drawing on the wall, "And pray who may that shrewd-looking man be with the domed and ample cranium? He ought to be a man of mark." I said that it was my father, whom I regarded as a man of very exceptional intellect, though he had neither had the opportunity nor the ambition to care to make his voice heard beyond his own private circle. He resumed, "And so it was with my father, and I can say that in native wisdom neither I nor any son of his came near him, and yet he cared only to go about his little land, and exercise his judgment upon its state, to settle the order of his crops, and to watch that they were defended from all the evils that threatened them in their course, and to see that the home was well ordered. Yes, at times he would talk about the news of the town, of its men, the sage, and the crankie, and yet I can honestly aver he was well fitted to be a counsellor to kings."'

B

I

J

S